To the Atlantic Posse

Thanks for the
Many years of
Shmaltz — and to
Many more —
L'Chaim!

Dec 2010

CRAFT
BEER
Bar Mitzvah

Shmaltz Brewing Company was awarded the gold medal for 2010 as "Best American Craft Beer" and the overall "Best in Show" by *Beverage World Magazine*. A recipient of the "Distinguished Business Award" from the Brooklyn Chamber of Commerce, Shmaltz was also ranked one of the "Top 20 Fastest Growing Bay Area Companies" in 2009 by *San Francisco Business Times*.

Established by Jeremy Cowan in San Francisco in 1996 with the first batch of 100 cases of He'brew Beer® bottled, labeled, and delivered by hand, Shmaltz has sold over eight million bottles of beer to date. Along with the acclaimed line of He'brew Beers®, Shmaltz introduced its sideshow-inspired Coney Island Craft Lagers® in 2007. Proceeds help Coney Island USA, a 501(c)(3) Arts Non-Profit fulfill its mission to defend the honor of lost forms of American popular culture in Brooklyn's historic Coney Island neighborhood.

He'brew Beer® and Coney Island Craft Lagers® are available in over twenty-five states through more than thirty wholesalers at nearly two thousand retail specialty shops across the U.S. including Beverages & More, Whole Foods, Total Wine, select Krogers and Publix, and Cost Plus World Market.

Shmaltz Brewing beers have appeared in such distinguished media outlets as *The New York Times, CNN Headline News, The Onion, Beer Advocate Magazine,* NPR's "Weekend Edition," *Men's Health, MSNBC, San Francisco Magazine, The Jerusalem Report, New York Jewish Week, Washington Post, Forbes,* Entrepreneur.com, and Epicurious.com.

Praise for **Craft Beer** *Bar Mitzvah*

"Jeremy Cowan has emerged as a noteworthy, march-to-the-beat-of-your-own-drummer personality within the craft brewing world -- no mean feat in an industry with no shortage of personalities. The fact that he's managed to build an award-winning brand from its genesis as an inside joke and is here to write about it 13 years later is a testament -- Old Testament, of course -- to how far the combination of passion, talent and a sincere sense of humor can carry artists and entrepreneurs. Cowan's story of Shmaltz Brewing, as told in *Craft Beer Bar Mitzvah*, mixes comedic self-deprecating anecdotes with general acts of badassery -- which pretty much sums up the brands he has created."

-Jeff Cioletti, Editor-in-Chief, *Beverage World Magazine*

"When I first met Jeremy, I couldn't believe he was a member of my shul in Los Altos Hills, California. A young kid, with a wacky but interesting concept that my beer partner Mark Bronder had coincidentally discussed years earlier -- a beer for Jews with the same name (HeBrew), but our initial image was a muscular bicep with a Star of David tattooed on it. Well, we went in a different direction, and I was enthralled with Jeremy, his idea, and his incredible sense of humor and passion. This man knows how to build a brand from scratch, and reading his story is a fascinating, can't-put-the-book-down read. Just don't read it from right to left."

-Pete Slosberg, founder of Pete's Wicked Ale

"Jeremy Cowan is the Philip Roth of craft beer and *Craft Beer Bar Mitzvah* is his *Portnoy's Complaint*, a hilariously mind-blowing account of a young Gen J entrepreneur who, armed only with vision, love of things Jewish and few bucks, turns his "He'brew Beer" label into an American cultural institution. *Craft Beer Bar Mitzvah* will bootleg inspiration straight into your heart."

-Alan Kaufman, author of *Jew Boy, a Memoir* **and editor of**
The Outlaw Bible Of American Poetry

Praise for **Craft Beer** *Bar Mitzvah*

"Jews believe in tikkun olam, repairing the world, but in a world beset by natural and man-made disasters, it often seems impossible for individuals to make a meaningful impact. While he may not have cured cancer or ended the Middle East conflict, Jeremy Cowan has performed two exceedingly worthy deeds -- creating a world-class beer and telling a compelling, entertaining, and engagingly transgressive story. L'Chaim!"

-Richard Block, Senior Rabbi, The Temple - Tifereth Israel, Cleveland, Ohio and president-elect of the Central Conference of American Rabbis (CCAR)

"In his new book *Craft Beer Bar Mitzvah*, Jeremy Cowan combines the heart of a brewer with the soul of a two-thousand-year-old rabbinical *mensch*. A must-read on how to get from there (a crazy dream) to here successfully in beer."

-Tom Dalldorf, Publisher, *Celebrator Beer News*

"A funny, irreverent account of one man's quest to build a beer brand, wandering the desert landscape of bad beer to let his people drink the good stuff. A wry tale of how it took thirteen years to turn Shmaltz Brewing into an overnight sensation."

-Jay Brooks, Brookston Beer Bulletin

"Cowan transforms San Francisco into the land of Malt and Hops with humor, an edge and a deep sense of biblical intoxicity."

-David Katznelson,
Co-Founder of The San Francisco Appreciation Society

"This is a powerful tale of how one man turned a passion -- and a pun -- into a durable brand. It is also a touching illustration of how hard work is really the root of all success."

-Gabriel Kahn, Professor of Journalism,
University of Southern California

From the beer label for Bittersweet Lenny's R.I.P.A.:

"Satire equals tragedy plus time." – Lenny Bruce

Emmis, Shmuck! 40 years alive. 40 years dead. And shares of Lenny Bruce commodities are still long-term performers – *solid!* Sure there's been books, posters, films, plays, a box set of course. But the big Four-O inspires innovation, something hip, modern – *unorthodox* – a taste that really swings. Ladies and Gentlemen, Shmaltz Brewing Co. is proud to introduce **Bittersweet Lenny's R.I.P.A.** Brewed with an obscene amount of malts and hops. Shocking flavors – far beyond contemporary community standards. We cooked up the straight dope for the growing minyons of our nation's "extreme" beer junkies. Judges may not be able to define "Radical Beer," but you'll damn well know it when you taste it. Bruce died, officially declared a pauper by the State of California, personally broken and financially bankrupt simply for challenging America's moral hypocrisies *with words.* The memorial playbill read: "Yes, we killed him. Because he picked on the wrong god." *–Directed by,* the Courts, the Cops, the Church... and his own self-destructive super ego. Like Noah lying naked and loaded in his tent after the apocalyptic deluge: a witness, a patron saint, a father of what was to come. Sick, Dirty, Prophetic Lenny: a scapegoat, a martyr, a supreme inspiration. From Burlesque to Broadway, Carnegie Hall to the Courtroom, Long Island to Lima, Ohio to L.A., savor the provocative spirit of **Bittersweet Lenny's R.I.P.A.,** our HE'BREW monument to the richness, the bitterness and the sacred sweetness that is life... *L'Chaim!*

- Jeremy Cowan, *proprietor*

ALSO BY JEREMY COWAN

Fiddler on the Roof, (Tevye) Menlo School spring musical, 1987
Projector, 'Zine, New Orleans, 1992
Beer Label Shtick: 1996-present
Press Releases 1996-2006; edits to Jesse's 2006-present
Shmaltz Business Plan, 1999: leading to complete loss
of all friends-and-family investment by 2001
Maxing out all personal credit cards, and surviving to shatter
all previous Shmaltz Brewing sales records, 2003-2010
Decision to ask close friend James Sullivan
to co-write *Craft Beer Bar Mitzvah*, 2009-2010...
because check out what he's handcrafted:

ALSO BY JAMES SULLIVAN

Jeans: A Cultural History of an American Icon
The Hardest Working Man: How James Brown Saved the Soul of America
7 Dirty Words: The Life and Crimes of George Carlin

CRAFT BEER
Bar Mitzvah

How It Took
13 Years,
Extreme Jewish
Brewing, and
Circus Sideshow
Freaks to Make
Shmaltz Brewing
Company
an International*
Success

by
JEREMY COWAN

with
James Sullivan

Malt Shop
PUBLISHING
NEW YORK · SAN FRANCISCO · BEYOND

Because making a character "alive" means getting to the bottom of his existential problem. Which in turn means getting to the bottom of some situations, some motifs, even some words that shape him. Nothing more.
– Milan Kundera, *Art of the Novel*

Or, to put it a little crudely, how will your private pleasures connect with your public responsibilities?
– Kirk Varnedoe, curator at the Museum of Modern Art, from a commencement speech at Stanford, 1992

Malt Shop Publishing
912 Cole St., Suite 338
San Francisco, CA 94117
www.maltshoppublishing.com
info@maltshoppublishing.com

ISBN Hardcover: 978-0-9829325-1-3
ISBN Paperback: 978-0-9829325-3-7

Library of Congress Control Number: 2010934612

Ordering Information:
Quantity sales: Special discounts are available on quantity purchases by synagogues, homebrew clubs, sideshow schools, MBA programs, and others. Orders by U.S. trade bookstores and wholesalers, please contact Malt Shop Publishing, info@maltshoppublishing.com

First printing December 2010

Book design by Matt Polacheck
Cover photos by Todd Huffman
Cover photos shot at 4th Ave. Pub in Brooklyn - thanks Kirk!

Printed in the U.S.A.

* "International": Since this is the legalese page, I can in fact confirm that we consistently ship beer to Western Canada (which does not count as part of the United States). We also sent two shipments to London but that kinda fell apart so I'm calling us "International" for now, and we'll work on more exports to justify the bombast. I just think it sounds too cool to pass over.

Craft Beer *Bar Mitzvah*: Today I am a Man.

This book is dedicated to my Mom. I love you!

And to my Dad and to Granny, I miss you.

Except for all the pages that have drug references
and bad language -- those are for the amusement
of my friends. I love you and often miss you too.

The work-related parts, which are always
personal for me, are dedicated to my co-workers.
I could not have done it without you all.
I love you too. Now get back to work.

JUNE 2003, NEW YORK CITY

I emerged first thing Monday morning from the crush of the Eighth Avenue subway line walking west through bright already-moist summer air. I don't remember thinking about the $50,000 I'd charged to two credit cards that month. For a guy who hadn't had a full-time job in over six years and had already lost $135,000 of his closest friends-and-family investment, I felt surprisingly optimistic.

I don't remember any back pains from the month spent on Peter's fold-out couch in Park Slope. I don't remember being concerned about our lack of AC at my current sublet above the wood-burning pizza place in Williamsburg. What I do remember is a brand new size-large black Beefy-T with a simple, powerful, one color metallic gold screen print declaring to anyone coming toward me that HE'BREW -- The Chosen Beer was back in business.

It's unlikely that even one person walking toward me would have known about the hiatus, but I certainly did. Seven years after taking a shot at creating a beer that had grown out of an inside joke with some high school friends, my little one-man company had received local and national media coverage, expanded to multiple states across the country, brewed with one of the highest rated craft breweries at the time... and done nothing but lose money year after year. I got married in the middle, and then divorced before the end. I had been paid to talk about He'brew Beer at the most prestigious Jewish museum in the country, and I'd failed out of a Buddhist meditation retreat, only to find a small sense of revelation in a two-dollar-a-night grass hut on a beach in Thailand.

That summer morning, I mistakenly thought I was meeting the sales rep from my newest wholesaler to finally strike the mother lode -- the most populous Jewish neighborhood in the country on the Upper West Side of Manhattan. Walking west from Midtown, I realized that instead I was heading towards Hell's Kitchen, maybe twenty blocks south of the heartland of the Jewish Diaspora.

Nidal, my guide for the day, was born in East Jerusalem to Palestinian parents. After the 1967 Six Day War, his family moved to Jordan for nearly a decade before finally settling in northern Italy, where he'd lived from high school until he was thirty years old. He'd recently immigrated to Coney Island and met, then married, a Dominican woman who had converted to Islam.

Our first stop for the day would prove to be about the same as the rest: little bodegas that mostly sold lottery tickets, individual cigarettes, egg and cheese sandwiches, and beer. Most of the beer crammed into impossibly small sliding glass door coolers was Bud, Heineken and Corona.

After a quick introduction by the sales rep to the young guys behind the counter, I launch into my first pitch of the second coming of Shmaltz Brewing. "Hi, my name's Jeremy and this is my beer and how about bringing in a couple cases for your customers?" From behind a wall of overloaded clear plastic shelves, the buyer looks down at my new shirt and the He'brew Beer in my hand and asks, "What is this, some kind of Jewish thing?"

Turns out the owners of nearly all the small corner stores in the neighborhood are from Yemen. The kid snaps a look over at his cousin… and suddenly an old man pops out from the back room… and another guy appears from the front of the store. Everyone is speaking Arabic fast and loud with accompanying hand gestures while I stand in the middle with a salesman's grin. A pause in the action and the buyer looks at the sales rep: "Dude, what's the deal?" Nidal shrugs, "It's just a beer. Just business."

Everyone looks at me. Everyone looks at each other. Back to me, back to each other. Then the kid says to me and Nidal together, "All right, send me a case of each and we'll see how it goes."

We walked out the door and shook hands on our first sale of the day. I figured if I could sell Jewish beer with a Palestinian refugee to Yemeni Muslims in Hell's Kitchen, maybe everything would turn out just fine.

CONTENTS

Craft Beer *Bar Mitzvah*

(needs an INTRO: why beer??)

From the beginning, my co-writer, Jim, included this note in the first line of the first draft of the manuscript we'd been swapping for many months. I'd been looking at it knowing that this particular question is one of the easiest to answer.

Many more questions have been much harder to approach. What to include, what to skip, and what the hell is a struggling, only-recently-profitable small-business owner doing writing a several hundred page book, instead of sticking to his already-way-more-than-full-time job running the company? Given that Shmaltz Brewing only recently broke $2 million in annual sales of specialty beers with dancing rabbis and sideshow freaks adorning the labels, the better question might be, **why a book?**

Several quick and easy answers pop into my head. My grandmother published a few, and I thought that was simply one of the coolest things. I have letters from her to William Styron and Anais Nin -- more social than literary, but retaining the aura of a literary life. For a college english major, ironically, I didn't even read much until well into high school. I had to take a speed reading class just to keep up.

A customized gift when I was four or five, *My Birthdayland Adventures* cannot really count as my first book. That honor must go to *Conan the Liberator*, the first book I remember picking out myself, at the old Kepler's Books in Menlo Park, California. The cover portrait displayed the warrior, showing off huge pecs and cut abs, enthroned, grasping a shining steel sword, presumably liberating a number of half-naked women in the foreground -- from what, I never discovered. I don't remember ever opening the book. Hey, I was ten.

But I do remember being forced to make choices for book reports in elementary school, so I labored through sports biographies of my heroes, from Terry Bradshaw to Dr. J. I suppose more a Soc than a Greaser (though truly neither in suburban '80s Bay Area), I discovered S.E. Hinton's *The Outsiders* and finally started to enjoy reading.

Similar to the Three Pillars of Shmaltz Brewing, I don't think I'm giving anything away by acknowledging the four pillars of *Craft Beer Bar Mitzvah*. More in tone and imagination than in substance, I felt these works floating like planets around my literary world: *Kitchen Confidential*, by Anthony Bourdain, Lenny Bruce's autobiography, *How to Talk Dirty and Influence People*, Dave Eggers' memoir, *A Heartbreaking Work of Staggering Genius*, and *Invisible Cities*, by Italo Calvino.

The answer to *why a book?* comes surprisingly close to the answer to *why beer?* Honestly, I just thought it would be fun and, I hoped, kinda funny.

It has proven to be much more work than anything I ever imagined.

I've been asked many times when mentioning this project, "Who is your 'target market?'" As with Shmaltz Brewing, I have no data to offer. Given that craft beer finally broke a paltry five percent of overall beer sales (including Sam Adams, Sierra Nevada, Fat Tire and all the other huge small-beer companies) and that Jews hold steady at two percent of the population (with half of them too young and half too old and half who truly don't drink beer), my market adds up to somewhere in the vicinity of zero percent of the general public. Less than a blip on a rarely, if ever, watched radar.

As a purely niche entrepreneur, I have no fear of small numbers. I, personally, don't find much meaning beyond momentary entertainment from most mass marketed blockbusters. I've stopped even bothering with the best-selling beers. Why should I worry about volume with my own creations?

Even presuming the intimacy of the group that may gather to hear this tale, I am likely to disappoint a portion of whoever shows up for the party.

Religious or even modestly traditional Jews, after reading what I hope shines as sincere commitment to our traditions and texts, will be disappointed with some un-orthodox behavior in several chapters. Atheist Jews may mock my attempt at mystical spirituality in the Holy Land and dismiss the ongoing struggles with Torah interpretations embedded in our beer labels.

Business readers might laugh at, or empathize with, the amateurish attempts at starting a venture, but will likely want a more serious examination of ROI (Return on Investment) and EBITDA (Earnings before Interest, Taxes, Depreciation, and Amortization). There should be some helpful moments, but unlikely enough to merit required M.B.A. reading.

Some friends, so many of whom have been vital to the life force of Shmaltz Brewing, will be disappointed not to be included. I apologize and owe you a round, or several. Plenty of others will be horrified to even be mentioned.

Certain business colleagues will recognize the compliments, and perhaps nod at the digs. Others will likely be way too busy to even open the email about the book, much less crack open the book itself. At least one business owner will likely say, "That bastard still owes me thirty-five grand."

Beloved beer geeks will crave more details on original gravities and finishing hops. Those who love Blue Moon or Stella will think *I'm* the asshole for generally thinking they show poor judgment.

All I can ask is forgiveness and indulgence. Take what you will, and wipe up spilled beer with the rest. Either way, I will certainly take it personally. This business and this book have been nothing but a deeply personal journey for me.

As we all know, sometimes it's the small moments that make the larger picture come to life. So special thanks to David "Yo Idea Man" Boyer for first suggesting self-publishing, even while I kind of hosed him by bailing on a promised sublet in Brooklyn. He also said, "Well, does it pass the Mom-test?" for my concerns about certain details. I've simply removed those pages from the copy I've sent my own Mom, so please keep the rest just between us.

Having long ago lost the right to say anything I do anymore is a one-man show, I need to acknowledge those responsible for bringing this project into the world. Without Leah's willingness to record my brain-spew chronology, covering the first thirteen years of the business and forty years of my life, this book would not have happened. Without Noah stepping in, and stepping up, at a particularly crucial moment (the last minute), daring, urging, and supporting a frantic re-re-rewrite of so many elements of the manuscript, this book would have been a lesser version of itself. Without Matt, my creative brother, as always pimping out everything he touches far beyond anything I could have envisioned, this manuscript would have remained just a Word doc printed on copy paper bound with a binder clip. And Jim, who spent hours and hours over months and months translating my rambling stories into a coherent narrative, brought his own well-honed craft to the myths and moments of Shmaltz Brewing Company.

The prayer in Hebrew is called the *Shehecheyanu,* which more or less says thanks so much to everyone who got me to this moment. Amen.

Let's get on with the show. Cheers,

J.C.
September 2010
San Francisco, Brooklyn, beyond

CHAPTER 1

Genesis Act 1: Beers In The Garden

For underage kids in the suburbs of the San Francisco Bay Area in the mid-to-late-'80s, the Holy Grail of fake IDs was a state-issued identity card from the California Department of Motor Vehicles. Not an actual driver's license, which would require an in-person test and legal snags far too advanced for the average college-bound scofflaw. Not a giant posterboard cutout from the back room of a head shop in the Haight, or someone's brother's fraternity basement at Cal. A DMV ID card was the real deal. You could hold your head high and buy-up anywhere -- bars to bodegas to the biggest grocery store chains on the Peninsula -- without so much as a whiff of trouble. No parking-lot veterans demanding a two-cans-on-a-twelve-pack commission, or worse yet, simply walking out the back door with your beer *and* your change, laughing about grifting the high school boys. DMV IDs were bulletproof.

They were, that is, until all five of us who had ID cards were accosted by two plainclothes inspectors from the California Department of Alcohol Beverage Control, several pitchers into our favorite Friday night ritual: frozen strawberry daiquiris at Compadres Mexican Cantina on the El Camino Real in south Palo Alto. It did not help that most of us had taken gag names pulled from TV personalities and dead poets we studied in junior-year English class.

It also did not help that not one of us was carrying a second form of ID, or even a wallet, except for Henry, who had mocked up a frequent flyer card for America West Airline to match his phony alter-ego. One ID, one twenty-dollar bill each. Henry's mother had to vouch for all of us at the police station, and nearly everyone's golden tickets got punched. Except mine. The Man giveth but somehow forgot to taketh away.

Luckily, Jews don't believe in Hell. After almost meeting his maker, Tom Lacy's belief system was his own concern. My concern was making sure Tom typed up the form on his parents' manual typewriter correctly so we could be the masters of our own beer destiny, and procure wine coolers when the girls asked. At age seventeen, Tom "Exploding" Lacy had casually walked into the Christian Bookstore on Veterans Boulevard to obtain two certificates of baptism. One of my closest friends, and a very smart and creative young man, Tom had demolished his parents' living room a year or so earlier when an experiment with model rocket fuel went terribly awry. He also blew a hole in his own guts and had the scars to prove the tale. A couple years later, Tom would escape the wrath of the Atherton police when an officer asked for his driver's license. "Tom Lacy... ? Tom -- Exploding -- Lacy?! Oh, man, I was the officer at the scene that day. Great to see you're still alive, kid. Now, just be careful and go straight home. Tom 'Exploding' Lacy... go figure."

Baptism certificates. Yes, through some extraordinary quirk in the known universe, the California DMV accepted certificates of baptism as proof of age. So Tom sat in front of his parents' old manual and worked his magic.

As I nervously attempt not to fidget in line at the Mountain View DMV, there are glossy color posters on the walls strongly declaring fake IDs to be a crime punishable by something I don't remember fearing enough to dissuade me from applying for my VIP beer pass. The large gal hunched behind the desk asks in a disinterested voice, "Which one of these birthdays is correct?"

Umm, whhaaat?

Just an hour earlier, Tom and I had discussed what birthdays to use. Cunningly, we decided it would be easiest to use our real ones, dated four years earlier. Somehow he'd misheard me and used April 20th -- not April 24th, which is my actual birthday -- and I hadn't noticed. When I filled out the application, I'd written April 24th.

2

GENESIS ACT 1: BEERS IN THE GARDEN

"So which one is correct?"

What to do? I could bolt: hurdle the lane lines, crash through a huge room of bystanders past the warning posters, and hope to bust out the glass doors and down the street, perhaps to the Tower Records across the street or the mini-mall down San Antonio Blvd., to escape the security guards chasing me.

Instead, I said, Oh, ha ha, I must have been thinking about my, uh… zip code. Of course, the baptism date is right. Lemme change that.

Without a blink or a pause, she slams the stamp on the form and says, "Go to Window Six and get your picture taken."

Several months after La Debacle de Compadres, I still had not heard from the cops or received a summons. On a whim I called the DMV, mentioning a lost ID. Another disinterested voice: "No problem. You're still in the computer, so just come on in, fill out the form, and take a new picture. No baptism certificate needed. You're in the system."

The story of He'brew, the Chosen Beer, begins, naturally, with a creation myth: This one involves volleyball, manicured lawns, the glorious sunshine of youth and, predictably, underage drinking.

Josh and I stood taller than most in the front yard of Rob and Ben's parents' house in Atherton. The town, which has one of the richest zip codes in the country, was not what you'd call a hotbed of Jewish activity. Robert had started an annual volleyball tournament in honor of the family's dead Rhodesian Ridgeback. One afternoon after school, his brother Ben discovered Leo, lifeless in the entry hall. He'd eaten most of a neighbor's big metal garbage can and died from the internal wounds.

The volleyball games were serious business, an unsponsored version of our own NCAA tournament. Someone had stolen an official CBS Sports banner from Stanford Stadium, and we draped it on the front stairs as a backdrop. Each year Robert fastidiously plotted the winners' and losers' brackets on two oversized wipe boards. It was considered a privilege to design the yearly custom-printed t-shirt. It was considered a necessary evil to endure the summer's rotation of ringers who showed up in the form of older brothers

3

back from college or new girlfriends who just happened to be 6'1" with an unstoppable overhand jump serve. Bob and Dodie Mullin, surrogate Mom and Dad to many of us, generously hosted the fest for fourteen or fifteen years, until so many of the players were chasing their own children that there was hardly anyone left to play the damn game, or drink the damn beer.

Josh was a good athlete, and an outspoken young man. I remember him taunting the other guys, saying how badly we were going to beat them. During the clowning someone pointed out that our two-man team was all-Jewish.

"What's the deal -- Jews vs. Gentiles?"

Henry, Andy, Rob, and Ben were all goyish (though Henry and Andy have since batted both ways by marrying nice Jewish women). Affectionately, they called out "Go Team Jew," or "the Jew Crüe," or "Two Live Jews." Shmaltzy from the beginning.

Eighteen-ish in the late 1980s, on a good day we would be drinking Coors Light. That was a step up from the more common suitcases of shwag from the Redwood City bodega that sold to minors. And then came the Bartles & Jaymes wine cooler phase – a trunkful for a U2 show at the Cow Palace, and the same for Howard Jones at Kaiser Pavilion. Twice. Hey – one of the blondes from history class flashed me at the first Howard Jones show, so I figured number two was worth a shot. Turned out not to be.

Around the volleyball net, the idea just kind of popped out. "This team needs its own beer. You know what: *The Jews need their own beer*. Every other ethnic group in the U.S. has their own beer."

"We'll call it He'brew. And the tagline will be Don't Pass Out, Passover."

We all remember it as a collective effort, although I will claim that I at least blurted out the punchline. I can't really take credit for the whole thing. Thirteen-plus years of my life and career spawned from ambiguous beginnings at best. In any case, the joke stuck. For years, we'd trot it out alongside choice lines from *Blazing Saddles* and *The Blues Brothers*, *Fletch* and *Caddyshack*.

Cut to years later, on vacation with my girlfriend and her family. Tracy's father was a lawyer and a bit of an entrepreneur, having once operated a small franchise of sub shops in Cleveland. He always floated killer family trips, and

I'd started getting the hook-up. We went to Australia for three weeks, cruised through nature parks, saw a kangaroo, held a koala. One day we fished for crocodiles with bacon out of the back of a four-wheel drive Land Cruiser.

We were on a boat in a river, bird-watching, I think. Somehow, the volleyball game and the idea for a Jewish beer came up. When the words came out of my mouth -- "We had this joke about a beer called He'brew" -- I remember Tracy's father sitting in the boat and saying, "Huh, a Jewish beer. That could be pretty cool. There's nothing else like it. If you made it tasty and fun, why wouldn't everybody like it?"

I'd just gotten my first official career-ish job, in a company that I really liked, in the exact professional direction I'd been aiming. My first reaction to Bob's suggestion was, That's an absolutely terrible idea. Why would I ever give up the new art gig to start... a beer company? A Jewish beer didn't seem like one of the products the world desperately needed.

However, when I came back from that vacation with Tracy's family, there was a persistent, nagging itch in my brain. After trying unsuccessfully to ignore it, I finally decided to scratch it just a bit. It was May, 1996. I figured I'd at least start looking into whatever it might mean to make a beer without owning a brewery or becoming a brewer.

So I took the most basic pass at a few phone calls. It's a very common question -- people will say, "Hey, we have an idea for a beer. What do we do now?" Especially with beers specifically targeted to ethnic or minority groups. Today, I get that question more than most -- from Korean-Americans, Chinese-Americans, Mexican-Americans, Gay Americans and, most recently, Cajun-Americans.

I'd call up northern California and Central Valley brewers and say, Hi, I have a weird question: Can you guys make some beer for me?

In the beginning, I probably just looked up "Breweries" in the Yellow Pages (this, of course, was before the Internet was fully cooking), or went to the grocery store and grabbed all the bottles I could find. I made chicken-scratch notes, trying to figure out the questions I should be asking.

I got people like Dan Gordon of Gordon Biersch on the phone (nice Jewish boy trained at the renowned Weihenstephan, brewing German-style lagers), and I connected with Pete Slosberg of Pete's Wicked Ale, who, unbeknownst to me, was a member of my synagogue. Dan's new production brewery in San Jose produced five hundred barrels per batch, about eight thousand cases, much more than I was looking for at the time -- and more than I would sell in any given year until seven years into the business. He offered encouraging thoughts, and I moved on. Pete, a maverick in the industry who has since become a good friend, was struggling at the time through some challenging times with his company, which, like several others, had gone public in the mid-'90s. He said, "Get a million dollars and spend it on advertising. Then get another million dollars and spend it on advertising." I had two grand in the bank to start.

It became apparent fairly quickly that our best option to get this experiment off the ground was a tiny "brew-on-premise" (BOP) facility off the Rengsdorf exit of Highway 101 in Mountain View, forty-five minutes south of San Francisco. Brewmakers stood next to Petco in the mini-mall. A new In-N-Out Burger would shortly revolutionize the neighborhood, but at the time a bunch of rather forgettable businesses sprawled across the big-box footprint.

Tim owned, or at least ran, the operation. It was the kind of place where a fraternity, an ad agency, or a non-profit would go and brew five-gallon batches of beer. They had all the ingredients, and a binder filled with recipes. You'd brew on the first day, get it into the white plastic fermenters, and leave it in their cold box for a couple of weeks. Then your group would come back, after the staff had filtered and carbonated, and you'd hand-bottle your beer and put your wacky, one-of-a-kind, official beer label on it.

I wasn't telling anyone yet about the specific idea for Jewish beer. We tend to think that the minute you put your great idea out in the world some loser, or some genius, is going to steal it. At the time, Tracy and I were going to be fifty-fifty partners. She was going to handle the art, and I was going to handle the "business" side, though I had no idea what that really meant.

Brewmakers was the perfect place for me to start. The brewer there, Simon, would go on to become the head brewer for Pyramid Breweries, in Berkeley. At Brewmakers, Simon had a little seven-barrel brewing system, which made about one hundred cases of twelve 22 ounce bottles. Your fraternity could make a couple cases or so in the five-gallon system, or Simon could make a bigger, semi-commercial batch.

GENESIS ACT 1: BEERS IN THE GARDEN

At the time, it was the tail end of the initial explosion of craft beer -- not that I had any idea then that the first microbrew "bubble" was bursting. Brewmakers had started amid the enthusiasm of the early-'90s, while the initial craft-beer wave was still growing. By the time I got going, the business was starting to tank. But for a while, they were making their own beers, selling them in grocery stores -- 22 ounce "bombers," hand-bottled, hand-labeled.

At our first meeting, Tim was charismatic and extremely passionate about what he was doing. He made me a believer. He gave the most detailed explanations of the brewing process I've ever heard, to this day. I've gone on a lot of brewery tours, and not one person has gone into the detail that Tim did when he was just talking to me and Tracy. Unfortunately, Tim turned out to be, shall we say, a compromised figure.

I knew next to nothing about brewing. I'd worked at a brew pub in New Orleans, so I knew the absolute basics. I knew there were a bunch of stainless tanks, and some hoses… um, grain, and yeast. Right? But I had no idea about the details, and had never brewed a batch myself.

I put together what I saw as a crucial confidentiality agreement based on one I'd finagled from my day job, and I told Tim and Simon what I wanted to do -- my big secret. Given the hindsight of thirteen years of Jewish brewing, I had very little reason to worry about someone stealing my idea. Most of the time your nice little idea is not worth the effort for anyone else. The reason it's creative and unique is because it's a giant pain in the ass, and no one else is gonna believe in it like you believe in it.

Logically, I didn't really think there were hundreds of people sprinting out the doors of their businesses to create a Jewish beer. But there certainly were a couple of Jewish wine and food companies at the time that had ideas which, if they'd chosen to pursue them, could have put me out of business before I got started. They already had the distribution network, the reputation, the graphics department, the PR, the sales staff -- everything necessary to do it.

As a brewer, Tim certainly fit the bill. He drove a beat-up Jeep with beer stickers on the back, and he wore his Carhartt jacket and a pair of duck shoes. He hand-delivered a lot of the beer himself. He told me he'd raised a million or two to start, and he'd just gotten another million. His plan was to build Brewmakers all over the west, to franchise it out. It was a great business model:

Make beer for nine cents and sell it for four dollars. He was going to set the world on fire, and he sounded reliable and confident. I really liked talking to him. His enthusiasm was contagious.

And then there was Simon, the brewer, who actually made all the magic happen. I learned in retrospect that when the frontman is talking a mile a minute, but the people who do the actual work have a slightly sour look on their faces and a hard time meeting your eyes, there's potential danger looming. Little did I know, the business was perpetually thirty to sixty days from going out of business.

But Simon was awesome to work with. My first meeting with him was pretty embarrassing. I started to realize that I'd never before consciously, carefully, methodically... *drank a beer*. Even in the brew pub where I worked in New Orleans, we never did any staff trainings or beer tastings. We never talked to people about hops or malts, or balance, or flavor contrasts and complements. At the time, if you'd put glasses of Sierra Nevada, Anchor Steam, and Sam Adams in front of me, I couldn't have told you the difference.

To this day, Simon and I still joke about it. I wasn't at all sure what I wanted, but I knew what I thought the *experience* should be like. Leaning over to him, I exclaimed: It should be like biting into the most delicious, perfectly grilled, wonderfully dressed turkey Reuben you've ever had! The flavor should fill your mouth in an utter moment of Manna.

"Turkey Reuben."

He looked at me like, "This guy's out of his fucking mind." Here's a brewer who had nothing to do with Judaism, didn't know Jewish food or Jewish shtick, and he's listening to me wax allegedly poetic about this journey we were gonna go on with our new beer. When I was finished, he paused a moment and then deadpanned, "Uhh, malts? Hops? Anyway, why don't you bring me a bunch of beers you think you like, and we can taste them together."

I probably brought in about thirty beers, and we "researched" together -- pale ales, ambers, red ales, ESBs. Everything in the category that was darker than golden and lighter than porters. It's amusing to know now how little I knew then.

There were a number of niche microbrews, generally contract-brewed, much like I would be doing, popping up in the Bay Area at the time. Queer

GENESIS ACT 1: BEERS IN THE GARDEN

Beer, waving the rainbow flag, was started by a very experienced marketing guy, and quickly disappeared. Brothers Brewing, one of several African-American micros that popped up around the country, had a good run for a few years in the Bay Area before running out of steam and closing up shop. Nationally, Three Stooges beer set the bar high, or low, depending on your perspective, for gimmick contract-brews. The partners, from outside Boston, sold truckload after truckload of licensed product that stacked high everywhere it went and sold out in cheap and furious bursts, until finishing its career a few years later, marked down, discontinued, never to return. But they sold some humongous numbers, for sure.

New labels for dogs, fishing, buxom blondes, a frog flipping the bird... Pretty much everyone who's done stuff like that, if they were successful, made their nut in fast and short-lived blasts of initial orders of inexpensive beer, or even t-shirts, and got out. More commonly, they ran into all the headaches and difficulties, and ran out of interest, and bailed. And for all the right reasons: They ran out of money, like I did. They ran out of hours in the week, like I did. Some had family problems, and some had drinking problems. Because of the reduced margins on contract brewing, there's very little money to be made on truly gimmick-y labels slapped on often forgettable beer.

From the beginning, I've known that I wanted to be a contract brewer -- but using my own version of what I thought could be a tasty collaboration with the right brewers. I certainly didn't have the money, but I also didn't particularly have the desire, to build a brewery. As my friends and ex-girlfriends love to joke, I can barely lift a finger to cook for myself. I've never been fascinated by the mechanics or the chemistry. I love experiencing and exploring the flavors, and I love the product as it moves into the world. I love the creativity, the imagination, the concept, the excitement. My energy comes from everything outside the vats, so that's where I figured I'd invest and spend my effort and my time.

Even with my admittedly limited beer knowledge, the goal has always been to make a truly high-quality beer that was interesting, flavorful, something I could be proud of and, of course, something I'd want to share with friends and, most importantly, drink myself. But I didn't know enough about brewing to know what that meant.

Simon would ask me specific questions about flavors, and I never knew how to answer him. I'd wander around in these terms I didn't really understand. He was great, and very respectful, considering the gibberish that was pouring out of my mouth. At the time, pale ales like Sierra Nevada set the standards. And amber ales from all over the west coast were extremely popular; every brewery had one. So I said, Let's make it in between the two styles. I could not describe it at the time, but I have since used these words on all our marketing shtick for Genesis Ale: "Crisp, smooth and perfectly balanced between a west coast-style pale and amber ale, with a supple malt sweetness and a pronounced hop flourish." Nice shelf talker. Yum.

My first beer ended up being a kind of hybrid. It didn't fit any particular category or style, which has been pretty much the same with all our beers since. We didn't know what to call it, so we made up the name "Light Brown Ale." I remember Simon was standing on the brewing ladder, and he said, "Brown ales like Full Sail and Newcastle and Negra Modelo are all a little darker." This beer was definitely lighter in color, had more of a malt flavor, with enough of a hop presence, though it wasn't a pale ale. The phrase "Light Brown Ale" has been on the label ever since.

Like many other things in He'brew history, it didn't exactly catch on. As it turns out, there was and still is no "light brown ale" category -- not at Great American Beer Festival, or World Beer Cup, or in Beer Judge Certification Program style guides. And no one jumped on it, any more than other companies jumped on the category for Jewish-themed beers. No sweat -- I'm happy as usual to be the only fish in a little pond.

I started doing my research in June, and I finalized the relationship with the brewery by the end of the summer. Simon brewed the beer, and we put out our small first batch of cases by the end of November. The whole thing took about four months. Looking back, that seems like an impossibly short time, given that I knew nothing about what we were starting. It became clear there was an endless, dizzying amount of details I never even imagined to try to get one little Jewish beer into the world.

I figured I was going to spend two grand of my own savings and see what happened. Hopefully, I'd cover my costs. And if people liked it, great -- maybe

I'd keep it going. Writing this down, it seems pretty straightforward. Then why at the time did it all seem *so damn hard?*

I was working on the stuff I was pretty confident I could pull off -- the shtick. I talked to some friends who worked in advertising agencies. We had a beer tasting at my place. I wanted to decide how outrageous to make the packaging, and the consensus was to make it as over the top as we could. Why not go for it?

I knew the beer was going to be called He'brew, and the tag line would be "Don't Pass Out, Passover." Every writer, radio voice, or amateur blogger who has ever interviewed me has asked, "So, do you ever get any negative feedback about the catch phrase?" The answer is, hardly ever. However, there was a brief period at the very beginning when I got some confused letters and comments. Once in a while, people would say, "I think I'm offended, but I don't know why. There's nothing in particular that I find offensive. Is this blasphemous?"

My original intention for the product was to reach those in the Jewish world called the "non-affiliated" -- those who are Jewish by birth, who will define themselves as Jewish, but won't do much about it. They don't have the education, or the tools, or typically much desire to participate in the community. Quite often they have never had a particularly positive Jewish experience to justify any concern or curiosity for a more meaningful Jewish life. For them, identity has felt more a burden than a birthright.

I had a very personal connection to that precise feeling: knowing you're Jewish, being proud that you're Jewish, but not doing, or even knowing how to try to do, much about it. We wanted the product to provoke a response. We wanted to riff off the Beastie Boys, Mel Brooks, *Seinfeld*. The whole point was to reach skateboarders, video gamers, smart-asses, hipster girls who were involved in the environment or politics or art or fashion -- whatever subculture all we Jewish kids were jumping into.

There was nothing else on the supermarket shelves that was relevant to celebrating that type of Judaism. Instead, we were aiming for the realm of literary magazines, art shows, indie-band side projects. The idea was intentionally outrageous. We never thought the product would show up at a

11

Jewish community center or at a synagogue. Tracy and I thought it was going to be for outlying pop-cultural Jews, much more like the future new-school-Jew projects of *Heeb* magazine and J-Dub Records.

I was conscious from the beginning that we were trying to infuse the beer itself, the labels, the events we chose to participate in, with content so people could use it as an occasion to explore Jewish culture. The only other specifically Jewish products were matzoh, gefilte fish, and Manischevitz. There were some kosher wines that were great quality, but with nothing particularly Jewish about the content. It was kosher, made by Jews, for Jews, but with no added layer of education through the product itself. That was an important part of what I hoped to accomplish.

In fact, kosher is not really an issue with beer. When it comes to beer, three rabbis will offer four answers. When I started, I didn't even get the beer certified kosher. Most products made with only grains, hops, yeast, and water would be kosher anyway. Wine, with its sacramental tradition, demands intricate regulation, Talmudic discourse, mystical interpretation. Beer, perhaps considered the drink of the Egyptian overlords (or, more recently, the German beer hall-ers), was barely even regulated.

Though the bumper sticker "Jews Don't Drink Beer" loomed, I knew from experience that the stereotype had enough exceptions to disprove the rule. With varying levels of Judaic identification, plenty of Jewish guys populated microbrewing. Just at the top were Ken Grossman at Sierra, Pete Slosberg of Wicked Ale fame, Alan Newman and Matt Cohen from Magic Hat, Alan Sprints at Hair of the Dog, Jon Bloostein at Heartland Brewing, David Myers at Redstone Meadery, Alan Shapiro (J-Bro -- now Sr., for our brethren in Seattle) of S.B.S. Imports, and of course the Rheingold family (not of the craft beer tribe, but from an earlier era of American brewing history). Countless brewers, reps, and staff have swung by the He'brew booth or a pint night to share the secret handshake. Each time that happens, it reinforces the existence of an unspoken, and rarely documented, underground Jewish brewing conspiracy.

But five thousand years of beautiful tradition -- "from Moses to Sandy Koufax," as John Goodman says in *The Big Lebowski* -- nevertheless could not muster a fraction of the rabbinic attention for beer that wine had earned.

GENESIS ACT 1: BEERS IN THE GARDEN

Anyway, the percentage of people in northern California who were keeping kosher was minimal. But as I expanded to L.A., Chicago, and New York, I knew it would be important to get the certification. It wasn't necessarily a huge selling point, but it was an obvious question. Every retailer would ask, "So it's a kosher beer?" Almost a year later, I began working with a kosher supervisor[1], Rabbi Lisbon at Kosher Supervision of America in L.A. Wonderful to work with, a real *mensch*, he cut me a deal on the Rabbi Seal of Approval, and he even let me slide on payments when I hit financial bottom a few years later.

Looking for a way to make the beer, the beverage itself, somehow more *Jewish*, I decided to use pomegranate juice in the brewing process. Pomegranates are one of the Seven Sacred Species listed in the Torah (Deuteronomy 8:8). When Moses leads the Hebrews out of Egypt through the desert to the edge of what Abraham had known as the Promised Land, he sends spies into Canaan. They return with a famous remark: "It's a land flowing with milk and honey." They bring back what become the seven sacred species -- wheat, barley, pomegranate, figs, dates, grapes, and olives. Pure, delicious, unadulterated malted barley (or wheat) is the base ingredient in all high-quality, adjunct-free craft beers. I figured I'd work from that.

I'd grown up with a pomegranate tree in a neighbor's yard, which helped me imagine a connection between California and the Middle East. Putting pomegranate in the beer was intended more for symbolic purposes than flavor, although I did think the sweetness and tartness might complement the sweeter malts and more bitter and spicy hops. (Of course, I didn't exactly *know* that at the time.)

I went to the wholesale produce market at the edge of the Mission District at five a.m. and bought eight crates of pomegranates. A group of friends gathered around the floor of our apartment and squeezed the pomegranates by hand, cutting open the crowns and squeezing them into a five-gallon white bucket. We were watching *ER* to pass the time. On the show, the hospital doors fly open, and blood is spurting everywhere. Meanwhile, rich crimson pomegranate juice is pouring over everyone's hands, dripping into the vessel

---

1 Especially with my original intention to reach unaffiliated Jews, kosher was even less important. However, as comes up later, when the organized and religious Jewish communities embraced He'brew, it became a priority to make sure everyone had confidence in the certification, so they could in fact include The Chosen Beers in the "sacred rites and rituals" of their lives.

between us. My cuticles were stained for weeks.

At the brewery the next day, Simon tossed the juice into the kettle. To pull out more of the flavor, we probably should've thrown it into the fermenter, but the boiling process basically pasteurized the pomegranate juice, which we figured was safer. (Didn't need an Odwalla-style E. coli outbreak, which had happened that same month.) We thought it was a beautiful way to add a hint of uniqueness to the beer, and it gave some Jewish content to the actual liquid in the bottle.

Though I was set on the name of the beer, I still needed a name for the company. I looked around at other beer companies and came to the conclusion that the way Sam Adams did it was pretty effective. The Boston Beer Company made Samuel Adams, which had several beer styles -- Boston Lager, Boston Ale, Cherry Wheat, etc. Each beer had individual names, and the brand was Samuel Adams.

I have a perfect visual memory of the exact moment I thought of the slogan "The Chosen Beer." Standing with the bathroom door slightly ajar, a couple feet from our bed, I was taking a leak, thinking how Budweiser claims to be the "King of Beers." Miller is the "Champagne of Beers," and Coors calls itself the "Banquet Beer," however outdated that may sound. Shlong in hand, it came to me: We'll call our baby The Chosen Beer. It seemed so obvious.

From there, the shtick just started pouring out fast and furious. Our first creation should clearly be Genesis Ale. And the first question at Passover every year is "Why is this night different from all other nights?" In town at one of our tastings, my buddy Eli's brother, a Jewish doctor from Seattle named Cookie, dropped the suggestion, *Why is this beer different from all other beers?* To this day, Cookie's inspiration remains the first line on the Genesis label.

In the beginning, there was an idea, and it was good. A beer to celebrate the Jewish-American experience. For the company name, I truthfully can't remember when I came up with the word *shmaltz*. Everybody loves to ask about that. It seems familiar and evocative, but most people are not exactly sure why. And it's just fun to say. Inevitably, someone at a sales meeting will say, "Doesn't that mean lard?"

Shmaltz, in fact, is Yiddish for "chicken fat" -- an old-fashioned Jewish comfort food. Grandmothers would spread it on black bread as a snack, a nostalgic standard of Jewish cooking. I quickly realized Shmaltz worked as the company name on at least three levels. Besides the idea of a nouveau hand-crafted comfort food, comedians like Sid Caesar, Mel Brooks, Henny Youngman are often referred to as having a shmaltzy sense of humor -- that Catskills shtick that I thought was so appropriate for the brand. On top of that, as a dedicated craft beer, we've always said up-front that we don't use adjuncts like rice or corn as fillers or cost-cutters. Though the origins may have started otherwise, these days major brewers use these other grains to make their beer cheaper and lighter (and less flavorful). The primary ingredient of every craft beer is malted barley, or wheat, or rye, and the word *malt* is right there in the middle of *shmaltz*. So it was, quite literally, a triple threat, a power trio: the trinity of Shmaltz.

The way I wrote the first label is the way I wrote the thirteenth: I sat around doing research with the Torah open, and I started grabbing passages. The Genesis Ale label came together like a dream. I tried to tie together the cultural crossroads of the Middle East as the birthplace of civilization -- every major empire, from the ancient world through the World Wars, has crossed paths right in the land of Israel -- with the idea that California represented a cultural crossroads of its own, where east meets west, convergent energies and philosophies, a sense of opportunity and history and destiny. *From the Golden Gate to the City of Gold.*

Just as I had my own identity crafted by my parents and my environment, by the pop culture around me and the history of California, the beer too has its own identity. I am proud of the fact there aren't a lot of beer labels that quote from the Torah. And it's not just irreverent. I was very serious about trying to make something that was funny, contemporary, and relevant to the Jewish experience I'd had, and wanted to share.

I wanted the product to create experiences for people. I wanted somebody to be drinking He'brew and think, "Sweet, this is a cool moment." Anchor Steam has an incredible history behind it -- they're tied into (and in fact have helped create) an authentic San Francisco tradition. So much about that brand has meaning and substance. Through something as commonplace as beer, my brand allowed me to draw on the history of an entire civilization and make it my own playground, my own canvas -- to cram as much shtick as I could on a beer bottle and all the stuff that would go on around it.

We wanted the label to shock and engage people. I used to say it was "flamboyantly Jewish." We felt like we were targeting customers like ourselves: young, creative, the Lollapalooza, X- and Y-branded generations. Yet very quickly, and totally unpredictably, I would get a deluge of requests for the beer from some of the largest, most established Jewish community groups around the country -- which made for some interesting reactions, given the art that we ended up using.

We were talking to a couple of artists down the hall from us about creating an image for the label, and all of a sudden Tracy said, "Why are we having someone else do it? I can do this." I said, I think that would be amazing.

Tracy's paintings have always been urgent and expressive, balancing structure and anarchy. Her work is abstract, for the most part -- very physical and lush. We talked about something referencing Chagall's iconic painting of a modernist green violinist dancing through the center of a village. We wanted something that would be a kind of *Fiddler on the Roof* meets the Mission District. She did a bunch of prototypes, and the one we liked best looked like a giant dancing green rabbi looming over a cityscape from San Francisco to Jerusalem.

It was supposed to be a bold statement -- "Wow, what is *that*?" Admittedly, it's a pretty aggressive image. I liked everything about it, though I did appreciate that the green face was rather intense. Whether the average beer buyer looking at the bottle-wielding friendly Godzilla would get the Chagall reference was debatable, though over the years I have heard a few people make the connection. But we weren't creating a product for the average beer buyer.

On the shelf, you couldn't miss it. The artwork definitely grabbed people walking down the beer aisle. At the time, many of the other craft-brew labels featured a dog, or a mountain, a fish, a sunset -- a lot of regional landmarks, usually reflecting the topography or the local wildlife. There was nothing like our label when it came out. I thought it did the job. But it also scared a few people.

All these years later, the labels for our Coney Island beers now get a similar reaction. Nobody walks by without looking at those labels. If I put my business card on the bar, someone three stools down will holler, "Wow, what's that?"

The office manager at my wholesaler in Kansas recently blurted, "It's kind of scary, and I'm afraid of clowns." Luckily, when we put out He'brew, not many people said, "It's scary, and I'm afraid of Jews."

We actually did clean up the image a bit. The rabbi had a slightly mangled mouth, so after we got the digital image we had a friend put a smile on his face. Our graphic-design friend Ramon made the lips red and straightened the rabbi's teeth a bit. We trimmed up the Rasta-dread earlocks, and we were ready to roll.

It certainly got us some instant recognition, some notoriety. For the most part, grocery store packaging is not the most provocative artistic endeavor. If that same image appeared on a *Playbill* for a Broadway production of *Fiddler on the Roof*, nobody would have batted an eyelash. But because it's a beer label, people didn't know how to take it. A few people thought it looked like the caricatures of Jews from Nazi Germany, but Tracy borrowed the rabbi's nose directly from her father and me.

The original artwork was probably three to four feet wide by two to three feet high. We rolled it up and brought it to my grandmother's house to show it to her and my mother and my aunt. Sitting around a suburban coffee table at my Granny's retirement community, it did not go over well. We unfurled this gorgeous, bright, powerful statement. All three women kindly complimented the background and cityscape, but they felt the face was grotesque.

As an artist, Tracy wasn't making Hallmark cards, and we weren't trying to sell He'brew to grandmothers (or even mothers). Between the shtick, the outrageous label, the ridiculous names, and the hint of pomegranate, we felt we definitely had a one-of-a-kind story to tell. We had a narrative that would be my most complex, multi-layered attempt to create art, commerce, and meaning. And to create a party.

CHAPTER 2

The Old Country

My love of words must be genetic. My dad was a big verbal game-player and a relentless practitioner of clever, often-corny vocabulary antics. He had all of Tom Lehrer's records and he worshipped Mel Brooks. I used to wear his *Young Frankenstein* t-shirt whenever I visited him. Most of his t-shirts came from those stores at the mall with iron-on graphics along the entire wall, and little felt letters you could use to whip up your own shtick. He personalized a pair of bright red shirts, his reading *Father and Son* and mine *Son and Father*. One my favorites was a true custom job: a picture of a cartoon turtle humping an army helmet, emblazoned below in felt lettering: "HOPE SPRINGS ETURTLE."

He also started a fake running organization. After my parents' divorce, my dad moved into a tiny studio apartment above an alleyway in Beverly Hills. To find his new pad, you went down Reeves Drive, entering the alley on the left. So he called his jogging club the "Reeves Gauche Athletic Club," and of course got t-shirts made. Even got a PR mention in *Runners World* magazine for finishing close to last (seven hours, baby!) in the New York City Marathon, "wogging" across the finish line with his running buddy and my stepsister, proudly sporting their RGAC shirts.

One thing I did not inherit from my father was his joy of running.

THE OLD COUNTRY

My mother and father met at Beverly Hills High School in Los Angeles. My grandmother -- my mother's mother -- taught tenth grade English through the late '50s to a roster of students including David Cowan (my dad) and his group of rambunctious, smart, and irreverent Jewish friends -- clean-cut class clowns and class presidents alike. My grandmother always told me how much she loved those kids[2].

My mom, Michael (yes, Michael), was born in Ross, in Marin County, north of San Francisco, while my grandfather was stationed in northern California at the end of World War II. After graduating from Berkeley, Jehiel "Jay" Lehman served as an engineer working on huge construction barges, man-made islands in the Pacific. While he was overseas, my grandmother brought my mom as an infant to L.A. to stay with my grandfather's extended family, a gaggle of lovely Jewish aunts who would fawn over me even through my bar mitzvah years. My mom's family would stay in southern California through her junior year of high school.

My grandmother, Anita Jacobs -- Granny to me -- came from a vibrant Jewish community on the Upper West Side in Manhattan. In their world, everyone was Jewish, perhaps traditional, but not particularly religious. Her parents likely kept kosher and went to synagogue for the holidays, but for the most part, they were interested in being American, in assimilating.

Her parents' generation, like so many other Jewish immigrants, started and ran a rag-turned-garment company on the Lower East Side, winning a coveted contract to produce uniforms for the Army in World War I. Granny loved to tell how her father had described horse-drawn carriages carting the raw materials across the Brooklyn Bridge. She said you could still see the sign for Jacobs Woollen on the side of the brick building all the way from the bridge. A rare example of a businessman in our family still alive by the time I was growing up, her cousin Bernie Jacobs became a titan of Broadway, president of the Shubert Theater organization. My mom and I got the sweet hook-up for third-row seats for *Cats*, *Dreamgirls* and *A Chorus Line* on my first trip to New York at age eleven.

Granny, whose mother had passed away when she was very young, went

---

2 My grandmother mentioned she taught Rod Serling, which I never could confirm, though I'll claim it, since I watched *The Twilight Zone* marathons religiously every year during my Thanksgiving trips to Los Angeles.

to college at sixteen, but she soon dropped out to care for her ailing father, who would also pass away within a couple of years. She moved to Boston to stay with her older brother, Len, and his wife, one of my favorite relatives, Aunt Alice. My grandmother met my grandfather in Boston at a party, while he was there for military training.

My mom always told me that she got her Jewish identity from Jay, her father. Jay's father, Alexander, moved to America from St. Petersburg, Russia, a rare Jew in Czarist-era dental school. Family lore suggests he traveled to the U.S. for a dental convention and stayed, landing in Kansas City, where he became the dentist for the sheriff's office. They'd bring in the drunk-tank brawlers for dental work; as I understand it, he had to get deputized. My grandmother kept a tiny pistol she said he'd been given by the Kansas City cops. I think my mother still has that in a lockbox somewhere.

My mother's grandfather, the dentist, was deeply invested in Jewish life, and he seemed to pass that along to my mom's dad. We have a box of his notebooks coordinating young men's Jewish groups and the local Reform movement push for a state of Israel.

My father's mother, Lola, was also born in New York, to a well-to-do Jewish family in Manhattan. Her father made his money owning horses and race tracks, and I remember photos of an infant Lola dressed to the nines in little white princess gowns. Her brother, Howard W. Koch, became a big *macher* in Hollywood, producing *The Odd Couple* and *Airplane!*, among other movies. He served as president of the Academy of Motion Pictures for a time. Uncle Howard was a family superhero, with a mansion in Beverly Hills and a big pool in the backyard that my dad and I would cannonball into on sweltering summer vacation days.

I got the impression that there was tension between Lola's family and her husband's family. My grandfather -- my dad's father, Sidney -- just never managed to become all that successful. I guess he made enough to get by, but compared to the other side of her family, his success must have seemed rather modest.

It's a bit hard to describe how so many from that generation, especially those who emigrated west to assimilate to our land of milk, honey, and Hollywood, could look and act and *feel* so Jewish without really *doing* anything very Jewish. When my parents got divorced, I celebrated Christmas with my extended southern California cousins -- definitely not the religious part of Christmas, but still with the Christmas trees, the presents, and the football. My dad was never bar mitzvahed; it just hadn't been a priority. We celebrated Passover together, and the chopped liver certainly smelled and tasted "Jewish," but that was probably the extent of it.

His father, Sidney, opened and ran a men's clothing store, a haberdashery, in L.A. Later he started his own small factory making stone benches and garbage-can holders for public spaces, which I remember seeing around the city when I was very young. I still have a two-pound piece of granite from his business that he drew a smiley face on, giving it to me after a forklift ride -- one of those impossibly vague memories that seems more like an old movie roll than one's life. Sidney seemed to have gone through a couple of failed businesses. They said he died of a heart attack.

Though they didn't live in the district, my mom attended Beverly High while my grandmother taught there. My parents met a couple years after my father had been in my grandmother's English class. They dated a bit in high school, eventually breaking it off when he went to college.

Before my mom's senior year, my grandfather got a new job in Sacramento building tract homes, and the family headed north. The differences between west L.A. and Sacramento must have been striking for her. Having to leave her friends and life behind at seventeen, the summer before senior year, sounded grim. I know she was excited to reconnect with many of her friends, and of course make new ones, the following year when she went off to school at Berkeley.

My father also had gone to U.C. Berkeley for his first couple years of college. Halfway through, his parents started to worry, and judge. He joined a Jewish fraternity, acting like your average early-'60s animal, getting so-so grades and wearing *cutoff jeans* and *sandals* to class. It was not what the generation of the '40s and '50s thought their kids should be doing, or how they should be looking. So they brought him back to finish up at UCLA, closer to home, where they could keep an eye on him.

My mom always said she was a "good girl," doing what she was supposed to do, studying, getting good grades. Perhaps she was a bit of a late bloomer.

Half her friends in her Jewish sorority were engaged, or even married, before graduation. While dating a guy named Phillip Michael, her friends wrote her a song imploring her not to marry him: If she did, her name would be Michael Michael.

Her first name came from her grandfather, Alexander ("Goc"), who was convinced the unborn child would be a boy. When she came into the world, they just stuck with Michael. I always thought it was a cool name, that it gave her just enough edge for a suburban mom -- though I didn't envy every single phone conversation I ever overheard, as she tried to make a reservation or a donation or an appointment: "Yes, it's Michael Cowan. Yes, Michael -- M-I-C-H-A-E-L. Uh huh, like the boys' name. Yeah, but I'm a girl. Yes, Michael…"

Far from the Summer of Love in the Haight, and farther still from Woodstock, I was born at Cedars-Sinai Medical Center in L.A. in 1969. We lived in West L.A., on Stearns Drive off Pico Boulevard in a Spanish-style duplex. Then a mostly-Jewish (if not particularly religious) area, Pico Blvd. became a little more of an African-American community in the late '70s, before later changing into an orthodox-Jewish, middle-class neighborhood, a little gourmet kosher shtetl, with tons of kosher markets and specialty shops. I head to Factor's Famous deli on every trip south, and the rabbi who certifies our beer kosher has his headquarters down the street.

My parents got divorced when I was four or five. After my mother's father died, my grandmother moved to northern California and got remarried, to a short, white-haired, well-to-do doctor from Stanford who would be the only grandfather I knew growing up. Though Marshall was definitely not Jewish, strangers used to approach him fairly regularly, shyly asking if he were George Burns.

My mom and I moved into the apartments just down the street from my grandmother, a five-minute ride by bike or skateboard. In the mid-'70s, most of the neighbors were divorcees and young families, and we had a gang of kids from five to fifteen in any given year taking the run of the small pool, the tanbark playground, and the hundred-foot football pitch inside the two-story, brown shingled compound. My mother got a job as a typist in the medical school at Stanford making three hundred dollars per month. She would eventually work her way up to become an Associate Dean for post-docs at the medical school.

I don't remember being traumatized by my parents' divorce, but they had a pretty shitty relationship after we moved to northern California. My mom was really not happy about the way my dad's parents had treated her during their marriage. She was also plainly pissed, disappointed, and frustrated with him. After they broke up, he slipped into a bachelor life, living a kind of beatnik/post-hippie lifestyle, forever buying, crashing, and buying another in a series of motorcycles to cruise around southern California. While my mom was becoming more and more professional, and more conscious of style (she read *Vogue* every month, and I remember the fat fall style issue arriving every September, much to my mother's excitement), my dad was dressing himself (and often me) in overalls, old Army fatigues and too-far-ahead-of-their-time ironic t-shirts. At home in Menlo Park, my mom encouraged, and I generally went along with, the *Preppy Handbook* fashion of the era.

As had my grandmother, my father started teaching English and history at Beverly Hills High School, before becoming a Special Ed teacher for most of his career. I'd go down to visit him every three weeks like clockwork, often for school vacations as well, bringing my homework and crashing his wild classrooms of ever-changing alternative teaching methods, which usually included a stray beanbag chair and a "KISS vs. Led Zeppelin" art project for the "remedial" students of the late '70s. I loved it.

Always the first "unaccompanied minor" on the PSA commuter flights Friday afternoons from SJC to LAX, I'd grab the first-row seat and let the attentive stewardesses check in on me with punch and peanuts. Sometimes my dad would come up for a long weekend or a big soccer or baseball game, and we'd go cruising around in his 1972 VW camper or, later, the Chevy conversion van, overnighting at Fort Baker or Big Basin. We talked on the phone twice a week, and he mailed me a letter every week, usually including a comic book or some other tidbit.

Yet despite his playful personality, when I went through that pre-teen, embarrassed-about-my-parents thing, it was more about him than my mother. He was a bit of a hippie outside his time. He was constantly smoking cigars and growing varying stages of beards. He carried man-bags before it was even vaguely faddish, and he sprinkled wheat germ on everything he ate. At his school, it was definitely a *thing* -- "Mr. Cowan is one of a kind." For a while he drove a humongous '66 Ford cab-over camper to work every day, chugging down the side streets of Beverly Hills with nonchalance.

He'd been in ROTC to help pay for college, and he stayed in the Army Reserves throughout his life. According to family tales, he served when the U.S. invaded the Dominican Republic. Story goes, he saw his commanding officer getting the Dominican women to do the laundry, but not paying them for the labor. He complained, got reprimanded for being a loudmouth about it, and got summarily dismissed back to the States.

Every summer he went on active duty as a teacher in Army Intelligence, Sixth ITASS, a boys' club with a few far-outnumbered women in uniform as well. I would visit him at Ft. MacArthur in Long Beach, and later at Los Alamitos, staying on base and generally playing mascot for the crew. The whole thing seemed like my own real-life sitcom. Chomping cigars and drinking scotch, everything to them was FUBAR -- Fucked Up Beyond All Recognition -- and the muckety-mucks were MFICs -- Motherfuckers in Charge. They had this pseudo-

THIS IS THE KIND OF IRREVERENT SHIRT MY DAD WOULD HAVE LOVED. THANKS TO FRED GROTENHUIS FOR SHARING THE SHTICK.

secret society, five to twenty-five of them in any given summer. With mock initiation rituals and half-baked award ceremonies, they called themselves the Mushrooms -- kept in the dark and fed nothing but bullshit. He wore these two little silver and turquoise mushroom necklaces for years. I can neither confirm nor deny my father's use of the magic variety.

Like his father before him, and his father before *him*, my dad was an alcoholic, though I didn't quite know what that meant back then. Grampa Dave (my dad's grandfather) and Grampa Sidney both had to finally stop "drinking" -- which meant hard alcohol -- and just stick to wine and beer. Whenever I visited my dad, at the end of every day, we'd go to the well-appointed liquor store across the alley from his apartment and see the very gracious, slightly stooped older Jewish couple who owned the shop. The Levys had been seemingly transported straight from the Old Country to Beverly Drive. He'd get a bottle or two of scotch, and they'd always give me a candy bar on the house. I would go to school with him, and he would spike his morning coffee with anisette. Judging by a couple of later, unsuccessful attempts to get through AA, he seemed to know he was a functioning alcoholic. I have the faintest memory of him mentioning that the stuff about God in the program just seemed… irrelevant.

As a kid, it drove me crazy that he was always such a slow driver. We'd be on the 405, going fifty-four miles an hour while everyone else was hauling at breakneck pace. It took us forever to get anywhere. Looking back on it, he probably thought he was "playing it safe," keeping it together.

There are a lot of father issues in the running of my business, in the way I deal with older men. My dad was nurturing, friendly, playful, and consistently loving. Rarely do I remember him disciplining me, saying no. He certainly challenged me -- whether in sports or hikes, or in school. But it would come as something of a shock to me when I began to navigate a competitive and adversarial beer world overflowing with strong-willed, older men, none of whom, understandably, were particularly interested in my emotional well-being.

I find that people have widely varying ideas about being an only child. Some will say all the best things -- that we're independent, responsible, ambitious, self-motivated. Others think only children are clearly spoiled and self-indulgent, bordering on narcissistic, obnoxious, demanding, and incapable of sharing or compromise. I'm sure they are both right.

If my father was my special weekend entertainment, with go-carts, BMX rides, barbecue and Taco Bell, my mother was my rock -- a rock of loving, encouraging, and patient support, and plenty of fun as well. She loved music and had a huge cabinet full of R&B records, from Motown to Michael Jackson, Teddy Pendergrass, and Al Green, as well as classics from John Lennon to Simon and Garfunkel, and of course, the ultimate, Barbra Streisand.

She went to work every morning and came home every day at the same time. As a classic latchkey kid, I called her every afternoon the moment I got home after taking the key from the Velcro pocket on my shoes, or climbing the balcony to dig up the spare buried in the planter. We ate together at the dinner table every single night, from the first day of kindergarten until the end of high school.

The only two nights she was gone through all those years were appropriately replete with adolescent debauchery. One of those two nights, I had some friends come over, and we got trashed. I made out with my friend's ex-girlfriend, and he climbed a tree to spy on us. The other time, my mom unexpectedly came home early and found my friend Jim and I intently playing quarters, with a case or so of empties between us on the kitchen table. She thought we seemed... *funny.*

My mom encouraged and supported the rather typical Reform synagogue Jewish education that I got in Sunday school from about fifth grade through my sophomore year of high school. Not a big percentage of the class to start with, I was generally one of only a handful who would miss class for the Jewish holidays. We lit Chanukah candles every year, went to family friends' for Passover, and occasionally found other ways to participate in the limited Jewish life on the Peninsula. In my room, a beautiful artist's rendering of an Israeli fighter jet flying over the Golan Heights hung alongside my own handmade collages of supermodels cut out from *Sports Illustrated* swimsuit editions.

My bar mitzvah -- April 24, 1982, on my thirteenth birthday -- did not make me a man. But after chanting a passable Torah portion and speechifying on the lessons of the *parsha* of the week on leprosy, I did accumulate, predictably enough, multiple Cross pen sets, Swiss Army knives, and savings bonds, as well as my first Walkman. The background soundtrack pumped out from the kings of the Los Altos bar mitzvah circuit, winners of the Most Appropriately-Named Band award, Hot Borscht. My parents and family were glowing.

My friends from junior high evidently felt otherwise. Over the next few months, and through the entire year of eighth grade, I would become exiled from my social world, excommunicated and ostracized from my group of friends, many I'd had since my first days of school. Though I am confident that my exile was unrelated to Judaism, my bar mitzvah certainly marked the beginning of an adolescent trauma that, even at forty-one years of age (come on, man, *get over it* already), makes me cringe.

Purely Guilty Pleasure time: Vote for the most appropriate Rush lyrics for my seventh grade:

1) "A modern-day warrior, mean, mean stride/ Today's Tom Sawyer, mean, mean pride"

2) "Living in the limelight, the universal dream, for those who wish to seem/ Those who wish to be/ Must put aside the alienation, get on with the fascination, the real relation, the underlying theme"

3) "He's old enough to know what's right, but young enough not to choose it/ Wise enough to win the world, but fool enough to lose it"

In seventh grade, I was balanced on the mountaintop: hottest girlfriend in the class, stylish middle part with slightly feathered hair, perfect scores in diagramming sentences. Just after my bar mitzvah, I ran for class president. *(Bear with me. I know this will all sound truly pathetic, but come on, people -- it was junior high. Feel free to grab a beer and skip ahead).* One of my good friends, arguably the best athlete in school, Danny came to my bar mitzvah despite the fact that we were on the outs with each other. We were in a bit of a power struggle, which involved several other close pals, and was played out through baseball, girls, and riding bikes. Looking back, I know he'd suffered a bit of his own temporary but painful exile during the year.

That spring, Danny led a revolt against me. My friend Andrew (coincidentally also Jewish) was running, like me, for president. In top adolescent form, tearing down my posters and marching through campus with signs reading "Andrew for President," Danny got everyone -- all our close friends, teammates, girlfriends -- to agree to vote against me. One of the girls, after becoming a good friend again in college, over a few too many beers once admitted to me, "I don't know why, but suddenly everyone decided that they would hate you."

Needless to say, I didn't win the election. Guys tried to push me around, throwing out bullshit anti-Semitic comments, not even really knowing what they meant. (Danny's father and another good friend were Jewish, anyway, so it all seemed pretty stupid.) Through most of eighth grade, I had few to no friends, until sweet, smart, and skinny Andrew, the victorious class president and an old carpool friend from Sunday school, along with his cadre of the "un-cool" kids (read: smart, creative, quirky, and also slight outcasts) gradually allowed me to hang with them. They saved me from despair.

Dovid, who would become one of my closest friends, had gotten booted from his own school and came to my junior high. We would cut PE to eat lunch and watch *Perry Mason* reruns at my apartment, across the street from school. (Dovid would later save me again, after my divorce, but those are tales for a later page.)

I bore my After-School-Special slings and arrows with glum endurance, and a lot of studying. Watching the whole scenario unravel, I think my mom was equally, if not more upset than I. When it was time to start high school, I can't remember who suggested it first, but she offered to get me into a different district. We were set to move when she heard about Menlo School, a small private high school.

Now a true Cadillac of prep schools, at the time Menlo was still a bit funky in its academic rigor. My 6'3" geometry teacher had been a linebacker at Stanford, and he taught us about Pi and hangover remedies while sporting a dyed mohawk and combat boots. By night he was a bassist in a punk rock band.

From my very first class through four years of Latin, my guardian angel and Magistra, Brigit Kubiak[3], whipped us into academic shape while letting Henry and me slip out to bring back donuts for class and play hopscotch on chairs for vocab quizzes. Her husband, Russ, also on staff, was famous for his salty talk, burly wit, and demanding curriculum. He once caught Jim and me with the same sentence in separate term papers about intercalary chapters of *The Grapes of Wrath*. Knowing the closeness of our friendship and trusting our word that it was an accident (which it was), we got off with a firm verbal spanking, and an A-minus for letting it happen at all.

---

3 Mrs. Kubiak still likes to remind me of a conversation we had near the end of senior year, in which she asked me what I really wanted to be good at. She remembers me responding, "Partying." Though plausible, and this may be a rationalization, I'm gonna say I likely meant being able to achieve maximum fun and extroverted, interconnected energy (not necessarily boozing), with a group of friends and strangers alike, specifically in an effort to seek truth and beauty... Not simply what I think she assumed was my goal, to merely drink as much as possible, whenever possible. I still like to imagine the moment she heard about the beer company, and thought to herself, "I knew it!" Win-win, I suppose.

I ONLY RECENTLY STUMBLED ON THIS GEM PASTED IN MY HIGH SCHOOL SCRAP BOOK

Maria Degnan, my freshman English teacher, schooled us in the ways of writing just about any type of academic paper -- and demanded we do it better and better, over and over… and over… throughout the year. And Steve Gill -- outrageous, intense, nurturing, brilliant, a recovered alcoholic, and yes, I don't think he'll be upset if I add, slightly crazy -- my ninth grade drama teacher, who would become my surrogate dad by senior year, as my teacher for literature and history (the Russian Revolution and the rise and fall of Nazi Germany) and, most memorably, the director of our spring musical, *Fiddler on the Roof.* His musical direction was famous in our "little village," and when he pulled me aside to say he wanted to put up *Fiddler,* but only with me as the lead, I said, No way -- the big-nosed Jewish kid playing a poor, singing milkman in a prep school full of Atherton gentiles will not be my destiny. But Steve proved to be a hard guy to say no to. The show, and I, did in fact go on, and the *L'Chaim*s at the curtain seemed to signal success.

A tight-knit group of ninety-one graduated in the class of 1987: Jim, Cristi, Ben (technically '88, but an honorary member of the '87 tribe), the fake-ID club and the amateur volleyballers, and a world of others I still stay in touch with -- amazingly only through phone and email, and not the wonders of Facebook. (Zak, Leah, and Melissa handle our Shmaltz fanpage, however, so sign up. I'm not *that* stubborn.)

In the summer before my senior year, my father was diagnosed with lymphoma. By this time he had a second family, having reconnected at his own twentieth high school reunion with Dale, who would become his second wife. After dating for seven or eight years, they tied the knot on New Year's Day, 1986. I had a good friendship with her younger daughter, Michelle, a year older than I, who once came north to be Jim's date for our junior prom. I covered for her one night in L.A. when she came home plastered and puked all over the bathroom tile. We told the parents it was bad Chinese food. Is it weird to have a crush on your stepsister?

Michelle's older sister Dena, was just old enough that I didn't get to know her very well. I still think of her as a cool '70s chick in Santa Monica. For some reason I always associate her with Foghat. Her boyfriend drove a killer 1976 Camaro, bright yellow and bitchin'.

My father died just a few months after his diagnosis, on November 4, which was the same date my parents had gotten married, and the day after his mother, my Grandma Lola's, birthday.

The date had yet another significance, which I found out about by mistake. Late the night before my dad died, my stepmom came into the hospital room, saying, "I can't believe this. What a ridiculous coincidence -- the same date his father killed himself."

I looked at my mom and she said, "Uh... right." We had to have a little chat at the Burbank airport the next morning, at five a.m., on our way back home for the moment.

Apparently, when my dad was about thirty, his father, Sidney, left a note at my grandparents' house, and my dad and his cousin had to go look for him. They discovered him after-hours at the plant, with the door to his office closed. He'd shot himself in the head with a shotgun.

For years while I was growing up, my dad had a painting in his apartment -- a five-foot orange canvas with streaks of color, shells, and all kinds of talismans attached to it. I found out later that he painted it after his dad died.

People often ask if I grew up in a family business, or if I had a lot of businesspeople around in my life when I was younger. I tell them I really knew nothing about business as a kid -- it just never came up, with my dad and grandmother teaching for all those years, and my mom working at a university. I guess the only connection to an entrepreneurial impulse would have traveled through my grandfathers, neither of whom was particularly successful professionally, and one of whom was clearly a troubled and tragic soul.

For years, until very, very recently, I've felt that at any moment my business was simply going to fall apart. Perhaps one phone call, a piece of mail, a meeting, and it's all over. All the hard work and hours invested for nothing, the money truly lost, the project over and done. Failure.

For some people, worrying makes them depressed. Luckily, whether from genetics or by training, like many entrepreneurs, fear forces me to work. Anxiety makes me sublimate. My response is to pick my fingers in nervous habit and start jamming on projects, writing out schemes on scraps of paper, and then banging down the lists, trying to juggle as much as I can possibly load up with. It has rarely been elegant, and often ineffective, trying to crank it over and over, ram it down the world's throat, in the perpetual terror that if I don't do enough, it could crumble at any moment.

In the summer after my sophomore year of high school, I went to Israel for six weeks with my confirmation class and hundreds of other teenagers from around the Bay Area and the country. The "teen tour," at least when I was at that age (long before the Birthright program), glistened as the crown jewel, a much-anticipated rite of passage for Jewish teenagers. After finishing your bar mitzvah and going to confirmation class on Monday or Tuesday nights for a few more years, this is the big payoff.

Well-adjusted and comfortably sarcastic guys traveling in close quarters with cute, smart, and funny girls. No drinking age in Israel meant many of us were ready to pound Maccabees the minute our chaperones turned their backs. Later, returning at twenty-five, I realized I'd retained almost no meaningful Jewish education growing up. I went to Sunday school every weekend. I felt Jewish, I guess, or at least I self-identified as Jewish. But I had no substantive skills or knowledge about anything to do with religion. I knew that Jews think education is important, they think family is important, and that Passover is a holiday that celebrates freedom. Basic stuff – nothing, say, a Unitarian or a Baha'i couldn't get behind.

Still, the trip proved transformative. Traveling out of the U.S. for the first time, I lost twenty pounds, grew a few more facial hairs, made out with two or three girls over the course of the summer. Marla from Cupertino let me put my completely inexperienced fingers down her pants, kissed me, and said it was OK that I had no idea what I was doing.

We drank too much. One night, walking home at one a.m. through Tel Aviv streets after sharing multiple jugs of cheap Russian vodka, with even cheaper orange drink as a chaser, somebody shouts that it would be a great idea to run home. I'm barreling downhill, running in the full glory of youth, buzzed with the breeze of the world in my face. All of a sudden there's a car coming straight at me. Clad in cargo shorts, I fall to my knees on the asphalt in a perfectly executed disco slide.

We got back to the hostel and I fell into bed, straight asleep. When I woke up, the sheets had caked to the huge, bloody scrapes on my knees. The following week I would receive the perfect punishment: freshly scabbed knees bobbing in the concentrated salt of the Dead Sea.

That kind of stuff wasn't what you'd call a particularly Jewish experience. But everywhere you went in Israel, everyone was … *Jewish*. (Except, of course, for the twenty-five percent of the population that was *not* Jewish.) We saw all kinds of Jews, all shapes and sizes, attitudes and colors. Young old skinny fat rich poor dark light religious atheist, soldiers and protestors. A far cry from Menlo Park.

We were lucky enough to spend four or five days living with families in Kiryat Shmona, a town in northern Israel. We experienced a bomb scare late one night and packed into the family's air-raid shelter. Hanging out at a swimming hole one afternoon with ten or twenty Israeli boys, all thirteen to seventeen years old, reinforced how different our lives might become. Some were just spazzing out, wrestling and horsing around like any other summer day. Others were talking about going into the Army shortly for their mandatory three-year military service.

Our religious education went in waves. To the counselors' credit, they consistently tried to infuse our daily experiences with references to Jewish history and thought. We'd be doing something that seemed secular, and they'd put a little Jewey twist on it: "By the way, this is where Abraham and Sarah walked after leaving their homeland for the promise of a new life." We'd go to a hillside near Tel Aviv to a scenic lookout for a gorgeous sunset, and the guides would point out a Holocaust memorial or a 1948 War monument. Holding a falafel in Jerusalem, they'd drop, "This is a spot that King David, Jesus, and Mohammed likely stood on."

As young, clueless, and enthusiastic as we were, we couldn't help but be inspired. I definitely had those moments where I'd think, I'm gonna take a year off and go into the Israeli army and be a hero. We're going to save the future of Jewish people!

Was it brainwashing propaganda? Absolutely. We saw a bit of Arab life and some Palestinian towns, and learned a sanitized version of the creation myths we were there to be fed.

But the stories of a culture and tradition and an evolving civilization going on every day, with our sixteen-year-old selves seemingly able to make even the slightest impact on the momentum of the life surrounding us -- this felt too profound to dismiss. For a teenager raised on the hero-worship of rock stars and quarterbacks, the history being lived as daily life there felt urgent and vibrant in a way far more compelling than Stanford Shopping Center or MTV.

I was growing more conscious of my Jewishness, though still without much substance. It was more the *style* of Judaism that attracted me. Living as an assimilated Jew, you go to popular culture to discover what you like, whether it's Einstein, Sarah Silverman, Jon Stewart, or Krusty the Clown. That's where I drew inspiration, but I didn't know the difference between morning and evening prayers, or the interpretations of kosher or Shabbat, or any rules about sexual relations, marriage, the way one might interpret stories from the Torah. None of that would happen until I went back to Israel when I was twenty-five.

That first trip was more like *Dazed and Confused* than *The Chosen* -- with a piercing. Before we left Jerusalem, my friend Jamie and I got our left ears pierced. I got a little gold Jewish star that even made it into my junior year high school headshot, above the Aca Joe canvas sport coat, collar snapped up, and a burgundy lizard-skin skinny tie.

For the rest of summer and the school year beyond, we felt like we owned the suburb. I basically raced everywhere I went, driving my pumpkin-orange 1970 Mustang convertible. The 302 had been my aunt's car and then my mother's until, with the help of my remaining bar mitzvah money for insurance, it became mine. Equal parts teen romance and teen horror flick: An afternoon with a trunk full of wine coolers for a U2 show; a different late night with a stolen handicap parking sign; the pilfered headstone from the Redwood City cemetery for our unsanctioned scavenger hunt. And finally one night, hauling ass down the El Camino, clowning with friends in cars behind me, glancing up just in time to stand on the brakes before slamming into the back of the car turning left directly in front of me.

Over smashed metal and glass, our cars limped onto the side street. In a moment of terrible coincidence, two other guys from my high school class stepped out of the car, all of us shocked and shaking. I realized I'd been a split-second away from killing all three of us.

I know I'm lucky -- my teachers and my parents made sure I knew what *hubris* meant. I've had recurring lessons that have brought me back down to earth, that let me revisit how I want to be in the world. The stupid, small-minded, potentially hurtful and destructive shit that we give and receive offers a chance to change, to mend, to choose. There's a difference between being confident, positive, and outgoing -- aggressive, even, in pursuing one's vision (or creating that vision in the first place) -- and being arrogant, blind, immoral, disgraceful.

And then my dad died.

But having my dad die at that age didn't feel like a lesson, it just fucking *sucked.* In July, during his usual summer Army stint, he'd complained about some stomach pains, which suddenly became a diagnosis of fast-moving lymphoma. By the fall I was sitting beside his bed, again in the hospital in L.A., after a brief period at home in which it looked possible that he might somehow recover, only to have his body fall apart completely.

Through those last three months, his wife, Dale, spent every minute beside him praying for a miracle and lovingly nursing him, along with my aunt, his sister Jill, and my grandmother Lola. Both my grandfathers had passed away before I was old enough to realize it. I had never experienced death before, and it just didn't seem possible. I had no idea how to respond. I don't know why I thought this, but at the time, my response to it all was the thought that I just needed to be... *strong*. I tried to be what I thought was the sturdy and steady Man among all the women in my life -- my stepmother and stepsisters, my aunt (my dad's sister), my grandmother, and even my mom. I even went to school that very day. I tried to act like it was all OK. I'm not sure why.

I had so much angry bile inside me after my dad died, bottled up, occasionally gushing out. Given how soft-edged and open he was as a person, it's particularly strange to me that I responded by shutting down that part of myself, something that I recognized and valued in him, that I think he passed along to me. I had spent a fair amount of time with him throughout his illness and was able to slowly and lovingly say goodbye. Perhaps it's natural to overcompensate for a pain that's so unanticipated and deep. So astonishing.

But I also had absolutely everything else going so great for me at that age. School, friends, success, and the promise of more of everything. I think I thought being *strong* somehow made me *better* -- or at least safe. His death brought a darker, even more sarcastic edge to my humor. It definitely blocked much of my emotional growth for many years. I think I clamped down on anything other than fun, curiosity, and imagination. Was it an escape, or was it just life?

My grandmother often called herself an "existentialist." Growing up, I heard that all the time from her. I think I was beginning to feel like I knew what she meant.

CHAPTER 3

Let There Be Rock, Blood, And Revelation

All through college and up until the time of my second Israel trip, I didn't even know where the Jewish student union was at Stanford. But my grandmother, my mother's best friend, and I sent my mom to Israel for her fiftieth birthday, and when she came back she got involved with the Jewish community on campus. Just a few years later, I was offered the job of temporary executive director of the Stanford Hillel, which I turned down. I've always wondered if I'd taken that job, would I have started He'brew at all? Probably not.

At Stanford, my major became a hodgepodge of everything I could justify under the theme Theories of the Individual. Technically the B.A. says English with an Interdisciplinary Emphasis, which came to mean, as I was scrambling to graduate on time, that I could justify credits for everything from literature to psychology to history, art history, philosophy, Greek mythology, and even earth sciences (how we *experience* the earth). Classes on Jung, Marx, Freud, central European novelists (just as the Berlin Wall was coming down), religious rituals across world cultures, the political art of the French revolution, and of course the great western canon, from man's state of nature through predestination vs. free will and deconstructing post-modern pop culture. Everything, that is, except business and economics, hard science and math. Advanced volleyball

-- two separate quarters -- counted as class credits, though not toward my major. I tried.

Starting school, I was all the way into a full-blown Jim Morrison phase. Sitting in the dark in my dormitory bed, writing poetry. Awful shit I never want anybody to see. My girlfriend at the time, Olivia, led me on our bikes out to a construction site on the edge of campus, where she had spray-painted a quote from the Lizard King's book of poetry for me on a thirty-foot plywood wall. By far the coolest thing anyone had done for me up to that time. Cool, for the moment -- she ended up dumping me and sleeping with this jack-off, one of those pseudo-genius psychologist types everyone knows in college. He was so... *intense.*

Spring quarter of freshman year, I joined the ranks of the worst college DJs ever. We had three lectures a week for Western Culture, the core block of my Humanities higher education class, and I cut one session each week to spin records. At KZSU in the basement of Memorial Auditorium, I'd bring three beers with me and play wonderful, terrible classic rock. They still had a set format, with jazz from six to nine a.m., classic rock from nine to noon, and progressively wilder, newer (and better) music though the afternoon, wrapping around to "anything goes" from midnight to six a.m. Normally the newbie DJs got stuck with the three a.m. shifts, but since no one wanted to play classic rock, I got lucky (for me, not for the listeners). I went head to head with KOME, KSJO, and KRQR (the Rocker!) for morning AOR attention. I invited friends to guest-DJ, including Jim in his post-operation Frankenstein neck brace, and Ben, who cut class from spring semester at my old high school to judge such epic battles as Randy Rhodes vs. Angus Young and themed shows such as the Rush Hour (all B-sides). I consistently left the microphone off by accident, most notably during a three-minute dirge tribute to the death of Andy Gibb, and played records at the wrong speeds. I got a lot of angry, disgusted phone calls. But I gave them free tickets to local shows, which seemed to calm the raging beasts.

I did a little college theater as well. I played Creon, the Greek king, in a play that was this guy's senior thesis. I got to play the ruthless, one-dimensional tyrant in Bertolt Brecht's version of the myth. Never able to really get over myself to commit to any real form of acting, I'd started in high school with whatever Steve Gill called his introduction to acting class. Trust exercises, the mime box, and simple scenes, along with some experimental stuff I likely didn't throw myself into. Generally, I stared at Pammy Brown, at the time the most beautiful girl I'd ever seen up close, not really knowing what I could possibly ever do about it. She was a senior.

At college, I played rugby for two years. My buddy Gabe told me, "Seriously, our team sucks. (Not true for long: Just a few years later, they would start making the regional and national playoffs consistently, with no help from me.) But you'll get into great shape. Then you drink a bunch of beer and try to pick up girls, who for no understandable reason like hanging around muddy guys singing about incest and bestiality." The bumper sticker sounds heroic: "Give Blood. Play Rugby." Over the course of my career, I had a couple of nasty injuries. One time I went up to catch what's called an up-and-under, a high kick, and the ball came straight down from two stories up, directly onto my pinkie. I got a spiral fracture in the third joint of my little finger. It fucking killed, like the end of the world, every time I had my hand in the scrum. I tried unsuccessfully to play with a finger cast, so I went on injured reserve for a few weeks, until the bone fused.

The only blood I gave through injury actually happened the night before a match. In a particularly intense game of Nerf Hoop in our dorm, my friend Matt went up for a jump shot and threw a huge right elbow that smashed me flush in the center of my face. Bleeding uncontrollably, I went to the campus clinic, and they stuffed it with gauze and sent me home. On Saturday morning, we drove to Sacramento for the game. I played the position known as a lock, where your shoulder supports the ass of the guy in front of you and your head is jammed between everyone else's knees in the scrum. Rather uncomfortable with a broken schnozz.

In the spring quarter of my junior year I went to Italy, which, of course, had a whole lotta Christianity going on. I'd taken a captivating art history class the quarter before, and I loved the three months in Florence and the nearby towns, going from church to church, seeing variations on the Annunciation to the Pieta, all the Bible scenes created to glorify the wealthiest ruling families and educate the illiterate masses on the ways of God. A few years before at Stanford, one afternoon we were tripping on acid, floating through the main quad. I remember staring at Memorial Church, with its huge mosaic of preaching Jesus, and thinking, *I'm so glad I have my own thing and don't need to be a part of that whole thing.* What a heavy trip, man. Well, gotta go play frisbee!

By the time I went to Italy, I'd stopped freaking out about churches so much and became fascinated with the history and creativity pouring out of these institutions. I lived with a cool, very "modern" Italian family -- as in, the mother was rarely around, and the father was never discussed. When I arrived, speaking no Italian (even after over a year of classroom language instruction), a slightly hunched older woman in a house dress greeted me at my new home. I assumed she was the Mamma and stumbled through some very very basic greetings and thanks. Took me about four or five days to realize she was the maid, and that the mom was out of town. There was an older sister who was my age, a hot Florentine, who would come home after her job, get food on the table for her younger brothers and me, and then go out every night, dancing and smoking hash until two in the morning. She had no interest in talking to yet another American college boy. I played soccer with my "brothers," who were maybe eleven and fifteen, and we had a blast. They let me use the family scooter, just fixed after a recent crash, and I'd cruise through five hundred-year-old streets to meet friends at the college bars cranking Pink Floyd and Led Zeppelin.

My growing curiosity about art and the hero-worship of Michelangelo and related artist rock stars led to a senior thesis on two paintings – Velazquez's *Las Meninas* and Picasso's late-career reinterpretation. Turned in only two months after graduation (thanks for letting me walk, Professor), my opus, termed "A Question of Meaning," studied three sets of critics looking at the same paintings, each reaching wildly different conclusions about what the art, and the artist, meant. The possibility of multiple, even contradictory, truths embedded in the same text or tradition feels so reasonable to me. This openness to an intuitive struggle with interpreting ideas, images, and culture has long informed my sensibility about so many parts of my life, from rock lyrics to beer flavors to a crafted sense of my own Judaism.

During college, Ben and I had crashed a spring break in New Orleans with our high school friend Jim, who was in architecture school at Tulane. There was no last call, and extensive funk possibilities beckoned. After graduation,

Cristi and I decided to relocate to the French Quarter.

I had a vague notion about doing something with art or literature, maybe music promoting, or even theater. I had a spectacular time in New Orleans, though Cristi, I know, had less of a great time, at least when I was around. Longtime close friends, we were roommates on Toulouse Street only briefly. In a serious relationship with a good friend of Jim's, Cristi got a job as a paralegal, for which she had to wear panty hose to work every day, and be at the office at eight a.m. A major damper on our weeknight festivities. What the hell? I thought. We were going to be artists, right? Or at least committed bohemians, low-level hedonists, blah-blah-blah Dadaists. Justifiably so, Cristi never tires of calling out my hypocrisy for giving her shit about being a paralegal -- and then later becoming one myself in Washington, D.C.

I got a job in the Quarter at Crescent City Brewhouse, which would be my first specific exposure to craft beer. The older brother of a guy we knew from Stanford had opened the first brewpub in Louisiana with a German brewmaster, Wolf, who remains there to this day (and is now, I believe, the exclusive owner). Kent planned to road-trip to New Orleans to work at his brother's pub, surviving and thriving in what would be a skanky, cockroach-infested summer sublet. The last week of school, Olivia, my ex-, and Kent's current girlfriend, introduced me to Peter, his New Orleans co-conspirator. Never knew the guy during our four years of college, but when we started talking, Peter and I realized we'd been at all the same parties and knew all the same people. We'd both gone to the Neil Young-Sonic Youth concert, the same Grateful Dead and Pink Floyd shows; we were both regulars at the same jam-band Happy Hours. Peter would soon become one of my best friends and, eventually, the most consistent and generous donor to the Shmaltz couch-surfing foundation.

The Brewhouse was my first real bartending job. I think the management thought I was better friends with Kent and his family than I was, so with my comment about having "bartending experience" (two shifts for my dorm R.A.'s bartending scam for campus events), they let me get behind the bar right away. After my first preposterous attempt to make a Dewars and water (this story only works with the thick New Orleans accent -- come to a book reading), I spent most of my time pulling drafts. They made all their own beer, and it was good stuff -- the beer was better than everything else they served there. They made three styles: a pilsner, an amber, and a dark beer called Black Forest that was my favorite.

The job itself wasn't the greatest, but it was a hell of a lot better than most others in the Quarter. I'd just gotten my second and third ear piercings, but management didn't let you wear earrings. I told the boss some story about a fictitious girlfriend getting it for me for sentimental reasons while we were apart. I worked every shift for nine months with a Bandaid on my earlobe, covering the new studs.

This being the service industry *and* New Orleans, the staff had some eccentricities. All the chefs seemed to have gout -- chubby fingers swollen over wedding bands after a lifetime of too much decadence and too little fruit. One manager hawked his five thousand dollar crotch-rocket motorcycle to buy an engagement ring for his girlfriend. A month later, she ditched him but kept the ring. Understandably, the guy was pissed, but I guess he was too much of a pushover to get it back. Instead, he chose to direct his bitterness at the staff.

Another manager was doing a ton of blow, and later smoking crack, in the downstairs bathroom. One night he grabbed the entire night's cash sales and split town. Unbelievably, after he returned to town and set up a payback plan, they actually let him come back several months later and return to his old position. The last manager played it cool and plotted quietly, finally stealing over fifty grand -- basically all the money the place earned in a week -- never to be heard from again. Rumor had it they sent the FBI after him.

Creatively, I tried my hand at a few different things during my time in New Orleans. My first paid acting gig came as Dead Body #2 in a Bourbon Street dinner-theater murder mystery. A plant from the get-go, I came in with the audience and made small talk like I was there to see the show. In the middle of the salad course, I jumped up to escape the lead "detective" and got shot in the back, my corpse dragged off by two plainclothed "policemen" (barbacks). Twenty-five dollars a night, free dinner and booze. We opened with three performances the first week, two the second, one the third, and closed. One more night of work on a paddle boat for the same show, and that was the last of my working actor-slash-bartender career.

Though I lacked the lifestyle commitment of the originator, I started taking some Bukowski short stories and turning them into one-act plays. I planned to start a little theater group, and even got one of the hottie waitress/actresses from work to agree to perform. After a botched tryout reading of Ginsberg's "America" for a well-respected regional theater group, I closed the curtain on my short lived acting career and started a literary magazine instead -- well, a 'zine, during the early-'90s self-publishing renaissance.

I had no idea how to do anything in publishing or graphic design. I got a job answering the phone at the office of the New Orleans Symphony, which, as it was going out of business, needed one lone soul to sit in a grubby little room in an anonymous Central Business District building. It was very slow, but a guy next door ran a computer center, training arts groups to use technology. Extremely encouraging, he let me learn how to use Pagemaker for free while I waited for Symphony calls to come in. I started soliciting writers and artists to contribute (mostly my non-starving, non full-time-artist friends), and I called the magazine *Projector*. I got a few of the architecture professors at Tulane, local poets, and grad-student friends of friends to submit stuff. I'd print maybe a couple hundred copies. I sold subscriptions to my friends and family -- I think I sold seven, or twelve -- and I put out five issues. I used to walk around the French Quarter and Uptown and sell them for a dollar on the street. Sweet margin. My most illustrious sale was to Richard Ford's wife, who was evidently staying in the Quarter. I said, Hey, want to support New Orleans artists?

"I already do," she replied.

Here's how little I knew about what I was doing: I had a friend in design school at UCLA, and she suggested, "Why don't you change the font? It all looks the same." Already on my third issue, I said, What's a font? She made me some gorgeous pieces that I put in the next issue. (Where are you now, Kelly?) I wish I'd kept it going. I was quite proud of the last issue of *Projector*. By then I had moved up to the position of Desktop Publishing Assistant at Kinko's, doing resumes and menus for po-boy shops for $6.50 an hour, by far the most I ever made in town.

I stumbled into another part-time job on my block, selling tickets to shows at a new-ish club on Decatur called Storyville. Named after the notorious red-light district that had been closed for nearly a century, respected movie director Taylor Hackford (*An Officer and a Gentleman*, *Ray*, the video for Lionel Ritchie's "Say You, Say Me") opened a comedy and music club that mildly referenced the days of much wilder jazz and legalized prostitution.

I worked in a tiny cubbyhole overlooking the sidewalk for $4.50 an hour, plus a few drinks each shift and free shows. After the manager with a far-too-large coke habit died at way-too-young an age in the bed of his not-previously-disclosed mistress, the joint went under and was remade as Jimmy Buffett's Margaritaville. Insert snide "Cheeseburger in Paradise" comment here.

Watching the acts come through sort of deglamorized what I imagined was the whole show-business gig. Many comedians had plenty of talent, but as regional guys without TV fame, just grinding out the comedy tour, most of them underwhelmed, if not flat-out bombed, with the southern tourists and suburban Metairie couples the place tended to draw. Many of the comedians ended their week-long runs bitter, insulting the crowd. The bands usually got the same treatment. We were no Tipitina's or Maple Leaf, and there just wasn't the right vibe. I saw Dream Theater, sort of a minor-league Rush, who went on to have a long and successful career as a working rock band. At the time, they stacked an enormous wall of amps in the huge echo chamber of the main room. Besides me, I really don't remember anyone else watching the show. Deglamorizing for me. Demoralizing for them.

Working at Storyville was the first time I experienced the sideshow shtick that would become such a big part of the success of Shmaltz. When Jim Rose's Circus Sideshow opened for Lollapalooza in New Orleans, the crew threw a private party at the club. I believe it was Mr. Lifto who had somebody come up and drink beer through a straw stuck through the tip of his penis. That someone was not I.

I also met a long-haired, fresh-faced bartender recently arrived from Boston who stepped into our manager's office to apply for "whatever shifts you have." Jim Sullivan (professionally, these days, James) and his sweet, hilarious, and lovely wife Monica would become some of my dearest friends during our New Orleans days and beyond, as we both moved from city to city over the next two decades. Jim/James, who'd started writing record and band reviews for a local Boston music paper, plugged away at freelancing with the New

Orleans music rag *Offbeat,* among so many others, eventually committing to the craft in San Francisco, where he would serve for many years as the Pop Culture Critic at the *Chronicle.* Back on the east coast, he would become a consistent contributor to the *Boston Globe* and settle into writing books. *Jeans: A Cultural History of an American Icon*; *The Hardest Working Man: How James Brown Saved the Soul of America*; and, most recently, *Seven Dirty Words: The Life and Crimes of George Carlin.* And now the tale of Shmaltz Brewing.

Other than the violence, the crime, and the entrenched poverty, I loved the whole experience of living in New Orleans, and have tried ever since to continue making as much of life as possible an adventure. Standing on our raggedy front porch overlooking Decatur Street near the French Market, I remember a lady hollering from the street below, "Do any of you people have real jobs? How the hell do you live like this?" It never occurred to me that a career should be the most important thing. Whenever I have to choose one over the other, I'll always choose less money and more flexibility, lifestyle over cash.

However, after a year and a half or so of the Big Easy, I decided, along with so many enthusiastic young peers, to flock to Washington, D.C. Bill Clinton had just been elected, and I wanted to share in the excitement of what we thought might be true progress. I was nothing but a voter -- I hadn't taken any responsibility for the victory that past fall. Still, I figured I was young, eager, and smart enough, and I had one or two connections in D.C. I would become a White House whiz kid, fixing the world.

I arrived into Union Station on February 1, 1993. It was thirty-one degrees and raining sideways. Other than skiing a few times, I had never been in cold weather before. I walked around in my dyed-burgundy Army jacket, in a turtleneck and tennis shoes with two pairs of socks. Walking down the Mall to check out my new home, I thought, Shit, it's cold. Wow, it's really cold. Holy crap, I'm fucking freezing!

To make a few dollars, I got a lousy temp job, working in an open-air warehouse putting together flowers for Valentine's Day. The locals took one look at my chilled California bones and said, "Hey Man, what are you doing? Get boots and a heavy jacket, a scarf and some gloves."

I went to a Democratic National Committee job fair with a resume highlighting my 'zine, the New Orleans Symphony, Kinko's, and some assorted volunteer stuff. I got in line with about a thousand people. All the guys in front of me were carrying briefcases and wearing suits. All the women behind me, too. The guy on one side of me was talking about how he'd run Clinton's campaign in Kentucky, and the one on the other was doing some innovative project for the Department of Education. I had on my turtleneck and wool sweater -- the nice one -- and my Army jacket and my spit-shined, slightly battered Doc Martens.

Not surprisingly, I didn't get the hook-up with the White House whiz kids.

The closest I could come was to get a job as a paralegal, for a woman whose husband was the junior senator from New Mexico. Anne Bingaman served on the board of trustees at Stanford, and she liked to pack her staff with as many Stanford kids as possible. The Friday before I was supposed to start, I read in the *Washington Post* that she'd been appointed to the Justice Department as the assistant attorney general for antitrust. And just like that, my vaguely glamorous connection was replaced by a nice-enough, but generally uninspired, Jewish lawyer from the Atlanta office. I'd been hired to work on a contingency-fee case against the phone company in Florida, which had bilked millions of people out of $1.75 a month apiece for ten years. Added up, the scheme raked in something like $500 million. I started in a cubicle before moving up to a tiny shared office, where my officemate and I eventually installed a dart board and a Nerf hoop.

It was my first time in a professional office. On the first day, I wore my Docs until a smiling, passive-aggressive H.R. manager quietly suggested I go out and buy a pair of business-appropriate shoes. I went to a mall in northern Virginia and bought two pairs of slacks, one black and one dark green, that I don't think I ever bothered dry cleaning. It was just work anyway, and who would even notice? I had two ties from high school, got another as a gift from Mom, and bought one more on the street for three dollars.

As corporate law firms go, Powell Goldstein was rather progressive. They took on projects like Democratic housing proposals and health care, but of course with the usual *Fortune* 500 clients as well. We took classes with paralegals from other offices, learning things like how to use Lexis-Nexis.

They'd say, "You have it good. We have to put on our jackets just to go to the bathroom." Still, the hierarchy was brutal. Most of the partners would not even look at you in the hallway. The "lowly" paralegals, most of whom had Ivy League degrees, would go to Happy Hour with the young associates, who soon enough would need to decide if they should get off the track to pursue their intellectual and professional passions, generally guaranteeing a sizable pay cut. Either that, or they would ride that train to partner-land, with a fat hourly increase… and spiraling expenses, perhaps a mortgage on a second vacation home, private schools, newer-bigger-swankier cars, and rare breaks from their own rain-making grind.

We went to Anne Bingaman's appointment announcement in the Justice Department courtyard, which included the infamous Lani Guinier thumbs-up moment. I got to shake Clinton's hand, and at the party for Anne's confirmation, my co-worker and roommate Porter and I approached Janet Reno when no one happened to be around. I told her my mother and my grandmother, being staunch feminists and huge Clinton supporters, would be so thrilled that I'd met her. And she blurted, "Well, when your mother comes to Washington, make sure to look me up, and you can come over for a drink." Porter and I looked at each other thinking, these folks don't get out much.

I lived at first in Adams Morgan in a rented room on the top floor of the house of a woman who was slowly going crazy. One time I peeked in her fridge, and it looked like somebody had thrown a bucket of wet mud inside. Next I moved into a place in Dupont Circle, where I lived with six guys – my first pseudo-fraternity scene. Everyone in D.C. at the time was young and idealistic, very fired up. At a house party in New Orleans, you'd be drinking beers, talking shit, chatting up on girls with fresh tattoos. In D.C., the girls would be working for, say, Al Gore, the guys all excited about a new supercollider project, or strategic plans for a bullet train in their home state. I thought, Wow, these are my peers.

Uninspired by work and a little cooked from the office routine, after I'd been in D.C. a year I took a couple months off and went back to San Francisco. I officially informed my mother and grandmother that I would not be going to law school, not pursuing the path we'd all assumed I might follow.

When I returned to D.C., they kindly let me work part-time at the law firm, and I grabbed some evening bartending shifts at a couple of cafes on U Street. There were no rooms left at the house, so when I got back to town I moved into the walk-in coat closet. It was big enough to install a single bed, a chair and a tiny desk over a defunct radiator. I offered to pay $275 a month. My roommates accepted; only later did they tell me they'd never planned to charge me for the closet. They thought that was hilarious.

Dr. Dre had a banging video at the time showing a fridge full of glowing green forties and scenes of an ongoing house party. One weekend, the roommates all went to the 7-11 across the street, ordered twenty cases of Olde English, Mickey's and Colt 45, took the shelves out and filled two fridges. We invited everyone we knew. Awesome sight, to see cute girls standing in the hallway, talking about healthcare reform while pulling straight from the Bull.

Needless to say, I wasn't exactly focused on craft beer at that point.

My plan at the time was to move from city to city and see the world: Rio, Sydney, Shanghai, and just keep rolling. I picked up some flyers for Jerusalem and came across a program that looked like a ridiculously inexpensive way to get to Israel and live near the center of town. Livnot U'Lehibanot -- "To Build and To Be Built" in Hebrew -- ran a three-month program of studying, hiking, and doing public service. Sounded like an interesting way to live, and I figured we'd have plenty of time outside of class to check out the country. There were sixteen of us when I signed up for the program. None of us had any idea how intense the experience was going to be.

The first day we got there, a little posse of us went to Tel Aviv, swam in the Mediterranean, drank strawberry daiquiris, and slept on the beach. That was our idea of going to Israel. But we proceeded to have a three-month experience that proved to be life-changing for nearly everyone on the program, certainly for me.

Of the sixteen, there were only three guys: myself, Tony from Australia, and Phil, still in college, from Colorado. A few of the girls were friends from college, and others flew solo, from Chicago, Baltimore, Florida, and Cleveland. Jill and Stacey, Jen and Jenny -- pretty much everyone had had the same lame Jewish education: enough to think they wanted to go to Jerusalem, but not enough to know much more than that.

I ended up liking it so much, I stuck around as a counselor for the three-week version of the program. So I got to see it from the inside as well. It's still not quite clear to me whether Livnot was designed as a cult, or whether real Judaism simply *is* like a cult. Which doesn't have to be bad. In many ways, observant Judaism can be nearly totalitarian in its regulations about everything we do -- what to eat, what to do on weekends, how to interact with family, how to handle your sex life, what to do when you get up in the morning, or what to pray for every time you get on a bus. The goal is to elevate one's daily life, one's labor, and one's ritual life, to seek the sacred and to increase the spiritual aspects of our experience in the world. That idea sounds pretty good to me.

But it's also true that if you choose to live outside self-contained, intensely religious neighborhoods, most Jews simply choose not to follow every, or even most, of the rules. There's 613 *mitzvot*, or commandments, just from the Torah, not to mention thousands of years of traditions, texts, and teachings beyond the Hebrew Bible. Everything from love to work to food to idolatry, incest, bestiality, clothes, courts, slavery, kingship, death, birth, crops, holidays, and so much more. (It's fun to read the list; check it out in the Appendix.)

Many say they keep kosher at home, but not outside the house. Or they'll celebrate Shabbat every Friday night, but head to kids' soccer games on Saturday. For the vast majority of Jews, it's a balancing act. Numbers suggest that about ten to fifteen percent or so of world Jewry is Orthodox, with another sixty to seventy percent claiming some type of "religious" affiliation, such as synagogue membership or celebration of the main holidays. Most Jews are picking and choosing, engaging and struggling (or not), even while they're being faithful to the concept of identifying as Jewish.

The people running the program were spectacular. Many, though not all, were Americans who had moved to Israel and made *aliya* -- become citizens and made their homes in the Holy Land. They had an incredible passion for Jewish civilization and were able to communicate it, each in his or her own way. Some through cooking, others through conversations about history and politics through the lenses of religion, culture, philosophy, psychology. Still others just had amazing voices. There were times, singing and dancing, that brought back the feeling of being at the Maple Leaf in New Orleans at three a.m., watching the Rebirth Brass Band, high and happy, jamming the hardest you'd ever grooved. Hang on, we're going for it tonight! You're overflowing with joy. I had those experiences fairly regularly in Israel, with music and celebrating (and without drinking), that touched what I guess I would call the holy and the sacred.

The day trips offered a different kind of deep encounter. Crawling through caves dug out by hand in the foothills outside Jerusalem where the Jews hid, prayed, and lived, trying to escape from Roman soldiers hunting them after the final destruction of the holy Temple around 70 C.E. Camping on the banks of the Kinneret, the Sea of Galilee, where Jesus performed his water dance and many sacred Jewish writings emerged after the exile from Jerusalem. Waking to hike for three days over the mountains to the Mediterranean, over fifty miles west, all while busting open the Torah to understand, for example, why the name of a certain flower might share the same root in the Hebrew language as a character from Genesis, revealing some thematic and mystical connection across thousands of years, right to the sky above your head and the landscape beneath your feet.

In classes, we'd explore deceptively simple questions: "Why keep Shabbat?" or "What is kosher?" What might the calendar mean, or the holidays reveal? And there were more academic or literary questions about possible interpretations of the exile from Eden, the Flood, the Exodus -- and how they might relate to us sitting around the table. And: how *do* they make challah taste so damn delicious? Then we'd walk out the door into Jerusalem or Tzfat and see people struggling or rejoicing, living those questions, and that life, every single day.

It was a relatively quiet time -- optimistic, even -- in politics, during what are sometimes referred to as the Oslo years. Rabin and Arafat had won the Nobel Peace Prize, and the Second Intifada was still several years away. Though there were plenty of overcrowded refugee camps, institutional discrimination, brutal bus bombings, and consistent border clashes, for many people hope seemed possible, perhaps even more realistic than despair.

For one of our free weekends, we rented a car and headed north to explore. On our way back to Jerusalem, we decided to take the fast way through the West Bank. That year, Jordan and Israel had signed a peace treaty; new roads had been opened and tensions were seeming to wane.

There were six of us in an Israeli rental car, which had yellow license plates.

The cars from the West Bank had blue plates. We were the only yellow plate on the road as we suddenly came into the middle of a small Palestinian town -- myself, the two other guys, and three nice Jewish girls -- on what seemed to be market day in Jenin.

People are pulling and pushing their donkeys and ponies attached to carts, schlepping goods. A few cars, bikes, and hundreds of people, all presumably Palestinians and Arabs -- many looking directly at us -- and we had nowhere to go but onward. We crept through Jenin and passed through Nablus (Schem, in Hebrew, where Abraham, Jacob, and Joshua all spent time) and Ramallah (future capital of the Palestinian Authority), before returning to the car rental office in Jerusalem.

When we got back to Livnot, we took out a map and showed the teachers where we went. They said, "OK. Jericho just opened, and there's a new road along the Jordan River. And while you are with us, you will never go back to those places again."

Three weeks later, two Israeli soldiers on patrol in Jenin got cornered in a cul-de-sac and were killed by a mob hurling rocks and bottles. Several years later, these towns would see some of the bloodiest battles of the Second Intifada.

We also spent some time (usually Shabbat, or after some hiking) in the settlements in the West Bank, on the far side of Bethlehem. Many families there often just moved for more affordable housing, and not necessarily ideological reasons. If you could ignore the wider conflict, the foothills and valleys were gorgeous places to live, reminding me of the hills of northern California. However, a lot of the other residents, particularly the younger ones that I met, were pretty aggressive, saying, "This is our land. God promised it to us." The settlements often stood literally within minutes of Arab villages, their pastures for animals and groves and orchards for farming stretching out towards each other's homes.

A lot of the cars from the settlements had steel mesh grates over the windshield to protect from the rocks often hurled at passing cars by the Arab teenagers. I heard sixteen-year-old settlement boys who said, "I can't wait to get into the Army and fight for my country. Why don't the Arabs go live in Jordan, or Syria? We're the ones fixing the land, creating agriculture and technology. What have they done to the land in the last five hundred years?"

Perhaps this is a good time to take a deep breath and grab a beer. It was heavy stuff, quite a complex world, compared to the playlands of Palo Alto, the French Quarter, and Adams Morgan that I'd been used to.

After months of studying and hiking, painting houses for older folks, and joining an archeological dig near the Western Wall, the culmination of the program came as we set off for an overnight in the Negev desert in the south of the country. The desert in Jewish tradition has been the place of revelation, and of defining one's personal and collective identity -- Abraham and Sarah leading their nomadic clan to a new homeland; Jacob's dream of the ladder to heaven and wrestling to become Israel; Joseph's brothers throwing him and his dreamcoat into a pit before selling him to slave traders heading to Egypt; Moses' burning bush talking him into leading a revolution; or the wandering Hebrews surviving the Golden Calf to finally receive the Torah. The prophet Elijah escapes to a cave in the desert to hear an eternal voice whisper his destiny.

With shorts, t-shirts, hiking shoes, and loaded with pita and hummus, we head into the canyons to explore, as we had in many other parts of the country. There are gorgeous red sandstone hillsides, carved paths and dry riverbeds, and beautiful lookouts as we descend to the desert floor, walking deeper into the valley.

A couple hours in, we notice a dark cloud rising over the edge of a distant cliff. Beginning to blow in toward us, a grey, brown, and black line in the sky growing perfectly defined, literally coloring in the horizon. We could see it coming, this massive wall quickly covering the entire sky. A towering sandstorm soon broke on the desert floor, filling the air with a sea of sand and rocks from the ground beneath us as far as we could see. Winds so violent you couldn't open your eyes, the sand and stones pelting any uncovered flesh. I wrapped my thin rain jacket around my head, sealing my glasses, so I could witness the spectacle swirling for what must have been well over an hour.

Then came the rains -- a torrential downpour with huge drops that soaked us instantly and began to pool and run across the desert floor, gathering into well-worn rivulets that grew into larger streams, and finally into rushing rivers of red dirt bursting over the paths we'd crossed, flooding into waterfalls over the faces of the cliffs. I wasn't scared until the lightning came, flashing on the desert walls seemingly not far from our tribe, thundering through the waves of the deluge as we finally agreed that it would probably be a good idea to return to camp.

One of the directors was a guy who'd gone to journalism school in St. Louis before coming to Israel. On his own first trip to Israel, Michael went to work on a farm, put his hands into the soil and felt a shock run through his body. He said, "This my life's calling. I'm staying here forever." He'd been going on the desert hike for years, and he said, "I've seen a lot of crazy things in this country, but I've never seen anything like this before."

Later that day there was a sunset that looked like blood-red lava pouring over the universe. The singing and dancing that night was nuts. We all felt electric.

> *Kings 19:11 "Then a great and powerful wind tore the mountains apart and shattered the rocks but the divine was not in the wind. After the wind there was an earthquake, but the holy was not in the earthquake. After the earthquake came a fire, but the truth was not in the fire. And after the fire came a gentle whisper. When Elijah heard it, he pulled his cloak over his face and went out and stood at the mouth of the cave. A still small voice said to him, "What are you doing here, Elijah?"*

At the end of my five months, my friend Michael, the director who had given up journalism for farming and then cultivating young Jewish sensibilities, said to me, "I've got to tell you, Jeremy -- this was real. This was not just a vacation meant to be filed away in a photo album."

"There's a way to have a Jewish life in America. But in Israel, fostering and advancing Jewish civilization is potentially the most profound thing one can do with one's life. So think seriously about it."

This was a man I deeply respected. My dad was gone, and I had few male role models in my life. At Livnot, the group of guys between five and fifteen years older than I -- Shmuel, Yehoshua, Gabi, and several others -- were intellectual, emotional, and spiritual, serious and supportive, but also a ton of *fun*. They were a different kind of "strong" than I had come across before. The experience rocked my world. It seemed holistic, and I wanted to keep that multi-layered energy in my life back home.

The Livnot staff were smart and experienced. They didn't encourage people to freak out and throw away their past lives. They said, "Go home and see what it feels like. Don't get mad at your parents for ordering a bacon cheeseburger, which was probably *your* last meal before you came here. Take it slow, get involved with the Jewish community, and create a Jewish life for yourself."

When I came back to the States, I was committed to jumping into the Jewish world. I volunteered for the Jewish Museum in San Francisco. I worked for organizations doing cultural programs out of the Israel Center -- concerts, art shows, readings. I volunteered for the Jewish Film Festival, and I helped out a bit with *Davka*, an alternative Jewish literary magazine. Eventually, I started the beer business to create my own unique kind of Jewish community organization, to put my own small (less *still*) voice into the world.

CHAPTER 4

Underwater Kabbalah And A Mission Burrito Of Love

A s I was preparing to leave Israel, a good friend of mine from Livnot told me a story about how she'd once stood in line with her mother to see Rabbi Schneerson, the head of the Chabad-Lubavitch movement. A revered and adored Hasidic rabbi, looked upon by many believers possibly as the Messiah, the Rebbe throughout his life emphasized outreach to a broad community and opened his *shul* to anyone who wanted to attend, occasionally offering a moment of personal teaching or advice to those seeking it. My friend and her mother went to hear him speak and to request a private thought. When she got to the front of the line, he leaned over and whispered something to her alone. She later understood it as an opening and a beginning. It was as if she'd been told the exact thing she needed to hear at that moment to move forward with the rest of her life.

Coming back from Israel, I felt that same sense of urgency, anticipation, and possibility. I got to New York and stayed overnight in their rat-trap apartment on Bleecker Street with Peter and his then-girlfriend, Moni, with whom we'd worked and raged in New Orleans. I was overflowing with the wildest enthusiasm that happens to so many people coming off the Israel trip. I remember sitting in my friends' tiny living room at 8:30 in the morning, after Peter had gone to work, trying to explain to Moni everything that had happened in Israel. I was gushing five months of life all at once. Even *I* knew I sounded a little crazy.

When I was working as a counselor for the program in Tzfat, the group of guys took an opportunity to go to a famous *mikvah*, a ritual bath -- a natural spring diverted into a stone basin in a cave on the hillside, far below the giant cemetery near the city walls[4]. We went early one morning, in January, I think. I remember for a California boy it was freezing. Tradition says that you go under the water, naked, put your hands on either side of the walls of the bath, and make a prayer for the thing you most want in life.

If you're outside that world of Jewish observance, I can see how this could sound ridiculous. But in the throes of the journey, we were seekers. History held that this was the *mikvah* of Rabbi Luria, the Ari, among the most famous Jewish mystics of Kabbalah in the sixteenth century. Spiritual warriors purified themselves here and prayed for their deepest personal yearnings. The idea is not to wish to end world hunger, or to demilitarize the military-industrial complex. You wish for something you have some control over, something that you personally can act on afterwards.

I decided I wanted to pursue two things: a stronger appreciation of humility, and a deeper sense of truth. I figured that's why I liked art, literature, and trying drugs -- why I liked talking to all kinds of people and traveling. I was not necessarily looking for absolute truths, but a better entry into the spectrum of truth.

In Jewish tradition, this combo platter of humility and truth is often called "awe." It usually comes from nature -- realizing how powerless we are, in some ways. Not in a negative sense, but in a connective sense. Jung's archetypes, or the sublime in the Romantic poetry of Blake and Wordsworth, or even the ravings of Dr. Bronner's soaps (All one!). I'd already had the feeling that boundaries, and even opposites, are perhaps less rigidly defined than common sense suggests. Dropping acid and running around the beach in northern California, you intuitively know there seems to be no separation between the molecules inside your body and out, in the sun and sand and wind. Unlike

---

4 Recently this bath has been renovated and looks almost fancy and cleaned-up, though at the time it was a very basic stone hut at the bottom of a long rocky path, with no one around but hundreds and hundreds of gravestones painted sky blue as a reference to the Zohar, the book of Jewish mysticism.

the Matrix, with a cold, digital on-off switch, I'm thinking about the obvious interconnectivity of matter, from the Big Bang to Eden to the present day.

For me, this *mikvah* experience was the first time I said, OK, I can make a conscious decision about what it is I want out of this life. Create the moment. In a different way, and with many more opportunities than my existentialist grandmother ever imagined, I yearned to squeeze the juice out of life. I wanted to figure out *what's going on*. But of course it's just your own personal journey. It's not a revolution, or a religious movement.

It's in my nature to be pretty cocky. My verbal style and my personality thrive on performance; call it playfulness, gaming, theater. But I also seem unlikely to forget the exile of eighth grade, however childish it may sound. So this was a great counterbalance for me, and I try as much as possible not to let that get the best of me.

That, in the end, is what the business is about. I'm trying to be provocative, outrageous, and colorful, but also sincere and thoughtful, precise and composed. Well-crafted.

Back in San Francisco, I moved in with my mother and took a temp job with an organization that managed money for non-profits. I'd sit and go through tax returns. It was tediously detailed, boring stuff, but I really liked the people I worked for, and I was grateful for the generous hourly wage.

As in many offices, we did a lot of verbal game-playing. I remember we did some work for a Mormon group, and the people had the most improbable names, like Imelda Fishhook and Mosiah Nibley. Poring over tax returns became a scavenger hunt for bizarre, seemingly impossible combinations of names you could never make up.

At the time, I was going through a list-making phase, much like that scene in *High Fidelity* where the John Cusack character's girlfriend reads his list of dream jobs: manager for Led Zeppelin, 1971-'72 American tour; Bob Dylan's agent from 1964-'65. His girlfriend tells him how utterly ridiculous and unrealistic his lists are.

Oh, yes, I had lists like that.

I finagled enough money to move into a three-bedroom shared flat on

24th Street in the Mission District. I got an internship at the SFMOMA, in the Education Department, and a paying job from a friend parking cars at the Marriott. Wearing a full polyester monkey suit with clip-on bow-tie, I got my exercise running with the younger guys there up and down the garage, waiting for shift change for pooled tips and a chance to check out my colleagues' lowered Hondas with under-body neon tubes and kicking stereos.

At the Museum, I wrote wall descriptions of pieces for a new exhibition. Unfortunately, to me the pieces were just terrible -- contemporary, allegedly conceptual artworks by guys like Mike Kelly, who did the Sonic Youth album cover with the crocheted doll. We had a three-foot square blankey with a moldy stuffed animal tipped over in the corner. Even worse was Richard Prince. His claim to fame came from working in the basement of a magazine and taking old Marlboro ads, cutting out the words, blowing up the images, and calling it art. He got so lucky, emerging during a moment in which bored and unimaginative critics, more interested in their own power than in creativity or originality, felt a kindred malaise. Deconstructing pop culture was a big part of undergraduate my major, so I understood the concept: what is "authentic," "real," "true"? I liked the idea, perhaps as a high school wall hanging or a screen saver. But not as a several-hundred-thousand-dollar piece of art.

When I worked on a show that combined rock music and architecture, I talked to the guy who did the Grateful Dead's lighting, and I was on the phone with the poster artist Frank Kozik. Making those kinds of connections felt entrepreneurial, though it was a huge help to have the reputation of the institution to lean on. I realized then that I could call just about anybody and justify asking for ten minutes of their time. It doesn't always mean they're going to give it to you, but as anyone in sales knows, the worst thing they're gonna say to you is no.

The museum led to my first salaried job in San Francisco, answering phones part-time for a start-up that made audio tours for museums. It's amazing to think how ahead of the times these guys were, and how ultimately unsuccessful that would make the company.

Other interactive tours at the time were using CD players, but we were using cutting-edge technology: Apple Newtons. In 1995, we were trying to turn these hand-held, hi-tech bricks into touch-screen audio players. We bought them for a thousand dollars apiece, and probably spent five or six hundred modifying each one. Inevitably, half of them broke the first few times inexperienced consumers yanked on the audio cord or jammed their thumbs into the glass screen.

A typical start-up, the company was pretty much all people in their late twenties, and I remember thinking, Wow, that guy's, like, thirty (as in, old). This was just before the Web boom in the Bay Area, but the company founders raised a million dollars from their parents and their parents' friends, and a couple million more from venture capitalists. I kept thinking, Where's the adult here?

Launching quickly from receptionist to office manager, and then Technology Purchasing Manager (they asked me to make up the title), I was shortly buying everyone computers on my personal credit card, racking up frequent flier miles, and getting reimbursed by the company. (A minor detail, but this would prove vital to my future ability to crank up huge credit card debts later in the Shmaltz saga. Read on.)

The company ended up bombing, but not before the principals landed several impressive contracts for the National Air and Space Museum and the Smithsonian's 150th anniversary traveling show. Some great successes, for sure, but the product never reached its potential. Around the time the company folded a few years later, suddenly a three-hundred-dollar pocket P.C. did everything they ever wanted to do and more. Today, even the oldest iPhone can cram together a hundred times more apps than we ever imagined possible.

One of the last projects I worked on was an audio tour of Chinatown in San Francisco. The content was fantastic, even with a somewhat awkward audio device. We found a gallery run by a friend of mine at the gate of Chinatown and convinced her to rent us a booth upstairs. We put out a sandwich board on the sidewalk. One small ad in the tourist rag, and that was the extent of our initial business plan.

We arranged a chitchat with the city's Concierge Association, on the sky-high roof deck at the Embarcadero. The woman presenting ahead of us was representing a dry-cleaning and storage company for fur coats. The company was offering money toward a full-length mink for any hotel staffer who could bring them a certain amount of business. The arrangement came as a big surprise to my naïve mind. All the services of four-star hotels in San Francisco were scratching each other's backs with minor (and not-so-minor) kickbacks -- a little palm grease here, a smidgen of "incentive" there. Just a little something to say We Value You.

You might get in a cab in San Francisco and ask the driver, what's a good Italian restaurant in North Beach? If he says, "Oh, I know the perfect spot," when he drops you off, he makes sure the doorperson sees him. Then he whips around later that night and collects his five or ten bucks. It was a good education in seeing how things are done.

If, at age twenty-five, I'd even ever pondered it, I likely assumed the presence of beers at a given store was played on a level pitch. Of course, popularity and success had to be based on taste and flavor (after all, it does taste *great* and have superior *drinkability!*) and, of course, a little marketing muscle. All right -- I probably wasn't oh so innocent, and blind, but if Bud or Coors or MGD is getting extra shelf space, doesn't that have *something* to do with the contents of the product? Why is there a fifty-case display of Becks instead of Heineken, or Sol instead of Corona, at your neighborhood grocery store? Why is one brand on sale, stacked and tagged as "Special"? Is it really "special," as even the blandest dictionary from Microsoft Word defines it: "distinct, different, unusual or superior in comparison to others of the same kind"?

Yes, I was a newbie, and I had no idea. After starting in the beer business, walking through the grocery store became an entirely different, and often depressing, experience. Looking around at everything -- macaroni and cheese, mustard, water, apples -- you wonder who is making the deals. In the real world -- the big, bad business world -- it's pay-to-play. And isn't that special?

Kellogg vs. Post, Coke vs. Pepsi, Fender vs. Gibson at Guitar Center, Durex vs. Trojan at Walgreens. That's how business gets done, unfortunately. If you were talking about pure supply and demand, you could say, OK, here's He'brew. Let's say it's ten dollars a six-pack. And here's every other beer that costs the same. Put them all on a shelf (that somehow doesn't have dusty bottom rows that make some poor brand suffer), taste them, and buy the beer you like better.

But it's rarely like that. The companies with the muscle say, "Stack 'em high and make 'em fly." Yes, perhaps it sounds naïve -- and I was precisely that.

Throughout my first year in San Francisco, and when I started working on He'brew full-time, I cobbled together a succession of part-time jobs with catering and bartending companies to make extra money on the side. Nothing spectacular, generally cookie-cutter weddings ("La Bamba" into "Brick House" into "Y.M.C.A." into "We Are Family"[5]), bar mitzvahs (not much had changed since my 1983 rendition), or some huge corporate junket, with Willie Nelson or Dana Carvey performing for thousands of consultants slurping giant prawns from ice-filled silver punchbowls.

At many of the bigger events, I would encounter this watery-eyed slightly past middle aged guy from somewhere back east, New York or nearby, who ran an on-call staffing company for caterers and bartenders known as Barry's Angels. Gravel-voiced, flamboyant, and unmistakably Jewish, Barry Seigel was always *on*, always running the show, throwing his commander shtick around. And always surrounded by a squadron of men -- tall, thin, athletic or artistic, all good-looking, and all very *clean*. His boys would be hired to beef up the staff of our catering company for big events.

Barry was truly one-of-a-kind in this world. Someone needed to do a documentary about him, and I was disappointed that he wasn't my bananas older uncle. One night I gave him a ride back to his infamous condo in the Castro, where I'm sure he kept all kinds of exciting things with which a sixty-ish-year-old man could entertain his young gentlemen callers. I was not one of them, however, and I think he got a kick out of my straight, California-Jewish lack of flair.

In his vintage New York tenor, he told me he'd been straight for his whole adult life. I think he worked at a bank or something, had a wife and kids, the whole bit. At the age of fifty, he realized, "I can't do this anymore." So he moved to San Francisco, came out of the closet, got a job as a waiter, and eventually started this staffing company.

It was such an interesting dynamic. Here's this old queen, a total hedonist,

---

5 But best first-dance song EVER... was it on purpose, inside joke, I'm hoping at least a Jesus reference... but turned all our heads at the time: Stephen Stills' "If you can't be with the one you love, honey, love the one you're with."

doing the thing he wanted to do -- partying and screwing and working really hard running his own gig. And being damn successful, seemingly less stressed and more fulfilled than so many others I saw around me.

I rarely smoked weed then, but after the lift, he offered to smoke a joint and drink a beer, and I figured, what the hell. Standing in the kitchen, he looks over and launches this fatherly grilling, really laying into me: "Seriously, what are you gonna do with your life, kid? Come on, you better get on it. I've got fifty guys working for me, and they're all gorgeous, smart, healthy. And they have *no fucking idea* what to do with themselves. They're confused, and they're excited. They're inspired and they're lost. *What are you gonna do?*"

I didn't have an answer for him. Real life was a bit more complex than grabbing the walls of a mystical stone bath and praying for insight and inspiration.

I was sad to hear a few years later that Barry had passed away. Undoubtedly with a load of cash in his bank account, lines on the mirror, and plenty of Angels surrounding him.

One evening after working at the SFMOMA, I was heading to a show by these genius lunatics called Survival Research Labs. They're well-known in San Francisco for putting on art shows involving aggressive fire-breathing robots and blowing shit up.

Walking down the alley behind the museum, I saw the guy who owned a tiny café on the block -- we'd chatted a couple times before. He was sitting in the open doorway with a good-looking young San Francisco woman, drinking a beer. I asked if they wanted to come see Survival Research. They closed up the shop and we strutted over to the show.

Afterwards, they said they were going to the Mission to get burritos, and they asked if I wanted to come. I lived half a block from the taqueria, so I said sure. Rebecca popped into the café to call her friend. I would hear later that Rebecca told Tracy, "Stay there, we're coming to meet you. I'm bringing your future husband."

Walking through the glass doors of Taqueria San Jose #2, I followed Rebecca up to a small posse of twenty-something guys, everyone clearly baked, chowing gigantic burritos. Seated in the middle of the dudes, Tracy was wearing this faded orange t-shirt, slightly too small. I'll never forget it. She was gorgeous. I thought, Holy shit, who is that?

Later that night we went to the Latin American Club for a beer. Looking back, it's hilarious that we were at a bar. Tracy hated bars. After the first few times, I don't think I ever set foot with her in a bar again. When we were leaving, I said, We should hang out some time.

A couple days later, I heard a knock on the door downstairs. Tracy is standing there, and she says, "You said we should hang out, so let's hang out."

I was making macaroni and cheese for lunch, and she said, "You'll never believe it -- that's my favorite food." We walked around the neighborhood, got some fruit popsicles from the Mexican guy with the bell-ringing cart. And we spent nearly every day together for the next five years.

An artist -- an abstract painter -- who was studying at the San Francisco Art Institute, Tracy had just moved into a live-work studio on Cesar Chavez and Valencia. I'd researched and written academic work about art; I'd been interning at the SFMOMA. Art was already a huge part of my life, and yet I had never really experienced it from the creative side. Seeing her paintings, her studio, the fact that these ideas came from inside of her and then she birthed them, made them available for the rest of the world (and me) to participate in, felt beautifully powerful. I was completely turned on.

I was overwhelmingly attracted to her creative drive. It was awe-inspiring, and it tied right in with everything I'd been thinking about since the *mikvah*. She was Jewish, and actively engaged with her Judaism, but in a very personal and evolving way. She was serious about exploring creation myths. She was smart, hilarious, provocative, and hot. I fell directly in love with her.

CHAPTER 5

Genesis, Act 2: West Of Eden aka Exile Never Tasted So Good

For a small company selling a consumer product, it's no stroke of genius to acknowledge that your packaging is critical to your success. Apologies for stating the obvious. It's just that, given how complex and multi-layered our designs have become, and how much packaging and collateral we crank out each year, I'm astounded to look back at what it took to produce one single label for our first creation.

Given today's technology, to take a picture and put it on a piece of paper seems eminently doable. But in 1996, the process of transferring anything in the real world to a piece of paper actually proved to be infuriatingly complicated. (I can hear any designer over thirty-five groaning with empathy.) It certainly took more resources -- more time, more energy, and much bigger nightmares -- to get the paper beer label made than it took Tracy to paint the picture in the first place.

Neither of us having done a project like this before, we first needed to learn to simply ask the question: How do we do it? First we needed a photograph, a positive transparency slide, of the painting. We went to a commercial photographer Tracy had worked with, a guy with a grubby little studio underneath the Tunnel Top bar, next to the Green Door massage parlor, near Chinatown.

Next, we took the slide to another business, a place where we would use something called a drum scanner, which of course I'd never heard of. It turned out to be a hundreds-of-thousands-of-dollars piece of technology. A new set of hands slaps the transparency onto the drum roller, and through some twist of digital magic, it manages to take all of the analog layers of color and composition and texture from the slide and transfer this data into the digital pixels that we so take for granted now. Today, any grandmother with a digital camera can do a passable version of this whole process in about three minutes.

At this point, we're two steps removed from the artwork. In 1996, the next step up from floppy disks was this exciting technology called Syquest discs, which ran through a little tape drive. We transferred the drum scan onto this portable disc, which I kept for years buried in the files, before finally realizing there's no way to access the disk anymore.

So now we're three layers removed, and we still haven't output a picture. To accomplish that, we went to a third business in the South Park neighborhood of San Francisco. This new shop was tasked to make what was called an Iris print for us. They claimed the process had a twenty-five to forty percent margin of error. If they tried to fix the color in one area, they might be screwing up something in another place.

They print it out, and it just looks awful -- like the worst color copy you've ever made at Kinko's. We hold it up to the painting, and it's muddy, too blue or too red, completely out of whack. They're clearly not in control of the technology they're using, and they basically admit as much. And Tracy is freaking out.

Next they try to color-correct the file. By this point, we've had six or seven people involved, and they're all frustrated. You'd say, What's fire-truck red look like? And they'd show you twelve different Pantone swatches, none of which match up with what you're looking at on the computer screen. Still, we were assured it would be all right in the end.

Meanwhile, a friend of Tracy's younger sister was doing some graphic designing at his job using Quark Express, the next evolution of the Pagemaker-style program that I'd used in New Orleans to create my little 'zine. Ramon helped me learn Quark, and he gave me a pirated copy of the program. I put it on Tracy's 356 Hewlett-Packard laptop, and I used it to design our postcards and our sell-sheets for the first couple of years.

Ramon started the process of fixing the mouth on the dancing rabbi and cleaning up his hair a bit. We used a Hebrew-looking typeface I'd found at a stationery store servicing the advertising ghetto near Levi's Plaza. We put the text on the side and the government warning on the right. (I copied the government text from a Sam Adams bottle, figuring they knew a hell of a lot more than I did.) Finally, we thought it looked presentable -- gorgeous, even. Now the question was, how do you print it on the labels?

Labels for most products at the grocery store are run by the tens of thousands, or even millions, at a time using "offset" printing on huge professional machines run by experienced eyes and hands, tweaking and massaging the calibration for clinical consistency. We were going to do one hundred cases with twelve bottles in a case and one glued to the outside, so we needed 1300 labels to get through the first run. But the minimum order from the manufacturer that Brewmakers worked with was 25,000 labels on a "gang run" -- many labels cobbled together to fill up a larger sheet. This is a cost-effective solution -- and often the only one that Shmaltz, even in 2010, can afford. However, in the hands of a less-skilled printer than our current long-time masters at DWS and 48 Hour Print, gang runs often result in inaccurate finished jobs, given the multiple demands of ever-rotating labels on any given sheet.

We couldn't afford to do that many anyway. As it happened, upstairs from my job at the audio tour company there was a print shop that had just bought an advanced technology called digital printing. In 1996, this miraculous and rare machine didn't use film and didn't use traditional four-color ink. Most importantly, they could do smaller runs, like five hundred flyers for your corporate outing, or 1300 labels for your Jewish beer.

I think Tracy went to pick up the labels the first time. And we both had the same reaction: What the fuck?! Possible tears, likely outrage. The colors were dark and murky. The orange was burnt and brownish, the blue was too purple, the red was chalky burgundy, and there was a coat of dusty tan over the whole thing.

We asked the guys upstairs to rerun the labels. Though they still never made it to the rich, popping colors they should have been, we did what most novices do -- complained and compromised.

There were several questions I probably should have asked before bringing the labels to the brewery. Number one: what happens to the paper when it gets wet? That hadn't occurred to me.

What happened, not surprisingly to anyone but a bright-eyed English major: It wrinkled. It shrunk. It shredded. It turned into goo. As it happened, the paper we used was not appropriate paper for beer labels. It was uncoated, not glossy – only slightly thicker than stock ink-jet printer paper.

However, we wouldn't realize that... yet. We took the labels to the brewery and brought a little crew of friends to help hand-bottle the beer and hand-label the bottles. In that era, new small-batch beers often came in 22 ounce bottles. Because the beers were novel and limited, it was possible to charge a bit more, with modest costs to start: one beer label, a bottle cap, and a box. For me, the expense of six-pack art and set-up charges remained prohibitive. The whole point was that people could sample a beer for three dollars or so, instead of buying six at a time for seven or eight bucks.

The flip side was that they didn't sell as fast, so it was a lot harder to gain momentum and sales volume. Twelve purchases cleared a case of 22s, while it only took four to move a case of six-packs. He'brew, of course, would have been considered a novelty either in six-packs or 22 ounce bottles, but the packaging definitely limited the market. Though 22s -- "double deuces" -- have had their ups and downs as the craft-beer industry ebbs and flows, they are now a permanent fixture in any good beer set. Still, most packaged beer is sold in six-packs. (In the mid-'90s, just before I started, small craft brewers such as Anderson Valley, Mendocino, and North Coast had all started by using 25 ounce champagne bottles, which were even more unusual, and more expensive.)

We rolled the kegs over and set up filling stations. Everyone stepped up and took turns cranking away. One bottle, one cap at a time, over and over... and over... It actually went pretty quickly, was relatively painless.

The labeling, however, was a bitch. The brewery had one or two of these simple mechanical devices, about six inches by a foot, one side of which held a pool of glue. The label moved through two rollers picking up the adhesive before getting slapped by hand on the bottle.

Glue -- another one of those things we take for granted. Sticking to the theme, I had no idea there were hundreds, if not thousands, of kinds of industrial glue. And you've got to identify the precise glue style to fix your type of paper to glass, in just the right environment. Can it get cold and wet? How does it do when it's dry and warm? At Brewmakers, Tim, for all his talk, never mentioned what kind of paper to print on or what glue would work best. Once again, I didn't know enough to ask.

Corrugated cardboard boxes with uncoated cardboard separators between the bottles inevitably rub the labels, and can catch the edges or scuff up the sides. We also quickly found out we couldn't put the beer on ice, or the labels would disintegrate. In a refrigerator that got any condensation, the labels would slide around and wrinkle up. At this point, everything that could go possibly wrong was, in fact, going wrong.

So much of surviving the process of starting a small business is managing your own hysteria, your frustration, your disappointment. It's never what you think it's going to be. And really, that's OK. It should be a bit of a point of pride to survive the uncertainty with anything resembling grace.

Unfortunately, Tracy and I had such high expectations for ourselves, and the world. At the same time, we were both glass-half-empty people. It was a dangerous combination: We were constantly, painfully disappointed and angry, and underwhelmed by our own ability to overcome the little failures that creep up relentlessly.

On the other hand, I must say that finally -- finally! -- holding the finished product -- *our beer!* -- was pretty damn cool. After all those headaches, you've got a beer -- *your beer* -- in your hand. You take off the cap, and you think about how much you're spending to drink that one beer. To life, suckers!

I wasn't officially following a plan to start a business. Originally, I'd been thinking I'd make thirty cases for Chanukah of '96. But the smallest batch Simon could make was one hundred. As the days got closer to having an actual product, the thought certainly crossed my mind, powerfully and repeatedly: I bet I'll sell ten cases, and I'm gonna have ninety cases left, stacked in our living room, to give out as Super Bowl or Valentine's Day gifts.

But if we were going to have a business, we figured we should have a business card. One afternoon Tracy hand-drew the logo, and we took it to the little black-and-white print shop directly in front of our entrance (aptly named Your Printer -- thanks again, Shepard and Alfred), and they scanned her line drawing and added a little red hat. It was adorable. People would see that and say, "Awww!" Then they'd see the beer label and go, "Whoa... uhhh..."

New entrepreneur in 1996, get yourself a forward-thinking marketing tool: email. We signed up for a new local email provider. Continuing the adorable trend, we combined last our names and added the contact cowberg@sfo.com to our first cards.

Initially, we had our home phone on the business card, but we quickly realized that having strangers call your home any time of day or night can be a real drag. So I grabbed one of those cheap voicemail services off the back page of the *Bay Guardian* for maybe $2.95 per month. I left this crazy-old-Jewish-guy-from-the-Catskills message on the system: "HELLO! YOU'VE REACHED SHMALTZ BREWING COMPANY!"

It was a big hit. Somebody would call, and then they'd call back, and I could hear them on the speaker phone: "Dude, come check this out," or "Hey, mom, listen to this!" Soon I was leaving long-winded outgoing messages with everything I could think of, from stores that carried the beer to punchlines about "no preservatives or gefilte fish added!"

Next, we decided to make a postcard to promote the product. I think I just looked in the Yellow Pages for someone in the Mission who could do it. Once again, who would think how complicated it could be just to make a simple postcard? But there were so many questions. Did we want the postcard to be horizontal or vertical? Did we want it printed on one side or both sides? Three-by-five, or four-by-six? Matte, glossy, aqueous coating? Sixty point, one hundred point paper stock...

I did the design, and when we got it printed, it was even darker and murkier than the first beer labels. Plus, at the time it cost us somewhere around ten or fifteen cents per postcard, which seemed like a fortune. I didn't even want to hand them out.

Of course we needed to have t-shirts. You can't form your band without a t-shirt. Everyone from your softball team to your co-ed naked lacrosse team (to your fake "Reeves Gauche" running club) needs a t-shirt. A buddy of mine, one of my very first friends in high school, co-owned a t-shirt shop in Lower Haight. The screen printer he worked with was a self-professed country boy -- evidently he had some land in logging country somewhere, though he seemed to spend all his city time skateboarding, drinking forties, and making some of the most professional four-color t-shirts I've ever seen. Mike would connect with Tracy at one of our house parties after she went out on the roof and thought she saw a UFO. He said, "Oh, I definitely saw one a few years ago," and they spent the next two hours consumed in the topic of UFOs (I'm fairly certain no probing was involved).

One of the guys at the t-shirt place had a buddy, a guy who had done a little home-brewing and some service industry work, and had talked vaguely about creating a beer line. I found out later that the night I brought all my designs to the t-shirt place, these guys immediately began scheming. They decided to do another Jewish-themed beer, and they concocted a rip-off brand: Bagel Beer – The Beer You're Bread For. (More on this, including a jail sentence, later).

The next week, they ran our first batch of white shirts with the four-color rabbi image on the front. As a nod to the old t-shirts from Israel that had "Go Fuck Yourself" printed upside down and backwards in Hebrew font, we printed our kinder, gentler slogan, "Don't Pass Out – Passover," in big Hebrew letters on the back. They were a big hit at the beer festivals. In fact, sometimes I felt like I should've just been running a t-shirt company. I'd sell out however many we printed, and I'd walk home with the cash. It was more or less how I paid the rent for several years.

So now we had a beer label, a business card, voicemail, a t-shirt, and a postcard. I thought, I'm going to go for it and place an ad. I'll place the absolute biggest ad I can afford in the Jewish newspaper of northern California (then called the *Jewish Bulletin*, now the *J*). The paper's office was about ten blocks from my job, and I would speed-walk down there during lunch to get things just right.

The biggest ad I could afford was the smallest that they had: a one-and-a-half by one-and-a-half inch corner, at fifty-seven bucks a pop: "Now available: He'brew, the Chosen Beer." With the line-art rabbi drawing and the phone number. That was it.

The *Bulletin*, bless them, decided to feature the beer in their Chanukah gift guide, as a cool gift idea under five dollars. That mention was seen by a writer at the *Chronicle*, who put it in her weekly column. One sentence. Her piece went on the *New York Times* wire service, which goes out to every major newspaper in the country. The week before Chanukah, fifteen newspapers across the country dropped half a sentence into their holiday guides.

I'd put the voicemail up maybe forty-eight hours before. Literally the day after the *Chronicle* item ran, the calls started coming in. On the first day, the sweet electronic voice said, "You have… one message." It was a welcome message from the voicemail company. The next morning I checked before work: "You have… thirty-two messages." I scribbled them all down, erasing them afterwards.

At lunch, I'd check again: "You have… fifty-one new messages." In that first week, we got probably four hundred messages, from people all over the country: "Hey, I read about your beer in Baltimore," or in Denver, or St. Louis. "When can we get it? Where can we get it? Can we do a fundraiser? What is that crazy voicemail? Grampa Lou, is that you? Is this a joke?" It was fantastic. And the cat was out of the bag.

Again, I'd been doing all of this on the sly, while still working at the audio tour company. All of a sudden, everyone in my office knew. My bosses came up to me and said, "What the hell's going on?" Lamely, I said, Well, we're having a party. You should totally come! They were disappointed that they'd given me added responsibility at the office, and here I was seemingly working my way out of the job. Still, they were pretty cool about it. They allowed me to cut back my hours and told me not to work anymore on the beer on company time. It was actually a pretty tough decision – this was my first "real" job in an arts-related business. But I would be out of there within a matter of months.

The momentum was hard to fight, and too exciting and excruciating to ignore. The official launch was at a party thrown by the people behind a local alternative Jewish magazine, *Davka*. Thinking back, it was definitely a model for what I've done over the years -- bringing together bands, performance artists, literature, and beer, and making it a real cultural gathering. It was their Chanukah party, which they called, appropriately, Challapalooza. It was perfect: one of the bands, Charming Hostess, even had a t-shirt with an illustration of a woman in a slinky red dress offering up a pomegranate on a silver tray.

Between bands, they let me jump onstage for a quick shout-out, which I stumbled through awkwardly over the din. Then I stood at a little table in the corner and poured samples while the bar sold the bottles. The beer seemed like a big hit. Halfway through the party, somebody walks up to me with a glass and says, "Hey, is this your beer?" I looked into it. What was left of the beer looked like apricot juice mixed with a bit of vomit. And it smelled nasty. I said, Oh, no, that's not my beer. I don't know where they got that.

I immediately realized that during the hand-bottling, some percentage of the batch had already spoiled. And there was no way to know which bottles or which cases were affected. Thankfully, the problem seemed to stop with a few bottles of spoiled beer, as I had already started to deliver cases of The Chosen Beer to stores.

The theme is consistent: I didn't have a clue how I was supposed to go about actually selling the beer. According to Tim, most stores have a person who is responsible for buying the beer, and he or she often hangs around in the beer section. I walked into four accounts, if I remember correctly -- Whole Foods and Mollie Stone's in Palo Alto, Whole Foods in San Francisco, and maybe Draeger's in Menlo Park. I'd introduce myself and say, Hey, I've got this product. We're making it right here locally. Can I sell some to you?

Ironically for the great-grandson of a *schmatte* salesman, I didn't know the difference between wholesalers and retailers. I simply didn't understand the concept, the language. For one thing, I figured those huge trucks with beer logos were owned by the beer companies themselves. Not so. Tim, at Brewmakers, explained to me the concept of wholesale distribution, but when he told me what they charged for it, I figured, Oh, well, I'll just do it myself. I didn't know how much to charge for the beer, either. Luckily, I set my price the same as Brewmakers was selling their beer for, $26.95 for twelve 22 ounce bottles, which landed $2.99 on the shelf. So for the first nine months of the company, while I was self-distributing, I kept that margin. At the time, most grocery stores took a firm twenty-five percent margin. Now, generally most stores take thirty percent or more. In New York City, it's often fifty percent.

Mollie Stone's in Palo Alto sold a lot of kosher products, so they were excited to bring in He'brew. With a local story to tell and my obvious enthusiasm, my first accounts placed five-case orders. Living in San Francisco, I'd had no need for a car up to that point, so for those first rounds of deliveries, I borrowed my grandmother's pristine white Volvo 740, with its rarely touched burgundy leather interior, a sunroof, a cranking stereo, and a deep trunk. I shoved as much beer as I could in the car and ran the cases to most of the accounts. My mom made the first delivery to Mollie Stone's for me.

My mother's car fit about ten to fifteen cases, my grandmother's about twenty. The brewery was an hour drive in traffic on the 101 freeway in the morning. It was brutal trying to get anywhere through the peninsula's tech-boom traffic. The stores weren't open for deliveries in the evenings, so I had to schlep to Cupertino and drive around desperately, carrying cases in the front doors. Then I'd haul ass to work, in commuter traffic, without time for a shower.

One of my immediate problems was that I didn't know how my new accounts were going to pay me. I'd never bothered to ask. I suppose I thought I could walk in the front door and they would just hand me money from the cash register. The day I was supposed to make my first delivery, to the Whole Foods in San Francisco, a small still voice of Jewish businessmen past whispered in my ear… and I heard the word *invoice*. I went to an office supply store and bought a generic book of invoice blanks, and I wrote my name at the top. I'm pretty sure you'd have a difficult time doing that now to a spot like Whole Foods.

On the voicemail that week over klezmer music in the background, I hollered that the beer was available at Whole Foods and Mollie Stone's. After they ran the blurb in the *Chronicle*, all the stores called immediately: "Five more cases! Bring me *ten* more cases!" Well, cool. Though I wasn't exactly prepared for it, we were suddenly off and running. Was it just that easy?

CHAPTER 6
Conan The Distributor

Fortunately for me, California passed forward-thinking laws when they legalized microbrewing. They allowed small brewers to self-distribute, which meant you had the right to pimp your goods as best you could, door-to-door, to anyone who had an alcohol license. Without going through traditional beer wholesalers (the biggest of whom sold Bud, etc., and the smallest of whom usually had someone like Anderson Valley, North Coast or even Sierra), you could get off the ground and at least begin to create your own destiny. It was a foot in the door for the littlest guys.

On the one hand, that kind of alternative sales model can be a cool way to get your budding project off the ground. Like many entrepreneurs, I thought, I'm going to be *different.* I won't need to play by the same rules, because my baby is so special, damnit. Hustle, sweat, cajole, crank, beg, promise, smile, push push push. Over and over. This is small business at its best, starting from passion and labor, ingenuity and chutzpah. Call it birthing, bootstrapping, and all the other clichés that exist for a reason: the early explosive energy of so many small businesses I've come across can light a spirit for the future enterprise, providing a pool of stories that flow through the project for years to come. Even a book, sometimes.

But it also has been an utterly tragic way for people to try to live their lives, if they're not really up to the task of being their own wholesaler. I realized rather quickly that I was just such a person. Nine months of distributing gestation was plenty. Today, one of my favorite things to do is to have my wholesalers take a margin on my products so I don't have to be the distributor, ever again. Doing it by myself, I was on a very steep learning curve, and I had a terrible time trying to wrap my brain around the logistical nightmare.

For the first nine months of my business, I'd go to the brewery in Cupertino, pick up some beer, and drive around and deliver it. I had a "distribution network" that was the antithesis of what a smart distributor should do. Still, it would become a business model for the rest of my company to this day -- to sell a little bit of beer in a lot of places, to the few people in each spot who would be interested in it. I had about thirty-five or forty accounts -- a few little neighborhood grocery stores, two accounts in Santa Cruz, Draeger's in San Mateo and Menlo Park. I probably had about five or ten accounts in San Francisco, a few as far away as northern Marin County, and some out at the edge of Alameda County in the East Bay. I would drive an hour to deliver five cases, then schlep ridiculous distances to bring another account a case or two.

Around this time, my grandmother and Tracy's grandfather both got sick. Tracy's grandparents lived half the year in Arizona and the other half in Cleveland. We were all in Arizona for Thanksgiving that year, and after dinner, her grandfather said, "I don't feel great. I'm going to go lie down." He never got out of bed again. He was quickly moved to the local hospital, slipped into a coma, and passed away early in the new year. Tracy had been extremely close to her grandfather, the patriarch of their close-knit family, and his illness was devastating to her and her family.

At the same time, my grandmother was in and out of the hospital, recovering from lung cancer and surgery. She got pneumonia and all these disturbing side effects from the drugs they were giving her, and it soon became clear she was just winding down. So while Tracy was going back and forth to Arizona to see her grandfather, I was running to the peninsula to see my grandmother. Within a few weeks of each other, they both died. It was an intense process for us to go through with our families and with each other. In sad and meaningful ways, it kind of helped cement our relationship.

This was all going on while I was starting the business and still working full-time. I finally quit my job, taking freelance catering and bartending gigs to make some money. I drove my grandmother's car another few weeks and then gave it to my aunt. I bought a little old stripped-down, faded tan mini cargo van from a guy in Pacifica. Eleven years old, two seats in front, rubber mats in back, that was it. No air conditioning, no radio, roll-down windows. It had low vinyl seats, so if you stopped short and anything came flying out of the back, you were guaranteed to get smacked in the head. I put a little boombox on the seat next to me to keep me company.

As the joke goes: "Q: What do you get when you cross a Jewish guy with Arnold Schwarzenegger? A: Conan the Distributor." I was certifiably not Conan, nor cut out to be Distributor (whether steroids and a tiny Speedo would have cured my back problems, I'll never know). I had no organizational skills in the area of distribution. I basically went wherever anybody called to order the beer. I wrote voicemail messages onto binder paper in a three-ring folder, with scribbled notes on how to get to the store. I should have set up a route -- Monday, I'll go to the South Bay, Tuesday to Marin. Not sure why I couldn't figure out that pretty damn basic plan. Just add it to the list of things I just never thought to consider. Do as I say, not as I did.

The initial burst of orders and re-orders thrilled me and gave me hope, the promise of a bright and successful launch -- and future. Very quickly, however, I realized that filling the shelves and the existing vacuum are very different than building a steady and growing sales pattern.

Everyone who read the PR ran straight out to get their bottle or case for Chanukah, and I'd sold out of the first hundred cases -- a great run, compared to handing out Genesis Ale as a St. Patrick's Day gift. It's amazing and true that after all that hard work, months of creating the product out of the ether, pulling it from inside our heads to placing it on retail shelves -- all the zillions of steps, the little heartbreaks and giant accomplishments that brought me to, say, March of that year -- that's when the real work started. That's when it went from a funny idea and a cool little project to, "Hot damn -- this is really happening. I better get the hell up again and again and force this thing to life."

Getting paid was similarly disorganized. I'd hand-write an invoice when I delivered the beer and keep the receipt in one little flip book. I was operating under Tim's license, so my accounts would mail the checks to him. He would cash the checks and give me the profit. But he was, let's say, spread a bit thin -- running around doing some sales and marketing himself and a fair amount of who knows what.

After selling the first batch and deducting the costs of the labels, business cards, postcards, shirts, the tiny ad and the monthly voice mail, I'm a bit astounded to think that I probably broke even. As we put the next batch into production, I was probably selling fifty cases a month, maybe not quite that much. I chucked in three grand for the van, the insurance, gas, old classic rock cassettes from the gas station, and a lot of Advil. I was taking home five hundred bucks a month, maybe.

There were a lot of things I liked, or that at least were instructive, about that period. The depth of the personal connections I was making with the buyers, where you're actually showing up at the back door, personally hauling in three cases and putting them on the shelf, talking about the beer, putting up flyers -- that education would prove to be priceless. I did what were called "dry tastings" at Whole Foods in Cupertino, standing next to the beer section on a Saturday afternoon, trying to hand-sell bottles of He'brew to customers walking by. Since they did not have the necessary license, this was all without the help of actually pouring samples of the beer. "Trust me, I'm Jewish, you're gonna *love it!*"

All these years later, I still see distributors, some of them running sophisticated machines, others with chaotic systems. Within both models, that personal-relationship, customer-service aspect of the business remains absolutely critical. For small businesses, strong personal connections can overcome a ton of problems. Though the incentives, the grease and the back-scratching are so prevalent in the beer business (and I'm sure, so many others), the real-people part of much of the craft beer world often helped (and still helps) us to sidestep some of that payola. In fact, it makes our cottage industry stand out that much more in contrast to how things get done in the Big Boy beer world.

There are different ways of responding to the logistical problems an ignorant, inexperienced small business owner is inevitably going to face: 1) Curl up in a ball and hide, 2) Argue and rage against the machine and never change, or 3) Take some feedback and adjust, hopefully getting better through each crisis. In the beginning, I sort of did all three, all the time. The hardest part was that I was still learning what I needed to do at the same time that I needed to be doing it.

I was totally stressed all the time, and I started to have back problems from carting beer up and down so many flights of stairs, onto loading docks, into back rooms. In the mornings I'd wake up, roll over, and my back would seize up. I remember one massive tremor caused by a simple movement to towel-dry my hair. Some tough entrepreneur. But an account in Berkeley needed three cases and I'd promised another guy in Albany I'd be there. So I'd creep toward the van. In the driver's seat, I couldn't turn my neck or look over my shoulder. It felt like I had to force everything, jam everything, crank everything, just to get *anything* accomplished. There was no elegant flow to the business, or to me, at that point.

Over the next few years, like so many other small business people, I'd obsess about every detail of the project. It sometimes thrilled and inspired me, but mostly it haunted and terrified me. I could often barely slip into sleep at night after scribbling down a few last reminders about the morning or grand schemes for future success, and I would easily snap awake without an alarm and feel far behind before my toes even hit the ground. I also developed this annoying habit of constantly forgetting two or three small items that I would need for the sales day or for an event -- my one banner or laminated press clips, the invoice book or zip ties. I constantly found myself running up and down the stairs, in and out of the apartment, three or four or more times before finally pulling out of the parking lot. Tracy got to counting my re-entries and re-exits while I'd be sweating and swearing, trying to check more details off than I'd ever had to organize on my mental list. I was essentially hysterical for the first three years of the business. (My co-workers might say thirteen.)

I'm always amazed whenever I come across small business people who aren't panicked out of their minds. It's refreshing to think there's a human who can go through it, and then I get jealous and resentful. How the hell did they pull that off?

One key distinction with beer, as opposed to many other products, is that it needs to sell through the store between sixty and a hundred twenty days. That's especially true for the kind of beer I had -- hand-bottled, unpasteurized, perishable, particularly unstable. It needed to be fresh to taste good, and not blow up in the bottle. That was the gist of one of the more frustrating ongoing conversations I had with Simon: I'd ask, in all honesty, What's the shelf life of the beer? And he'd just say, "You know, a month or two or so. Just get it out there and sell it, and it'll be OK."

I was always trying to figure out the effect of heat on the beer. Coors famously brags about being "cold-filtered." Well, except for some exotic naturally-filtered styles, nearly every beer is cold-filtered. The question is, what happens when it warms up? Beer is a living, breathing organism (especially with the fantastic growth of wild, often sour, and barrel-aged beers). The mark of a truly quality beer shines when it remains enticing and enjoyable even when it warms up. The obsession with keeping beer ice cold undermines the big beers' claims of superior flavor. Simon kept saying, "Just don't let it warm up very much, or for very long."

I'd be in the van at six in the morning, and I'd get to the brewery to pick up the beer. If it was warm out, the bottles would take on condensation pretty quickly, so the labels would get sticky and grubby. I'd be stuck on the Bay Bridge, sweating, not being able to turn around to look at the beer because my back would be seized up. On an unusually hot San Francisco night, one stray bottle from Brewmakers exploded, shooting beer onto the ceiling and all over the seats. After that, I couldn't help but fixate on when the next one might blow.

I poured a lot of beer for a lot of people, at fundraisers and parties, in stores, festivals, bars, and delis. It was as guerrilla-marketing, hand-to-hand combat as you can get. Luckily, people loved the shtick. Unfortunately, I got a lot of people telling me they'd already bought a bottle -- and still had it. I'd say, Well, did you ever drink it? Did you ever buy the beer again? It's not intended to be a gag, or a museum piece. The point is to buy the beer, then drink it, then buy the next beer and drink that one. Repeat! A lot of people thought it was so cute, they didn't want to open it and ruin it. I'd say, if you don't ruin it by drinking it, I'll be ruined out of a job.

Maybe four or five months into my arrangement with Tim at Brewmakers, it became clear that things were not right with his business. Checks to his suppliers and employees bounced repeatedly, and Tim was getting harder to reach on the phone. At the same time, he was still telling these tall tales of growth and the future. He kept going away somewhere to meet with "investors." All the while, the staff was showing up less showered and more stoned, cranking even louder speed-metal, and doing more skateboarding in the brewery.

The bitter end came later that summer. I'd heard that the grain supplier, who hadn't been paid for several shipments, showed up one day with a baseball bat, saying, "I think it's time to get paid." Shortly after, the sheriff's department put large metal locks on the front doors, officially seizing the property and everything in it. Luckily, I had most of my profits, but there was still a fair amount of beer that would never come out of the building.

Tim essentially disappeared, went underground. I heard he ended up living in the basement of a buddy's rented storefront. Once in a while I would see his red Jeep around town. The glass guy, the label guy, the grain guy, the cleaners -- he owed everybody money. There were some seriously pissed-off people.

For the last few months, I'd been talking to one of Tracy's friends who was curious about brewing. In the spirit of It Takes A Village to Start a Jewish Beer Company, Matt generously agreed to help me call every small brewer in northern California, trying to research a new agreement. Would they contract brew? If so, how much would it cost? Could we fit into their distribution network? What was their batch size? We had a lot more questions to ask than the first time I'd called around, the year before. I remember asking the brewers, How many microns do you filter down to? I'm pretty sure I still have no idea what an actual micron is, but I know it's important.

Some brewers liked contract brewing for the additional revenue it generated, filling their tanks and keeping production humming and overhead steady. Others were doing well and didn't have the capacity to brew extra beer. And some were in between. We researched everyone we could reach and came up with a short list, four or five places that had the ability to do small batches, were willing to do contract brewing, places that could do 22 ounce bottles and could do what I was looking for in the actual brewing process. We whittled the list down to a few breweries.

Coast Range in Gilroy brewed some very quality stuff, though sadly, they'd be out of business within a handful of years, unable to keep growing their core brands or stay afloat exclusively through contracting. As with Coast Range, I really liked the people that ran Golden Pacific in Berkeley (later bought by the Gambrinus group to produce Trumer Pils), which made a few exceptional beers, and others that were a bit more standard.

Then there was Anderson Valley Brewing Company, which at the time stood out as one of the premier microbreweries in the country, if not the world. They had been making very innovative and ambitious beers -- flavorful, complex, experimental, small-batch. These were "extreme" beers before the concept even existed. They had a great reputation, won tons of awards, and inspired admiration in the craft beer community. The founder, Ken, was heavily involved in the national craft beer trade group, the Brewers Association. I loved the idea of combining my crazy shtick with a brewery that was able to make me a product that would be really special.

As has happened so often in my life, I stumbled on a piece of advice that could have been very instructive, had I only listened to it. I met a friend of a friend, this young urban-warrior, pierced-and-tattooed dude, who said he'd worked the previous nine months in the Anderson Valley brewpub. Right on, man. How was it? I asked. And he said, "Oh, that scene was nuts -- just way too difficult to work with. I had to get out."

But I figured, how nuts can it be? The company is so well-respected. Aww, c'mon -- I'm sure it'll be fine.

Many times during the next four years, I'd think back on that moment. I often wonder why, once I get a plan in my head, I rarely give enough credence to other voices. At the time, however, I was whole-hog gung-ho psyched and ready to kick ass. Being brewed at Anderson Valley was the selling point that allowed me to get into wholesalers, to expand around the country, to get many excellent reviews and win awards. The World Beer Cup had just named Anderson Valley one of the Top Ten Breweries in the World (along with North Coast Brewing, the only other American brewer to make the list), based on the collective quality of all beers coming out of the brewery. The next year they would be the first American brewery to win that award two years in a row. Hell, yeah. I hollered their victories far and wide. I pushed their reputation in every press release, flyer, and postcard, and I added it to my ranting-old-man voicemail message. It wasn't even bombastic shtick aimed at mocking the beer world -- it was the truth: He'brew Beer was now being brewed at one of the Top Ten Breweries in the World.

Seemingly overnight, He'brew had all this front-of-the-house awareness and legitimacy, all due to Ken and Loren's offer to bring me into the Boonville brewing family. Behind the scenes, though, what was in the beginning a promising level of mutual enthusiasm would turn into an on-going struggle.

I found out much later, from a newspaper article, that Ken's ex-wife must have been Jewish. Loren, his son, told the reporter, "We were interested from the beginning because our mom is Jewish." I was thinking, whaa-aat? The town of Boonville, located in lower Mendocino county, is famous for its esoteric dialect called Boontling (a pidgin of Scottish, Gaelic, Irish, Spanish, and Pomoan Native American languages). The place is filled with farmers in overalls and guys in trucker hats (because they're actually truckers), with a lot of weed being smoked and cultivated -- typical rural northern California. I was shocked. They never mentioned anything about their Jewish connection when we were working through our negotiations.

In the beginning, when everyone had the best of intentions, it seemed like a good fit. I'd drive up to Boonville, over to the old ten-barrel brewery beneath the pub and soon to the new thirty-barrel down the street, which seemed huge at the time. At first I was buying the beer from them directly, then selling the cases to my wholesalers. Eventually it would become a licensing deal -- Ken would help me with working capital -- but in the beginning I had to write a check.

Once we had a contract in place, I had to function for the first time as a legal entity, a legitimate beer company. I had to register as a San Francisco business, create an employer ID number, and get federal, state, and local permits to actually run this little operation. That part was completely overwhelming. To this day, I don't quite get the rules and regulations, though sometimes the enforcers will admit that they don't either. I'm not so naïve to overlook the fact that most of it has to do with who gets taxes out of the transaction. At the same time, we're supposedly living in the most liberal, aggressively capitalistic society, yet there are all these labyrinthine, overlapping jurisdictions. I'm not a businessperson, but as a Stanford literature grad I do know how to read fairly well, and I *still* found it next to impossible to wade through all the details.

Most of this was before the Internet was tuned up and googling along, so I was working with agency pamphlets, poorly photocopied sheets, trying to figure out what I had to do. I didn't even know what an excise tax was. (Do I now? Don't ask.) I had to apply for alcohol permits from the federal government and the state of California. If you take ownership of the product at any time in the process, you have to have federal, state, and usually some type of city license to operate legally.

So I applied for what's called a Federal Wholesalers Permit, which was handled by the old Bureau of Alcohol, Tobacco and Firearms (ATF). At the time, they had a field office in San Francisco. When they reorganized several departments of the federal government at the end of the Clinton era, they closed the west coast offices and moved everything to the Cincinnati headquarters. Throughout the process, I had to call the HQ several times a day for several weeks in a row. Each time, to get through to the right agent who was handling my file, I had to go through the front desk: "H-hello, the B-b-b-bureau of Alc-c-cohol, T-t-t-tobacco and Fire-fire-fire-firearms."

Now, I consider myself pretty progressive, and I absolutely think everyone should be entitled to equal access to jobs. But come on -- just as you probably shouldn't hire a person who has no arms to be a brain surgeon or a hand model, you probably shouldn't hire a person with a very severe stutter to be the telephone receptionist. It seemed rather cruel to both of us.

Trying to navigate these new worlds, I was usually sitting in my kitchen, white-knuckling the phone and gnashing my jaw. I couldn't help but wonder if they did it on purpose to keep people out of the business and reduce their workload.

That said, in fact I got through the ATF permitting fairly quickly, after they did a background check, registered my fingerprints, and loaded me into the system. Onto the state of California, my beloved home state of three generations of Jewish grizzlies.

I walked in the front door at the old office near Mission Bay and asked how I could obtain a permit to contract-brew.

"What exactly will you be doing?"

Paying a brewery to make beer for me and then selling it to wholesalers.

CONAN THE DISTRIBUTOR

"So you wanna be a wholesaler?"

Why would I be a wholesaler if I'm not self-distributing anymore?

Every week they'd tell me something that was the opposite of what I'd thought I'd been told previously. I'd say, I'm only doing it this way because you told me to. And the rotating representative at the "help desk" would say, "Well, I can't take responsibility for what you think you heard." At one point I'd sent a letter explaining my new venture to the neighbors that turned out to be unnecessary. Because I lived in the Mission, for several weeks they'd mistakenly told me I'd need to petition the Board of Supervisors, since there were too many liquor stores already in the neighborhood. But the moratorium was on retail, not wholesale. It took months of conflicting information to get through the process. In the end, I got my California ABC Type 17 Wholesalers License, which allowed me to sell contracted beer to both wholesalers and retailers.

Thankfully, my building was zoned for combination commercial and residential live-work spaces. I established the offices for wholesaling in our kitchen. The state stipulated that the business had to have a filing cabinet. So our home address was registered with the state of California as the global headquarters of Shmaltz Brewing.

I was also supposed to have a separate warehouse, even though I wasn't going to be warehousing the beer -- Anderson Valley would be doing it. But they were in the middle of a move at the time, so I found one of those refrigerated warehouses in an industrial section of San Francisco. They had aisles and aisles of deep-frozen fish and ice cream, and one small section for refrigerated goods. They were willing to fill out the paperwork for me, so I mounted the same sign for He'brew I'd put on the outside of our loft building, took a picture of it, and submitted it with my application. After filling out the paperwork, not one time did I ever go back, nor did I ever ship anything from there. I assume I'm still registered there to this day.

After 9/11, the federal government transferred the duties of taxing alcohol businesses to the newly re-organized Alcohol and Tobacco Tax and Trade Bureau (TTB). As one of George Bush's tax cuts, they rescinded the tax of five hundred dollars a year for the stamp that certifies us to sell wholesale alcohol. Currently, they don't mail us any paperwork. We don't send any money, and we don't have any updated physical permit. Every year I just call the TTB office and ask, Hey, am I still in good standing? "Yep, you're all set," they said on my last annual checkup.

In California, they still send you paperwork every year, and they keep raising the price. Still, it's only $300. If you can jump through the hoops to get permitted, it's actually shockingly inexpensive, and mysteriously legal, to run the business once you have everything in place.

Still, there were snags. For one thing, I learned that I would not be able to call the company Shmaltz Brewing Company on the label itself. I didn't own the facility, and I didn't personally brew the beer, so I couldn't call myself a "Brewing" company. Pete's Wicked Ale was produced by Pete's Beer Company, and Sam Adams was made by the Boston Beer Company; they weren't allowed to use the word "brewing" because they didn't own their breweries, either. But "Shmaltz Beer Company" didn't have the right ring to me. I settled on Shmaltz Enterprises, like an umbrella mothership, a grand scheme that could morph into anything that we might dream up moving forward.

The beer label had to say "Brewed for Shmaltz Enterprises by Anderson Valley Brewing, Boonville, CA." The agencies were on a kick for truth in advertising. In reality, some of the best beer makers in the world don't own their breweries. A lot of Belgian ales, for example, are contract-brewed at other monasteries, or at family-owned (or even corporate) breweries in neighboring regions. At the time, Budweiser was arguing through aggressive advertising that Sam Adams and Pete's Wicked were "just" contract brewers. They were using it as a dirty word, even though Sam Adams and Pete's were clearly as responsible as anybody for the explosion of craft beer. Even some of the growing microbreweries would bad mouth the concept, but both those guys, Jim Koch and Pete Slosberg, were originally homebrewers, and clearly passionate about small-batch brewing and the fledgeling industry.

I had to go through another process with the city to get a Fictitious Business License, a DBA (doing business as): Jeremy Cowan DBA Shmaltz Enterprises. I got duplicate DBAs with Shmaltz Brewing and Shmaltz Enterprises, so that nobody else could call themselves Shmaltz. (Why would they? I wonder, looking back). To this day, when I want to access my bank account, if I get the wrong teller, they get confused: "Are you Shmaltz Enterprises or Shmaltz

Brewing?" The whole process was much more convoluted than it seemed like it had to be.

I published the fictitious business name announcement in the cheapest rag I could find, filed the paperwork for the name in San Francisco, and received my business license. That allowed me to get my ABC license from the state of California to sell alcohol, which allowed me to get my federal wholesaler's permit, which allowed me to ship the beer throughout the state and across the country. At that point, I guess I more or less felt like I had a business, barely legal or otherwise.

Regardless of how things ended up with Anderson Valley, it can't be overstated how important that initial relationship was for me. The fact that they were willing to take on my beer proved critical to getting the company off the ground. Their reputation for great beer was widespread, and they didn't really do any other contract brews. On top of that, everyone knew how tough Ken was. Everyone, evidently, but me.

In fact, I was mostly dealing with his son, which was fantastically easy. Loren served as the *de facto* general manager of the brewery. The company was going through their own changes at exactly that moment, moving out of the little ten-barrel system in the claustrophobic basement of their roadhouse pub on the side of the two-lane country highway running through Boonville out to the Mendocino coast. They could fill about twenty kegs at a run or pull in the portable bottling machine, running bombers, having evolved beyond their original 25 ounce champagne bottles just a few years prior. In the first couple of years I was with them they moved from the basement to the other side of town, building an impressive new brewery, raising their output from ten to thirty to a hundred barrels per batch. In very short order, they got ten times bigger. It's a strain on any small business when things happen that quickly, and they were no exception.

Within a year or so Loren left, simply saying, "I'm done." His departure had little to do with me; however, with no experience in the flow of the beer business, I was definitely a pain in the ass to him while he was there. Uncertain about timing and priorities, being my usual persistent self, I typically asked him for everything RIGHT NOW.

I never had a mentor to tell me that every little problem was not the end of the world. I was forever asking for emergency deliveries, last-minute changes, minor and not-so-minor tweaks -- all this while they were trying to run their own rapidly expanding business. In a bit of a reflection on my personality, I figured out a way to ask for much more than was probably reasonable up front. Maybe that's the only-child syndrome: You just keep doing it until somebody says no, and if nobody says no, you keep going anyway.

It's a rather constant theme for me: to ask for more than I should likely expect, or probably deserve. So many friends and colleagues have repeatedly gone so far out of their way for me, allowing me to accomplish things I never would have without their help. Dozens of friends who've volunteered to work in a pinch, advisors offering hours of time, shoulders to bitch on and doors to open, all the free artistry I've cajoled. Whether dealing with supply catastrophes, recipe design, government compliance, trucking, or a million more details, Bob and Paul at my current brewer, Olde Saratoga, spend hours upon hours helping me build my growing concern. In that first full year of business, Loren was one of those people who went pretty far out of his way to make my new beer life manageable for me.

The move from self-distribution to the bewildering world of the wholesale network marked the next evolution of my baby business -- and the disappearance of half my margin and income. Who are these people, and would their services be worth it?

I had a conversation with a beer rep, a friend of a friend who worked for the Boulder Beer Company, one of the oldest craft beer companies, from Colorado. I sat down with this guy over a few rounds at Gordon Biersch on the Embarcadero and said, Tell me about your job. How does it work?

In the beer business, we have what's known as the three-tier system. It dates back to the repeal of Prohibition, in an effort by the federal government to keep monopolies from controlling the entire alcohol trade. The three tiers -- the producers (breweries), the distributors (wholesalers), and the retailers (grocery and liquor stores, corner markets, bars and restaurants) -- must remain independent of each other. Certain states allow exceptions for small microbreweries and brewpubs, which can self-distribute their own products to retailers or, for example, host a tasting room. In practice, a brewpub spans all tiers as the manufacturer, the wholesaler, and retailer, selling their goods directly to customers. The state of California allowed for self-distribution, which allowed me to operate under Brewmakers' microbrewery permit. But most self-distribution remained small scale, so it rarely undermined the common structure of the beer industry. The vast majority of the money spent on beer continues to pass through the three-tier system.

I needed to find out what it meant to have a wholesaler. I thought if I didn't have to schlep the beer anymore, maybe my back would stop seizing up on me, and I could focus on what I was clearly better at: selling the shtick. This guy from Boulder was a "supplier" rep. (A supplier is a brewery that supplies beer to the industry.) He worked for the brewery, doing sales and marketing in northern California to promote and sell their brands.

Right off the bat, he says, "I gotta tell you, wholesalers are a fucking pain in the ass. I bust my nuts every day trying to make a sale. I go to the stores and get them to agree to bring in the beer. And inevitably, the wholesaler screws up the order. He has the wrong beer on the invoice, or he just drops the few cases at the back door and walks away, or he doesn't follow up on re-orders. I go back a few weeks later and it's always messed up, and I end up wasting my time and looking like a jackass."

It was another one of those moments where you see the extreme edge of one perspective on the industry you're playing in. It should have pretty much terrified me as an initiation into the supplier fraternity. Now, many years later, of course I know each tier complains that the others are consistently at fault for dropping the ball. Don't get me wrong -- I've had plenty of times I'd love to jam a shiv into a wholesaler sales manager or a street rep for a perceived injustice, a lost opportunity, or a major fumble. Or, even worse, simple disinterest. I love hearing even the bigger craft suppliers complain about how impossible it is to get attention when steering through the beer distribution world. (Though this, of course, is cold comfort, thinking that if the big craft companies can't get it rolling, how the hell do the little guys ever stand a chance?)

Really, though, he was being rather unfair to the wholesalers. They bust their asses all day, too. They build up the brands in their beer portfolio, especially in the craft houses, none of which have big advertising or marketing budgets, or huge demand. There's so much that can go wrong every single day. Given the maximum margin available based on the market, nearly every wholesaler has to run on a very tight budget, limited resources, and even fewer of the perks and giveaways so common among the biggest companies. They deal with cracked pavement, slippery floors, dank back storage rooms or basements. Hard physical work no matter what the weather -- sleet, snow, dark of night. Some of the retailers are always slow to pay, or they're not going to pay at all. Or they're trying to pry money from bars that are run by night owls -- guys snorting their A/P funds or getting robbed by their staff and managers, like the New Orleans drama. Endless mechanical issues with the fleet, and endless injuries on the job. There are so many moving pieces on the wholesale side, all for twenty-five to thirty-five percent margin.

And then there's all those demanding *suppliers* -- constantly wanting attention and focus, tap lines and shelf placements, distribution spread and volume. So, so needy and insistent, proud of their award-winning beers and confounded because you're not flooding the market with their clearly worthy offerings. Whether it's a fair, smart, or just system, there are a lot more suppliers than wholesalers; inevitably, the funnel is overflowing. Even distributors with the best of intentions end up with a price book packed with more valuable commodities than they can reasonably push.

Though the Boulder guy's monologue included some valid advice about the industry, his entire perspective proved precisely why I don't want to do that job -- to be the distributor. I don't want to be there at six in the morning or eight at night, picking up everyone's broken, moldy cases for return, or chasing down money legitimately owed. I'm very happy to have wholesalers take their cut, so I don't have to.

But I didn't really understand that until probably six or seven years into the business. For me, at first, letting a wholesaler take their slice -- half my pie -- just seemed like money flying out the door. In time, I came to realize that if you set your expectations low, you might be pleasantly surprised at just how effective they are at doing the job. If you assume your wholesaler is essentially like UPS or FedEx, if the absolute least they do is deliver your product to someone you managed to sell to or someone who actually knew enough to ask for it, you're ahead of the game. I'm exaggerating a bit, but as a small, unknown, non-advertising niche product, if I ever got them to actively talk about, represent, or acknowledge that my product was in their portfolio -- if I could walk into a bar or a grocery store and someone said, "Oh, the distributor sales rep was here, and he mentioned your beer" -- that was an accomplishment.

When the guy from Boulder told me his troubles with wholesalers, I kept thinking it would somehow be a little different *for me*. I thought, I'm working with a different model. I have a different attitude, a different brand, different consumers -- *different shtick*.

In reality, however, it's still the beer business. Tom McCormick, a longtime friend of the craft beer industry, past owner of a craft distributor, and co-founder of an organic beer company, endured years of my calls and emails and often talked me off the ledge, simply to remind me that there are plenty of ways to be creative, and to risk innovation for the sake of vision. Generous in spirit, advice, and support to this day, he has been consistent in reminding me that it's still "the beer business, after all."

As much as I did what I thought of as my "alternative" marketing and PR, I kept getting dragged back to the fact that I was simply making beer, and working with a wholesaler to get it into the stores. The laws are in place to force the model to exist. I could struggle against it or throw myself under its wheels. Or I could make a bit of peace with it and realize that at least I don't have to chase down (too many) derelict accounts receivables or pallet-jack half the load the trucking company tipped over on the side of the loading dock. My job, every day, is to wake up early, stay up late, and push the hell out of my product.

CHAPTER 7

Business School 001: Catholic School Girl Meets The Candyman

One of my favorite tales of wisdom and woe from the Shmaltz Brewing saga involves my first label approval with the Bureau of Alcohol, Tobacco, and Firearms.

I know now, that with zero exceptions, every beer label must be submitted for review and approved by the federal government before leaving the brewery doors. Each one must contain specific language, no fewer than two millimeters in height, stating the Government Warning aimed at pregnant women, drunk drivers, and general alcohol abusers. I agree one hundred percent in principle and damn sure comply in practice on every label we produce: GOVERNMENT WARNING: (1) ACCORDING TO THE SURGEON GENERAL, WOMEN SHOULD NOT DRINK ALCOHOLIC BEVERAGES DURING PREGNANCY BECAUSE OF THE RISK OF BIRTH DEFECTS. (2) CONSUMPTION OF ALCOHOLIC BEVERAGES IMPAIRS YOUR ABILITY TO DRIVE A CAR OR OPERATE MACHINERY, AND MAY CAUSE HEALTH PROBLEMS.

As I was preparing to move my production to Boonville, Anderson Valley asked me to submit the Genesis Ale label to Washington for approval. While I was self-distributing, still operating under Brewmaker's license, Tim never felt the need. I know now we should've done it, but I didn't know any better then, and anyway it was his license that was at risk.

When I started with Anderson Valley, Tracy and I did one more minor round of graphic design adjustments, brightening some colors and changing the language to show that Anderson Valley was now contract brewing for me. The way the regulatory world works, every year, it seems they adjust the things that might come up as red flags in terms of what's OK to print on your label. In my experience, when you shoot for approval, it's a moving target. The good news is that today I have a fantastic inspector at the Tax and Trade Bureau. He's utterly reasonable, highly intelligent, and able to communicate what the issues are, now through email, instead of physically mailing copies back and forth across the country, routinely stretching over several excruciating weeks or even months.

But the people I dealt with in the early days, before the TTB was established, were something else altogether. My "inspector" seemed to be the type who probably couldn't have kept a job at the DMV. In their defense, before the expansion of small breweries, a new label approval historically meant a new label for Keystone Light or a Busch line extension. These were companies with huge legal departments, who had longstanding relationships with the ATF, knew what to expect, and knew how to work the system.

Over the past few decades, though, in the late '80s and '90s, there were literally thousands of new beer labels for microbrews that never existed before, many of them groundbreaking, thought-provoking, original, and unique. Rarely is a government bureaucracy well equipped to deal with such an overwhelming surge of innovation.

However, that doesn't excuse the utterly ridiculous process I went through to get my Genesis Ale label approved.

The first problem was really my own, although it was painfully exacerbated by the inspector's inability to communicate about the regulations she was bound to enforce. If a brewer uses any ingredients other than malted grains (barley, wheat, rye, oats, etc.), yeast, hops, and water in a "traditional" brewing process, the brewery must file what's called a Statement of Process, an S.O.P. (Of course, they don't consider the high-gravity brewing and corn and rice adjuncts of the Big Beer companies a problem.) The form outlines the specific brewing process and lists all the ingredients, and the bureau decides exactly what to call the beer: for example, a "flavored malt beverage," or a "fermented malt beverage," or "malt liquor," depending on the latest regulatory decisions.

In 1997 the debate was still raging about the use of the words "ale," "beer," and "lager," not to mention all the styles, from porters to stouts, ESBs, and IPAs, which just seemed to confuse the officers. At the time, many brewers had started producing a range of fruit beers, such as apricot and blueberry, using varying techniques and ingredients, from the actual crushed fruit to concentrates and extracts. to commercially available juices. Because we were using pomegranate in our Genesis Ale, we were required to file a Statement of Process. The trouble was, I couldn't get a straight answer out of anybody about what to submit and what might come back for the label demands. Every year the guides changed for fruit beers, and on top of that, Anderson Valley had never filed a Statement of Process before. I didn't know if we needed to describe the entire brewing process, textbook-style, from grain-in to bottling, or just list our ingredients.

Stumbling through the bureaucracy, scrambling for time, weeks went by. I got contradictory feedback, or simply no response. After a long conversation with Loren, I finally realized we weren't likely to continue using pomegranate anyway: I couldn't afford the time and money to squeeze it all every few weeks, and there were no sources of juice we could find at the time. (Antioxidant elixirs would be the sole kingdom of blueberries and cranberries for another decade, before the widely advertised magic of Pom and its free-radical-fighting brethren.) So we abandoned the S.O.P. and just decided to bump up the malts to sweeten the flavor and add more hops to reproduce the bite and hint of tang to best match and hopefully even improve the flavors.

One hurdle hurdled. Then the inspector challenged me on our punchline, "Don't Pass Out, Passover." The slogan appeared on the side of original labels, floating above the stones of Jerusalem. The buyers loved it, and at beer fests, people ate it up, pointing, laughing and buying the t-shirt with delight. The inspector says, "There's no way I can allow that." Why not? "You're not allowed to have sayings that encourage drunkenness."

Pregnant pause. I try to explain that it's a pun based on a most sacred and widely celebrated Jewish holiday, and that, if she is worried about encouraging drunkenness, it actually says *don't* pass out. She says, "Yeah, but *pass over*." I say, well, exactly.

It was comical. Tragic. Brutal. A most ridiculous conversation about what the English language may or may not mean, like Bill Clinton and the precise meaning of the term "sexual relations." This woman was completely uninterested in having one iota of fun associated with her job, or mine. I thought, there is no way I'm going to convince her, even though her logic is precisely backward. Catch 22, Yossarian -- the more you prove you're right, the more it proves you're wrong.

Those conversations made for some very uncomfortable mornings on the phone. I started the company sitting at Tracy's desk in a big open part of our living-room loft, using her laptop and the landline. After I quit my job, I went to my mother's house and brought back my old desk from high school, and set myself up in the corner of our kitchen. I organized myself by yellow stickies, which I stuck absolutely everywhere -- all over the desk, on the wall, overflowing the space. I felt like I was dreaming about having wallpaper made of yellow stickies, each one reminding me how behind I was, and/or how little I knew.

Tracy was a total coffee fiend, though I didn't drink coffee in the morning. Didn't need it: I was wide awake, frustrated, terrified, and consumed with motivation. I am not generally a morning person, but something about the nagging entrepreneurial venture has woken me up without an alarm clock every morning for fourteen years. So I'd be in the kitchen, on the phone, ready to strangle myself. And Tracy would wake up, mosey into the kitchen, and grind her coffee beans every morning. A totally reasonable thing for a person to do. But I remember both of us being ready to murder each other over this. I'd be on the phone with somebody from the east coast, and right when I was about to make my point -- "GRRR-CHHHHEEE-CHING!!" -- she'd hit the grind button.

When I'd complain, she'd say, "Dude, you're in my kitchen. It's not my fault you can't get your shit together and get an office." She had a point there.

I could see that I wasn't going to win this battle with the inspector, either, as absurd as it was. Finally, I buckled. I figured we'd just continue to use the slogan on our t-shirts and postcards, but take it off the label.

So now we have no pomegranate juice, and no "Don't Pass Out, Passover." I'd been really proud of the fact that we had something inside the beer that actually answered the question, Why is this beer different from all other beers? To this day, I love saying that we have the only beer in the world that has a certain process or ingredient. We created Rejewvenator using other "sacred species" listed in the Torah, and using multiple lager and Belgian ale yeast strains. We have a couple of Coney Islands with truly unique lager recipes, and the ridiculous malt and hop lineup for Jewbelation every year is a one-of-a-kind brewing enterprise. But now, with the new-and-improved Genesis Ale, I just had an amber ale with a funny label on it. I was veering dangerously close to representing the much-maligned, perfectly average "contract brewer."

But the last little nightmare undoubtedly took the cake. The ATF inspector had one more problem with our wording. She says, "You can't call it 'The Chosen Beer.'"

Me: Huh?

She: "Well, I mean, who chose it?"

Next pregnant pause…

Astonished at this latest bit of pretzel logic, I sputter that Budweiser calls itself "the King of Beers," Miller is "the Champagne of Beers," and Coors is "the Banquet Beer." As the first and only Jewish celebration beer, I very much felt like saying, Listen lady, this is priceless beer-industry-mocking fun -- damn straight this will be The Chosen Beer.

With confidence and total sincerity, she explains that those companies have spent "literally millions" on market research to prove their claims.

So I say, How many mile-high banquets did Coors have to host to prove their claim? And exactly which region of France would certify Miller High Life as "the Champagne of Beers?"

This goes back and forth, not just for one long phone call, but over days and days. Meanwhile, Anderson Valley kept pushing me to resolve things, because the new brewery was just about finished and we needed to hit the play button on Genesis Ale, version two, batch one.

I'm in the kitchen with Tracy grinding coffee beans, feeling like my head is going to explode. What could possibly go wrong today? How am I going to force this product into the world which, ironically, has already been in the world for nine months?

Finally, I ask the agent to connect me with her supervisor. I figure she couldn't possibly be the final authority. It seemed absolutely crazy that a base-level government worker could say thumbs-up or thumbs-down to anything she pleased, based on her arbitrary understanding of a truly convoluted set of regs. If you have a lawyer, or a pack of lawyers, like the big beer companies certainly do, you can spend your time and money arguing this sort of thing. They walk in the front door and glad-hand the staff and build relationships over many years. They smooth things over and invest time and money to get what they want. In fact, they generally draft the legislation and language in the first place to ensure their position in the market. But if you're a small businessperson and they say no, you're just supposed to live with the decision. I kept thinking there's gotta be some sort of recourse.

After all that back and forth, I finally just wore her down. She says, "This label needs to get off my desk. You can't use the pomegranate juice, and you can't use 'Don't Pass Out, Passover.' But I'm going to allow the use of 'The Chosen Beer.'"

I was dumbstruck. I say, Wow, OK. I'll agree to those terms. And then -- and I'll never forget this -- she closes with, "Just so we're clear, I'm approving this. *But I don't think the Catholics are gonna like it.*"

I'd just endured six weeks of mental anguish over this one label. My back is killing, I've quit my day job to throw myself full-force into this venture, and my money's buried in beer. I was silent. I felt like screaming, If that was the issue from the beginning, couldn't we have addressed this crusade early on?

The troubled origins of He'brew Beer have given me some priceless material over the years. Not that birthing pains ever go away on new products. But now that I'm well past the first baby, it's great stuff. You can't make that shit up.

Now that I had actually learned what they were, it was time to find myself some distributors. I'd had an introduction from Tim to a business called A&D Distributors, south of San Francisco. They'd started ten years earlier in a tiny warehouse space they'd sublet from a bigger San Francisco distributor called Consumers Distributing. Bill, the owner, started the business like so many other small distributors: He and a buddy got a truck, pretty much like

I did, except they picked up five or ten new products to deliver together. They schlepped and hustled. By the time I got there, there were probably four people in the office, and maybe eight or ten salespeople in and around San Mateo and Santa Clara counties, with a handful of drivers working out of a five-bay warehouse around the block from See's Candy headquarters.

A&D covered two counties selling Sierra Nevada, Newcastle, Spaten, and northern California brands like Anderson Valley, Lost Coast, and North Coast. They had a ton of quirky smaller brands and imports from all over the world. A volunteer fireman and doting father to an aspiring baseball star, Bill proved to be a really nice guy, at least to me. He helped facilitate a little network of independent beer distributors around northern California for He'brew, and I started pursuing those connections.

In San Francisco proper, three young guys bought Consumers from the previous owner, who wanted to retire after decades of the grind. One twenty-foot roll-up door in and out, but half a city block long, their brick warehouse at the base of Potrero Hill, just down the street from Anchor Steam, held some hope of turning a contract-brewed brand and a handful of craft beers into a reinvigorated business for the partners. With the web boom just beginning, they were mostly sitting on a gold mine in that building. The distributor lasted maybe a couple years. Surprisingly, they retained the right to sell the building, which they did, for a large chunk of cash, to a real estate developer.

My first official sales day with a professional distributor sales rep started with a visit to a nicer liquor store in the Castro on Market Street with Sean, one of the owners of Consumers (now a successful owner, with his wife, of Mammoth Brewing). Standing in front of the cash register, he introduced me to the buyer, and I launched directly into a fever blast of every selling point I could throw at the guy. Even after he agreed to bring in one case of beer, I kept on selling, making sure he understood *everything* about the beer. Even Sean, who is a great talker in his own right, pulled me aside afterwards and said, kindly, "Great job on the sale… but you probably don't need to tell every buyer every single thing about your entire concept for the one beer. Take a breath."

In the North Bay, Morris Distributing handled Marin County and parts of Sonoma and Solano counties. In addition to many years of successfully wholesaling craft beers and a slew of non-alcs, Ron also owned a fertilizer company, and I'd always heard he made most of his money selling chemical dung to farmers up north. I can't imagine this guy's internal clock: The first sales meeting I went to, I had to be in Petaluma at 5:15 in the morning, so I had to leave San Francisco an hour before. And these were beer guys. I'm not much of a morning person, so I was barely functioning, explaining the merits of Jewish celebration beer and kosher certification in a dreary room full of jaded route salesmen. I'm pretty sure they used five o'clock kickoff meetings to punish new suppliers and keep the future visits to a minimum. But the fact that Anderson Valley was brewing my beer would make a huge difference for me there, as it did in so many places, and they eventually got the sales ball rolling.

In that era of craft beer in northern California, there were only one or two options for small brewers in each area. By law, each distributor had exclusive rights to sell brands on a county-by-county basis, and most of the guys focused on two, or maybe three, counties. It's changed a bit over the years -- some smaller distributors have stretched out, especially for specialty beers that don't need deep penetration into B and C accounts. (It's called "high spotting" -- avoiding convenience stores and non-craft accounts to focus on the better specialty accounts that will do the vast majority of your business.) The big beer distributors had the big brands that controlled the biggest part of the trade at the biggest stores. But these little distributors had popped up, ran with smaller new quality brands, and both created and followed the craft beer movement as it developed from tiny to slightly less tiny to modest-but-growing. All these niche players knew each other. It was a small world.

In the East Bay, I first went with a company called Geyser. They concentrated on distributing bottled water and juice, and then they slowly dipped their toes into beer. About a week into working with them, I realized the sales manager, maybe ten years my senior, was a rare bird among these smaller distributors: a Jewish guy. Welcoming and patient with my inexperience, he showed a few of us milling about the sales room one morning a new product they were bringing in: a little aluminum can and a stack of flyers for this stuff called Red Bull. They called it an "energy" drink, like some combination of Gatorade, Coke, vitamins, and caffeine. He said, "It has taurine, man." I'm a proud Taurus, and I still wondered why anyone would market something that sounded like it came from bull's nuts. They had samples, and most of us thought it was disgusting, like old Flintstones vitamins, liquified. They said they were selling it for two bucks for an eight-ounce can. Branding and marketing guru that I was fast becoming, I said, Yeah, right. Good luck!

My best distributor from the get-go, Geyser just *sold*. In my first sixty days with them, they added something like seventy new accounts. (When I was self-distributing, I had maybe thirty-five accounts from Santa Cruz all the way north of Marin.) Even after such a successful start, within the year, I had to leave them for a new wholesaler.

When I got He'brew into Safeway, Geyser didn't have any other beers approved there, and they didn't want to put up with the headaches of delivering one case at a time to twenty or thirty Safeways. I said, If you don't want to take advantage of this opportunity, I need to find somebody who will. I can't pass this up. And the sales manager said, "Fine. Find somebody who will."

So I go over to Bay Area Distributing, which covers the same counties. The sales manager's name is Keith. He reminds me of a captain on *Hill Street Blues*, except Hawaiian. There's nothing you can throw at him that he hasn't seen before. He just keeps bulldozing through this job. Bay Area had some SKUs in Safeway, and of course they wanted more, so he agrees to take on my little one-man, one-beer operation.

I go back to talk to Sil at Geyser, who drove a pimped-out white Lexus with gold-plated trim. I suppose he thought of himself as a bit of a player. Perhaps he was. I ask if he could transfer my beer to Bay Area Distribution, and Sil gets seriously pissed.

In the beer business, there's exclusivity county-by-county, which tends to mean that if you want to switch distributors, your old company has to agree to let you go, or the new company has to buy the rights to your brands from your old one. Or you can finagle, bitch, argue, and ram your way out. If it's a small supplier and a small distributor, the stakes are low enough, and nobody has the money for legal battles. But over the years this has become a bigger and bigger point of contention in the industry.

Franchise laws, as they are called -- enacted to protect small, family-owned distributors from the much bigger and more powerful national brewery suppliers -- can often lock small brewers into distributor agreements, even if the distributor underperforms or cannot handle the distribution for a brand, as was my case with Geyser and Safeway. State laws can make it difficult, if not impossible, for a brewery to switch wholesalers, and some states even enforce this relationship as a birthright, to be inherited by future generations. Luckily, California law left most of the business decisions to the parties involved, allowing the companies to negotiate based on success and failure, not arbitrary state rules, which, whether by design or simply in practice, benefit the bigger businesses, who have the resources to fight it out.

For the most egregious causes, there are generally ways to sue to break the contract. Limited exemptions exist for particularly small companies, and there are rather common standards for compensation for purchasing brand rights. All this would become clear after several more years of experience, but at that moment I just needed to get paid.

Obvious lesson to any vaguely experienced business person: Never tell somebody bad news in a business relationship until you've gotten your money. In the case of Geyser, I had one outstanding invoice for one pallet of beer. They'd already sold much of it, and I was owed maybe $1100. Sil says, "Forget it, I'm not gonna pay you. Get out."

But your sales manager *told* me I should go, I said. You guys invited me to do this.

I pick up the rest of my beer, put it in my van, and drive it to the other distributor. I'm still thinking, They've at least got to pay me for the beer they've already sold.

I head back to Geyser a few days later thinking, Seriously, grown people can't possibly behave like this. It's not like I'm Pepsi, or Sam Adams. What's the big deal if I leave? If you can't or won't do the job, and it's certainly not threatening the life or success of your business for me to leave, why all the hassle and headaches? But I quickly realize that when it comes to pride, it doesn't matter how big or small you are.

On the way over, I call them from a pay phone near the Oakland airport. Again, lesson learned: If you're coming with bad news, don't tell them you're coming.

I pull up to the warehouse. Sil's Lexus is out front, so I know he's there. I walk up to the office door and yank the handle. Nothing. It's locked. At 2:45

in the afternoon. I'd felt so powerless for so long, and suddenly you realize that even though you may feel powerless, other people don't necessarily think you're powerless. I put my hands over my eyes to see inside, and there's the warehouse manager's face right there in the window. We're nose to nose, with a pane of glass between us. I can hear his muffled voice yelling "Go away," and I realize they've locked the doors because *I'm there*. They think I'm gonna do something.

I'm shocked. I say, Open the damn door! I can see Sil's car right there. When he wouldn't budge, I holler, Fine, we'll take care of this in court.

In the end, I took their business to small claims, and we went through the whole process. Hours, days, several weeks of my time. I kept thinking, what is his defense possibly going to be?

On the court date, Sil shows up with the sales manager and a big, chubby, older *Death of a Salesman*-looking guy they identify as their industry "expert." The three of them are on one side, and I'm on the other. The judge says to Sil, "There's an outstanding invoice. You've sold the product and been paid for it by your customers. Is that the case?"

Sil is actually counter-suing me for $1700 arguing that he should be paid for back profits and loss of future sales. The judge asks if in fact his sales manager suggested I should go to another distributor that could handle Safeway, and Sil says, "Well, yeah." The judge says, "Countersuit is dismissed, and this case is found in honor of the plaintiff. Now pay him."

Hell, yes. Justice served.

Potentially the worst risk about small claims remains that there's nothing to force a defendant to actually pay you. Once you get the judgment, if he doesn't want to pay, you have to go through another round of shenanigans -- put a lien on his property, hire a collection agency, whatever you can do to yank that cash.

Thankfully, the next week, without comment, Sil mailed me a check for the rest of what he owed me. All that just to get back to even.

In my head, sitting at my high-school desk in the corner of our kitchen, trying to become a businessman and run my own show, I was thinking, Wow. So that's business. This is what we're all so proud of in America? Business capital of the world, entrepreneurial spirit, picking ourselves up by the bootstraps. And generally being assholes, just for the sake of it.

In nearly every neighborhood of San Francisco, many smaller corner stores and specialty shops, liquor stores, and even simpler bodegas are owned and run by Arab families. Throughout the Mission, Noe Valley, the Haight, off Divisadero -- pretty much all over the city, in fact, these stores for years have carried the better beers that gained so much market share for craft brewers, from Lagunitas to Speakeasy to Full Sail and many more.

When I started self distributing, not realizing much of the landscape yet, I just went in to the shops closest to our apartment to try to sell them the beer. Glancing up at a poster for an Arab film festival or cultural event, maybe a map of the Holy Land that may or may not have the state of Israel represented on it, I would quickly realize that most owners were Palestinian or Lebanese, perhaps Jordanian or Syrian.

From the stories they shared with me, whether they were Christians or Muslims, many of these Arab shopkeepers had moved to the U.S. in the '60s and '70s for economic opportunity. For them, most of their daily decisions, including carrying the beer, was simply a business decision. It was a more optimistic era for the Middle East in the late '90s, and the peace process was looking like it would move forward more than backward. Some would say, "Oh, we're all cousins, anyway." Tensions in Israel weren't nearly as polarizing as they have been recently. It was not necessarily a kinship, but at least there remained a modest respect. They seemed to look at me as a small business owner, much like themselves. And it wasn't like I'd served in the Israeli army or built settlement housing.

I quickly discovered that this network of shops represented a diverse association of extended family businesses. If my pitch went well, the owner inevitably would recommend a next stop: "My cousin owns a liquor store off Fulton," or down in the Tenderloin, or over in North Beach. "Tell him I sent you." Hopscotching store to store offered a valuable lesson in how the economy of the city operates. It's well known that so many immigrants and ethnic groups start out and often grow to economic success by running these corner shops that get sold to the next cousin or the next generation. Traveling for sales through these many years, I'll typically hit a streak of Korean, Indian, Pakistani, Turkish, Chaldean (Christian Iraqis), Yemeni, or Russian owners. Not that most of their products are ethnic, though sometimes a small shelf or back wall will carry some special items or holiday gifts. Mostly, they sell the everyday basics that chug through our economy -- soap, toilet paper, frozen dinners, milk, razors, lottery tickets, chocolate. And beer -- ideally, craft beer.

As reasonable as most of these shopkeepers were, I was always a little cautious not to open the door to a conversation I didn't want to have. Best to avoid any ideological battles, since we're clearly not going to solve the political problems of the Middle East standing in a corner store on Market Street. I generally led with the neighborhood pitch, moved on to any attempt at humor possible, and just kept dancing with my audience until he gave me the green light to bring in a case or two and put up a poster.

On occasion, I'd get an upsetting comment, but there were no more than a handful. For the most part, the younger generation was pretty cool, often interested in the product and new beers. A few of the older guys would tell me that the profits from the beer supported the building of settlements in Palestine. I'd say, I'm sorry, why do you think that?

"Well, it says so on the label."

And I'd have to explain that, since I personally wrote the label, I can assure you it doesn't. And since I was far from profitable, they had very little to worry about anyway.

It took some time before I understood just how much Public Relations (PR) is involved in getting a start-up off the ground. When I was looking for jobs a few years earlier, I put on my resume that I'd "done PR" for the symphony in New Orleans. I'd been hired to work in the office by myself. I thought that because I was dealing with the public -- answering the phones -- I was "doing PR." Like so many of my preconceived notions about business, I was completely wrong. Later, at the audio tour company, they had a part-time person who did PR, and I came to understand that PR meant *media* relations.

My earliest advice came from Alan Kaufman, who started the short-lived but provocative and influential *Davka* magazine in San Francisco, edited *The Outlaw Bible of American Poetry,* and wrote a memoir, *Jew Boy.* Best known as a pivotal Slam poet, child of a Holocaust survivor, and nephew of the founder of the Jewish *Forward,* Alan also had a gift for PR and promoting. He laid it out for me: "Create a story to tell the media. They love to write -- and it's their job. They have to write about *something* today. It might be a tech company, or a car crash, or some celebrity. Or they might write about your beer."

I asked for advice from everyone I could get my hands on. An investment banker familiar with the drinks industry, the father of a guy I knew growing up, shot off one of my favorite quips: "Any whore with the cash can advertise, but it takes real *cojones* to get the media to cover you for free."

Another advisor, an independent marketing consultant not much older than I, came to me through a friend of a friend, offering a free bull session over lunch. Eytan told me that I should pick two or three things that define my company, and that I should drive those elements home over and over and over, in every aspect of everything I put into the branding, marketing, and PR about the product and the company. His advice proved fundamental to everything I've consciously tried to create through every beer style and label, every press release and all the events Shmaltz has ever cooked up.

I went home and thought about it, and I came up with the "Three Pillars" of the Shmaltz Brewing Company. At Livnot, I'd heard about the Three Pillars of Judaism -- the people, the land, and the Torah. (Alternately, from Pirke Avot -- Jewish ethical teachings -- it's Torah, worship, and *tzedaka*, acts of loving kindness.) I thought, if it's worked for five thousand years of Judaism, maybe it'll work for the next year of He'brew.

My three pillars were, and remain, Quality, Community, and Shtick. Everything I did, I'd put those words in bold. I'd use them in every pitch and presentation I gave. I wanted -- still want -- to make sure the quality of the beer is as good as the best craft beers on the market. That's why I went with Anderson Valley. That's why I push Paul at Olde Saratoga to use so many ingredients, and constantly urge him to add complexity and uniqueness to our recipes.

When Genesis Ale started winning awards and garnering positive reviews, I was thrilled. My first year at the Sausalito Beer and Chili Cookoff, He'brew took second place for best beer of the festival. The second year Genesis grabbed a first-place gold. Of course, this wasn't the World Beer Cup blind taste test, but I already had Anderson Valley for that pedigree. And this was a mainstream audience, not a Jewish fundraiser, deciding the People's Choice awards. Highly gratifying -- and I had a blast.

As for community, I spent hours and hours in Jewish Community Centers (JCCs), at Jewish museums, in federations and hillels around the country, sponsoring Jewish film festivals, comedy shows, literary readings. We intended to appeal to non-traditional Jewish people, so I had no idea it'd be picked up so quickly by the organized Jewish community. Within a year of starting, I was giving talks about being a Jewish entrepreneur at synagogues, grad student events, Hadassah gatherings, Jewish education fundraisers. Given my severely limited business experience, the events mostly focused on beer-label punchlines and free samples. People loved it.

He'brew was my unique angle on being as Jewish as I wanted to be. This was my own form of worship, my own celebration of a Judaism that felt relevant, compelling, and communal.

Finally, front and center, stood the shtick. I wrote an early press release when we were still with Brewmakers, but I didn't spread it around much. I wrote a new version upon the move to Anderson Valley, and another version after we expanded to southern California, Chicago, and New York. I figured the press release should cram as much Shmaltz as I could fit on one page (see Appendix for the original). I wanted to put He'brew in the context of wider traditions -- the craft beer movement, and Jewish humor in America. And doing that seemed to demand being bombastic, outrageous, even a little ridiculous.

I tried to balance all the puns about gefilte fish and bar mitzvahs with the seriousness of working with Anderson Valley, of paying more for my ingredients. And I infused all that with what I thought was a very sincere effort to celebrate Jewish tradition, tying into the Jewish calendar, the Torah, and sacred Jewish text. Was it all possible? What would the public's response be?

The first real press release I sent out got an incredible response. I went to the bookstore and started looking in magazines, writing down the addresses and names of the editors. I got such enthusiastic replies, I often thought I should've started a PR company, not a beer company.

Bay Area producers called from several radio stations, including KFRC, the local oldies station I'd grown up on, listening to Wolfman Jack. Jewish newspapers all around the country mentioned the product, and even ran longer features. The *Chronicle* ran an enormous article, several print columns wide on multiple pages, that even got most of the details right. The *San Jose Mercury News* ran an entire top-of-page fish-eye-lens photo of my face, with my prominent Jewish nose front and center for the readers.

Oy vey! For this he spent four years in college?

TYPICAL SHMALTZ: EVERYONE GETS TO THROW IN THEIR OWN PUNCH LINES. © HEARST COMMUNICATIONS INC., 1999

For years I'd pull the quote from one of my favorite buyers and early supporters, Loren at Mollie Stone's: "Genesis Ale is one of the best microbrews we carry." Local neighborhood city and peninsula papers, from the *Noe Valley Voice* to the *San Mateo Times* to *Stanford Magazine*, just kept plugging the beer. Northern California's *Celebrator Beer News* gave me a ton of love in those early days and continued to feature Shmaltz news, particularly when esteemed editor Tom Dalldorf could throw in his own well-constructed shtick to go along with announcements, reviews, and hype. Most astoundingly, even *Newsweek* included a hit about the new beer -- half a column, right in the front of the magazine. Equally astounding, though utterly appropriate: they included a full color photo of the beer -- *backwards!*

But one of my all-time favorite features ran in the *Jerusalem Report*. Their west coast correspondent met me for a chat about Jewish identity and my niche business at the Crowbar, a punk-rock dive that had taken over an old Chinese diner, just down Broadway from all the strip clubs in North Beach.

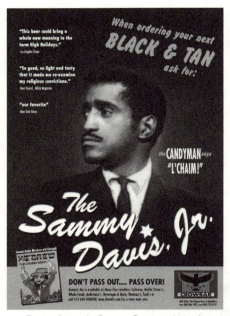

Poster design by Jeremy Ortega, 1998-ish

A down-and-dirty neighborhood hangout with a killer employee-curated jukebox, the Crowbar's Joe and Sage and crew were some of our biggest supporters, and a longtime draft account. One night a driver for my San Francisco distributor was hanging in the bar after work, getting loaded after his shift. They were one of the few places that had Genesis Ale on tap, and he said to the bartender, "Give me one of those Jew brews. Actually, make it a Black-and-Tan. Guinness and He'brew -- make me a Sammy Davis, Jr.!"

From that point on, the bar flew through kegs of Genesis. We designed and mounted a gorgeous poster for the Sammy Davis, Jr. at the end of the bar. A local Jewish group booked a gathering there, and I hired a Sammy Davis impersonator – a white guy, thankfully not in blackface -- who still managed to offend nearly everyone there by turning "Mr. Bojangles" and "The Candyman" into pervy renditions more appropriate for the clubs up the street.

So I suggested to Ori, the writer for the *Jerusalem Report*, that we meet at the Crowbar. Ori wasn't strictly observant, but as we talked I could tell he clearly took his Jewish identity seriously. We seemed to have a kindred sensibility. He got it all, what I was trying to do with He'brew. And he wrote a glowing article, covering everything from the Kabbalistic interpretations of the color green on the beer label to the beer's acceptance in a tattooed-urban-warrior bar.

It was so satisfying that he could weave together the disparate elements of the brand. I felt I'd reached a real milestone. I'd been driving this idea through the packaging, the beer itself, the marketing and PR, the community events. Reading the article made me feel that I had been able to communicate my entire vision for this project to at least one other human being.

CHAPTER 8

Business School 002:
Success For Dummies

Somewhat to my surprise, I got extremely lucky with two bigger retailers in northern California. The first was with Beverages and More, a chain of warehouse-style package stores selling liquor, wine, martini mixers, gift baskets and, of course, beer.

When I first met Jay Brooks, I think they had eleven stores. Jay worked as the main beer buyer, and everything had to go through him at the corporate office before trickling down to the store-level buyers. He'd cut off his hair -- evidently it had been much longer at one point -- but he'd kept a thin rat-tail in back. We hit it off right away. I really enjoyed telling him my vision for He'brew, and he turned out to be a big cheerleader for me, a mentor, a colleague, and a friend. (Jay has gone on to produce one of the premier craft beer blogs, and he writes for several publications nationally.) He gave me a shot even before I had wholesalers, which was a huge coup for me at the time. He approved me as a direct supplier, allowing me to deliver straight to any of the stores that wanted to bring in He'brew.

If high-spotting was the name of the niche-beer game, BevMo was about the highest spot I'd reached. Access to the destination beer stores helped sales, and it definitely helped legitimize my brand. My subsequent conversations with wholesalers took on a very different tone, and a wider spread of retailers were happy to follow the leader and bring in my booty. Sales picked up almost immediately.

But some of my loneliest, most pathetic in-store tastings were at BevMos. I remember one particular demo in the back of their giant store in the Bayshore industrial section of San Francisco. In the state of California, stores need a self-contained area to taste products. At Bayshore, the tasting corral was all the way in the back. Few customers wandered that far into the store. So I would stomp around, trying to lure people to come try my beer. After they got to know me, the staff let me jump on the intercom to make announcements: Attention Bev Mo shoppers, FREE BEER NOW!

The other retailer that gave me a shot when I didn't deserve it was Safeway. Publicly traded, a behemoth even among the eight-hundred-pound gorillas of the grocery world, Safeway was the top shelf of craft sales volume-wise, which counted far beyond high-spotting.

Whole Foods and Mollie Stone's did their buying individually, store by store. At Andronico's, you had to go through their corporate buyer, but they had specialty, high-end niche products that worked well with He'brew. The higher-end northern California chains provided by far the best outlets from specialty brewers like me. To this day, every time a new Whole Foods opens, another Shmaltz angel sprouts its wings. Without these types of stores around the country (Total Wine, Binny's, Wegman's, Cost Plus, QFC, PCC, Heinen's, AJ's, Bev Max, Big Red, Hiller's, Haskell's, Gomers, Hi-Vi, Canal, Lowe's, Harris Teeter, New Seasons, Balducci's, Sendik's, Woodmans, and so many others who gave craft beer a shot and then made it a priority), we literally would not have survived.

But Safeway, a Fortune 500 company and the biggest chain, by far, in the region, was a new level of business for me.

One of the buyers at Safeway was known for being tough. She was well-respected, and slightly feared. Unlike many others in the buyers' chairs at the time, the chain's two beer buyers were women. Safeway had a modest selection of alternative beers -- Sierra Nevada, Sam Adams, Pete's Wicked Ale. They had a few other craft beers, like Lagunitas, Deschutes, and Full Sail, but the really small craft beers hadn't quite gotten in yet. (Ironically, after a brief golden era of craft authorizations around that time, a massive change in corporate strategy resulted in many fewer small brands in Safeway, even all these years later.)

When I went in to present to Loretta and Janice, I put together a little Microsoft Word presentation and stapled together some recent press clips and customer emails. (I didn't know how to use Powerpoint, and still don't, probably more out of spite toward the lingo of consulting firms than anything: "How's that *deck* coming?") I basically made up a bunch of reasons why I deserved to be on the shelf at some of the biggest stores in northern California. None of them had anything to do with hard sales numbers, retail penetration, IRI scan data, or a marketing plan (read: dollars to spend). In the scheme of pure business decisions, there's no reason I should've even gotten a meeting with them.

But in the right moment with the right people, having a unique angle -- and the chutzpah to pitch it -- can give you entrée in a way you might never achieve if you have a product only slightly different than everyone else's, or the (quite reasonable) fear that you don't "belong" in the conversation.

One of the Safeway buyers, I believe, was of Middle Eastern descent. She and the head buyer ended up being incredibly hospitable to me. I tend not to approach my pitch like a legitimate business issue. The way I look at it, you're just trying to massage a friend into doing you a favor -- trying to get them to see your idea, and get into it with you. Come on, gimme a hundred of the biggest stores around. It'll be a blast.

I was always much better at the idea level, anyway. Numbers: cold, dry. Beer ideas: Bubbly, delicious!

In the heat of conception, I got a bit spoiled. For the first couple of years, pretty much nobody ever said no to me. Everyone I approached to stock the beer, bring on the brand, brew the beer, or give me a hand agreed to do it. (It's humbling to know how many hands were involved helping my one-man show get off the ground.)

Early in the history of Shmaltz Brewing, there was a moment when I had He'brew approved at more Safeways than Anderson Valley did. Sometimes it's better to be the new kid on the beer block, unencumbered by fear (or experience).

One big pitch for me to retailers was, Look, you've got a hundred fifty or two hundred other beers -- Dominican beer, Jamaican beer, twenty German and English styles and, of course, Japanese, Italian, Australian, Chinese brews. One of my common punchlines was that you really haven't made it in America until you have your own beer. I believe it was Frank Zappa who said, "You can't be a real country unless you have an airline and a beer. It helps if you have some kind of football team or some nuclear weapons, but at the very least you need a BEER." Jews make up two percent of the population, so with one three-inch-wide 22 ounce bottle, I felt I was asking for *less* than our fair share. Totally reasonable.

That to me was the fun part of the business -- sitting around bullshitting about the ideas. Once it becomes a numbers game, it doesn't matter what the beer is. It's more about who's on sale -- who's got a yellow discount tag this week. I still didn't know enough about the industry to realize that's how it was mostly done.

I've been awful at that part of the business over the years. It's always depressing to me when it comes down to price or money, and not surprisingly, I'm not good with managing that side of the sales and marketing. I always approached it as if we -- myself and the retailer, or the wholesaler -- were talking about doing a project together. When pitched at the right moment, I think it was a little refreshing for a lot of the people I talked to. Relying on enthusiasm and ideas can create a powerful momentum, especially within an industry built on the grind. The difficult truth is that this is simply a beginning: Those who maintain that level of passion again and again must eventually also master the ongoing routine to achieve any solid, long-term growth.

But at that moment, I felt like I had some momentum. I had good wholesalers and a great brewery. And I was convincing the retailers down the line why they should take this risk. It's a critical part of being an entrepreneur -- a lot like how in the early stages of a relationship, you'd better have some romance, some newlywed days. The beginning is the time you should be freest to go for it. You're struggling, and it's mayhem, but it's also very liberating. And as an entrepreneur with your own product, you should be able to communicate that exhilaration. That's what they'll remember for years to come. Everybody has those stories -- "I met the guy from Dogfish (or Stone, or Sam Adams) on his first trip out. And now look at him!"

Safeway approved He'brew in a hundred stores. And then the hard work started. Getting that next big break was always going to be the solution to my problems. I'd say, If I could just get into all the Whole Foods, I'll be off and running. All I need is to get into wholesalers and I'll have it made. No, seriously -- Safeway, that's the answer, that's the big time. Everything sells at Safeway! If they have the beer in a hundred stores, and each one sells a case a week, and a few sell a couple, I'll be golden.

That's the game I played in my head. But in my experience, every goal I set, as soon as I achieve it, I turn the corner and realize it's only created access to a whole new world of moving targets and rising hurdles.

A key point: just because you're *approved* in all those Safeways doesn't mean the beer's *in* all those stores. The receiving clerk at the back door -- that guy's job, essentially, is to turn people away. If he doesn't know you, he does not want to see you: "I'm loading fifty pallets of merchandise today, and you're hassling me about two cases of beer?" On the other hand, some guys made the time. You talk to those guys. You shoot the shit, crack some jokes and get them to let you bring in two cases instead of one, four instead or two.

The year I made it into Safeway, between those accounts and the BevMos, Whole Foods, and so many specialty stores around the Bay Area, I probably had well over two hundred fifty accounts with He'brew on the shelf. That was up from thirty-five at the height of my self-distributing. However, the reality set in rather quickly: The beer was not flying off the shelves like it had those first two weeks around Chanukah for the introduction. Five- and ten-case orders were very rare, and sales were averaging to about a case per month at better stores, even less at many more. I was so crazy hectic, however, that I never made time to stop and look at numbers or try to "analyze" my business. I figured everyone was saying yes, the media kept pouring in, and there were voicemail messages every day. It seemed like things were slamming.

However, I certainly did see the bank statements, and I soon realized that with only half the margin from the self-distributing days, selling a bit more than a hundred cases a month at four to five dollars per case, I was barely better off than I had been.

As soon as I realized that Safeway alone wasn't going to be my salvation, I started thinking that I had to go into L.A. My Aunt Laurie knew Sam

Bronfman, whose father was the C.E.O. of Seagram's. (Industry gossip held that after Prohibition, the Jews got the liquor business and the Catholics got the beer business.)

The Bronfmans are an international powerhouse, but Sam turned out to be one of the most humble guys I ever came across. He was worth a gazillion dollars, and he had access to everybody. I was pretty aggressive in asking for advice every step of the way, and I was thrilled to bend his ear. I gave him a He'brew t-shirt, and years later friends told me they'd see Sam playing basketball in it. He made some introductions for me to some southern California wholesalers, and I was able to get one of the largest liquor distributors in the world to pick up my beer.

Southern Wine and Spirits, at the time, sold $2.3 billion worth of booze. And that was before they got *really* big. They repped Bacardi, Absolut, Kahlua, Cuervo. They offered a wine portfolio that was hundreds, if not thousands, of wine SKUs. They had previously distributed Guinness as it grew to be a staple at American bars. They had established Pete's, and some innovative boutique brands, like Samuel Smith's.

S.W.S. reigned as a monster distributor, but the beer department was almost an afterthought. In fact, at the time they were scaling back on their beer portfolio. We got some good accounts; we did some business in West L.A. But it was tough being with such a huge distributor. Anyone who has ever sold through such a huge company knows exactly what's called "supplier math." If you looked at their org chart, you'd think, Man, if every sales rep just sold one case of mine this week, this month, or even this year, I'll be swimming in it. There must have been several hundred street reps, managers, beer specialists. Of course they can each sell a case or two.

But with the way the industry and companies of that size work, ninety percent of those guys won't have any interest in selling your product. Some of them won't even know it's in their price book. As a small supplier, you're not paying them incentives, and their base commission on selling a case of beer is almost nothing. The big brands are pimping big-screen TVs or trips to Europe, hundreds of dollars cash, or a cruise for the high sellers. Even the not-so-big brands kick back five or ten or more bucks for new placements. So "supplier math" ends up being a cruel joke you need to avoid playing on yourself.

Southern had maybe ten guys who sold between one and ten cases of He'brew a month. As would happen for many years to come, my first ride-with to sell He'brew with S.W.S. fell to a nice Jewish salesman named Ira who covered all the kosher accounts, mostly with wine.

Ira helped me out a lot in the beginning, introducing me to many of his Jewish contacts and better retailers who might appreciate the beer. Somewhat ironic, given that the company was owned by a Jewish family, but Ira was the *only* go-to Jewish connection on the sales staff. He had his successful niche, though he never seemed especially pleased about it, and would soon break into a wider role for the company involving high-end wine education.

I went on another ride-with on the west side of L.A. with a team manager that my first employee, Rob, and I crowned the "Best Shaved Man in Hooch." It seemed like this guy must have been shaving three times a day to stay that smooth. Gold and ivory cufflinks, a brand new Lexus, a Rolex. Tight.

He ran a team of twelve to fifteen salesmen. He told me his numbers had to be up month over year, every month, and Southern did not mess around. There was heavy pressure from the top. If you were up, you were handsomely rewarded. Down, and you were out. As we stopped into a few delis and some nicer bottle shops, placing a case here and there, he recounted an incident from a couple months back.

It was the last day of the month, and his district manager says, "You guys are down thirty-eight grand. Get it fixed." That was more than I'd sold in the entire year of He'brew at that point. So John gathered his second-in-command, and the two of them personally called in favors, barged through doors, and nailed it. By four o'clock that afternoon, they'd blown past the thirty-eight grand and actually went twenty grand over their target, all before Happy Hour. Brass balls, baby! Coffee's for closers. That was a completely different scale than anything I had seen before.

It seemed like all I needed to do was to get to all those Jews in L.A. and I'd be killing it. I drove down from San Francisco time and again, slept on the couches of friends from high school and college, crashed with cousins and anyone else who would indulge me, trekked around an enormous expanse of territory, did all kinds of Jewish events.

Still, in 1998 or so, the Jews in southern California were a very different breed than those in northern California. They drank a lot of Corona, a lot of cosmopolitans. There were a lot of Israelis who didn't get the shtick, or didn't think it was funny, or didn't drink beer. (I certainly found *some* customers and cheerleaders even in those days, but it has really been in the last few years that the LA area craft beer scene has truly taken off. Better beer days indeed.)

The next step was Chicago. In a minor miracle, a wholesaler who read about the beer in one of the Jewish newspapers actually *contacted me* to ask to rep my brands. That was good progress.

Chicago has a huge Jewish community, and it's a great beer-drinking town. Pacific Wine and Spirits appeared to be a miniature version of Southern; in fact, Southern eventually bought them. Pacific had a robust beer portfolio with a lot of quality brands, so it was enlightening to go to Chicago to see the way they did business there. In California, by law, case one to case one hundred had to have the same set price, which needed to be posted with the state. Specifically forbidden to cut deals and play games, the smaller craft distributors and suppliers ostensibly sold the concept and the product.

But in Chicago, perhaps evolved from its notorious traditions of bootlegging, there simply were no laws regulating pricing. Everything was about "the deal." The official printed price book meant next to nothing. The web of relationships between buyers and sellers, sales history, promises kept and/or broken, and likely some waft of simple corruption meant the pricing at any given moment fell into convoluted categories, defined by an unseen hand of the margin god. Pacific had the "frontline" rate, which no one but the most desperate or foolish ever had to pay; the "mid-tier," the "mix-and-match," the "family plan," and, my favorite, the "deep discount."

Pat Collins was Master of the Deep Discount, or at least he was in my mind. Everyone knew Pat. He seemed to have gone to school or played sports, drank beer or gone to church with the entire city. He took me to a huge liquor store called Sam's, north of downtown, whose owners were Jewish.

In the late '90s, Sam's claimed the mantle of the largest single freestanding liquor store in the country in terms of volume and dollars. While it was generally illegal to ship beer across state lines, they created a legal-enough way to sell beer by mail-order, which proved a boon for me. I put the 800 number all over my promotional materials and on the web site. It was very expensive to ship, probably forty dollars for a case of beer and another thirty for shipping. Still, it was worth it to many as the only way to get the beer, and people paid. If someone wanted six bottles of The Chosen Beer for a bar mitzvah, or for a boozy Chanukah present, now they could have it shipped to most spots around the country. Sam's sold a boatload by mail-order for me, and as a favor, Brian, one of the family owners and managers, even kept He'brew shirts under his desk to sell to customers if they wanted the add-on.

Back in San Francisco, I also had an account with the Wine Club south of Market, which took a ridiculously low margin on beer and gave me a huge boost by selling my He'brew Starter Kits (beer, glass, shirt, stickers) to customers all over the country. I sold the gift packs directly to the store, and even with a little kickback to my local wholesaler, the profit on those goody boxes paid my rent several times during the holidays.

In Chicago, many of the Jewish community groups in town threw together parties that featured He'brew as a special attraction, and many friends (some of whom had been on the Israel trip with me) provided couches and showed up to offer hugs and support by drinking the goods. I threw together my first official "History of Shmaltz Brewing" shpiel (covering, oh, maybe eighteen months) for the Young Adults Division of the Jewish Federation, pulling together enough material to stand up in front of about a hundred people for an hour, riffing on the genesis of He'brew. Chicago offered a glimpse of what I thought the business could be like if the beer were in all the major Jewish markets in the country -- and if I had my shit together.

In the spring of 1998, with beer on shelves and wholesalers in place, I worked on creating a naïve plan to market this product. Unfortunately, I still couldn't have given a succinct definition of the word *marketing*. The buzzwords were things like "brand awareness," "brand identification," and "creating pull," none of which I knew what the hell they were talking about, and didn't particularly care for the vocabulary.

With much trial and many errors, I attempted to plant the hat of the marketing department on my head. With the very limited desktop publishing skills I had from my 'zine days, I transitioned from Pagemaker to Quark

Express. I got a couple of quick lessons from some friends who were graphic designers in San Francisco. The designer from my last job at the audio tour company, having moved on to his own freelance gig, consistently let me come into his office, bother him for advice, and pirate software. I created a one-page black-and-white flyer with bullet points (well, Jewish star wingdings), the one-color outline logo, and some hype from the media hits. I thought I was pretty damn clever, customizing the same one sheet with different headlines for different targets -- Jewish organizations, beer wholesalers, retailers, and finally customers. I had to remind myself with still more yellow stickies which one was which and what I wanted to say to them.

Looking back, my strategy was so basic it's embarrassing. I wanted to get those flyers out there, but I had to be very stingy. I dropped some off at the front desks of synagogues and posted some on bulletin boards on campuses. I faxed them to chain buyers and handed them out to distributor reps and retail accounts. For a wider "marketing campaign" to reach consumers, I found a local printer who specialized in club cards -- little glossy, double-sided four-by-four-inch cards -- and ran five thousand postcards for a couple hundred bucks. They were mailable, but I barely did; it was too expensive for postage. I left them at bars and coffee shops, on windshields outside stores or events, and I'd hand them to employees at the retail stores that surrounded the accounts I was selling to -- the nail places and sub shops in the mini-malls around BevMo or near Whole Foods.

I still don't know if any of this was the most effective, or even cost-effective, way to spread the word. I was working on pure intuition. Though the business has progressed a fair amount from those early days, our tactics have not really changed all that much. I don't wander down University Avenue or 24th Street handing cards to strangers anymore, but we do in fact use that strategy over and over and over at beer festivals and on the Coney Island boardwalk.

Though providing cash "incentives" at the wholesale level is one of the most important elements of the success of certain brands, I've really shied away from paying distributor reps to focus on our brands. Especially in the beginning, I figured, Wasn't it their job to sell the beer every day? After all, I was cutting my margin in half to go with wholesalers, so I innocently assumed they'd do their best. Some did and still do. But when I started, Sierra Nevada had a standing incentive for every new tap handle sold in northern California: a hundred dollars. That was big money for these reps. I didn't and still don't blame them -- they are working for money, not glory. I'd chase that dollar as well. And Sierra had a great product and a great brand, so it was worth the effort.

No doubt one of the most important things for a small business is to build a distribution network with people you can trust, people who are professional, who show up and do their jobs, and most importantly, pay their bills on time. It's utterly miraculous if you find people you actually like. After thirteen years, the vast majority of my distributors are reliable and professional. Most amazingly, I truly enjoy dealing with nearly all of them. And some of them I absolutely love. Since I worked more or less solo for over a decade, these people have been my primary co-workers and peers.

Though they were still a small company, at the time Lagunitas was probably 30 times bigger than Shmaltz. I clearly remember the day I walked in the door at A&D Distribution in San Mateo, and Ron, their sales manager, blew my mind: He had colored paper. In Day-glo shades.

Not exactly revolutionary thinking in the history of modern marketing, but I sure hadn't thought of it. So I started making my flyers using goldenrod yellow, to more or less complement the vibe of the Genesis label. At twice the cost of plain white paper, my flyer budget went through the roof. But those flyers stood out on the salesroom table and in the salesman's pitch book. What was my return on investment (R.O.I.)? I have no idea.

I did know from going to beer festivals that craft brewers are typically very casual and laid-back. From what I saw, they were not the most aggressive promoters around. They were intensely passionate about the beer they wanted to make; sales and marketing were just a necessary chore.

Though I wouldn't have been able to define it at the time, I had started a sales and marketing company. I knew, however, that I didn't have the liberty of sitting back and waiting for somebody to come to my pub and buy the beer. I always felt like I had to force people to buy it.

In the industry, it's called "hand-selling." The customer (or a retail buyer) might not know much about the product, but with a little information, and a lot of enthusiasm, you can get them fired up about it. In those days, I felt like

I had to hand-sell every single bottle of He'brew beer. Even after ten solid years in the business, I still felt like I had to be at the point of purchase for every beer being bought. Why would somebody buy a six-pack of He'brew if I wasn't standing right there, telling him or her how fantastic, funny, and delicious the product is?

Just being relentless is one of the most important parts of being an entrepreneur. Not everybody is an extrovert. It comes naturally to me, but whether you are or you aren't, it's helpful to think of selling and marketing as theater.

Even shy people on occasion like to do karaoke. Self-promotion is a skill that has to be learned, in the same way that I had to learn invoicing, even though I hate it and I'm terrible at it. You don't have to be the greatest promoter or emcee to walk up to someone and say, Hi, I'd like to share a little information with you. I say to my staff, Think about how you have a conversation with friends, when you tell them about your job or describe your favorite beer. Someone a little more understated than I am can still stand in front of the Whole Foods buyer, look her in the eye, and tell her a convincing story.

It's important to play to one's strengths, and the successful owners have found a comfortable and compelling style. Different entrepreneurs can be wildly successful in communicating their passion, in creating a feeling of cult following for their brands, in very different ways. Some are loud, boisterous party guys. Some are academic, quiet, and intimate. Even Adam Avery can't compete with Sam from Dogfish for rock star enthusiasm. But Ron from Jolly Pumpkin, or Rob (and Jason) from Allagash, project a compelling passion that demands attention and respect (not to mention sales). Patrick from the Bruery can share his homebrewer-to-national-specialty-brand story in a very different way than Greg from Stone might talk about his company's brewing attitude and explosive expansion. But both will draw devoted followers, and create believers.

One of toughest things for me about He'brew has been reminding myself not to take rejections so personally. Of all the people walking through the grocery store, plenty of them are going to have no interest in my product, and that's OK -- I didn't necessarily create it for everyone. But I created this beer with a very personal intention, and it just killed me when people didn't like it, or, sometimes even worse, simply weren't interested.

I had a particularly hard time with the quick dismissal, when they're not going to take five seconds to hear about it. I'd think, I'm spending everything I've got, busting my ass to bring this thing into the world. As Lenny Bruce defined the underlying drive of most entertainers, "Look at me, Ma! Over here! Ma -- *over here!*"

When I worked at the SFMOMA, the museum kept data on how long an average person will look at a painting. These are works that are worth, at minimum, hundreds of thousands of dollars, if not tens of millions. The answer: Seven seconds. And this is for the art that people actually decide to stop to look at.

I grew to remind myself on every sales call that I simply had an agenda to accomplish. Much like the journalist whose job is to write every day about *something*, the beer buyer similarly has to decide to say yes or no to a pitch. She can say yes, and that means something's going to happen. If she says no, she's stopped something from happening. In a sense, she is accomplishing a task there, too. If she says maybe, she's just really putting you off and creating more work for herself.

As a salesperson, I try to act like now is the time when we decide, and together we get work done. The purchasing cliffhanger is like a movie that isn't resolved -- not fun. Of course, you also *never* let the call close out with a no. At the very least it's gotta be a not today or, even better, *not yet...*

I think of myself as a performer. I won't usually acknowledge that the buyer said no. I'll jump to a different character, come at it from a different angle. If a guy says no for one reason, I'll try another. You don't like pomegranates? How about history? If not, did you home-brew in college? You went to the track one time in Saratoga? Knew a woman who joined the circus? Whatever.

It's a lot like improv. Give me a color, a season, an article of clothing, and the first car you owned. You just have to create a space for people to find a way they're going to be either comfortable or worn down enough to say yes.

If I was going to sell my beer with any sense of authority, I figured it would behoove me to get better at talking about the beer itself. I signed up for a class about beer, which was more about how to drink a beer than how to brew it. The instructor was Dr. Joe Owades, a fascinating, softly outspoken character who had been in the beer industry forever. One of the grandpops of modern brewing, he'd worked at Rheingold in New York, an iconic regional (and Jewish-owned) beer company. A chemist turned brewer, Owades invented light beer, unfortunately a bit before its time. His version flopped, years before Miller threw a ton of money and football superstars at the idea, creating what would become the number one category of ubiquitous and mediocre beer atop a mountain of interchangeable, supposedly competitive products.

As he would often profess during class, Dr. Joe was a true believer in the Church of Lagers as the only "true" beer. In what craft beer critics would likely welcome as a move away from the dark side, he also worked with innovators such as Anchor Brewing and Sam Adams, creating recipes and consulting on brewing techniques for brands that would fuel the craft beer movement.

He reminded me of the Jewish grandfather I never had, and I hit him up after each session: What the hell am I supposed to do to make this project work? I kept thinking there must be some secret to unlock this mystery. As so many of my early network of advisors can attest, I sent letters and emails and made calls and asked for meetings through each early stage of the business, just trying to understand what I should be doing differently to catapult into the black. John from Jupiter and Triple Rock, Ron from Thirsty Bear, Ernie from Hagafen, Mark from Real Beer -- so many offered up time and advice along the way.

During every single interview I've ever done about He'brew, the reporter will inevitably ask, "So, are you profitable?" The truth, potential entrepreneurs, is that I didn't break even until eight years into the business -- and that was only break-even for that one year. (To this day I still haven't covered the friends-and-family investments of the early days. Hang tight for details.) My standard comeback always went, Well, I'm on the cusp of profits.

Rob, who would soon become my first sales guy, used to give me endless crap about that. Every email I got from him would say something like, "Well, I'm *on the cusp* of selling a floor display and meeting you for Happy Hour."

By 1998, I'd long since run out of my original two-thousand-dollar investment. I'd taken the rest of my life savings, about fifteen grand, plus another five or so I'd earned while catering and working my various jobs. That last fifteen grand was from my father's life insurance policy. I'd used most of what I got from that to contribute to my college tuition and my living expenses, and I'd promised myself I wouldn't spend the rest. When I moved to New Orleans, I took something like twelve hundred bucks. After working at Kinko's for $6.50 an hour, I moved to D.C. with another grand or two. And so on.

When I was about twenty-two, I'd trusted my savings to a hotshot investor from Palo Alto who had a ton of seemingly smart and sophisticated clients. Everyone knew this guy. He started investing in tech companies, long before any Web boom was even imagined. At the time, it was all wildly speculative. The stocks went from two dollars to twenty, and then, suddenly, they plummeted to two cents a share.

I freaked, but he was calm: "Just ride it out." And then my grandmother sent me a clipping about the broker, whose other clients had lost millions. It was front-page news in our hometown papers. It still isn't clear to me whether what he did was illegal, or just really bad judgment. In any event, my fifteen grand was basically worthless.

I sent a letter to Merrill Lynch, and somewhat miraculously, they actually gave me my money back -- all of it. I took some of that money and sublet part of a guy's loft in the live-work space upstairs from us. He was a painter, and he had built a loft with a small, elevated desk space for himself. I think I paid him $250 a month to sublet the twelve-by-twelve-foot upstairs part of the loft he'd built. The only problem was, the ceiling above the space was only about five-foot-ten inches, and I'm six-one. I had to duck to not smack my skull on the exposed industrial pipes crisscrossing the ceiling. Still, it was a huge step for my microscopically small business, moving out of my kitchen with Tracy, attempting to create a little space for both of us.

I used that fifteen grand to get me through the better part of a year. I was still freaked out every day, working beer festivals every weekend. But at least the product was getting more and more exposure. Some pretty substantial articles came out when I switched to Anderson Valley and put out the press release about it. It felt like I was building some momentum. Yet at the end of the month, how many cases of beer did I actually sell? I didn't really know.

And then, in a matter of seconds, a friend of mine changed my entire way of thinking about the company. I popped in for some brotherly advice from my high school friend Rob, who had been the host of the original volleyball crew. At twenty-eight he was running his own successful investment fund.

Rob grabbed a scratch pad on his desk. He asked me how much I was making per case. I said, five bucks.

"OK. How much do you want to pay yourself? How much does it cost to run the company? Let's say with packaging, marketing materials and some travel it costs about fifty grand to run the company, and let's say you'd like to set aside a $50,000 salary for yourself. At five dollars profit, you need to sell twenty thousand cases this year."

My jaw hit the desk. First I thought, Shit -- math. Second I realized, I'm *never* going to sell that much. I'm nowhere close. Fuuuuck meeeeee!

Other than some short and expensive help while creating my business plan, it wouldn't be until my eleventh year in business that I took on an actual bookkeeper. Until then, I just made photocopies of my checking-account ledger, later a running laundry list in an Excel file. I never knew how much money I made or lost, or really how much sales I was doing. I didn't keep track of my expenses until the end of the year, when I threw together my taxes in an afternoon.

It just didn't seem like it made that much difference. All I knew was that it wasn't enough, and I wasn't going to stop. It was, I'll be the first to admit, a somewhat unprofessional attitude for running a business.

CHAPTER 9

Finally, Business School 101, Hold The Viagra

T hough it also happens to be true, I love to joke that it took me many years of craft beer drinking to begin to identify the nuances of flavor profiles and appreciate even the most basic technical brewing details. Practice, practice, practice.

I knew my strengths, interests, and desires, so I gladly handed over the recipe formulation first to Simon and then Anderson Valley and focused on what I did have in the early years: my idea, my intellectual property.

UNNN-fortunately, even there I made some nearly catastrophic mistakes related to trademark issues that would come back to haunt me, brutally and expensively, year after year. Finally, in our fourteenth year, I can say that I'm nailing down all our intellectual property issues. Yes, there's the current disco-dance group and biker-gang controversy, and the Evangelical Christian homebrew club ripping me off... but I'm working through it. In the beginning I was basically winging it, much like everything else.

When I started, looking up existing trademarks without a lawyer's aid meant heading to the public library. An intellectual property non-profit served the San Jose area for reduced fees, but the San Francisco public library was free, and on a BART (the subway) line. An eleven-by-seventeen-inch laminated paper sign sat between two computers -- *U.S. Patent and Trademark*

Office Database.

At the time, I didn't know the difference between trademarks, patents, and copyrights. It took me years to straighten out which was which, even having worked as a paralegal. Considering that I could not afford a lawyer, I jumped on the computer. I'd received a free introductory information packet from the non-profit, and I learned I needed to file for a trademark, not copyright.

From today's Internet: *A trademark is a word, phrase, symbol or design, or a combination of words, phrases, symbols or designs, that identifies and distinguishes the source of the goods of one party from those of others* (uspto.gov). Your trademark is your brand, the name that's front and center on your product -- what it's called, how it's referred to in the marketplace. Most importantly, I thought, I had to protect the He'brew name, though I didn't think Shmaltz Brewing or even Genesis Ale[6] needed to be protected. Who the hell would threaten "Chicken Fat Brewing Company"?

The Torah seemed pretty safe haven for beer names as well. I did every search I could think of on the fledgling Internet. Nothing came back for "He'brew" and "beer." I searched the Yellow Pages and called Information, and then I went on the U.S. P.T.O. database. Nothing matched, so I figured, Great, I'll pay the $275 and put in an application.

File under "Do as I say not as I did" and get your intellectual property straight from the beginning. Here's a little something to get you started, but seriously, unlike in 1996 when I screwed this up the first time, now just hit the U.S. P.T.O. website and get your act together. But here's an appetizer.

Trademark: A trademark is how merchants or manufacturers (i.e., brewers) present their product or brand to the market. This could be a word, phrase, symbol or design -- or a combination of these elements. Register the trademark(s) for your company's property with

REGISTER THE ENTIRE LABEL OR JUST THE NAME "CONEY ISLAND" AS A TRADEMARK.

---

6 See Chapter 18 for the one party after thirteen years who thought Genesis Ale was a problem: the pride of Rochester, Genesee Cream Ale.

the U.S. Patent and Trademark Office, either as an "intent-to-use" when still in the planning phase or as an "in-use" mark if it has been sold in commerce. After this is done, no one can use your trademark or a confusingly similar trademark to sell their goods. Unlike copyrights, trademarks do not have an expiration date -- they just need to be filed with the P.T.O., in continuous use, and renewed once every ten years.

Copyright: From an image to a book to a theatrical performance, a copyright protects the "original work of authorship" from being copied or drawn from by other people. The owner is the only one who can give permission for the work to be reproduced. Limited exceptions to this exclusivity exist for types of "fair use", such as book reviews and song clips. Copyrights do have an expiration date after which the product is free for the world to copy. You must file your copyright with the U.S. Copyright Office.

REGISTER JUST THE ARTWORK AS A COPYRIGHT.

Patent: A patent is the protection of a *physical invention,* whether a machine, a design style, or a chemical compound. Like a copyright and a trademark, a patent is simply to protect your invention from being copied by other people. Patents must be registered with the U.S. Patent and Trademarks Office and the also have an expiration date. Only the patent holder can give permission for their invention to be copied or drawn from. There are three types of patents: 1. Utility -- for machines, processes, or manufactured products; 2. Design -- a new/original design used on a manufactured article; 3. Plant -- used for a new variety of asexually reproduced plant.

TRADEMARK: Company brand and product names, logos, slogans, colors (The Chosen Beer, Albino Python, Maker's Mark wax drippings)
COPYRIGHT: Original works of authorship: painting/book (Coney Island Lager Freak Face, Rush "Tom Sawyer")
PATENT: Physical inventions (none from Shmaltz; nearly 500,000 applied for by others in 2009)

By the way, Ideas cannot be copyrighted, trademarked, or patented.

About a year after I started, when I began distributing down in L.A., I sold the beer to a little kosher grocery on Pico in West L.A., and the manager says, "Oh, is this you too? Did you change labels?" Another guy had a different beer he'd been producing for nine months called He-brew.

If my stuff was irreverent and a little corny, this stuff was downright schlock: "He-brew *Is-Real* Good Beer." A foil-printed Jewish star framed a picture of the guy's bearded mug beneath a "Chai" baseball hat, and he was wearing sunglasses and sporting a gold Star of David around his neck. He'd gotten a small brewery to relabel one of their lightest beers for him. He was doing exactly what I was doing -- contract-brewing.

I was dumbfounded. How had I missed him? I called around desperately, and finally got a trademark lawyer to give me a few minutes of free advice. She told me there's two databases -- the trademarks "in use," and those with "intent-to-use." I'd only used one of the two computers in the library. I had no idea there was any difference.

So I went back and searched again. Like a punch in the gut, I found not just the guy in L.A., but *three* other people in the U.S. with intent-to-use marks for the name "Hebrew," all of them ahead of me in line.

Was my pride most bruised for not being as clever and original as I assumed? Or was my true concern the fact that my life savings were suddenly at risk of being even more jeopardized than it already seemed? I still haven't decided if this legal wrinkle seems fair or reasonable. When filing an intent-to-use trademark, the person has to sign a statement claiming a "bona fide intention" to use it in commerce. This reserves a position in the lineup of registrations, and as soon as the product is sold, the rights and registration go back to the original date of the intent-to-use filing, regardless of possible delays and extensions. It could be years that one party does not use the actual mark (as in this case), but even if someone else starts using it and creates a brand and a product line, the registration will go to the intent-to-use filer.

Like so many contract brews at the time, the Is-Real Good Beer just seemed to disappear. I never heard from him, and on my next trip south, the account said he'd just stopped showing up.

Before folding, he'd been third in line for the trademark. The number two

Hebrews turned out to be a New York chef at a corporate dining room and his childhood buddy, a bartender. On a personal trip that became an emergency business trip, I met one of them at his workplace in Manhattan, where I discovered they hadn't even made any beer yet.

Their slogan was "Hebrew -- The Beer You Can't Pass Over." I'll admit a little shtick-jealousy. Theologically, their punchline spoke the truth, referencing the ban on drinking beer during Passover, because of the sprouted grains and the yeast used in brewing. Still, I thought mine had more chutzpah. For a hot minute, we kicked around the idea of entering a licensing agreement, but nothing came of it.

But the guy who was number one in line for the name quickly emerged as my biggest headache, by far. I'd started the process of creating my business plan to raise money, and it was clear I needed to straighten out the trademark issue. If your brand is constantly in jeopardy and you're guaranteed to have legal challenges, it makes it very difficult for potential investors to trust you with five, ten, or fifteen thousand dollars of their hard-earned money.

This guy had a full-time job at a national telephone company, and he sold used brewing equipment out of his garage in Atlanta on the side. He had a beer he called Evan's Hebrew, with a picture of himself inside -- what else? -- a Jewish star on the label. He had a big, bushy mustache and a *Welcome Back, Kotter* Jewfro. He'd contracted with an Atlanta microbrewery to make a few kegs of his beer, a rather forgettable golden ale, from what I'd heard. He'd applied for trademarks for both Hebrew and Evan's Hebrew. This guy ended up being the most expensive, and one of the most painful, thorns in my side.

We had a series of exasperating conversations over the phone. He claimed he and his "backers" had big plans for Evan's Hebrew that included contract-brewing in Puerto Rico to trim costs. They had professional baseball players lined up as corporate spokesmen. Cruise ships and grocery chains and extensive business plans, yadda yadda yadda.

Of course none of this had happened yet, but he would not give up on his claim. "Everything is in the works," he said. Back and forth, two, three, four times and more over several weeks. By this time I had a handful of investors lined up, with cash commitments that depended on me owning this trademark. Everyone loved the concept. There was no way I was going to part with the name.

I tried to reason with him. I pleaded, Evan, you've got one keg label, and it's a photocopy. I've spent two years of my life and all my life savings creating this product and spreading this brand across several markets. Cut me some slack here.

But he wouldn't budge.

I started to freak -- I had all my money, and so much of my self-worth, tied up in this thing. I saw no way to get it back without raising money and expanding the product line. In that final conversation, we were literally screaming at each other.

"YOU GOTTA GIVE ME FIFTY THOUSAND DOLLARS."

YOU'RE OUT OF YOUR MIND. I'LL GIVE YOU TWO GRAND.

It was brutal and pathetic, our haggling back and forth over an asset with zero true value to anyone other than us two. I was exhausted, inexperienced, and had no more fight in me. During the last bout I finally buckled, banging my fist against the support beam of my little loft office in frustration and resignation. Eventually I spit out, *Fine*, I'll pay you thirty thousand, but I need five years to do it.

He said, "*Fine*. I want five grand up front and I'll agree."

I started working with a lawyer, a friend of a friend of Tracy's dad who ran a boutique law firm in San Francisco. His client roster included companies like Lucasfilm and venture capital startups. Bill had already given me a lot of free advice, so I wanted to at least use his firm for creating the corporation, processing the financing paperwork, and finalizing the trademark agreement. Even with the additional cut-rate deal he kindly offered, the invoices added up to fifteen or twenty thousand dollars.

Through investment banker friends-of-friends, I got copies of the business plans for Pete's Wicked Ale and Sam Adams, when both made their initial public offerings. With one other generic business-school-type template as a model, I managed to cobble together my own business plan for Shmaltz Enterprises. One potential investor said it was "the most amusing and entertaining business plan" he'd ever seen. He did, however, decline to invest.

Compared to navigating the travails of the beer world, I found writing the business plan to be surprisingly straightforward. In fact, I found it to be pretty fun. In contrast to crying out for attention from my wholesalers and butting heads with retail buyers, spouting off one-liners about perceived marketing advantages and untapped Jewish markets demanded skills I'd already honed.

Crowing about the media success and visualizing a whole line of beers and other products under the He'brew brand (soda, coffee, tea -- anything "gourmet, kosher, and microbrewed") flowed easily. After floundering through CMYK and other previously unimagined technical demands of four-color process printing, and having survived the federal government's alcohol bureaucracy, raising money proved to be one of the smoothest, most satisfying projects I'd accomplished. Much like with the PR success that came so much more easily than any profits from beer sales, I noted to self that perhaps I should be in the business-plan-writing business, rather than the beer business. One of my investors even said straight out that he was offering money this round, but mostly to see what I did with my next venture after Shmaltz met its likely-limited destiny. I took the comment as a compliment and deposited the check.

I wrote the text of the business plan, explaining that my vision was somewhere between a Jewish community organization and a business. I got contributions from Tracy's father, my mother's friends, a few of my friends' parents, and three business guys I hadn't previously known who were very active in the Jewish community. Some had names on museums and Jewish community centers. Others were guys I played quarters with in high school.

The prospect of taking money from close friends and family was absolutely terrifying. Up until I started the company, I had never missed paying a credit card bill. I never spent more than I had in the bank. Never threw down the credit card for rounds of shots at college bars, or splurged on concert tickets I knew I couldn't cover.

Now here I was, totally broke. I'd spent the last of my dad's life insurance policy money. But I did have this idea and product that people still loved talking about. At beer festivals, people were total fanatics about it: "It's a million-dollar idea! You're a marketing genius!" Customer is always right, right? It just made me more frantic: There *had* to be a way to make this business work.

CRAFT BEER *Bar Mitzvah*

Executive Summary

In the Beginning:
In the beginning, there was an idea, and it was good: a high quality, hilarious beer to complement the Jewish-American experience. Shmaltz Enterprises proudly presents HE'BREW—The Chosen Beer and our first creation, Genesis Ale. Then we tasted it, and it was very good... *L'Chaim!*

Exile Never Tasted So Good:
In the past 2 years, HE'BREW—The Chosen Beer has grown from an inside joke to a viable consumer product brand. A successful 9-month test phase was followed by an very successful initial expansion period. Currently Shmaltz Enterprises (see "Company Background" below for explanation of Shmaltz names) is a wholesale contract brewer working with Anderson Valley Brewing Company to produce Genesis Ale, the first product under the HE'BREW brand.

Shmaltz Enterprises has signed distribution agreements with 5 wholesalers covering 11 counties around the SF Bay Area and all of Southern California. HE'BREW also hit the shelves in Chicago in March 1998, Minneapolis/St. Paul in June 1998, and Northern Virginia in October 1998. In early 1999, HE'BREW will begin selling in New York City. Genesis Ale currently sells in approximately 300 Bay Area accounts (including most of the smaller chains and 75 Safeway stores) and 70 or so retailers in Southern California. From October 1997 to December 1998, Shmaltz sold about 6500 cases of Genesis Ale.

Working with a retailer in San Francisco, Shmaltz also runs a successful mail order business shipping beer (where legal) and t-shirts, pint glasses, and posters directly to customers around the country. Our web site, www.shmaltz.com, which contains an array of fun, funky, relevant information, received over 250,000 impressions since October 1997.

Go Tell It On the Mountain:
Brand awareness and increased sales spread through two highly effective channels: word of mouth and media coverage. In the past year, Shmaltz had a presence at over 100 events, fundraisers, and festivals in the Jewish community and beyond. Kosher Food Festivals, receptions for Jewish theater groups and museums, numerous beer festivals, music concerts, comedy shows, and singles events have spread awareness and consumer trial and created brand loyalty.

A very successful PR effort splashed HE'BREW across local, national and international media. *Newsweek*, National Public Radio, the Sunday San Francisco *Chronicle/Examiner*, the New York *Times*, the San Jose *Mercury*, the LA *Times*, NY Jewish *Forward*, the International Jewish Wire Service (JTA), much of the beer press, and numerous Jewish publications featured HE'BREW over the past year. Sales and awareness increased significantly and the mail order business serviced customers from all over the country.

The Promised Land:
Shmaltz aims to become the premier producer of high-quality, hip products for the younger generation of Jews. After building a distribution and sales structure for the beers, Shmaltz will extend the HE'BREW brand into new products including microbrewed ciders, sodas, teas, and coffees all with the characteristic Shmaltz sensibility. Shmaltz will also continue to expand its line of custom merchandise in order to further solidify brand awareness and loyalty, as well as to increase revenues from these high-margin items.

Seventy Five percent of the Jewish population lives in 11 metropolitan areas. Eighty-Five percent lives in 25 metropolitan areas. These cities are the targets for retail sales of HE'BREW products. In 1999, Shmaltz will have a presence in the SF Bay Area, LA, Chicago, and New York with Washington DC, Miami, and other key markets on the horizon. Beer distributors from nearly every target market have shown interest in distributing HE'BREW. The challenge will be to obtain the resources to properly manage the growth of the brand and to maintain its presence in those retail markets.

Today in the U.S., Jews and Jewish culture are everywhere: Seinfeld, Speilberg, the Beastie Boys, the Supreme Court. Jewish humor and sensibility are an integral part of American culture, and HE'BREW plays on the connection between Jewish tradition and shtick and our American lives. Now is a time of great opportunity for Jews and Jewish culture in the U.S., and HE'BREW celebrates this exciting experience.

The Three Pillars of Shmaltz Enterprises:
The success of the HE'BREW brand rests on three integrated aspects:

Quality:
* Brewed at the renowned Anderson Valley Brewing Company, named one of the Top Ten Breweries in the World two years in a row by the World Beer Championships
* Consistently positive feedback from consumers, tradespeople, beer press
* Kosher certified and accepted by the highest Orthodox standards

Community:
* Proven commitment to community organizations (both Jewish and non-Jewish) through fundraisers, festivals, and community celebrations has built brand loyalty and repeat custom
* Constant grass-roots networking spreads brand awareness and gives customers a personal connection to Shmaltz and HE'BREW

Shtick:
* Puns, punchlines, literary references, and Biblical allusions entertain the consumer with a smart, sincere sensibility
* Artistic, flamboyant labels and marketing materials give HE'BREW a fun, funky and distinct personality
* In the upcoming year, Shmaltz will participate with even more hip Jewish popular culture through comedy showcases, literary events, and music festivals.

If Not Now, When?:
Within the next 12-24 months, Shmaltz Enterprises will take advantage of its unique opportuni to own the niche for quality hand-crafted beers with funky Jewish personality and flare. In 1999 Shmaltz will introduce a second beer product (Messiah Stout....It's the beer you've been waiting introduce Genesis Ale in 12 ounce bottles. The Company will immediately hire a Sales Manager to expand our retail accounts in current and future markets. HE'BREW e New York City market in February 1999 and other key markets will follow. Planned ns for 1999 include a Jewish Literary Series in New York City, a number of concert ns in various cities, and a series spotlighting emerging Jewish comedians. We are also g the line of Shmaltz Brewing merchandise as well as upgrading the web site to include e commerce (on-line ordering). Finally, we are developing packaging and marketing plan HE'BREW Starter Kit--2 bottles of HE'BREW, a t-shirt, and a logo pint glass--the ultim h present or grad-student care package.

I'd begun shopping for investors at the end of summer, 1998. By the spring of 1999, I started depositing the checks. My plan was to stop working on the side and to hire a salesperson who could help me expand the business. With a full-time salesperson, I assumed we could sell at least five, if not ten times more beer than I could by myself. I'd been so distracted with marketing and merchandise, learning the whole business at the same time as I was doing it, that I figured a full-time, focused, dedicated rep would push me way "over the cusp" of profitability.

I also wanted to put out a second beer style. I had to pay the trademark guy, and I paid Tracy for her work on the label art and the logos. From there, I would start to pay myself, whatever salary I could afford.

My goal was to raise $135,000. The linchpin of the entire deal came when Anderson Valley agreed to invest $35,000 in the form of profit sharing on future beer sales. The fact that I had them in the deal was my biggest selling point, by far. Ken had a successful business, and he knew what he was doing. I mean, this guy turned a little retirement project into a world-class boutique operation. He agreed to invest five dollars per case out of future beer sales, up to $35,000. At that price, he would cover his cost and throw the extra profit back to me as an investment.

For the other hundred thousand, one share cost forty-five hundred dollars. Most of my investors bought one or two shares -- my close friends Jim, John, and Robert, who would go on to become my salesperson (I did manage to get that back to him after I canned him), and Mike, one of Rob's banker friends, who had cash to spend on projects that interested him. Ben and his parents bought a few. Tracy's dad bought one each for Tracy and her sister Amy. Our longtime family friends Robin and Don bought two, as did a couple more of my mom's friends. The dean of the medical school bought one. One of my more-experienced angel investors bought one share, another threw in ten thousand dollars' worth, and a third, a local philanthropist and wildly successful businessman, bought in for twenty grand.

The plan intended to get me to break-even within a year. By the time we signed the final paperwork, I'd probably spent nearly half the money. Looking back, I can't believe how fast I dropped all that cash into the business, especially given my later experience of even more frugal bootstrapping, when I moved the production east and introduced six-packs.

Still, even then, carrying one little 22 ounce bottle and an overflowing bag of shtick, things were looking up. He'brew was seeing the makings of a cult following. My buddy Jon, who owned a small wine company, was very supportive: "You've got a tiger by the tail. It very well might be a million-dollar idea. You've just got to figure out a way to make it work." The problem was, I needed a lot more people to actually *buy the beer* -- and drink it. Then I needed them to go back and buy another and drink that... and another... and another...

With the sun having set on the exuberant decade of his twenties, looking to get serious about his future prospects, an enthusiastic, not-so-young gentleman got off his windsurfer for a moment and called Shmaltz Brewing Company. To his everlasting credit, Robert thought pulling a beer off a shelf at the only vaguely Jewish deli in San Francisco, and contacting the beer company directly on its Catskills-M.C. voicemail, would be a perfectly appropriate way to forward his career aspirations.

He left me a message in the beginning of 1999, as I was in the process of raising money. I told him I would in fact be hiring a salesman, and would be happy to meet with him.

Rob had done a little bit of a lot of things, from waiting tables to working as a sailing instructor and a health spa attendant in London. Most importantly, he had an aggressive sense of humor and irreverence, mixed with a profound appreciation for the Jewish traditions he'd grown up with in a Conservative family on the south side of Chicago. He had received a robust formal Jewish education and knew many more Hebrew prayers than I did.

Although Rob and I were both about the same age -- my twenty-nine to his thirty at the time -- we made the attempt to have a structured business relationship. I tried to play the role of boss, and I created a Sales Manager position for him. No org chart followed, but after several months of patience and follow-up, he began as soon as I sealed the deals with my investors. I had him create a sales and marketing manual for himself, and for the company -- how to approach on-premise bars and restaurants, off-premise grocery stores, corner markets and chains, how to work with distributors. How to prepare for the Jewish holidays and promotions, how to roll out new markets.

I was extremely excited, and nervous. Instead of me actively selling the product ten percent of the time, he'd be banging on doors one hundred percent of the time. It was a strange process for me, going from working by myself to having another human being I was supposed to be managing. I had to learn what I should and shouldn't say, when to get upset and when not to. Today, even with seven employees and many more years of experience, I still struggle with what I think a good manager should do and be.

In the beginning, having Rob on board was an endless source of fun. It was great to have a companion, a brother in Shmaltz, a fellow crusader. Though our sales didn't really skyrocket, as I had assumed they would, I just kept thinking that employees take a few months to pay for themselves, and we were bound to turn the corner.

I offered him a flat monthly salary. We weren't selling enough beer for either of us to worry about commissions. With my sincere hope to share profits and possibly equity as we grew, Rob was willing to work cheap for a time, which made a world of difference.

We're very close friends now, but to this day I can hurl shit at Rob for his first enthusiastic call about a sales success.

"Dude, we just made a sale!"

Kick ass! Where?

"Homeboy Liquors!"

Homeboy Liquors?

I thought, *That's* the first account my new salesperson gets? I have a brand-new sales manager selling one 22 ounce bottle of high-end and expensive Genesis Ale to a ghetto liquor store in the middle of the sketchiest skid row in the Tenderloin in San Francisco. I told him to get the hell out to Whole Foods and Andronico's, and to forget about Homeboy Liquors.

Rob and I did plan out what I think were all the right attempts to sell more beer week after week. He did ride-withs, in-store demos, sales meetings. He traveled to Chicago and crashed with family to keep expenses low. We expanded a little to some on-premise bars and cafes that would pull in a keg on occasion. Eventually that year our sales grew to the highest point by far: over seven thousand cases.

At that number, making five bucks per case, I had about thirty-five grand to run the whole business, pay Rob, cover rent on the new Shmaltz headquarters, and pay my own rent at home, which Tracy was subsidizing. Progress seemed certain, but with my lack of reporting prowess, I generally just kept my head down and kept pushing.

One morning we were in L.A. to do a presentation at Albertson's, at the time the third or fourth largest grocery chain in California. As predicted by the Southern account manager, the meeting went pretty quickly: the larger markets in southern California carried very little craft beer. They still considered Becks and Michelob to be high-quality specialty items.

So it's maybe nine-thirty in the morning, and L.A. is starting to get hot. We'd both been grinding away for several months, trying to build the business by any means we could dig up. In those days, I really didn't cut loose very often. I think I was so stressed and anxious that I just didn't allow myself to let up. Unfortunately, my back had not eased up much, and I had this developing neck twitch that kept my head from relaxing on the pillow when I lay down at night.

That morning, I just didn't have it in me to crisscross the flats of the L.A. basin, humping samples. I said, Rob, I think we need to bust out a little. How about Disneyland?

As a kid, I went all the time with my dad. I had not been in years. Rob said, "Hell, yeah."

As we rolled into the huge parking lot, I asked him whether he just happened to have any drugs in the car. He said, "Well, I have a joint, a hit of Ecstasy, and a Viagra." I said, Great let's split the first two, and I'll leave the Viagra for you and Alexandra.

Even with thousands of people swarming the park, I'm sure the second we hit the entrance the security guards were on the radio: "Uh, we got a couple of thirty-year-old men approaching with dark sunglasses and no children." Suspicious as we must have looked, we had a blast.

As fun as it was having Rob around, it wasn't long before we both started realizing that our partnership just wasn't working. It seemed like we were doing everything right, except the results part. I don't think he was the wrong guy. Maybe I was the wrong manager. There were just limitations on the brand at the time. The 22 ounce bottles never quite got off the ground. They were seen much more as a novelty than an everyday product. I also hadn't realized that though I'd only spent a certain percentage of my time selling every day, I had over those first two years reached a big percentage of the top beer accounts already -- and the market really didn't stretch a lot deeper when it came to niche beers. I had essentially filled the sales pipeline; now it would be more a question of selling off the shelves, which generally means relentless guerilla marketing, or simply throwing down the cash for big-buck advertising. "Yes" to number one for many years to come, and as I'd already hemorrhaged most of my cash, it would clearly be "no" to number two.

Rob and I would soon part, for all the right reasons. In fact, we became much better friends after I fired his ass. Pursuing his own small-business destiny, he opened a presentation skills consulting shop. Within a few years he was making amazing money -- tens of thousands per session coaching businesspeople about how to make better presentations. If his class speaks English as a first language (he trains a lot of foreign engineers), he tears it up, often breaking the ice with the story of the company he used to work with -- the Jewish beer with the slogan Don't Pass Out, Passover.

Rob has the magic charisma. No matter what he chooses to do, people love him. You can't teach that. He used to joke about the fact that he was getting paid to give talks about the process of talking companies into paying him to give a talk. When the economy went into the crapper in 2008 and his clients dried up, he and his wonderful wife Alexandra and their two kids moved to Mexico to ride it out.

Once in a while, you just gotta go to Disneyland.

GRAHAMCOMM *"Speaking and Selling Success"*

Robert Graham, founder and President of GrahamComm ("Experts in Presentation skills, Sales Training and Teambuilding Programs") adds his own shtick:

It's a good thing Jeremy is creative and persuasive, because his memory doesn't seem to serve him so well. Rather than discuss the fact that I quit vs. his claim to have "fired my ass" (he asked me to stay through Chanukah '99), we shall focus on the good stuff, as there was plenty.

The best thing to come out of my eight or so months as "the other He'brew guy" was undoubtedly our friendship. We were working on how to work together, and along the way much hilariousness ensued.

It's true that I got the idea for the job after drinking a bottle or two of Genesis Ale while watching the '99 Super Bowl in San Francisco. It's also true that my starring role as Queen Esther in my fourth-grade play had a big part in his decision to hire me.

My first sales call was a ride-with with Paul from our second of many San Francisco distributors. As we walked into Homeboy Liquors, he mentioned to me that the owner owed him a favor, as he was behind in his payments. Paul was pretty sure he could help me sell in a couple of cases, and we got a facing right between the Camo forties and the Olde English Malt Liquor. A more prime selling spot was rarely found.

Next stop was an equally suspect corner liquor store in the 'Loin. As we drove there, Paul told me the story of his attempt to reenact a scene from Dirty Harry. A couple of months before, he had walked into the store and had a somewhat terse conversation with the owner. He then yelled out the door to an imaginary sidekick, "Call 911, 'cause this guy's gonna need it when I get through with him." Suddenly, the air was knocked out of him by a sucker punch to his solar plexus, and he slumped to the floor. Pretty sure that's the last time he tried that line.

Another highlight from our Monday morning sales meetings: Having a new and very attractive girlfriend at the time, I wasn't always getting the requisite eight hours of sleep per night. One Monday, I staggered into his office with a forty-eight-ounce French roast coffee in hand, hoping to kick-start the thinking process. Jeremy took one look at me and asked, "You up doing the wild thing all night?"

As Jeremy points out, I still get plenty of laughs from my audiences talking about my days selling kosher beer. And the friendship that was fired in the kiln of the Shmaltz Sales Machine is still as strong as a bottle of Jewbelation Bar Mitzvah!

In the spring of '98, several people suggested I go to business schools to find free advice. I was invited to give a talk at Stanford Business School, and I told the M.B.A. students I could use every form of help I could possibly think of. Several classes used Shmaltz as a case study. The overriding theme was always the same: Just raise more money and spend more money, and you'll make more money. Brilliant.

I made up an internship announcement and sent it to Stanford, Berkeley, and a couple of Jewish college organizations. Amazingly, I heard from a guy who turned out to be a godsend to a Jewish small-business entrepreneur.

Social chair and then vice president of his Jewish fraternity at Stanford. Kevin was studying some humanities and some business. I let him make up his own title at the company for the project he worked on. He did such a great job for me that years later, I still got mail addressed to "Kevin Friedman, Executive Vice President of Shmaltz Brewing."

He said he'd work forty hours a week, and before I even raised the issue of compensation, he said, "If I can just sell a few t-shirts at beer fests now and then, I'll be all set." He spoiled me so much that he pretty much sealed the fate of every future intern I'd bring into the fold, including his underage cousin, Leah, who would take the torch several years later, and then come aboard full-time as the company's protean project manager.

That summer Kevin bought me my first computer (yes, first computer ever at age twenty-nine[7]), and we installed him in the walk-in closet downstairs from my five-foot-ten-inch loft. After mailing press releases and postcards to key buyers and organizing absolutely everything, we'd take our strategic business meetings outside, at the Whiz Burger on South Van Ness.

We went to beer festivals and bar promotions together. One bonus of being an even halfway presentable guy in the beer industry: you can talk to any woman at any bar. You can't be rejected, because you always have a fallback -- you're at work. So I sicced Kevin on all the cute college town girls. The instructions were simple: smile a lot, be nice, wear your He'brew t-shirt. Find out what they're reading, what movies and bands they're into. Since we're not going to have billboards, bus stops, and advertising any time soon, just reach people one at a time, and get them to buy our beer. Having Kevin was fantastic. If I could have a tribe of Jewish fraternity guys who were outgoing, smart, and motivated, I thought, I could really turn the company into something.

---

7 How old are you, Reader? As a generous gift for my high school graduation, Cristi's dad Mike gave me a top-of-the-line typewriter to take to Stanford. Not kidding. I guess this is my version of the old man crowing, "I remember when a beer cost a nickel and you got a pickled egg on the side for free."

After leaving Shmaltz, Kevin traveled the world, then went to business school. And he changed, from being the scruffiest guy in raggedy shorts, a floppy-haired Jewish kid, to a clean-shaven M.B.A. grad in suit and tie. Most recently he's even stepped off the corporate ladder to start his own venture. It's been very gratifying to see where people who get involved with the company over the years end up later in life.

The business plan called for a second beer style. From the beginning, I wanted to have a darker beer. When my grandmother passed away, I thought I'd honor her. She loved figs. In Judaism, it's one of the sacred species. (Fast forward to our twelfth year, when we finally did use figs, in our Rejewvenator beer.) My thought in 1999 was to make something I'd call Granny's Fig Porter. But I couldn't think of a good punchline, or how to buy the figs for any reasonable price for brewing, so the idea just sat there. It might have been a blessing. I don't know how many other beer drinkers would think of grandmothers as appropriate boozing inspiration.

We'd started at the beginning, with Genesis. I have no recollection how it happened, but eventually I came up with the idea of going straight to the end -- the Messiah. Messiah Stout: "It's the Beer You've Been Waiting For." For the second time, the process of creating a label with Tracy was both fun and excruciating. She made me stand naked in her studio, arms upstretched, holding beer bottles, while she sketched a picture of me standing on a globe. Then she added her own profile, all the while insisting that the characters looked nothing like us -- we were just for sizing and placement. We chose little icons from around the world to place on the globe -- the Eiffel Tower, a trumpet for New Orleans, Red Square, the Statue of Liberty. The beer would encompass the entire world in its breadth and harmony.

Drawing from Jewish tradition, the label referenced the coming of the Messiah as a return to a state of innocence and grace reminiscent of the Garden of Eden. The two figures represented Adam and Eve characters, globetrotting the world. The goal was not to have a naked picture of me and my girlfriend on the packaging. We just thought it would be funny, and we were cheap models. Besides, by design, the banner of the He'brew scroll would unfurl over our less modest bits.

However, we did a terrible job of planning the label. Given the characters' spindly arms and legs, the He'brew logo would cover the bulk of the artwork, so the composition never quite worked.

At some point (probably the minute I spoke to my kosher rabbi about it), I also remembered that in more observant communities there's a prohibition against seeing anybody naked, other than your own husband or wife. One element of an overarching concept called "modesty": women wear long skirts; men cover knees and wear hats.

My original notion for the brand, the punk-rock Jewish vibe, was still there, but we were doing outreach to Jewish community centers, and now the spectrum of the Jewish community, including Conservative and Orthodox synagogues and consumers, all the time. Even with kosher certification, I quickly found out that several observant groups weren't willing to have the new beer label at their events.

With strong relationships in place and buyers less concerned with modesty, I did manage to slide the beer into most Safeways and Whole Foods. Finally, we had two beers next to each other on the shelf. It allowed for the idea that He'brew was now a brand, not just a one-off novelty beer. It gave people an option. It made the whole thing seem real. For anyone who has ever endured the consumer-product market jargon: This was my double-size billboard effect.

Months earlier, when I told the guys at Anderson Valley about my idea for Messiah Stout, everyone agreed it was pretty funny. But they also said, "We don't know if you really want to make a stout. Dark beers are pretty hard to sell." I just thought it sounded cool. I ignored their advice, and asked them to brew a stout for me.

At that point I honestly did not have a lot of experience with the beer style. Anderson Valley made an oatmeal stout that I thought tasted fantastic, as did the many judges and critics who showered Barney Flats with medals and respect. But I didn't want one just like theirs -- maybe a little lighter-bodied, not quite as much coffee, a different palette of flavors. We only needed small batches, so I said, What if we mixed some of your stout with another beer to create a unique blend?

Now, I'm well aware that plenty of people in the beer industry will gag, laugh, and heartily mock the concept of combining two year-round beers to make a third, and calling it special. It certainly undermines my entire position that contract brewers can be just as ambitious, unique, and original as any other brewer. But if the beers are complex and high-quality to begin with, blending them can still create a unique and respectable beer[8].

As somebody who was desperate not to go out of business, I just wanted to promote a second beer. But Anderson Valley said, "Absolutely not. We would never bastardize our own products like that. We'll just create a new beer, and you tell us if you like it, and we can tweak it from there."

About a month later, they'd brewed a new recipe, and they called me to Highway 128, winding up into Boonville. So we're sitting around the conference table trying it -- myself , Ken, the head brewer, and a few other brewers and office staff. They pour it out of a unlabeled bottle. Everyone is sipping, holding up their glasses to see the goods, smelling, sipping again. It's good, a little drier than I wanted, not quite as rich. It's focused a bit more on the coffee flavors, not the sweeter caramel tones. In the scheme of things, though, it's a really solid beer. I mean, these guys are pros. That's why I'm here.

I say, Good to go for now. Maybe we can tweak it slightly for the next batch, but let's do it. Thanks so much, everyone!

Ken, whether in celebration or a typical five p.m. ritual, whips out his bowl and begins stuffing it with some Boonville kind bud. I figured, Fuck it, we have a new beer. Let's get a little peace and love working around here.

Half an hour later, Ken's pretty high, and I'm pretty high, beers in hand. He looks at me and says, "Well, kid, I wasn't gonna tell you, but I feel like maybe I should. That beer you tasted -- it's a blend. We used ninety percent stout, and added some wheat beer to it. We can adjust it if you want, but we didn't do a recipe for you."

Now, there are moments in a business relationship that, to this day, I don't know how to handle. I probably should have said, Are you fucking kidding me, old man? *I said* we should do that in the first place, and you guys made me out to be a douchebag for even suggesting it.

I imagined it like that daydream sequence in *High Fidelity*, when Tim

---

8 This isn't even taking into consideration blends from the most recent years of truly connoisseur offerings, such as Geektoberfest, our barrel-aged collaboration with Captain Lawrence and Ithaca for 2010 New York Beer Week, in-house projects such as Vertical Jewbelation, or highly regarded blends from Russian River, Lost Abbey, Allagash, Firestone Walker and more.

Robbins walks in to tell the record shop boys that he's the new man in John Cusack's ex-girlfriend's life. In a fantasy, the sidekicks hurdle over the counter and smack him in the face with the rotary phone: "Get your patchouli-stink out of here!" The entire scenario plays out only in your head, but instead you mumble, "Oh, uhhh... Yeah, umm... OK."

Ken seemed to see our business relationship as an endlessly combative attempt to get something from each other, as opposed to a collaborative attempt to move forward together. I once asked him for his wholesaler list, to see if I could dig up some desperately needed business.

"No way," he barked. "I've worked for years to create these relationships." I only learned later that many of them beyond California had very little ongoing communication with him. AVBC made beer -- great beer, for years -- and the distributors picked it up. That was it. But with Ken it was always a battle. It's too bad he thought that way.[9]

Though the He'brew Messiah got off to a rocky start, it has since settled in as a pillar of the He'brew brand. When I switched to Mendocino Brewing in 2003 and went into six-packs, working with Paul McErlean, the master brewer at Saratoga, we finally changed the recipe for Messiah from a stout to a nut brown ale. When I nervously drank straight from a twelve-ounce bottle of the initial batch of Messiah Bold at the brewery, that first sip had all the richness, the balance and flavor, yet the clean finish that would make it one of my favorites to this day.

Perhaps even more important at that moment was the enormous sense of relief, satisfaction, and hope that I was finally onto a new phase of the Shmaltz adventure. On so many levels, it was exactly the beer I'd been waiting for.

---

9 As I finish this, after many years of threatening to do so, Ken finally sold Anderson Valley. Brewing Co. In a fitting twist, the manager that he'd brought on after his son left, Fal Allen (no relation), who would later be forced to become the heavy for my problems with Ken, looks to be heading back to Boonville to captain the brewery again. Mazel tov and good luck all around. Might be time for a "Big Payback" Collaboration project...

CHAPTER 10

Snatching Defeat From The Jaws Of Victory

A rmed with a fresh infusion of investor money, in the late spring of 1999 I moved into an actual office, with a private door... separate locks... functioning windows... normal-height ceilings. The new global headquarters for Shmaltz Brewing. I had four hundred square feet above a hot dog stand and an ice cream joint. Glamorous digs, compared to the five-foot-ten loft.

I wanted to stay in touch with my investors, make it fun for them, keep them updated on the progress of the company. I wanted to use them for advice, references, and networking. I'd originally proposed a semi-annual gathering overflowing, in my mind, with bagels, lox, He'brew and success.

But despite my good intentions, I was never able to accomplish nearly what I'd hoped with them. I sent out long, detailed update emails for a few years and dropped off a case or two for the holidays, checking in personally when I could swing it. But the fact is, no one really wants to hear you bitch and moan.

Ah, the wafting smell of hot dogs, and the sounds of children squealing. My neighbor two doors down ran a Comedy Traffic School. It was unclear whether he'd been a standup comic who'd bought the franchise, but every morning a cross-section of San Francisco's pettiest offenders lined up to endure DMV re-education camp through the rim shots and smoke breaks. Several years later, I got a moving violation and the comedy-traffic-school guy signed off on it. No fence made for a great neighbor.

I don't remember the exact date we introduced He'brew to New York, but I certainly do remember the familiar sense that this was another milestone that would finally skyrocket Shmaltz into the brave new world of profitability. Something like thirty percent of the entire American Jewish community lives in this one, obviously very Jewish-influenced city. (Jesse didn't call it *Hymietown* for nothing.) At the time, the entire Bay Area counted about two hundred thousand Jews. New York City numbered over two million. I was now in search of the mother lode.

I got in through a small craft-beer distributor owned by Brooklyn Brewery, which has become one of the most successful craft brewers in the country. In addition to their own beers, they distributed only high-end micros such as Sierra Nevada, North Coast, Victory, Smuttynose. They had a unique business model. They were self-distributing much like I did at first, but with hundreds of thousands of dollars invested in tens of thousands of square feet of warehouse space, a fleet of delivery vehicles, and a full-time sales and delivery crew. While the sales reps and drivers were out hustling their own stuff, they could make money off other brands as well.

Years later, they'd sell the distribution company for millions, retaining their focus on the Brooklyn Brewery brand. At the time, they had a small, tight, rather exclusive portfolio of boutique beers. The owners were very selective. I wanted in.

Craft beer in New York was really just a blip on the radar at the time. The other distributors were typically huge companies, such as Manhattan Beer, with Corona, Coors Light, and Sam Adams; Anheuser Busch, which directly owned the Bud house in Manhattan; and the "smaller" guys, working with monster international brands like Bass, Newcastle, and Becks. The Brooklyn guys were by far the premier craft beer destination in New York.

Certainly from my roots in the suburbs, and even in San Francisco itself, I knew we didn't have hard-ass motherfuckers like New York does. Beer distribution in New York City was down-and-dirty, in the trenches. Most beer in the city was sold in the bodegas and the corner stores, and the bars were basically controlled by the big boys, with big budgets, big demands, and bland big-business beers. Unlike northern California, which already had forty or fifty craft breweries, New York City had just a couple of brewpubs at the time, and a few more regional packaging microbreweries.

Begun in 1987, the year I graduated high school, as second careers for an investment banker and a former war correspondent, Brooklyn Brewery started by contract brewing and self-distributing, much like Shmaltz. However, their business plan and multiple rounds of ambitious fundraising clearly aimed far beyond my humble beginnings and goals. Still, we had a kindred spirit. After all, their headquarters were in a brick building previously housing a matzoh factory. In their own way, they were very welcoming. I think they appreciated the shtick. Like many in those early days, they gave me a shot I probably didn't deserve.

The only way, however, that they would bring in my one and only SKU was if I could convince Ken to start distributing Anderson Valley's beers in New York through Brooklyn Brewery. That would allow us to ship a pallet or so along with Anderson Valley's order. We could combine loads and get better shipping rates -- especially given that Boonville was an extra dollar per case just to get it out of the winding hills of Sonoma County. Ken agreed, and we were off and running.

I flew to New York once to talk to Brooklyn, then I returned when they introduced the beer. The distributor (and a small draft-only brewery they'd installed on-site) was located in a post-industrial section of Williamsburg, a historically Polish and Puerto Rican neighborhood that was fast transitioning into a destination for more and more artists, musicians, and scenesters. Now the neighborhood has turned into an officially trendy shopping and tourist destination -- a foodie, craft beer and cocktail-culture mecca.

Back then, however, I was walking through blocks strewn with garbage, broken bottles, and puddles of ambiguous New York City goo. Partially to their credit and success, partially to many people's horror, the brewery now sits three or four blocks from million-dollar luxury condos in high-rise glass towers lining the waterfront.

I did my kickoff presentation at Brooklyn's office on North 11th Street. Though they operated the small draft-only brewery, ninety-five percent of their production came from upstate in Utica, at F.X. Matt. To this day, I often look at elements of their evolution as a model for Shmaltz.

The beer market in New York is so different from anywhere else in the country. The way people buy beer, the pricing, the fact that very few buyers at the corner store have any idea what these special craft beers are, or taste like. Even in 2010, Paul Catalano, the sales manager at S.K.I., loves to ask me what it's like to sell beer outside New York City, just to hear tales of a different beer life in not-so-distant lands.

But Brooklyn Brewery did a great job, sticking to their micro-guns, not cutting too many deals, selling their products on merit. When I introduced the beer in San Francisco, Portland, Seattle, and many other beer cities, craft beer already represented fifteen to twenty percent of overall beer sales in those markets. Brooklyn kept grinding away, doing a lot of the heavy lifting to increase that market share in New York, but it took a huge amount of patience, investment, and focus to pull it off.

Sierra Nevada, for one, was doing well in New York. And a lot of bars were opened by people who had actually worked at Brooklyn Brewery and left to start their own thing. There was an exciting, growing neighborhood beer scene.

But the problem for me was that we weren't really doing draft yet. I never thought of He'brew as a big draft product. I wanted people to take it home and have a private moment with it, to share it with a friend: read the label, laugh, think, drink, repeat. Maybe I over-pigeonholed: I probably could have gotten a little draft business. Brooklyn Brewery was about fifty-fifty, kegs to bottles.

My first real ride-with in New York, predictably, was with the one Jewish guy. I can't remember whether they called him "Bar Mitzvah" Bobby Levitt, or if I coined it myself, privately, in my head. Bob would soon become a friend and a colleague, but I couldn't blame him when he seemed bummed that first day. It was like, "C'mon, guys, you have to pawn the Jewish guy off on the only other Jewish guy?"

Still, we had a good time, even if we sold absolutely zero beer. We went to a bunch of punk-rock dive bars on the Lower East Side and in the East Village. At Brooklyn Brewery, their goal was to be friends with the people they were selling beer to. Bob was pals with everyone we visited, talking about movies they'd seen and barbecues coming up the next weekend. The strategy worked -- they had four or five draft lines at a lot of bars that otherwise served only Bud, or Bass, or PBR. It was wonderful to be able to drink their good beers in these neighborhood hangs.

From the beginning, New York City proved to be nothing like the mother lode for Shmaltz that I was expecting. The distribution channels were so clogged with competitive products -- mostly the big beers with billboards, TV ads, and greased palms -- and the existing relationships were so locked in that there was really not much room to get onto the shelves. Brooklyn Brewery was in the process of changing their business model away from self-distributing all their products. They cut a deal with a company called S.K.I. Beer to handle the bulk of the off-premise business so they could focus on bar and restaurant sales. (S.K.I. later became my exclusive wholesaler in New York after Brooklyn sold the distributorship completely.)

The retail accounts at the time were characteristically "only-in-New York." They had an Indian guy in the East Village who had five hundred beers crammed into a basement market, one neighborhood grocery store in Soho that had a respectable micro selection, a couple of impossibly cramped markets in Brooklyn, one small gourmet chain of four stores that only stocked a few microbrew brands. I think they had thirty-five total off-premise accounts that I had access to when we got going. There were, in other words, very few places for me to sell He'brew. It was a shining example of how important distribution is. If you can't get your product onto the shelf in the right stores, at best you're very limited. At worst, you're screwed.

I'd work two or three days in New York, and we'd sell two, three, maybe five cases each day or so. There weren't any Whole Foods or many other high-end grocery stores open to good craft beer yet. My He'brew home-away-from-home, Bierkraft, on Fifth Avenue in Brooklyn, was still a few years from opening. Unlike our suburban-style specialty stores in California, the "supermarkets" shoehorned into Manhattan or Brooklyn retail space had the tiniest aisles I'd ever seen, reminiscent of overgrown bodegas stacked to the rafters with everything you could ever imagine. Except craft beer.

I simply didn't understand how to work this market. New York had one unique problem in particular: by law, beer has to be distributed differently than wine and spirits. So there'd be a wine and liquor store and then, next door, a grocery that can sell beer. That means the consumer isn't looking at good craft beer in the same place they're looking at quality wine. Compared to markets such as California, Colorado, Oregon, and Washington, I'm convinced that pushed back the progress of microbrews in the city for many years.

I figured that with over eight million people (and almost two million Jews), even with just a modest percentage of buyers, a helluva lot of them should be drinking this beer. Like supplier math, there's also New York City beer-sales goggles. If there are eight million people and just one in a hundred buy one bottle once a month… you get the picture.

Yes, there are eight million people and a whole lot of Jews. But there are also ten times more products, spending ten times more dollars with ten times bigger budgets. Joe, a buddy who owns Spuyten Duyvil, one of the best beer bars in New York City, has another theory. "New York is wine and liquor," he said, recently. "Always has been, always will be. That's what the mobsters were drinking, and that's what P. Diddy is drinking."

✡　　★　　✡　　★　　✡

As I was finishing up my business plan, Tracy and I got engaged. We'd been living together for almost three years. I thought we'd survived some pretty tough times, with me starting a business and her pushing her art career, and neither of us getting to where we expected or hoped we'd be. My relationship with her was the most profound thing I had ever experienced in my life, and I was still completely in love with her.

But sometimes it was also the source of the most excruciating feelings I'd ever had, and we had some conflicts that we couldn't seem to resolve. At the time, I thought some of them might go away if we got married. I thought we might both calm down a bit. With the bridge and the headlands stretched out before us, I proposed to her on Baker Beach in San Francisco in the afternoon of New Year's Eve, 1998.

For the next year, besides raising money, hiring Rob, moving into a new office, and expanding to Chicago and New York, we endured the stress of planning for a wedding. We were both serious about planning every little detail -- me trying to combine the best of Jewish traditions, and she creating an artistic ritual that celebrated and reflected our own sensibilities.

We got married in October, on a bluff overlooking the Pacific in the part of San Francisco known as Land's End. It was a beautiful Indian summer day in the Mission, but by the time we got to the edge of the City, it was a blustery, freezing, typically fog-packed afternoon. Despite the abrupt weather change, we'd worked through plenty of disagreements about our Jewish identity, which rabbi we should use, and what the meaning of the word *wife* should be. I was actually optimistic.

The ceremony, the family, the friends, and a ton of great food -- that weekend, we threw the most decadent party I'd ever hosted, thanks to Tracy's father. At six a.m. on the third morning of the wedding weekend, I closed the door on the last of the stragglers. I sat down in front of the remains of my favorite cake and had this crazy revelation that I'd kicked a monkey on my back. On the morning after my wedding, after a wild night that was admittedly fueled by a few sweets heavier than the cake, I felt like a colossal weight had been lifted from my soul. I remember thinking that maybe things were going to be great from then on.

Right about the time Rob was transitioning out, I realized I was running out of money pretty quickly. I was hoping that I'd be able to get by, since I wouldn't be paying him anymore. But I was burning through the money just paying lawyers, accountants, and the trademark guy, not to mention our limited travel, sales, and marketing costs.

At the end of '99, I worked a San Francisco event for Chanukah called the Matzoh Ball, sponsored by the Young Adults Division of the Jewish Federation. They were expecting over a thousand people, and they agreed to put me at a table in the center barroom, selling exclusively He'brew from kegs. I figured we were going to kill it.

I think I had six or eight half barrels; on a really slamming night at a big club, you might go through that much beer. I drove everything over to 1015 Folsom at two in the afternoon -- the kegs, some posters, some t-shirts. It was

Christmas Eve, a Friday. I set up a jockey box (a cooler with coils and taps to run the kegs through) on top of the table and started connecting the hardware.

After loading in fifteen hundred pounds of stainless steel, beer, tools, boxes of flyers, and shwag, everything is finally set. I've got to jam home, shower, and hustle back to make it happen. I turn the crank on the regulator attached to the CO2 tank, to push the beer out of the kegs through the jockey box that will serve the night's Chanukah crowd.

Nothing.

The regulator says there's air in the tank, so it should pour just fine. As I'm trying to figure out whether the regulator is working, the screwdriver slips, and I gash myself on the hand.

Now I'm bleeding all over, sweating like a pig. Holy shit! It's 5:15, and the Airgas place is closed. Where can I possibly find another regulator? Or is it even the gas or the regulator? Maybe it's the kegs or the jockey box. The fittings, the hoses, the clamps... ?

In desperation, screwing and re-screwing, I try the tap one last time, and all of a sudden the beer starts flowing. True Chanukah miracle. I hurry home to clean up, and I come back with Tracy and a friend who is going to help us pour.

I'd done a huge Chanukah event in '97 in L.A., when I first switched to Anderson Valley. I figured there was no way a giant crew of Jews was not going to drink He'brew beer at a Chanukah bash. I handed out promo cards to everyone as they came in. I made the rounds to the eight or so bartenders to tell them about my baby, asking each of them to push the hell out of it. But as the evening progressed, I realized everyone was drinking cocktails and wine, or worse, Bud Light and Heineken.

And the same thing happened in San Francisco. I couldn't believe it. After the stress of the afternoon, I thought, This cannot fucking happen again.

At the '97 L.A. event, I left northern California with eight or so kegs to haul down to L.A. in the cargo van, aiming to hit the Palladium just in time to get set up. That night at two a.m., I brought the kegs out, turned on the taps and gas full-throttle. Not having the mojo to grunt all those full kegs back up the coast, I just poured all the beer into the gutter. I got into the van and drove back to San Francisco through the night.

Two years later, the Matzoh Ball in full swing, I let the disappointment of that night get the best of me. As I sat there cajoling people to come over to our corner and try one of our beers, I was thinking, Life has to be different than this. How much punishment does one person want to inflict on himself?

Other people think this is a million-dollar idea. I'm getting seemingly endless email, voicemails, PR. But nobody was buying enough beer to make the whole production worth it.

I had run out of answers.

At the beginning of 2000, I hired a buddy's dad, who lived in San Diego, to do some part-time phone sales for me. George had built his own business, selling anything he could get his hands on, from satellite systems to pallets of dented cans that had fallen off the backs of trucks. I trusted him and enjoyed his style, and I figured maybe he could dig up some business in southern California without me needing to grind it out there. I sublet the other half of my little office to another small business owner, and then proceeded to sublet more and more of the space to her. Right before I moved out, she brought in every personal item she owned, and piled it to the ceiling. I kept a desk in the corner. I was paying seventy-five bucks a month at that point.

Over the Thanksgiving weekend, a couple of months after our wedding, Tracy and I were walking through our neighborhood. In a little section called Precita Park, we went down a cute side street and noticed a house for sale. It was a little box house, built around 1900 and rebuilt in mid-century. Eighty-eight-year-old Helen lived there by herself; her husband had passed away many years before. She told us she was the tenth child of eleven, that she grew up in North Beach, and she shared stories of her father taking her and her siblings out to Ocean Beach in a horse-drawn carriage. For years she and her husband sold coal out of the garage, which also served as the neighborhood polling station for fifty years.

The place had a small, terraced backyard overgrown with weeds and wild gnarled rose bushes. Green shag carpet stretched wall to wall, a little fake fireplace insert running on a light bulb and colored cellophane. Helen couldn't get around very well and was moving into an assisted living facility. I think she said her husband paid six thousand dollars for the house originally.

It was a museum piece, a perfect little gem as the next step for us to move out of our live-work place, which we intended to keep so that Tracy could have her art studio all to herself. Tracy's family bought the house for us, and we set about making plans to fix it up a bit.

In the beginning, the work we were going to do was minor -- landscape the back yard, tear out a wall, replace a couple of windows. But both of us are very specific in our vision, and very ambitious about our hopes. The project, like many renovations, quickly grew until we were gutting the entire place. We had all this structural work to do to a house that hadn't been touched through multiple earthquakes. We were working with structural engineers, two different architects, dealing with the city on permits.

Many marriages are compromised, if not demolished, by renovations -- month after month, dollar after dollar. As a result, during the year 2000, all the things I thought would smooth out once we got married became more exacerbated. Cliché but true -- we had both changed, and seemed to be growing in different directions.

From the early stages of our relationship, when her art was about Genesis myths and Jewish mysticism, Tracy had developed an ambivalent relationship to Judaism. She began focusing her art, informed by her personal philosophy, with a much more critical angle on gender politics and women's spirituality. Her intellectual and emotional struggles, played out through her art, often seeped into our relationship.

I, too, had changed, from the laid-back, enthusiastic arts intern she'd first met, to an often-fuming bundle of stress, frustration, and anger. I was, in many ways, a failure. I'd spent nearly every weekend at beer festivals or work events, and I'd compromised my health and my sense of self, as well as my commitment to a life with her.

Our tensions and our arguments, her challenges and demands, felt like a burning hot poker stabbing my heart and guts. My response was to rage, often directly at her, with a fury I'd never experienced before or since, that shames me to this day.

I thought much of this would change if -- when -- I just got out from under the downward slide of the business, still assuming I could somehow turn it around. Through all this, I kept the company more or less in a holding pattern. I was relieved to see that, although I wasn't waking up in the middle of the night freaking out or spending every day begging people to buy the beer, the business didn't really drop off the edge of a cliff. The beer was on the shelf; the distribution was in place. Production was still set. I was very surprised to be selling anything at all.

In the first nine months of 1997, my first year of self-distributing, I sold about sixty thousand dollars' worth of beer. When I switched to Anderson Valley, I probably shipped twice that. Great growth, but nowhere near enough to break even. With Rob's help in 1999, we'd topped out at about seven thousand cases of Genesis Ale and the new Messiah Stout. But by the following year, no longer with a full-time rep, sales were down in the range of four or five thousand cases. The next year, down again.

After a weekend camping north of the city, Tracy and I came home to a resume and a hand-scribbled note shoved under our front door. The note said this person had been trying to contact Shmaltz Brewing and was desperate to intern for He'brew. Who would possibly go to these lengths?

The scribbler turned out to be a lovely young lady who had just graduated from the U.C. Santa Cruz. Her mother Israeli and her father a Berkeley rabbi, Shira was a distinctly northern California combination of an East Bay hip hop kid from Berkeley High School and a freewheeling Santa Cruz party girl. Yet she also had a very serious idea about what she wanted to do, and how she wanted to be in the world.

She became my next brilliant intern, and she saved my summer. For the next couple of years, Shira stepped in whenever I needed help for the Shmaltz cause. The graffiti-style plywood He'brew sign that she commissioned for the company remains a cherished and appropriate addition to my current home office in the Mission.

My letters to my investors became grimmer as the year went on. I wanted to be honest with them, but it was really embarrassing. These were some of my closest family friends and peers. The older guys were extremely successful businessmen. The younger friends had trusted me with their personal funds. It was so difficult for me to get through the process of having my hat in my hand, being so humbled. I'd done everything I could possibly think of, and it was failing. No doubt about it.

Finding an opportunity to sell the business was always in the back of my mind. People would say, "Hey, I saw that big article about your company. When are you gonna sell to Budweiser?"

Some who aren't entrepreneurs tend to believe that's the American dream. They see the business news anytime a guy who started (and may still be) in a garage or a kid out of college sells his idea for a million bucks. I have a feeling the number of people who've done that is about the same as the number of people who have won the lottery. It's so rare, but people think it's a constant possibility.

I started making the rounds. In '98, before I even finished the business plan, I was introduced through an investment banker friend of a friend to a gentleman who was chairman of the board of a giant international liquor company, United Breweries Group, which reigned as the Budweiser and Jack Daniels of India. They produced and controlled the largest percentage of the liquor business, as well as beer, in India. The UB Group did business in the U.K. and in countries all over the world.

The Chairman represented the third generation of his family-owned business. He'd looked into the U.S. and seen the microbrew explosion. In India, to protect the diversity of the industry, government regulation stipulated that one company couldn't own one giant brewery, capping the total production to keep the breweries smaller-scale. So they had twenty-five or more breweries around India, making Kingfisher and a number of other brands. They knew how to operate "small," one- to two-hundred-barrel breweries.

It seemed as though the Chairman loved northern California. He built a large home on the hillside in Sausalito. The group got involved on the financing side with Mendocino Brewing, which had built a bigger brewery than it could afford, and the UB Group eventually took over the pioneering company when it ran out of its own resources.

The Chairman was a high-powered guy. He went on to become a member of Parliament in India and served on the boards of dozens of companies under the corporate umbrella. He'd significantly expanded his family's financial empire around the world, began Kingfisher Airlines, and added a Formula One team and a professional Indian soccer team to his portfolio.

With one 22 ounce bottle of Genesis Ale to my business's name, I strolled into a meeting with him, the C.E.O., the C.F.O., the advertising and marketing managers, and the investment banker who had made the introduction. I made my presentation at the headquarters in Sausalito and told them everything about my vision for the company, not unlike my pitch to Safeway.

Wearing a royal-blue velvet track suit, the chairman stood out sharply from the rest of the group, who were dressed in traditional dark business suits. Hands clasped behind his head, he leaned back from the long, polished-wood conference table and looked at me: "I like what you're doing. Let's make a deal. I'll have my people send you the paperwork. Thanks for coming in."

Within a few weeks, the company sent me a proposal. They were willing to buy He'brew for fifty thousand dollars worth of stock options, though the shares could not be publicly traded until a future date and were valued at a price many times more than the stock was then trading for.

The deal included a job offer, and if we started making more money, I'd get paid a bit on back-end royalties. They were going to put the beer into their distribution channels, and I would likely sell their beer and remain the point person for my brand.

I don't know whether I was stubborn, or stupid, or sincere to my own vision. I guess I was personally taken aback. Looking back, I think that stands as the first time someone I was pitching didn't offer an enthusiastic "yes" and agree to my terms. These guys were serious businessmen and knew exactly what they were doing -- what they would offer, and what would work for them. They were not throwing a fun, wholehearted, "Wouldn't it be cool?" kind of party.

We went back and forth for a while, attempting to "negotiate." I couldn't get them to budge. I knew I hadn't started this brand just to have a steady sales job at a beer company. I could have just applied for a job two years before. For better or worse, I turned them down.

In the year 2000, we revisited the conversation. They offered me the same deal, but with fifty thousand in cash *after* the first year, *if* I hit a certain sales goal that I thought was possibly doable. They would also include a small budget for some administrative help and a limited travel budget to put towards He'brew. The first year's goal was two thousand barrels, or about twenty-six thousand cases – four times more than I was selling at the time. Even then, I'd be eighty-five thousand short on paying back my investors. I didn't see how that was going to solve my problem. Once again, whether sincere or short-sighted, I respectfully declined.

I went to a craft brewers' conference to see if there was anybody else I could find to buy the brand. I had conversations with friends and acquaintances at Magic Hat, Pyramid, Red Hook, even low-level business development guys at Miller and Coors. With the power of some of these companies, I figured they should be able to leverage the brand.

Even today, every so often, someone will say, "Oh, you're doing so well. When are you going to sell out to the big boys?" But until you're already a success, nobody else is going to make you a success. I was too small to catch the attention of the regional beer companies who had any money, like Gambrinus, which has acquired Pete's Wicked Ale. Gordon Biersch and F.X. Matt were making more beer in one batch than I was selling in nine months.

Shortly thereafter, so many of the publicly trade microbrewery stocks tanked, as the craft beer bonanza of the '90s fell through the floor. The bigger regional companies needed a lot more than my measly sales, and the smaller micros that could use a thousand barrels of extra business barely had enough money to run their own operations. Everyone was cash-poor, scraping by on anything they could cobble together to chase the dream.

In the fall of 2000, I was invited to speak at the Jewish Museum in New York. They had an exhibit on the history of alcohol from Egypt to the Lower East Side. I was invited to be on a panel discussion with a professor from the University of Pennsylvania, who argued that, in the history of civilization, beer was actually more important than, and even pre-dated, bread. A leading researcher on the topic, he told fantastic tales of ancient hunter-gatherers shifting toward an agrarian society, often accompanied by the discovery of spontaneously fermenting grains -- the birth of beer.

The other panelist was Garrett Oliver, the renowned brewmaster for Brooklyn Brewery, who went from being among the most well-respected homebrewers in the New York Homebrewers Club, which he started in the late '80s, to one of the most widely known beer commentators in the business. They were there to give authoritative historical and brewing perspective. I was there to give shtick. It was my first-ever paid speaking engagement.

The event went off without a hitch. It was a fantastic night. I did my shpiel about the three pillars of Shmaltz, the pomegranate, Messiah, everything I could squeeze in. Lots of my friends were there, and I was tickled to be sharing the stage with such legitimate luminaries. At the time, I was expanding distribution into Philadelphia and trying to expand our sales in New York. I had a whole plan for the rest of the week, to really nail some east coast sales and make some true progress. The event was a great start.

The next afternoon, Tracy and I went to a late lunch in the West Village. After a couple glasses of wine, she started getting upset about her own career. We'd had this conversation about her dissatisfactions and anxieties about her art and the art world so many times, and I'm sure she felt exactly the same way about my business.

That week would turn out to be the last week we spent any time together.

She flew home to San Francisco, and I stayed to close the deal with the distributor in Philadelphia, ship them several pallets, and do a little pre-launch kickoff. But the wholesaler abruptly decided it wasn't the right time, that he couldn't take the order we'd talked about.

Those profits, now lost, were supposed to cover my travel. Meanwhile, in Brooklyn, it was another series of the usual clusterfucks: the beer didn't leave the brewery on time, the trucker was slow cross-docking in the Midwest. We wouldn't be able to put on the big push we'd had all planned out.

It was the night of the vice presidential debate between Joe Lieberman and Dick Cheney. I thought, How much bad news can one damaged soul take? Already burned out and overwhelmed, this was one more shit-storm in a seemingly endless season of frustrating crap, overflowing the murky river of my life. I was spent, lost, beat. Not quite demolished, but just fucking sick of it all.

In an unusual move for me in those days, I just started drinking. Heavily. Setting off on a solo pub crawl wandering around the West Village, still wearing my He'brew shirt, I proceeded to get plowed. Good old-fashioned, grown-man shit-housed. I wandered through the maze of Village pubs and bars, a pint here, a shot there. A pint and a shot, a shot and a pint.

Trashed and appropriately distracted, before the debate begins I go back to the apartment of Tracy's friend Samantha, my consistent patroness on trips to New York. She's out of town, and I'm plastered. I stumble up the stairs of her pre-War walkup and find myself doing the one-legged drunken pirate dance in the kitchen.

I call the nearby Waverly diner and order a bacon cheeseburger, with sides of cheese fries *and* onion rings, a vanilla milk shake, and a slice of chocolate cake. I know Sam must have some weed in the house. I find her glass bong and prepare myself a little appetizer.

The delivery guy shows up, and I spread this feast in front of me. I sit down to watch the debate between two of the most powerful, successful individuals in the world. Lieberman is the first Jewish guy ever to run for vice president. Inspired by the historic moment, the month before I'd sent out a promo postcard for He'brew, for which I changed one of our taglines to support the Democratic cause: "Perfect for Bar Mitzvahs, Weddings, and Inaugurations."

Stoned, drunk, and pacified for a fleeting moment, milkshake in hand, staring at the mouths of the debaters seemingly lip-syncing their answers, all predictably pre-programmed, pre-digested, pre-tested for this epic job interview. Damn sure I'm gonna vote for the lesser evil… but these guys are both *total assholes.* They're both liars, or at least so ideologically wound up that they can't possibly show a chink in their dogmatic armor.

I yearn for an escape. Bring me the pre-survivalist, Bicentennial Ted Nugent: "Stakes are high, and so am I. Got me a rock 'n' roll band. It's a free-for-all!"

Unfortunately there would be no *deus ex machina* rock star to the rescue. I used to float in our bathtub in San Francisco trying to relax my back, and inevitably Beck's "Nobody's Fault But My Own" would shuffle through the playlist. His haunting refrains always felt strangely soothing, though a far cry from the days of my youth rocking out religiously to Led Zeppelin's riff on the original version of the Blues spiritual.

Things were seriously wrong with my relationship, and with my work. My last line of defense was to just get hammered, and to struggle with what it means to be successful and honest. (And what about happy?)

I didn't start the business to be a millionaire, or even a businessman. I wanted to create something that would be unique, artistic. Something a bit profound, and a hell of a lot of fun. All of that, it seemed, had failed.

I flew back to San Francisco, and Tracy went on vacation to Europe. I was supposed to go, but I just couldn't -- too close to Chanukah season -- so she took off with her best friend.

Meanwhile, I planned He'brew's fourth anniversary party. I figured I'd blow what I had left on my most ambitious party to date, at a rockabilly sushi place on Mission Street. I hired three members of the New Orleans Klezmer All-Stars to headline.

Tracy got home late on the Saturday after Thanksgiving, and when I picked her up at the airport she could barely talk. She was a wreck. I assumed she was jet-lagged and worn out. My party was Sunday night, and she'd had an art show at a friend's furniture gallery that was supposed to come down that day. She asked me to meet her to help take down the show, and she and her mom rented a U-haul.

Typically, it was a small disaster. They had a minor scrape with a building overhang, and when I met them at the gallery, it wasn't even open yet. At this point, it was early afternoon, and I had to get my own event set up. We spent the whole day snapping at each other through gritted teeth.

Later that night, after the beer bash had been raging for a while, Tracy walks in with her whole family, looking like they're all wearing death masks. I'm thinking, could we have a little enthusiasm out of you people?

When I get home, we start going at it. I ask what could possibly be wrong, and she says, "I'm really not happy. I think we need to take a break." I reply that you don't "take a break" when you've only been married one year. We argue and cry. In the morning, I say, We're not taking a break. And she says, "Well, then, maybe we should get divorced."

It turned out Tracy had spent her vacation realizing she didn't want to be in our relationship. It was obvious that we wanted very different things, and that we'd lost the balance of love and hope over fear that would have been necessary to move forward. In *The Snow Leopard*, Peter Matthiessen writes, "Yet love was there, half understood, never quite finished; the end of respect that puts relationships to death did not occur." We had passed that point.

SNATCHING DEFEAT FROM THE JAWS OF VICTORY

As painful as it was, I would come to appreciate the fact that she was willing to throw down the gauntlet. I didn't have the foresight, or the clarity of vision, to understand how to make things better. In my mind, this was what life is like. I thought you just had to suck it up and make it work.

I don't know where that idea came from, and I hope like hell it's gone now. But at that point, some part of me seemed to think that work and love needed to be painful and full of suffering to be meaningful.

Thankfully, she wasn't willing to do that anymore. It gave us both the opportunity to pursue the rest of our lives.

After living with Tracy for five years, on New Year's Day, 2001, I moved into the only thing I could vaguely afford: a room in a shared four-bedroom flat with three twenty-something strangers as roommates. It was the height of the Web boom. Trying to find an apartment in San Francisco proved agonizing. Trying to find a sliver of success with my company and my life felt even harder.

CHAPTER 11

I Don't Have The Cash For The Guns And Ammo, But I Do Have $50,000 Of Credit For The Beer

At the beginning of 2001, my good friend Peter and I were commiserating over our respective breakups. He'd just crashed out of the end of a five-year relationship as well, so he set out from New York to drive cross-country. I planned to meet him in Memphis to freeload at a friend's parents' house.

We went to New Orleans for New Year's Eve, then headed on to San Francisco. The trip came to be known as our "Guns and Drugs Broken Hearts Reunion Tour." Memphis boogie and New Orleans funk: check. Booze and drugs: check. But the guns turned out to be a "no" at our pit stop outside Austin. The rental fee and cost per bullet for the 9mm and machine guns they offered seemed better spent on a hungover brunch, more booze, and my newly doubled rent in San Francisco.

Somewhere in West Texas we formed a band called the Workaholics. High concept. Our gimmick: we would never show up. The Hardest Non-Working Band in Show Biz. And when the Workaholics bailed, we'd roll in to save the day with our alter-ego project -- the Taints. "T'aint got talent. T'aint got rhythm. Lean back and touch the magic -- the Taints!"

The car broke down in Flagstaff. On a late Friday afternoon, just at closing time, a middle-aged German mechanic flipped the fan belt in disgust, and the entire load of coolant flooded his garage floor. In an uncalled-for moment of anxiety and self-importance, I ditched Peter to get back to take care of some imagined, urgent work. I should have stuck around Flagstaff for a few more days.

Evidently, the big event I was racing home for was the nastiest flu I'd had in years. I monopolized the TV room in my new apartment and soaked myself in a germ-infested flannel comforter of sorrow. Great new flatmate.

When I finally came out of the haze, I went back to work, walking down Valencia Street from my office past the usual array of homeless guys sleeping in doorways and pushing carts. I was broke, heartbroken, and irate. I remember thinking, I could see how some guys end up in those situations. Sometimes you feel so hurt, you just want it to go all the way.

I've been so fortunate that, again and again in my life, every time something bad happens, I have an incredible support network anchored by a loving mother. She was fantastic during that era -- patient, nurturing, consoling. And so were my friends. As with so many breakups, there were endless hours of churning, reliving the steps that led to the bottom. Recriminations and realizations. Not fun, but necessary.

Having gone to Stanford and a well-connected high school, with so many resources at my disposal, no one I knew was going to let me end up truly broken. I started calling around to friends of friends to dig up some money. Once again Susan and Scott brought me back for the old temp job I'd had years before. Though it was pretty much straight out of *The Office*, I was grateful for the generous corporate hourly rate and the rather mindless routine, surrounded by nice, calm work friends, all happy to cut out for peach margaritas for anyone's first day, birthday, or last day.

Through the spring and summer, the business kept limping along. I was trying to keep my expenses as low as possible using frequent flyer miles for a couple of trips to Chicago and New York. I let all my investors know that it might be the end of the road. I told them I'd continue to keep Shmaltz alive, and to explore alternative directions. I was keeping the business going on fumes.

I started the year not quite firing on all cylinders, but by spring I'd moved into firing on way more than too many cylinders. After a cold and dreary three months of sulking into my pints along with Peter in San Francisco, I slowly crept out of my emotional fog and decided to make up for lost time by partying pretty much every night for the rest of the year.

Our house slogan was "I'd Rather Be Awake," and we declared 2001 the Year of the Bender. With my roommate Bari and his co-conspirator Basem (and sometimes visiting professor Hayim), and later Julie ("The Family Jewels") and EB and a host of regulars around our clubhouse, we managed to be out every night for months on-end, often hitting last call at Murio's Trophy Room on Haight Street, with the bartender breathing fire, the regular with the spiked-hair antennae talking about aliens, and the two hot Wendys shooting dirty pool (no luck, ever). Then we'd usually go to an after-hours house party or bring it home to ours.

Earlier in the winter of my discontent, a small group of damaged romantics had gathered for the first, and hopefully last, annual St. Valentine's Day Massacre, intended as a Tenderloin bar crawl. Well-oiled from stop one, Kim and Suzanne had enough already, and they left Peter, Eli, and me to hit the Overflow for liquor and pool with the regulars, and one tall, buxom, attractive prostitute on the arm of a guy who looked exactly like bartender Eddie from *Barfly*.

Closing time pushed us on to Eli's nearby apartment to scrape clean the remaining baggies and drain everything left in his personal bar. Three, four, five a.m., who knows? But my therapist, who'd helped me through couples' therapy, and then solo divorce therapy, did know (as did I) that we had our weekly appointment at his home office in Alameda the next morning. Stumbling out of Eli's, I grabbed a therapeutic donut and a Snapple Apple, crawled into the minivan, and made it all the way to the Broadway exit off 880 before pulling into the gas station and puking up my guts and any remaining vodka in me. Then I called my man counselor Ashley to cancel.

A month later, after another late outing, I was supposed to be in Marin for a 9:30 breakfast meeting with one of my investors. I woke up at 9:50, panicked.

I called the restaurant and got Russ on the phone, like in an old movie: "Sir, there's a Jeremy Cowan on the phone for you...?"

Russ, for the most part, was very understanding. To this day, we're more or less able to joke about it. It wasn't *that* big a deal to him, but it was a big deal to me. Rarely had I felt so irresponsible.

That, in a nutshell, was my 2001. In September, I went to Rob and Alexandra's wedding at a hillside retreat in Sonoma country. The night before, they had a rehearsal dinner, and everyone offered toasts -- loving, supportive, nostalgic, hopeful. Rob and I hadn't worked together for two years, but we'd become really good friends. I gave a toast that, to this day, is probably the low point in my sense of propriety.

I told a long, winding story that ended with the happy couple having sex on Ecstasy in the marbled bathroom suite at the Sir Francis Drake on my wedding night. I said something about how I thought that moment reflected their shared sense of passion and adventure, and how I hoped they would never lose that spirit.

And everyone join me in saying *L'Chaim!*

As I glanced up for the final toast, raising my glass, I noticed Rob and Alexandra's parents and grandparents staring, jaws in full drop, and Alexandra curling up trying to hide behind Rob in the middle of the room.

Pause, in slo mo.

Wow. I'm that putz at the wedding. I had honestly imagined my tale as clever, and true. Sure, a bit bawdy -- but sincere. I positively freaked out. The only thing that even slightly saved me was that right after me, Alexandra's closest friend went on and on about how excited she was about Rob, after all of Alexandra's "dark lovers" from her past. Misery, or at least the pathetically inappropriate, loves company.

Most of the time, when you stick your foot in your mouth like that, your friends will shrug it off. Not this time; not this crew. For months afterward, every time I saw someone who was there they'd say, "Dude, I can't believe you did that!" Maybe this year has gotten away from me a little, I thought.

So for the first time since I started drinking at fifteen, I consciously went on the wagon for a month, for the Jewish holidays. The first week, I was on a total high. The second week I crashed, hard. I had headaches, and I was just bitter and annoyed.

By the third week, I'd come back around. I was feeling vaguely human again. The fourth week, I was just kinda bored. I thought, If I have one more soda water-cranberry-and-lime at my neighborhood hangouts, I'm going to kill myself, or someone else. Gradually, I weaned myself back to having a few beers now and again.

The week after Rob's wedding was September 11. Not long after that, the anthrax scares started happening. I still had a small desk in the office above the hot dog stand, next to the comedy traffic school. One grey fall morning, I was walking down Cesar Chavez from my old parking spot at the live-work loft, and a squad of fire trucks and support vehicles were lined up outside my building.

My first thought was, Please, please, Lord, without hurting anyone, I hope you've sent a pillar of fire into my office and destroyed absolutely everything in there. I had general liability insurance. If nothing else, at least I would get some insurance money, and the whole sorry episode would be scorched out of my life.

As I got to the front door, a group of guys in full-body Hazmat suits -- white jumpsuits with bubblehead clear face masks straight out of *Outbreak* -- emerged from the stairwell. What's going on?

"Anthrax scare," the captain replies. "But it's all clear now."

I told them I just had to get a few things out of my office, and they assigned a guy to escort me. Inside there was an overwhelming chemical smell, and the guy said they were having trouble locating the source. The woman a door down from me had a small law office. She was doing some civil rights litigation, some ambulance chasing. They said she'd come to work that morning and immediately noticed this toxic smell. Then she noticed a white powder on her doorknob, and she freaked.

I thought, You've got to be kidding me. This small-time lawyer above a hot dog shop thinks she's being targeted by the anthrax terrorists?

As it turned out, a young woman who lived upstairs had a gas leak in her moped, sitting in the garage downstairs. She took the moped to the shop but hadn't cleaned up the gas, and it smelled awful. Meanwhile, somebody had sprinkled powdered sugar on the lawyer's door -- probably some traffic-school miscreant, bored in line for the bathroom at the end of the hall. I couldn't imagine how much the city spent on the whole ridiculous episode.

Not long after that, I gave up the dwindling global headquarters of Shmaltz Brewing and moved out of my office and into a desk overlooking the backyard at my apartment. I threw a couple of He'brew Chanukah parties, and a five-year anniversary party at Crowbar. Yet despite the brave-ish face, there was very little future I could envision for the brand.

Around this time I had a miserable incident in which I tried to sell the company to the guy who started Bagel Beer. Recall, if you will, my "good buddy" from high school, his LoopyWare t-shirt company, and the "friend of a friend" jackass who turned their knockoff spoof into a little contract-brewing start up.

All those years later, he had two or three Bagel Beers brewed in Gilroy, and by a really good brewer. Supposedly, this guy had a very big trust fund, and an eagerness to spend it. Tracy had mocked me for it, and I'd never told anyone else, but in spite of the fact that they had specifically tried to rip me off, I'd always kind of liked the idea of Bagel Beer. It was Jewish, but not *too* Jewish. It had nice alliteration. What can I say? I like shtick. And bagels.

Unbeknownst to me, Bagel Boy had name-dropped me as a reference to get into several of my wholesalers. Now this guy was cherry-picking off my business. Still, I thought, as much as I don't want this shmuck to have the business, if I could miraculously squeeze a hundred thousand dollars out of him, I could at least pay back most of my investors -- and be free.

We went back and forth for two months or so. I'd been introduced to a lawyer who specialized in the alcohol industry, and he agreed to help us put together a deal. I said, Let's do this thing.

The deal was one-time gross sales, which were something like $112,000. I was also going to get fifty dollars an hour for a certain amount of "consulting" which would have gotten me up to about $125,000. But after weeks of assuring me this was happening, Bagel Boy started to renege: "Ah, dude, I've got the coin, but it's just taking a while. Lemme get back to you."

Fuck! I can't believe I actually bent over for the goddamn Bagel Beer guy, and now he's jerking me around. So I told him, Forget it. I'm out.

There may be a God. Karma may exist. A year later, Bagel Boy turned himself into the Marin County Sheriff's Office and admitted to defrauding his investors of over a million bucks. I was thrilled at this revelation. And then I thought, How the hell did this guy get a million for that business?

At the end of 2001, I decided to take a big, fat -- or, more precisely, long and cheap -- vacation. I had a little bit of money from my divorce, and from the office job. Everyone around San Francisco at the time seemed to have just gotten back from southeast Asia, with stories of gorgeous beaches, four-dollar-a-night huts, and delicious noodle dishes for fifty cents. I figured I'd get a one-way ticket to Bangkok and go at it from there.

I cut a deal with Anderson Valley (or should I say, I accepted their only offer), in which they would effectively take over everything for the time being. They agreed to handle orders and shipping, plus some basic marketing. They would take the beer to the festivals to see if they could get the brand off the ground any more than I had. They reduced my royalty rate to two dollars a case, and raised the price to cover it. I only found out later that they kept producing and selling the cases and withholding the paltry royalties, even after I'd returned and moved the production to a new brewery.

When I left for Asia, I had no idea if I'd ever get back to working on He'brew. I thought it could go either way. I felt horribly guilty losing everyone's money, but I honestly knew I'd tried the best I could to make it successful.

I'd never paid myself a salary, just covered expenses. Before skipping town, I had one last work-related conversation with an acquaintance in San Francisco. Sean, a graphic designer starting his own company, had been bouncing around the beer shows and networking in the community. He wanted to get into craft beer, and he pitched me on doing a project with him. I had no money, and no need for new graphics. The only hazy notion I could muster for the future of He'brew involved the seemingly unrealistic goal of one day putting Genesis and Messiah into six-packs. Given my failures so far, the scheme seemed unlikely at best, but he convinced me to let him and his partner take a stab at re-doing the packaging -- if nothing else, to use for their portfolio and pitches to potential beverage clients. I acquiesced, sent him the graphics files we'd used, and directed my mind toward sunnier days.

In Asia, I kicked around Thailand, Malaysia, Vietnam, and Hong Kong. Gawking at giant Buddhas and hiking beside howler monkeys, swimming in the most beautiful water I'd ever seen, reading everything from the collected writings of the Dalai Lama to Italo Calvino's poetic imagining of Marco Polo and Ghenghis Khan in *Invisible Cities* to the backpackers' assigned reading *The Beach*, I knew I still hadn't gotten over Tracy and our divorce.

I went to what I thought was a yoga meditation retreat (I'd never done yoga, or meditation) in the foothills of Thailand, a place that had been recommended by Rob and two other friends who'd gone a few years before. They said, "You can't talk for ten days. It's an incredible spiritual journey."

After sleeping on a thin straw mat on hardwood floors, visitors meditated in full lotus position from five-thirty to eleven in the morning, occasionally walking in a small circular path around a dirt grove. Each morning, in his very strong accent, the esteemed elder monk offered a slow, monotonous teaching that was meant to inspire our concentration and learning for the day. The problem was, he sounded like a ten million-year-old man speaking through a ten thousand-year-old microphone.

I'd read one small pamphlet on the very basics of Buddhism, so once or twice I recognized a word he would mumble repetitively: "Ssuh-ringg... Suhh-ffrnng..." Yes, the core of human unhappiness: suffering. I had no idea what else he was saying, but I sat quietly, hoping to catch a phrase or thought to help me focus through the day.

Suffering: It was a hundred degrees and humid as a sauna every day. It was so hot that the ants were dying in the trees above and falling onto us. Unprepared for sitting for hours at a time, my knees were absolutely killing me. Practitioners were expected to actively think about nothing, all day, in silence. I barely got through one morning.

By lunch the first day, three people had dropped out. By day three, I couldn't take it anymore, so I shuffled out of the wooded monastery to a bus stop down the road.

I was very upset and disappointed with myself. Since the *mikvah* in Israel, and in many other times in my life, I have thought of myself as a seeker, open to diverse paths towards truth. The Buddhist goal of seeking enlightenment centered on letting go of one's unnecessary expectations, ending the clinging of the ego, and releasing the self to a natural state of oneness and grace. As the younger monk pointed out, "It took your whole life to get to this point. What's the big deal about ten days of something different?"

Though I was selling Jewish beer, I hadn't been as actively Jewish for the last year, or maybe more. This form of Buddhism, in a forest monastery, was so far from my experience, from what I thought I wanted to accomplish, or what I thought was exciting about Judaism. To achieve nothingness -- no high, no lows, just cool, distanced enlightenment -- this was so far from the ecstatic dancing and singing in the desert in Israel that I associated with my deepest spirituality. Or the precious moments of awareness I'd valued so much at shows by the Dead and the funky Meters. I found my monkey brain arguing loudly each day, ricocheting inside my head.

I also felt like a shmuck. Rob and our friends had loved the retreat, raved about it. What the hell was my problem?

I decided to go to the beach and meditate by myself, maybe just a few minutes a day, to see if I could do it on my own, at my own pace. I took a bus to another bus, to a boat to a walk to a place that had a handful of huts on the edge of another beautiful Thai island. I grabbed a bungalow and sat down on a mat inside and started... breathing.

I just kept breathing, slowly and smoothly, focusing on the wind moving into my body and out of my mouth. Easy, consistent, calm. A Jewish meditation technique I'd heard about focuses one's mind's eye and one's breath on one of the Hebrew names for the divine -- the Hebrew letters Yod-Hay-Vav-Hay. You actually follow the path of your breath as it moves from nose to throat to chest and back, all in the shape of the letters. Three to five to fifteen minutes of this exercise, just breathing and concentrating on the flow of the breath and the image of the letters...

And suddenly the entire fabric of my muscles, from the crown of my skull down through my scalp, to my neck and out to my shoulders, just released. It felt like the child's game in which you crack the "egg" over your friend's head and let the "yoke" of your fingers drip over the skull. My eyes and my ears, my whole face, my jaw, my neck and back all loosened up, literally for the first time in years.

It seemed impossible. Meditation school dropout, here I was in a reed hut in Thailand, having a completely unexpected transformative experience. It was the first time I felt I could let go of the shit that was tying up my insides. After about an hour, I felt like a newborn. One hour really changed my life, in the way that Israel had changed my life.

Coming out from the meditation, gingerly re-emerging to the world around me, somewhat more at one with the universe, I slowly opened my eyes and took one final deep breath, soaking in the serene moment. As my eyes came back into focus, I glanced at the walls of reeds, and I realized I was looking at a big cockroach crawling across the surface. It took me back to New Orleans, where the palmetto bugs were everywhere.

Then I saw four more, hiding on a post.

I went to the "office" hut to ask if they had any bug spray, and they gave me this huge, legal-only-outside-the-U.S., undoubtedly highly toxic can of bug napalm. Still high from my meditation jam, I sauntered back to my cabin, stepped in front of the post where I saw the first roach, and pressed the spray tab. In one instant, less than a second, hundreds, if not thousands, of roaches came flying out of the thatching. It was like the entire hut was made of roaches. They were scurrying all around me. It was *loud*. And behind them comes this huge millipede -- it must have been a foot long. The bugs had infested every nook and cranny of this spot, my previously sacred chamber.

I'd gone from one moment of utter, blissful clarity to another moment of complete, disgusting mayhem and terror. I'm sure I yelped like a terrified child and ran the hell outta there as fast as I could.

I slept on the porch the next two nights and never went back inside. I moved to the next beach, and for more than a week I played chess and volleyball with an ecclectic bunch of travelers, including an dynamic group of *kibbutzniks* from Israel, two British teachers-turned-beach bums, and a young English lad I called "Guv'nah" who'd grown up meditating, doing yoga, and learning Sanskrit at an alternative school outside London. I continued to meditate several times a day, sparking perhaps not total enlightenment, but at least the maximum relaxation fire.

Halfway through my trip, I arranged a stopover in Hong Kong, where one of my best friends from college was working for the *Wall Street Journal's* Asia bureau. I'd been traveling with a few quick-dry shirts, a couple pairs of shorts, living on ten dollars a day, at most. I generally weigh over two hundred pounds, but eating the cheapest rice and veggies, walking miles in the blazing heat, swimming in the azure water as much as possible, meditating every day, and rarely drinking beer (I was on a *vision quest*), I'd lost about forty pounds in six weeks. Backpacker chic and fresh off the beach, I emerged off the elevator high up the glass tower of the *WSJ*. Gabe took one look at me and said, "Dude, you've got to eat something. And by the way, you stink. Burn those clothes." Good to see you too, I said.

I crashed at his apartment on the twenty-first floor of one of so many vertical Hong Kong apartment buildings. He took me out exploring, and we walked all over the hills and neighborhoods of the city. Tracy's best friend, Samantha, who was still friendly with Gabe after a long-defunct relationship, happened to be in Asia and came to visit. (She was the friend who had been in Europe with Tracy.) Sam was willing to talk with me about what the hell happened to five years of my life -- to let me vent, and to remind me of my many faults and failures. Those couple days basically saved my emotional life. I started eating again, maybe even had a few beers. To life, Sam!

Over the next six weeks, as I moved through Vietnam and finally into southern China, I swapped a series of emails with Sean, the designer back in San Francisco. As he sent mockups of new labels, I began to take some growing interest in looking at them. They'd made some really cool progress. I began to allow for the possibility that it might be time to put the beer back into the world in its next phase -- a reincarnation, a new life.

By mid-summer, after attending Gabe and his lovely wife Laura's wedding back in New York, I returned to San Francisco and moved in, for the time being, with my mom. This would be the first of many times I'd crash her condo over the next several years. Patroness saint, no doubt, she even replaced the small foldout couch with an extra-long twin bed for me to sleep on.

The most recent report upon my arrival showed He'brew selling maybe a hundred cases a month. I had a booklet of potential designs that Sean and his colleague Nick had prepared for me, and not much else. I felt some rumblings of interest in re-engaging with the work, and I planned to respectfully follow through with Sean and Nick's new portfolio piece. Still, I remained very hesitant to throw myself back into the beer world.

I had a friend who was a standup comic and a cartoonist who'd long been supportive of the beer. While volunteering for me in the early years, he coined a name for my kitchen "office" -- the Shvitz Shop. Mike was hosting Jewish comedy nights, and he had one planned for a club called Rooster T. Feathers in San Jose. He asked me to bring the beer. It was the first He'brew event I'd done in many months. Planning it made me feel like I coming back to an old habit, wondering if it could possibly be good for me.

After I got the beer all set up, the staff informed, the postcards and flyers displayed, I plopped down at a corner table and waited for the place to fill up. Mike did a lot of marketing with Jewish singles groups, and as the crowd arrived, two thirty-something women asked if I minded if they shared my table. They sat down and made some small talk, asking me questions about myself. I said, I'm the beer guy. I just got back from Asia, and I'm kinda in between things these days.

As I heard myself talking, I was thinking, here are two good-looking women with real jobs and real lives. My own situation sounded more pathetic, if not alarming, with every word that came out of my mouth. Somehow I let it drop that I'd gotten divorced and gone on a vision quest with the million cockroaches, and that I was now living in my mother's den. I had no real job; I was temping again in Menlo Park. They asked me what I was reading, and I looked down at my novel of the moment... *American Psycho*.

Oh, yes. I was a real catch.

As I settled back into the Bay Area, I started working with Nick fairly regularly. He had come up with some great design ideas. I was, of course, broke, so the opportunity to work with Nick and Sean was certainly appealing from a budget standpoint. However, it soon turned out to be much more than simply a bargain. I quickly realized that Nick had a fantastic knack for generating multiple directions. He was flexible and willing to change, to evolve and try something different. He never got frustrated with me (and I do tend to micromanage). He got my creative juices flowing again.

I'd always thought of our labels being square -- up and down, left to right, horizontal and vertical. Tracy's artwork was typically front and center, but Nick flipped it so the He'brew logo took precedence. The brand name came forward in a powerful way, drawing one's eye to it. The label certainly had more of a traditional beer look, with the iconic beer "badge" shape. Yet to me, it seemed so fresh and unexpected.

The designs created an interesting tension. Suddenly, the brand was more understandable and approachable, though still embracing the potentially outrageous and provocative. It fits my disposition to have one foot in both worlds -- the more traditional mainstream, and the offbeat and unusual. By bringing those ideas together, Nick inspired me to see He'brew in a new light.

We did beer labels, six-pack carriers, even bottle caps and a "mother carton" design. Anderson Valley had always just glued a label on the outside of plain brown boxes, which was how most small breweries did it, and many still do. All of a sudden, the product started looking like a real thing -- a *real beer*.

My friend Chris, an artist and freelance graphic designer (and one of Rob's co-conspirators from U.C. Santa Barbara), agreed to help me change the color of the rabbi's skin, from Chagall-slash-Godzilla green to swarthy Jewish-looking white man. As I looked over his shoulder in his home office bungalow in Sausalito, Chris worked his magic in Photoshop. The technology had changed so much in five years that he could fix problems with the graphics file with a few mouse clicks that had proven so infuriating just a few years before. Now the dancing rabbi looked kind of tanned, with all the lush and evocative original brushstrokes still completely present. And the art still shone through, keeping the wonderful depth of character that Tracy had created.

I started making some phone calls to breweries to see what they were up to on the production side -- whether they had any extra capacity, and potential interest in brewing for me. I knew there was no way I was going back to work with Anderson Valley. I knew I needed to move on from that relationship. I decided to look clear across the country and began talking to brewers in Virginia, Washington, Pennsylvania, New York, Vermont and Maine. I wanted to find out who might be able to do six-packs, what price they might give me, how much I could sell them for.

With microbrews resurging in popularity, a lot of brewers were busier than they had ever been. They had less capacity; there were fewer people hungry for business. Next I did a round of west coast calling to friends at North Coast, Lost Coast, Speakeasy, and other northern California breweries.

I also talked to Rogue in Newport, Oregon. One of the grand poobahs and true mavericks of the industry, Rogue had created some of the most ambitious beers anywhere -- more examples of "extreme beer" before its time.

They cultivated the Rogue Nation, a tight-knit cult following that spread across the country.

The company founder, Jack, a lawyer who had been instrumental in sales and marketing with the early stages of Nike, had started the brewery as a second life for himself. He clearly understood brand-building, and he had a knack for being unconventional. At the time, Rogue ranked a step up from Anderson Valley in terms of national sales and distribution. They operated several brewpubs as well, and they'd started to expand to new locations around the Pacific Northwest.

A couple of years earlier, I'd visited Jack to talk about bringing He'brew to Rogue. We'd bonded a little, I thought. He was clearly an idea person, and I think he got a kick out of the vision and branding for He'brew. We'd gotten far enough that I put together a whole proposal to sell the brands to them and have Rogue produce He'brew in Oregon, put the beers into their distribution channel, and have me come work for them. Though he'd encouraged and entertained the proposal, it just wasn't the right fit for the brewery at the moment. I'd stayed in touch and admired their company's evolution from afar.

It was Thanksgiving weekend, 2002. On Friday afternoon, I'd been working on some of Nick's labels, and I thought, Let me call Jack and just put the whole scenario out there again. Maybe we'd be a better fit now.

I reached him on his cell phone at home and gave him my pitch. He said, "The project sounds fine. We'd want one thing -- a pub in San Francisco. If you can get me that, I think we can come to some agreement."

I wrote a proposal in which I would do the local sales and marketing for the pub, which might even include some Jewish menu items, perhaps a black velvet Lenny Bruce portrait -- enough to allow me to include He'brew in the mix. Rogue would buy the brand from me for a to-be-determined amount, and they'd put my beers into production at their brewery, then into distribution through their wholesale network. I would act as the national sales manager for He'brew, and I would help with anything else they might need for Rogue.

We bounced it back and forth, never quite finishing the paperwork. Meanwhile, I went up to San Francisco and spent every day for a couple of weeks talking to everyone I knew, walking the neighborhoods, talking to real estate agents, looking at storefronts. Finally, I found a restaurant I thought would be perfect for them.

Jack wanted a place that was already set up but about to go out of business, so Rogue could just bring in their signs and open as soon as possible. I found just the spot in North Beach, a restaurant that had been a really nice steak house, then flipped to a burger joint. It was in a high-traffic area, and it had the only outdoor patio at the time on that side of the city, which would have been perfect for a small beer garden.

Jack sent his lawyer and his west coast sales manager to check it out, both of whom were awesome guys. Amazingly, it seemed as though this might actually happen – a home for He'brew and Rogue in San Francisco. I started thinking about pairing gourmet Jewish deli food on the menu. And I let myself ride the fantasy.

Then Jack came down from Oregon to visit, and things took a significant turn for the worse. I guess I should have known when it became clear he wasn't interested in talking about Jewish deli food. He was starting to hint that he wanted me maybe just working on Rogue, helping with national chains, for example. Or I could manage the restaurant. (I had no interest.)

Despite all the hints, I tried to convince myself that it could still work out. I handed over the information about the restaurant, made the introductions to the lawyer, who went through due diligence. They got the space, bought the equipment cheap, and opened the pub. And I basically never heard back from them.

When I contacted Jack the month they opened and reminded him of our agreement, he said, "I never promised that. You misunderstood me." I pointed to the last drafts of my proposal. He told me he'd give me two tap handles at the pub, and let me bring people in to showcase the beer. I would have no expense budget and would need to pay for my own pints.

I walked into the bar one day and said, Jack, you better come up with a better solution, or I'll go to every neighborhood meeting and tell them how you took advantage of a local small-businessperson. I will try to make it very uncomfortable for you in San Francisco.

Admittedly, it was a low moment. It was a pathetic threat. I was just so disappointed. Once again, I felt so frustrated and hurt. He offered nothing. I left the meeting and went to my mom's friend, lawyer Robin, and asked, Is there anything I can do?

She said, "I don't know if you'd win a lawsuit, but let me write a letter." Robin, who is like my second mother, is a bulldog, especially when protecting her surrogate pup. In the letter, she demanded that Rogue follow through on their promises, including buying my brands for two times gross sales -- something like two hundred grand -- and a full-time job for sixty thousand a year, with a marketing budget as discussed. Or, she wrote, we can come up with a cash settlement and put this behind us.

All Jack needed to say early on was, "Sorry to drag you through this process. Thanks for the hard work. We love the place -- let me throw you a couple grand for all the time spent over the last month or so." I would have been disappointed but satisfied, at least to get paid for the hours I'd invested. But he offered squat -- didn't acknowledge that I'd done anything at all to help him get into business in San Francisco.

As she has done so many times for me, Robin was my superstar: She squeezed a settlement out of Rogue, more than I expected. Miraculously, I got a check.

While Anderson Valley was handling sales and distribution for me, I'd still managed to rack up debts for basic overhead, just to keep the thing alive. I used the money from the settlement to pay off all the debts for Shmaltz on my credit cards. Unbelievably, I'd managed to clear the books -- except, of course, the $135,000 from my investors.

After that latest debacle, I resumed my search for a brewery that could produce six-packs. Most brewers had a minimum batch run between a thousand and fifteen hundred cases. By the end, needing only a couple hundred cases at a time of He'brew, Anderson Valley had started simply blending (yes, blending) equal parts Boont Amber and Poleeko Gold for the Genesis Ale liquid.

Brewing so much more beer would be a huge risk, but if I could expand my distribution and sell that much, by the second or third run, I'd cover the costs of getting off the ground in the new era.

It was the beginning of the next wave for craft brewing, and there were a lot of businesses moving away from 22 ounce bottles. In the late '90s and into the early 2000s, many regional breweries became successful enough to get into six-packs. That made things a little clogged in the category, but everyone assumed you sold three to five times as much beer in six-packs.

Packaging trends have come in waves from those 22s when I started. Now, in 2010, we once again sell a huge portion of our beer in 22 ounce bottles, at margins that allow us to scrape out a living wage.

Eventually, I narrowed my choices down to two facilities. One was my old friends and two-time potential employers at Mendocino Brewing, in Ukiah. Their longtime and renowned master brewer, Don Barkley, still piloted the facility, cranking out their well-established brands. Unfortunately, they would only commit to huge batches -- almost three thousand cases for each style.

The other brewery was an outpost in King City, in the Central Valley of California -- Spanish Peaks. For many years, they had been a contract brewer, with a little brewpub in Montana, before opening their own production brewery. At one time as contract brewers, they sold hundreds of thousands of cases a year. But the years leading to 2003 had not been kind to S.P., and their numbers had been dwindling. They could use the extra business.

I met the brewer and manager, who would turn out to be one of my favorite beer-industry colleagues. Brian has been an endless source of scheming and imagining, and he's a bit of a self-avowed lunatic, and a loyal friend. They had the right packaging line, the right production facility, and Brian offered to put me in touch with their national network of beer brokers and distributors.

Just as we came to an agreement, it became obvious, even to an outsider, that their brewery was about to go out of business. In hindsight, it was fortunate I'd gone through all that *mishegoss* with Rogue, since it pushed me back a few months. Otherwise, I would have signed with Spanish Peaks, then been out of a brewer within months.

With the brewery likely to be sold for scrap any day, Brian's task was to close it down and arrange to have the Spanish Peaks brands contract-brewed again -- ideally, with one brewer on the west coast and one in the east. Producing only in California, they were losing money with every case they shipped cross-country.

In a weird twist, Brian ended up negotiating with Mendocino. But instead of brewing all the beers on the west coast, we flew to New York to check out

KIDS FROM THE LABEL FOR JEWBELATION BAR MITZVAH, 2009

DEAR TTB: THESE "CHILDREN" ARE WELL OVER 21.

GENESIS 1996

Positive transparency slides of the first Genesis Ale and Messiah Stout label artwork.

Messiah #1 design by Tracy and Eric Olsen Design ↓

Messiah #2 by Nick Bentley and Sean Ziegler, Voicebox Creative
Rabbi artwork revision by Chris Blair

1998 · MESSIAH · 2003

"CHRIST, THAT'S GOOD BEER!" - GOD

HE'BREW THE CHOSEN BEER.

ORIGINAL POSTERS HANDCRAFTED BY DAVID COHEN AND IAN GRAHAM.

PRINTED BY KIRSHENBAUM BOND AND PARTNERS

5760
1999

PERFECT FOR BAR MITZVAHS, WEDDINGS, AND CIRCUMCISIONS.

HE'BREW THE CHOSEN BEER.

HANUKKAH, CHANUKAH... PASS THE BEER.

HE'BREW THE CHOSEN BEER

RABBI LANGER, THE SELF-APPOINTED GRATEFUL YID AND NEWLY RELIGIOUS YISHAI ORDER A HE'BREW FOR THE CAMERA AT 7 AM AT BEN AND NICK'S IN OAKLAND

TWO JEWS WALK INTO A BAR...

HE'BREW
THE CHOSEN BEER.

MY GREAT-GRANDFATHER ALEXANDER (LEFT), AND GRANDFATHER JAY (ABOVE)

MICHAEL COWAN (MOM) IN 1968 AT BABY SHOWER

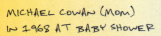

MEET
THE

BIRTHDAY ONE, EATING WITH GRANNY

NON-BEER BAR MITZVAH

MISHPOCHA

MY DAD (ABOVE);
PETER SCHMUHL
& JIM SULLIVAN
IN NEW ORLEANS
1992 (RIGHT),
MY APARTMENT
IN NEW ORLEANS
WITH CRISTI
THEN PETER
& B&D DRY
12-PACKS;
(BELOW) NOT MY
DAD'S CAMPER
BUT PRETTY
MUCH THE SAME
IDEA.

JAMIE THE MACCABEE AT 16. MY MOM SAID, "IS THAT A BEER?" I SAID, NO WAY.

(ABOVE) THE MIKVAH OF REVELATION. PLUNGE NAKED.

1997 – I COULD HAVE BEEN THE "OTHER HEBREW GUY" MAYBE A COLLABORATION?

(LEFT) ISRAEL, TAKE-TWO 1994: TONY, PHIL AND THE DESERT

MINI-CHRIS AND CHRISTA. NOT A FAIR TRADE FOR MY FIRST WEBSITE DONE FOR FREE. BUT A YUMMY BABY!

BIA HOI IN THE 'NAM, WITH MINI CHAIRS

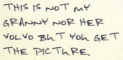

THIS IS NOT MY GRANNY NOR HER VOLVO BUT YOU GET THE PICTURE.

THE CONSUMERS

Examiner /Mark Costantini

BEARD AND MOUSTACHE COMPETITION:

1987 PRODUCTION OF
FIDDLER ON THE ROOF

JIM GOING FOR
THE MIRACULOUS
JEWBELATION

(ABOVE)
HEAD BREWER
PAUL McERLEAN
AND BREWERY
GM BOB CRAVEN

PHOTO BY CARL SAYTOR

DJ MIKEY PALMS

Why is this beer different from all other beers?

After 3000 years of civilization, finally a microbrew with the chutzpah to call itself The Chosen Beer.

In the beginning, there was an idea, and it was good: A microbrew to complement the Jewish-American experience. Whether at the shabbat table or at the deli counter, **HE'BREW** can accompany the sacred rites and rituals of life or simply inspire moments of joy and delight.

Our first creation is Genesis Ale. Like the Biblical spies bringing forth fruits from the land of milk and honey (Num. 8:23-27), we've added a hint of pomegranate to our brew. A smidgen of Middle East, a dash of American West.

Then we tasted it, and it was very good.

From the Golden Gate to the City of Gold, may **HE'BREW - THE CHOSEN BEER** join in the blessings of your lives. To our families, to our tribe, to our world. ...To Life! L'Chaim!

Shmaltz Brewing Company

✡ In accordance with Jewish tradition, 10% of our profits go to tzadakah (charity).

✡ Like your Bubbe's chicken soup, Genesis Ale is made with the freshest ingredients. Store it cold and drink it up within 3 months of bottling.

For more stick or to order chotchkies (t-shirts...) call (415) 3-HEBREW email cowberg@sfo.com surf www.shmaltz.com

HE'BREW
THE CHOSEN BEER

DON'T PASS OUT... PASS OVER

GENESIS ALE ✡ GENESIS ALE ✡ GENESIS ALE ✡ GENESIS ALE

WHAT'CHU TALKIN'BOUT, SHMALTZ?

CHANDLER, ROSS, AND... GENESIS ALE ON FRIENDS! SAVING THE GOOD STUFF FOR LATER I ASSUME.

"THE THRILL FROM ISRAEL" BUSTER MACCABI

ONE TIME INTERN, LONG TIME FRIEND OF SHMALTZ, JARED WITH JACKIE MASON AND TAKING HE'BREW TO THE WESTERN WALL

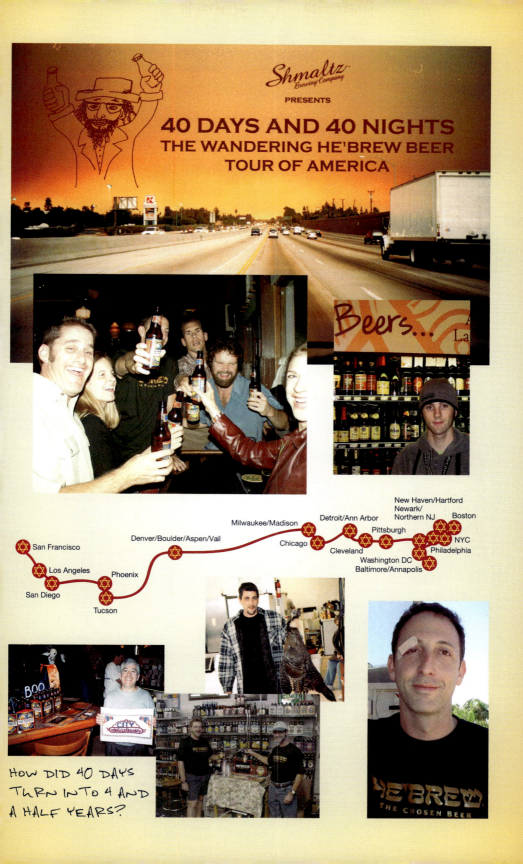

CHRIS HOLDING
JEWBELATION 9
BREW SHEET

TENTH ANNIVERSARY
PARTY AT FALLING ROCK
DENVER - GABF 2006

PHOTOS FROM THE BREWING OF MIRACULOUS JEWBELATION, 2004 (BOTH PAGES)

BRIGHT LIGHTS, SMALL SUBURB. PHOTO USED IN THE DESIGN OF THE R.I.P.A. LABEL

(BELOW) WITH MATT AT THE LENNY BRUCE & FREE SPEECH EVENT IN NYC.

LEAH WITH THE RYE WHISKEY BARRELS AT THE BREWERY IN SARATOGA SPRINGS, NY USED TO MAKE THE LIMITED RELEASE R.I.P.A. ON RYE

the ONION

The New York Times

WEDNESDAY, JULY 2, 2008

Dining Out

Coney Island? I'll Drink to That

By FLORENCE FABRICANT
Published: July 2, 2008

From the grinning funny face on the caps to the intricate labels designed by a tattoo artist, a collection of new beers by the Shmaltz Brewing Company of Saratoga Springs, N.Y., pays garish homage to Coney Island.

The Sword Swallower, a steel hop lager, is my favorite for its depth and bitterness. The Albino Python, a wheat beer, is light and refreshing with its hints of ginger, fennel and citrus. The Coney Island Lager is very pleasant.

The 22-ounce bottles are $4.99 each at Whole Foods stores and $6.50 at Bierkraft in Park Slope, Brooklyn.

LARS KLOVE FOR THE NEW YORK TIMES

DEAR NEWSWEEK: DO JEWS DRINK RIGHT TO LEFT?

BEER

And Kosher, No Less

JUST WHEN YOU THOUGHT you'd seen the most shtik-filled of microbrew-marketing gimmicks, along comes a beer label with all the subtlety of a stand-up act in the Catskills. Genesis Ale, the first beer under the new brand He'brew (the self-styled "Chosen Beer"), is wrapped in a Chagall-like label that has an Orthodox man straddling the Golden Gate Bridge and the ancient walls of Jerusalem. The founder of (what else?) Shmaltz Enterprises, San Franciscan Jeremy Cowan, 28, sold a couple of hundred cases of the stuff as an experiment last Chanukah. Now it's selling out in the Bay Area and is heading for Los Angeles and New York. "I want this to be a serious, quality brand," says Cowan. "Sort of a hip Manischewitz."

He'brew

Beeradvocate

BELIEVE THE HYPE!

MOST LIKELY TO MAKE YOU SHOUT "L'CHAIM!"

Jeremy Cowan

Founder, Schmaltz Brewing Company
shmaltz.com

puts it—"a little beer in a lot of places." Discovered almost on accident, it's become the secret to his success. "It's been really cool for the past few years, pushing the quality using innovative recipes. The more we do that, the more the best beer drinkers respond to us."

As the "English major behind the brewmaster," Cowan describes exactly what he wants, and then he and brewer Paul McErlean "taste an enormous array of beers" to find the next He'Brew. That's how they started making extreme beers—like Jewbelation Eleven and Bittersweet Lenny's R.I.P.A. "It's just a bummer that contract brewing got a bad name. It's really not that different in the scheme of things than the owner of a brewery who doesn't know how to brew."

Jeremy's latest project is the Coney Island line of lager beers, outfitted with provocative labels by Matt Polacheck and a Brooklyn tattoo artist. When an interviewer asked if he was selling out, Cowan summed up his philosophy: "Well, if circus freaks are more mainstream than Jews, then I guess we're going mainstream. I'm proud of sticking to my goal of digging deeper into the cult personality of the brand, using ingredients, shtick and themes that are close to the original vision for Genesis Ale." Such a mensch. —*Jay R. Brooks*

שמאלץ מהחבית

מה שהתחיל כגימיק של סטודנט יהודי במסיבת חנוכה, הפך למשקה מופולרי המוערך על ידי טובי מבקרי הבירה בארצות־הברית ● "היברו", הבירה היהודית שהמציא ג'רמי כואן, יצרה תרבות שתייה משל עצמה עם קריצה למסורת ולהומור היהודי ● אפילו הרב של חב"ד בסן פרנסיסקו הסכים לככב בפרסומת

"חשוב לי שהכיתוב על התוויות יהיה בהתאם למסורת ולהומור היהודי", מסביר כואן. "אני לא מנסה לפגוע לכלום, אלא בעיקר לאנשים עם חוש הומור, שאוהבים בירה חזקה ושטיק טוב על הדרך"

epicurious
for people who love to eat

Recipes & Menus | Articles & Guides | Community
WIN GREAT PRIZES FROM epicurious

Top 5 Holiday Beers

Greet the season with five robust ales and lagers that stand up to both sweet and savory dishes
By Stephen Beaumont

For as long as humans have brewed beer, they have also crafted special ales and lagers for holiday feasts and celebrations, a flavorful tradition that continues to this day. While there exists no precise definition of what constitutes a Christmas beer—some are spiced, others highly hopped, and still others crafted in conventional styles like bock and India pale ale—they are generally a bit stronger than conventional beers, and share among them a spirit of celebration and indulgence, much like the holidays themselves.

He'brew Jewbelation (Shmaltz Brewing, New York)

(About $5.50 for a 22-ounce bottle)

It may be tempting to write off this Hanukkah beer as a gimmick, but to do so would be a mistake, as this is one serious brew. Twelve malts, including rye and spelt, and 12 varieties of hop combine to make a potent (12 percent) and remarkably complex jigsaw puzzle of a brew with a forceful personality and long, lingering finish.

BREAKOUT BRANDS

MAY 2009

Stepping Right Up

Coney Island Lager is fast becoming a main attraction in the world of craft beer. By Andrew Kaplan

Craft beer has always had a strong grassroots, anti-establishment appeal. So you could say the launch of Coney Island Lager was a match made in heaven—or at least in Brooklyn. After all, can you think of a more anti-establishment place on earth than Coney Island with its sideshow freaks and carnival atmosphere?

While a developer has been negotiating with New York City to reinvent Coney Island, the beer's marketer, Shmaltz Brewing (which also markets He-Brew Beer), has craftily entered into an agreement to flow some of the brand's proceeds to the non-profit Coney Island USA, an arts organization trying to preserve Coney Island's unique culture. Both have benefited from sales which rose from 5,000 cases in 2007 to some 25,000 in 2008. Recently, *Beverage World* caught up with Jeremy Cowan, proprietor of Shmaltz Brewing, to find out more.

Coney Island Lager
PARENT COMPANY: Shmaltz Brewing Co.
HEADQUARTERS: San Francisco & New York City

BEVERAGEWORLD

Beer: Craft Brewer

GOLD WINNER
Coney Island

Yep, these guys again. The recipient of the inaugural Best in Show award is also the Gold winner in the craft beer category. For the past 14 years Shmaltz Brewing Co. has embraced the offbeat with its ever-growing He'Brew line. (A few years ago it expanded beyond the Chosen Beer's trademark and created Coney Island Craft Lagers, contributing some of the proceeds of the line to Coney Island USA, a non-profit arts organization designed to preserve the unique culture of the Brooklyn, N.Y. attraction.) It added a range of sideshow-themed extensions to the Coney Island Brand and instead of singling out just one, the BevStar Judging panel decided to award all three as components of one, grand, freakish whole. Those include Human Blockhead, a seasonal "Tough as Nails Lager," Sword Swallower Steel Hop Lager and Albino Python, a white lager with an innovative mixture of malts, hops and spices. It also recently released Mermaid Pilsner for the summer season. In late May Shmaltz opened what it's billing as the "world's smallest brewery," a nano-brewing outfit...

BEVERAGEWORLD

July 15, 2010

Best in Show

A Trio of Freaks

Shmaltz's sideshow-themed additions to its Coney Island Lager line earn the inaugural BevStar Awards' highest honor.

Beeradvocate

Q The term "contract brewer" is often misunderstood and tends to get a bad rap with some beer geeks and industry professionals. This could stem from the fact that companies who hire a contract brewer aren't considered actual brewers, but rather, marketing companies. Your thoughts?

Alan Pugsley
Master brewer, Shipyard Brewing Co. (Maine)

Dann Paquette
Owner & brewer, Pretty Things

Jeremy Cowan
Founder, Shmaltz Brewing Co. (California)

I am a craft contract brewer. Dirty word? I embrace it. English major behind the brewmaster, I thrive on the fringes. Dancing rabbis and circus sideshow freaks front our diverse, often ambitious recipes, rarely aiming for classic styles. Shmaltz Brewing began 13 years ago with $2,000 for labels, pomegranates, and 100 cases of 22s, hand bottled, labeled and personally delivered. With my credit card debt and their stainless steel, I can work with a truly world-class brewer and brewery staff on projects much more ambitious than anything I could cook up with my own knowledge or resources. Late at night, I dig deeper into our shtick (often hosting and hoisting the goods), and daytimes constantly and endlessly overflow with distribution, sales and more emergencies than I ever imagined possible. I get to run a tiny national beer company with seven fantastic coworkers and an award-winning lineup—all from a laptop in my studio apartment, couch surfing or subletting, participating in the best beer scene in the world.

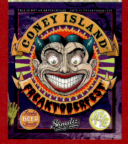

SALES MANAGERS ZAK DAVIS AND DARREN QUINLAN AT RUBY'S IN CONEY ISLAND

DONNY PERFORMING AT THE PORTER IN ATLANTA. MOLLY THE OWNER HIDING (ABOVE). I GUESS THAT'S HOW YOU WRITE CONEY ISLAND IN JAPANESE (BELOW).

JAMIE AND KENDRA AT MANITOBA'S, EAST VILLAGE, NYC

ついに出た！ **コニーアイランドの地ビール**

Coney Island Lagerの生みの親、Shmaltz Brewing Companyのジェレミー・コーワン代表（右）とアートディレクターのマット・ポラチェックさん（左）。「The Kettle of Fish」（59 Christopher St）で。

Coney Island Lagerが飲める店リストは、http://coneyislandlager.html でチェック！

CONEY ISLAND

LEAH, MATT AND MELISSA ROCKING THE BREWERS JUMPSUITS AT THE WORLD'S SMALLEST BREWERY.

FRESH CALF TATTOO

"DOWN THE HATCH WITHOUT A SCRATCH!"

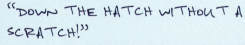

FREAKTOBERFEST 2009

ALEX FROM WORKOUT (LEFT), BURLESQUE PROS (RIGHT).

A FAKE JEW, A FAKE SANTA AND A FAKE CHASID WALK INTO A REAL BATTLE ROYALE OF BEERS: CHANUKAH VS. X-MAS 2009.

BARCADE THROWS IN THEIR OWN SHTICK BROOKLYN NYC

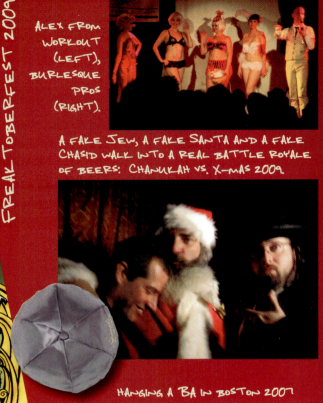

HANGING A BA IN BOSTON 2007

Beeradvocate
extreme beer fest
GUEST SPEAKER SCHEDULE Sessions 1 & 2 - Saturday, February 10

Guest Speakers:

2:15pm
Fred Hamp
Brewer, Hampton Brews

3pm
Larry Horwitz
Head Brewer,
Iron Hill Brewery and Restaurant
Meaningful Beer Analysis: Learn how to communicate what you taste, instead of what you feel.

7:15pm
Jeremy Cowan
Proprietor,
He'Brew Beer and Shmaltz Brewing Company
A Decade of Shmaltz: How it took 10 years and radical Jewish brewing to make He'Brew Beer a national brand

8pm
Sam Calagione
President,
Dogfish Head Craft Brewery
Enjoying big and bold beers with each of your five senses. World Wide Stout (18%) will be served and discussed … but not chugged!

DONNY AND HEATHER, AT CHURCH KEY SAN FRANCISCO 2010

BEER REVOLUTION, OAKLAND, CA (LEFT - PHOTO BY MICHAEL CONDIE), SUSANNAH PERLMAN AKA THE GODDESS (RIGHT)

their other brewery -- Saratoga Springs, about a half-hour north of Albany.

The guys there were easy-going and enthusiastic, real craft-beer veterans. Bob, the general manager, had originally built and run the brewery (then called Ten Springs) for the Nor'wester group in the late '80s. After Nor'wester folded and sold to Mendocino, Bob returned to run the newly-renamed Olde Saratoga Brewing Company. Paul, his master brewer, had years of experience brewing a wide array of their own beers as well as many contracts they had in house. He sported an impressive craft-beer-Santa-style beard and a trustworthy disposition. I was sold.

I made the decision to shift my production east. My goal was to use Brian's broker network around the country, and eventually revisit brewing on the west coast when sales justified the production. I managed to piggyback with Spanish Peaks, so we got incredible pricing. They were selling twenty times more beer than I was.

I began to make plans to shift my theater of operations eastward. Peter offered his Brooklyn foldout for my big arrival in New York.

The biggest piece of the puzzle was how any of this would get paid for. Thanks to the capitalistic generosity of the Federal Reserve and the largesse of Alan Greenspan, the credit card companies were still extending absurd lines of credit. Our Land of the Brave was wildly riding the economic bubble, long before the 2008 burst. I had two credit cards in my name, both of which were offering zero-percent introductory offers. Buying all those computers at my audio tour job years earlier made me look like a great credit risk. To a guy who had not had a real full-time job in six years, it's astounding to think I had fifty-seven thousand dollars of credit available to me.

The first two batches were going to be a hundred barrels each -- about fourteen hundred cases of two styles of six-packs. Those would cost me a little over fifteen thousand each. The packaging would be another ten thousand, so I was looking at about forty-plus grand just for the first two batches.

Obviously I was also going to have to support myself through the transition and cover some marketing and even my limited overhead. I had a few hundred bucks left from Rogue, a couple thousand from my temp jobs, and I wrote two checks to myself on my credit cards totaling fifty thousand dollars. I conveniently deposited them into my business account, crossed my fingers, and jumped on a plane to New York.

It was the summer of 2003. I figured I had nothing to lose. I really didn't have a plan. I'd just hit it as hard as possible right away, and hope for the best.

The fantastic new packaging, which created a reinvigorated spirit for the brand, opened the door to a new way of selling He'brew. With six-packs of twelve-ounce bottles, I finally felt I had the right product, the right packaging, and the right price. Now I could really see if anybody was willing to buy this product -- more than once -- and then again, and again.

At the very least, with this one last-ditch effort, I could be satisfied once and for all that I'd worked hard enough, and smart enough, to try to make it happen. I had three thousand cases to sell in a month, and another three thousand on order.

All I knew was, when the shit is rolling, you better get it rolling in the right direction.

CHAPTER 12

Genesis, Act 3, And The Messiah I'd Been Waiting For

June, 2003. The rebirth of Shmaltz.

I had given up my last sublet in North Beach in San Francisco and moved onto Peter's couch in Brooklyn. We'd completely redesigned the packaging and were introducing a new He'brew beer style. I had written myself checks from my credit cards for over fifty grand, and I was committed to spending almost all of that on the initial round of packaging and beer.

To get started, we shipped a couple of pallets to my new wholesaler in New York City, S.K.I. Beer. S.K.I. stands for Spanish, Korean, Italian. Three guys started a little sub-distributorship, much like many others in the beer business. Small warehouse, a few trucks, a few brands.

By the time I got there, the Spanish guy had been bought out by the Korean and Italian guys several years earlier. Their business model focused on doing the down-and-dirty work of distributing in New York that the bigger, mainstream-beer distributors weren't capable of, or willing to do. S.K.I. was expert at reaching into the tiny nooks and crannies of the retail world in New York. They distributed pretty much every product, including Budweiser, Miller, Coors, Corona, and Heineken, as well as soda, juice, and water, to the little bodegas and grocery stores throughout the city. They were the largest single customer for Bud in the city, even though they weren't really an official distributor. They bought products from the bigger wholesalers and took them into the guts of New York.

Before I found S.K.I., my first priority was to get myself into what I thought was already my wholesaler in New York, Brooklyn Brewery. We'd been piggybacking on Anderson Valley deliveries, doing business with them for several years now. I went in to meet with one of the owners, and it quickly became apparent that -- much to my surprise -- I was no longer actually doing business with him.

Tom told me that Anderson Valley had been too difficult to work with, that he'd effectively stopped doing business with them, and that he hadn't received a shipment of He'brew in four or five months[10]. He was actually very helpful, especially given how stressed out he must have been at the time. Brooklyn was in the process of selling the distributorship, breaking off their brewery business, splitting up the brands they'd represented for years in New York City, and finding homes for their suppliers, as well as themselves. Knowing more backstory now, it's surprisingly kind that he led me to S.K.I.: "The guy you want to talk to is Ralph Mauriello at S.K.I. Beer." He told me S.K.I. was a sub-distributor for Brooklyn Brewery; they distributed Brooklyn, Sierra Nevada -- a pretty significant craft beer portfolio -- to smaller stores off–premise throughout New York City.

Ralph was known as a bit of a rough-and-tumble guy. He and his long time partner, Charlie, had built their own business with a ton of sweat equity, a couple of trucks, one warehouse. Every year they added a little bit more. When I'd first cold-called New York distributors in 1997, I'd approached Ralph about carrying He'brew in 22 ounce bottles, but he wasn't interested. "When you have six-packs with twist-off bottle caps, come back and talk to me." Now I told him I had six-packs, but no twist-off. "That's all right, come in and we'll talk."

---

10 Brutal footnote to that specific moment came from Dana Ball, the Brooklyn rep who told me that after four years of us trying to get Genesis Ale into 2nd Avenue Deli, he'd fiiiinally one day discovered that the cleaning guy at a different account also knew the woman who controlled all buying for 2nd Ave. This cleaning guy led Dana to a small door that led to a tiny back office, with an older woman sitting among stacks of paperwork. Dana just had room enough to reach in with one lone bottle of He'brew. She took a quick look at it and said, "OK, send me five cases, and we'll see how it goes." Ecstatic, Dana went back to the office to place the order. Literally that week, Brooklyn had sold out of inventory and would get no more. By the time I got back to New York that summer, the Deli was not taking in any new products. Within a couple years it would close the doors of the famed East Village location.

The warehouse at Brooklyn Brewery still kept an industrial look, though it was on a block called Brewers Row, which had been pretty well gentrified by 2003, with condos and boutiques just down the street. The first time I went to S.K.I., it was a very different story.

The place was nestled in between blocks and blocks of garbage, scrap, and recycling outposts. There was loose gravel flying off the street at all times, chunks of cracked asphalt from the endless parade of overloaded trucks at dozens of warehouses in the area, broken glass everywhere, trash swirling around the sidewalks and in every corner and doorway. In the summer heat, the ripe stench from nearby plants filled the humid air, overwhelming even by New York City standards. Three-foot, bright yellow signs out front posted the warning: Beware of Dogs.

At the time, S.K.I. did all its own recycling in the main yard, so the giant brick warehouse, thirty-five feet high and a quarter city block wide, stood nearly obscured by mountains of garbage bags filled with aluminum cans and plastic bottles.

Stepping inside the warehouse, it's packed to the rafters with pallets of beer as far as I can see, from seemingly every brand on the market. Like the houses in Amsterdam, the only way they're standing up is that they're leaning against the house next door. There seems to be absolutely nowhere to move, and yet swarms of workers are loading up truckload after truckload every morning, pulling cases off beat-up industrial carts called U-boats, battered from the years of pounding. Two forklift guys are flying between the stacks, and they can't possibly fit another. Delivery drivers need to pull their orders for the day, so they are climbing all over the pallets to grab a truckload of cases. Few of them seem to speak English.

Mr. Kim, the Korean gentleman who runs the warehouse, is either storming through the aisles, flying through the offices, or yelling instructions at the top of his lungs in Korean (and possibly broken Spanglish). For several years they'd been in the process of expanding the business beyond reselling other people's products, into selling their own exclusive portfolio -- their "house" brands.

Ralph is an Italian guy from the neighborhood -- not mine, but someone's. He's got the heavy Brooklyn accent, when called for. I go in and say, Hey, how about this Jewish beer? Ralph says, "Good. We're looking for more house brands." It was one of the easiest presentations I ever gave.

S.K.I.'s street-smart business strategy was to hire sales reps and staff that spoke the languages of the customers they'd be selling to. When I did my first sales meeting on a Friday afternoon, there were about twenty-five sales reps -- a half-dozen Spanish-speaking, mostly from the Dominican Republic and Puerto Rico, a Chinese woman, a Russian guy from Brighton Beach. The rest of the staff were Arab, from all over the Middle East -- Egypt, Turkey, Yemen, Syria.

At the center of it all, Paul topped the roster as Sales Manager and played ringleader to the entire production. He ran the weekly meetings, doled out the incentives, and introduced a dizzying stream of new products from New York Minute energy drink to the latest Harpoon and Woodchuck offerings to my own Genesis and Messiah six-packs. S.K.I. is truly a different beast from any of my other wholesalers, and somehow, through it all, Paul manages to maintain a smiling disposition and always takes my calls with a robust "HAPPY Monday (or Tuesday, Wednesday, etc.)." After seven summers of sweltering New York City sales pushes, I'm still waiting for the invitation to his family's pool party in Long Island.

That first afternoon, Paul introduced me, and I broke into my comedy routine to introduce He'brew to the staff. I remember I was uncharacteristically nervous. This was a big step, my big reintroduction to New York, with a lot of inherent risk and no promise of success. But I figured it was the biggest Jewish community in the country, so I had to go all in.

Though the faces in the sales room weren't the white, post-college reps I'd known from Brooklyn Brewery, I launched into my usual shtick about Jewish humor and tradition, my references to the Torah, using all the puns. The stories of the genesis of Genesis, the three pillars of Shmaltz, Don't Pass Out -- Passover. Their reactions were a lot closer to blank stares than what I was used to, with one punchline after another falling on a cold room. It wasn't until the following week that I realized at least half the room simply didn't understand what I was saying.

On Monday, I had my first ride-with with S.K.I. Except you don't really "ride with" in New York City -- you meet the rep on a street corner and "walk with" all day.

The elusive mother lode of the Jewish community, which remained untapped from my days with Brooklyn, would, I assumed, be on the Upper West Side of Manhattan. There were more Jews living in one neighborhood there than in all of San Francisco combined. Every street corner has bagel shops, delis, a synagogue or a JCC. There's a rabbinic seminary in the neighborhood and Jewish law schools. In many ways, it's the heartland of the diaspora for world Jewry.

I thought Monday could fulfill my destiny. I'd probably sell more beer in one day than I had in several years.

So I'm meeting the rep, Nidal, at our first stop, on the corner of Ninth and 49th. I didn't know New York all that well yet. I get off the subway and I'm looking around. It slowly dawns on me that I'm not really on the Upper West Side.

In the last few years, Hell's Kitchen has turned into a remarkable foodie destination, overflowing with boutique neighborhood cafes and specialty shops. But in 2003, it wasn't nearly there yet. What was there was one crummy little bodega after another, selling lottery tickets and individual cigarettes.

When I meet Nidal, I realize he really doesn't speak English very well. Turns out he speaks Italian, so my two-and-a-half months of lame college Italian from thirteen years past ends up being about as useful as his English. He's thirty-three (a year younger than I), born in East Jerusalem, to Palestinian parents.

After the 1967 war, his family couldn't stay in Israel anymore, so they moved to stay with family in Amman, Jordan. When Nidal was fifteen, his father, unable to make a living in Jordan, moved the entire family again to Italy to live with cousins there. At age thirty, on his own, Nidal immigrated to New York to stay with some family out near Coney Island. There, he fell in love with a Dominican woman who converted to Islam, and they were married the next year.

So I'm standing in Hell's Kitchen with a Palestinian refugee, planning to sell Jewish beer. At the first stop, we walk in, with a bottle in my hand. Like a lot of places in the city, the cash register and the deli counter are elevated slightly, so they're looking down at customers, from behind big plastic walls of merchandise, a poor man's bulletproof glass. There are two guys behind this tiny counter, one furiously slapping together egg-and-cheese sandwiches and the other pouring coffee light and sweet, one after the other.

They know Nidal; he's there every week. He says, "I'd like to introduce you to this man." The guys look down at me. I jump into my first pitch of the new era: Hi, my name is Jeremy. I have this great beer, and I'd love for you guys to carry it. Can we find a spot?

The guy at the register looks at me, staring at my brand new black t-shirt, with a big, bright gold He'brew logo blazoned across the chest. It turns out all the bodegas in the neighborhood are run by Yemeni Muslims. Everyone calls each other "cousin," and they all seem to have known each other from back in the old country.

"What's the name again?"

It's called He'brew Beer.

"What is this, some kind of Jewish thing?"

Wee-e-llll....

I emphasize that we brew the beer in New York, it's great quality, top-notch packaging, great pricing...

All of a sudden, people out of nowhere are packing into the tiny bodega. Some dude from the back room, an uncle walks in, another guy from the cooler area, another through the front door. The Arabic is flying. I have no idea what's being said -- well, some idea. When there's a little break in the action, the kid looks to Nidal.

"Dude, what's the deal?" he says, in English.

Nidal says, "I don't know. It's just a beer. Just business."

The guy looks at me, looks at Nidal, looks at everyone else. Looks at everyone else, then Nidal, then at me. Time standing still.

Finally, he says, "All right, send me a case of each and we'll see how it goes."

We get outside, and my heart is pounding. I'm thinking, holy crap! If somehow I can manage to sell a Jewish celebration beer, standing next to a Palestinian refugee, to Yemeni Muslims in a bodega in Hell's Kitchen, there's an outside chance that things might just work out fine.

The rest of the day was very similar. We never did get to the Upper West

Side.

Later that afternoon on a cross-town bus, Nidal would ask me how I was involved with this company. I told him, evidently to his great surprise, that I started it. I'm the owner. The only employee.

I realized he had not understood most of my new product launch the Friday before at S.K.I. Over the weeks and months to come I'd revisit those meetings, going over the basic info the reps would need to present my beers. Actually, they could all speak much better English than most Americans ever speak a second language, but my fast-talking, Shmaltzy-loudmouth idioms would be a challenge for almost anyone. As I took it more slowly and repeated the selling points, they all got the pitch fairly quickly.

Except for one core mistake I made from the beginning. I originally insisted that He'brew was the *only* Jewish beer in this very Jewish city. True, for sure, but that claim would backfire, because the reps only thought of Jews ("Judio" in Spanish, "Yehudi" in Arabic) as the black-hatters, mostly in a few Brooklyn neighborhoods. They had no idea that Jews could look... like me.

I had to let them know where the "normal-looking" Jews lived. I even brought a picture of some Jewish looking "types" they could keep an eye out for: Jerry Seinfeld, Woody Allen, Mel Brooks, Mayor Bloomberg...[11]

Some of the sales reps are still at S.K.I. to this day. Making the rounds with them, I got to see a different side of our economy, a very different perspective on what I thought of as my beer world.

Most of the beer reps are hard-working immigrants who show up for work every day, early, and juggle complicated family lives. Particularly in New York City, it's a grind. They don't make tons of money, and the weather usually sucks -- either too hot or too cold. Before starting up with S.K.I., I'd mostly

---

11 My first mistake was to assume the reps would know who was Jewish and to understand that almost every New York City neighborhood has a Jewish community -- residents, shoppers, students, or businesspeople. My bigger questionable tactic for this crew was to call He'brew a "Jewish" beer instead of just a great craft beer, or a New York beer, and encourage them to put it anywhere better beer was sold. Over the years, I would learn to appreciate the subtle and not-so-subtle ways to change your angle, depending on your audience -- though with a burst of bravado, I figured S.K.I. would see what I saw (and everyone else who'd ever said "You must be killing it in New York") as enormous potential for a specifically Jewish beer. I won't know, and am honestly not that worried, whether this strategy limited my potential market. After all, there's still a dancing Rabbi front and center with Hebrew-esque letters pronouncing it The Chosen Beer -- rather purposefully specific branding. Once we started putting out our stronger, more ambitious "extreme" beers, we could truly say that these special offerings could and should go anywhere great craft beer is sold. We fight this particular battle to this day... And the punchline reads: Coming to convert you.

worked with white middle- or upper-middle-class, salespeople. Every day with S.K.I., I went out with a different sales rep from another part of the world. Hearing their stories, their wild and diverse tales of home, life, and New York City, would prove to be one of the most exciting parts about this new adventure for me.

One of the younger route reps was a Turkish kid who came to New York with his cousin at age nineteen to study at an English-language school. They traveled all the way across the world speaking next to no English. When they made it directly from the airport, traversing New York City, to the front desk of the school, they asked, "Where do we sleep?"

The director looked shocked. The school had no dorms: It was a day school.

I heard one story after another about how people had come to New York. One of my absolute heroes and favorite characters of the sitcom-drama that was S.K.I. was the company's salesman for "Home Ds."

Angelo is a one-of-a-kind human being. His job was to sell anything and everything he possibly could to the compact warehouse stores throughout New York City, which make home deliveries (thus, Home D) but also sell to neighborhood cafes and restaurants, churches, community groups, and anyone who has the cash. At the time, before the better beer stores and places like Gristedes, D'Agostino's, Met, Key Foods, Fairway, and of course Whole Foods, brought great beer brands to New York supermarkets, Home Ds were the primary destination for craft beer in New York.

I'm pretty sure Angelo's family was Puerto Rican, but he grew up in central Brooklyn, in a working-class neighborhood that was a true melting pot. His father owned a grocery store, and Angelo spoke just about every language spoken in Brooklyn -- but only five words apiece. Walking in the front door, he would shout out greetings in Chinese, Japanese, Korean, Italian, Spanish, German, Russian, French, Yiddish. He grew up around Jews in old Brooklyn. He would have been the perfect maitre d' at a Catskills resort. A day spent with Angelo was an education about generations and geography in New York City.

Angelo was also a restless entrepreneur, always working on a new project, even trying his hand at a line of New Age drinks that made it onto New York shelves. It also seemed like he had managed to get in and out of a bit of trouble, some of it not so serious, some more so -- fortunes gained and lost, casinos, wild tales of real-estate holdings and rearview mirrors. Those stories are certainly best left for him to tell. He was also a total biblical fiend. *Loved* the Bible. I had a blast sharing personal and historical philosophies and armchair theology with him.

To this day, Angelo will tell me what a cheap bastard I am. On my first day with him we sold about eighty cases, over a pallet, which was nearly what I'd been selling in an entire month. We were running fast and hustling. I was broke, and we were really busy -- and I didn't buy him lunch. On ride-withs, courtesy stipulates that you buy the rep lunch. To this day, he'll give me shit about that. Rightly so. Miss you, Angelo.

By the time I'd finalized an agreement with Mendocino Brewing to bring all my products onboard as a stepchild onto Spanish Peaks, I knew I wanted to continue to offer a second beer style. Recalling and finally heeding the Anderson Valley brewers' advice, I decided to change the Messiah from a stout to a nut brown ale.

In spring 2003, I started talking with Paul McErlean, the head brewer for Mendocino on the east coast. I told him I was looking for something in the category of Sam Smith's Nut Brown Ale, or what I remembered as the heartier days of Full Sail Amber, even a splash of beers like Negra Modelo. A fair amount darker than an amber ale, a little more robust, more chocolates, more caramels, more roast, a little hoppier. What I wanted would be a reference to brown ale styles from English tradition, but with a marked American craft attitude.

There was one problem: I couldn't figure out what to call it. I knew it was going to be called Messiah, but Brown Messiah? Messiah Dark... Negra Mesias... Nuts of Messiah... Chocolate Messiah? I spent weeks in thesauruses, spinning through options. Finally, by a war of attrition, in one of my least satisfying passes at wordsmithing, Messiah Bold won out. It's no Bittersweet Lenny's R.I.P.A. or Jewbelation, but it gets the job done.

Creating six-pack carriers was by far the biggest nightmare of the entire rebranding, a more painful undertaking than everything else combined. By sheer coincidence, my new printing company was then at the exact moment of transition from doing the same thing, year in and year out, to its first experience with a brand-new, highly complex, and utterly exasperating printing process.

Although the print broker kept saying, "Oh, it's gonna be fine," there were scenes of extreme violence in my head each time Jack took me back up 95 to the outskirts of New Haven. I forged a mutual bond of apologetic dislike of the pressmen, based on too many press-checks that failed repeatedly.

They had a brand new, two million dollar, top-of-the-line Italian press. They called it the Ferrari of printing presses. But with all its sophistication and elegance, the Ferrari simply couldn't do its job -- print. The blue didn't look blue; the burgundy wasn't *burgundy*. I felt bad for them -- they had to eat the cost of each round of mistakes -- though much worse for me.

Finally, we squeezed out enough carriers to get through a couple of beer batches, and then Jack -- crowned, to this day, after the initial *culpa sua,* as my prince of printing -- moved us to a less technologically-evolved (but more capable) print shop that ran my gorgeous new six-packs.

That's been a pretty constant theme with He'brew. In every production process that *should* be straightforward, that other breweries or vendors seem to crank out on a regular basis, our stuff always seems to be caught in some snafu or jam. It's happened again and again, from our t-shirts to label approval to simple stickers to fabric patches. Maybe it has to do with the way I operate in the world. The little Jewish beer always ends up being the square peg in the round hole. In an industry built to do the same thing again and again, we always end up being just slightly off.

When I started with S.K.I., they had three sales reps who sold draft beer in all of New York City. Now they have over a dozen, and growing. They covered Brooklyn, Manhattan, and a tiny bit of Queens. Now they're out on Long Island, in Westchester, in the Bronx. They're much bigger than when I started, much more tuned into the market, more organized, experienced, and professional. We've been growing together at a pretty good clip.

When Matt and I brought in the Coney Island beers in 2007, I think Ralph realized we were going to be a very different part of his portfolio. Our conversations about He'brew changed -- they became a lot more enjoyable, with a lot less friction. Those first few years, S.K.I. sold maybe five or ten of our kegs per month. In June 2010, we sold over four hundred.

Back in '03, Ralph connected me with a wholesaler who serviced Long Island, where more Jews live than in most of northern California combined. I figured we just had to get the beer to that area. This company, which shall remain nameless (may their name be cursed by all that is true, good, and powerful), distributed specialty beers and some non-alcs. Typical stuff. And it was run by Jewish guys. It seemed like a no-brainer.

I went out and did my presentation, and Ralph shipped them one pallet of each beer style. They took the beer and allegedly repped it for ten days or so. I went out on a ride-with with an older Jewish guy, a key accounts specialist, and we sold some cases. Everything seemed fine.

Then the sales manager, known throughout the territory as a Hall of Fame prick, calls me and says, "It's not gonna work. Take it back." Though he didn't say it, he did it: *By the way, I'm not paying you.*

I often wonder whether guys like this exist in every industry, or just the beer business. In situations like that, I get so angry at myself for not having an effectively strong comeback, or at least standing all the way up for myself. I tried to come up with a clever, vicious prank I could pull on them -- ten plagues kind of stuff -- but all I could think of was bringing a baseball bat to their office. Much like many other moments of perceived (and real) abuse and insult, I haven't figured out how to take off the gloves.

Finally, I sent them a letter that said, Luckily, I'm not you (you shmuck), and you have to live like this. Good luck with the heart condition.

Ralph ended up buying back the beer from them, saving my butt from my first financial catastrophe in the second life of Shmaltz. After that fiasco, I wouldn't introduce the beer on Long Island for several more years.

I'd brought some reports with me from Anderson Valley, indicating whom they'd sold beer to in the last eighteen months. To my surprise, they'd shipped He'brew to a handful of distributors on the east coast over the past year, in Boston, North Carolina, and a few in the Midwest. I'd simply not noticed.

I figured this out while I was scrambling to move three thousand cases in fifteen days. So I called these distributors and introduced myself. Most of them told me they'd been doing reasonably well with He'brew, unbeknownst to me. I said, I'm putting out six-packs, and the beer is being brewed in the east. I made five calls to five strangers, and they all said, "Sounds good. Let's do it." I quickly cobbled together a *Bad News Bears*-style distribution network, most members of which I happily continue to do business with to this day.

That was enough to get rid of almost all of the first two batches of beer. The first day of shipping was June 11, 2003. He'brew went to New York, California, Washington D.C., Philadelphia, and Pittsburgh. Later that summer, I'd add Chicago, Wisconsin, New Jersey, Colorado, Michigan, Virginia, Connecticut, North Carolina, Arizona, Florida, Ohio, and Tennessee.

In a lot of ways, it was like I was creating an entirely new business. Yet I felt much less unprepared and anxious, compared to the first couple of years. Frankly, I was just a little bit less hysterical. When there was a delay on a packaging issue, or a distributor about to be out of stock, or a trucking company that delivered to the wrong place, it was now just another problem that needed to be dealt with -- not the start of the apocalypse.

I felt better than ever about the product I was presenting -- the beer, the packaging, the pricing. I had a successful product, except for the minor detail that the business still wasn't nearly profitable enough to be self-sustaining.

Every day I needed to go out with a sales rep and walk the streets in Manhattan or Brooklyn, or jump on a bus to D.C. or Boston, and get in someone's car and go from store to store to store. Every single day. I hate to admit it, but I still hear Ken's voice loud and clear: "Kid, you just gotta go sell more beer!"

That's a solid, predictable way to get more business. Forcing the sales rep, who has one hundred to five hundred products to sell, to focus on mine, with the buyer standing right there, personally asking the guy for his business. Some distributors welcome the help. They love to bring in people who are passionate about their product, especially when they can say it's the "owner." But distributor reps out on the streets effectively act as their own boss, and some guys don't want to share that autonomy.

My first ride-with with my wholesaler in D.C. and Maryland, for instance, was an interesting test case. His name was Les Lupo, but everybody called him Lupes. Les was a nice Jewish boy from central Maryland, now a man, about ten years my senior. He'd been with the wholesaler several years, and he knew his world well.

We arranged for him to pick me up at a mini-mall off 95. The very first thing he says as I lean into the passenger seat is, "I gotta tell you, I'm not comfortable with this."

I replied, Good morning. Nice to meet you.

"Yeah, I'm Jewish, and proud of it. But I don't need to walk into every place I go and start inviting anti-Semites to put in their two cents. The fact that the company sent you out with the only Jewish guy should show you what people think about your product."

Evidently Les had grown up in a more judgmental community than I did, and he had a much more private sense of his Jewishness. Over the course of the day, however, I felt that I was able to answer his concerns, if not turn him into a Shmaltz believer. I told Les that he could check out how I present the beer, and at least we'd have a fun day.

There are so many products in this world whose message is bland and meaningless, so they can supposedly appeal to the widest audience. What's more offensive -- "I'm Jewish and really proud of it, and I'd like you to share that with me," or Coors Light having billboards in every single city, calling themselves the "official beer" and "proud supporters" of both sides of every blood-feud football rivalry? Blue state, red state, we'll sell ya all our beer (exclusively, of course) for eight bucks a cup. We're your hometown favorite!

Les turned out to be one of my all-time favorite success stories. By lunchtime on that first day, we were having a good time, and he was starting to see where I was coming from. By the end of the day, I think I managed to turn him into a bit of a cheerleader. And to this day, he has some of my most important accounts. I've stayed at his house when we've hosted Chanukah events in Baltimore, and he's shared his single-malt scotch with me.

As much as I could, I made every single conversation count. I still had no budget for advertising, so my voice in the store and on the road was one hundred percent of my marketing, as well as my sales effort. Me personally, standing there in that one exchange, trying to get another person to believe. And if not believe, then at least just buy the case, and let me put up a shelf-talker or a sign, or do a tasting.

That's something I've tried to impart to my co-workers as we've grown. If you see the same people every month, every week, every day, it's human nature -- you ask them, What's up?, and they'll say, "Ah, same old shit." That drives me crazy. Just dig a little deeper and ask a few more questions, and people usually open up. They drop these little tidbits or curiosities. Some of it is profound, some insane. All of it is the meat and spice of the life going on around us.

That was one of the real beauties of forcing myself to be on the road -- every day or so, a new city with new stories, new peculiarities, new points of view. The He'brew bottle served as a catalyst for a moment, a form of communication, an exchange. That was my magic carpet, my arts organization, my radio station, my psychiatrist's couch. All of this added new levels of meaning to the project. It opened the door to the diversity that was around me: Tastes great. More fulfilling.

CHAPTER 13

40 Days And 40 Nights...
And 40 Days And 40 Nights And...
Repeat.

Now that I had deconstructed Shmaltz world headquarters to a cell phone and a laptop, I went looking for what would be the first of many, many, many sublets in New York. Peter had graciously hosted the first month of my new life, but it was time to leave the nest.

I know Yahweh can be a jealous and vengeful God, but I think even the divine will appreciate my non-idol worship of Craigslist. Four and a half years of road travels, including countless trips between the west and east coasts, without a permanent address -- Craigslist was my sublet bible. After finding a few places that might be in my price range (the bottom), I narrowed it down to two spots, one in Chinatown and the other in Williamsburg, in Brooklyn.

At the apartment in Chinatown, I talked to a very nice, stylish young woman, Asian-American but not from the neighborhood. She and her roommate had a room open because her boyfriend was going on tour with his band. When I told her I made kosher beer, she said, "Oh, my boyfriend is Israeli. He's going on tour in Europe."

Williamsburg, that summer, was the global headquarters for the trucker-hat movement, filled with guys in ironic t-shirts and cutoff cowboy shirts. I walked into a nice-enough two-bedroom apartment, greeting my host, who had a bedhead Jew-'fro and five-day stubble. He was smoking a cigarette, sitting in front of a cobbled-together electronic drum kit. He was playing bass and looping guitar licks behind a woman's voice -- soaring, spiritual vocals, in Hebrew and in English.

I said, Wow, that's funny -- I just came from another apartment in Chinatown where the woman said her boyfriend is a musician going on tour.

Between drags, the guy says, "Oh, that's Ori's girlfriend. We're in a different band together." (Balkan Beat Box. Sweet.) Freakishly, the only two apartments I end up looking at in all of New York City are connected by zero degrees of separation.

I took the place in Williamsburg, which was above a small Italian tapas wine bar with a wood-burning stove. In the skanky New York summertime, the place had no air conditioning. There were multiple days when I took at least three showers. Five was my record. Every morning, I hustled to meet reps at S.K.I. or on their routes anywhere in the city, with subway platforms radiating the summer swelter and my new He'brew t-shirt collection getting a real workout. Door to door to door block after block, day after day -- I lived with the S.K.I. reps for weeks on end, walking every block in any neighborhood that had any craft beer, trying to ram my two new six-packs onto any overcrowded shelf I could reach. We made a respectable splash and sold about as much beer just in the city in three months as I had in the previous year in all my markets combined.

In August, I decided to throw a party to celebrate the new era of Shmaltz. My sublet-mate Itamar was friendly with a wild local klezmer-punk-funk band, which was going to be playing the Knitting Factory in Tribeca. We made plans to bring a few cases of beer for the band and to run a beer special on the night of their show. I ordered seventy knishes from Yonah Schimmel's and crossed Delancey to Guss' Pickles on the Lower East Side, where they agreed to give me a cut rate on seven buckets of their brined specialties. I invited everyone I knew, hyped up the event with a little local media blast, and planned to rock out for the night, from Genesis to the Messiah.

It was August 14, 2003. Before the party, I decided to take a mid-afternoon nap -- cool-down prep before the workout. I woke up around four to a commotion outside. I leaned out the window, saw a few confused locals, looked in the kitchen, and realized the clock had stopped. I tried to use my cell phone and couldn't. I soon learned that we were in the middle of the largest blackout in American history. The lights (and the amplifiers) would be out for a day to a week, as over 55 million people lost power.

The likelihood of my little rager going off was slim to none. I didn't have any way to get through to the knish place or the pickle guy; no way to call the club. The subways and buses weren't running. The city had come to a standstill.

With no electricity needed for one more cold shower, I hosed off before walking to the foot of the Williamsburg Bridge, where I witnessed the spectacle of tens of thousands of people walking across. I later learned that something like 250,000 people walked across the bridge to get home that day. It was a hot, sticky summer day, and a big group of Hasids with their sleeves rolled up handed out cups of water to everyone, sweat dripping from their earlocks.

Halfway up the bridge, I noticed a very cute woman in front of me taking photos. Suave: Hey, are you taking pictures?

"Yes."

Clearly an opening, so I invited her to walk across the bridge with me. A tourist from Berlin, she'd just arrived that morning. We walked on the upper deck above the flow of foot traffic, trekking through the old Jewish Lower East Side into the Village. I was headed to Peter's girlfriend's house to eat by candlelight.

I asked where my new acquaintance had been planning to eat, since everything was going to be closed. "Why?" she asked.

Uh, the blackout.

"Ha! Uhh, I had no idea," she said. "I thought it was impressive that so many people walked across the bridge every day."

Unbeknownst to me, the band did show up at the Knitting Factory that night. They couldn't be inside the building, so they ended up having a punk-rock-klezmer throwdown on the sidewalk. Wish I were there, but we made our own happening.

At the end of the night, carrying a few last beers and snacks, we strolled over to Washington Square Park, where a giant, mellow gathering was taking place. It certainly wasn't the wild party I had envisioned to celebrate the culmination of re-entry to New York. But it was an only-in-New York moment, between the eerily darkened tall buildings and the rare silence of traffic and white noise.

At about one-thirty in the morning, I glance over, and there's a couple sitting on the edge of the fountain. Just as I look, the woman bends her arm and takes a big swig of a twelve-ounce bottle. It was straight out of a movie moment -- a slo-mo, absolutely perfect label shot. She was drinking He'brew Messiah Bold, the new nut brown ale.

The moment launched a reel of images in my head. I thought of all the sales calls I'd made, all the stress and sweat. I thought about getting divorced and traveling, trying to get rid of all those ghosts. The risk, the money, the uncertainty. And after all that, here's this stranger actually consuming my product, on this mythical evening in New York City.

Part of me wanted to run over and grab her, howl at the sky and give her a huge hug. Instead, I casually asked, Hey, how's that beer?

She looked over, paused, looked at the beer, and said, "It's really good."

Instead of making a public spectacle of myself that night, getting blasted and stuffed on knishes and pickles, dancing on the bar, grabbing the mic, and bellowing "Hava Nagila," that quiet, tiny personal connection served as the climax of the first chapter of this new era for Shmaltz Brewing. For all the sound and fury every entrepreneur feels going through these epic, often private battles, it's a profound sense of satisfaction when you see your little drop fall into the pool of the world. That one experience justifies all that effort and energy. A minor, unexpected marvel.

Within the next week, I was on a plane back to San Francisco to set up shop in my mother's den for a few weeks. Age thirty-four, once again moving into my mother's house. This time, however, I was doing so with a renewed sense of purpose and optimism. I was in a much better place than I'd been the year before, awkwardly chatting up two Jewish singles at a comedy show while attempting to hide my copy of *American Psycho*.

I reconnected with all the wholesalers who serviced northern California retail stores that were willing to bring in the six-packs. As part of the typical wholesaler consolidation in the beer industry, the local Miller and Coors distributors had merged. With some of my wholesalers going out of business or selling to the big guys, I came back to the west coast to some pretty big holes in my network.

But I did the best I could. I took that same sales focus I'd had all summer and started making the rounds through Bay Area accounts, many of whom I hadn't seen in years, some of whom I still knew from my early self-distribution days. Rick at the Menlo Park Draeger's was still an enthusiastic supporter, and there were specialty stores from Marin down to Santa Cruz that I could now pitch six-packs that *should* sell faster than 22s, with only four purchases to move a case, instead of twelve, to get a re-order. Keith at Bay Area and Ron at Morris both agreed to pick up my new packages. I got nowhere with the new Miller/Coors manager on the Peninsula, so I fell in with a very nice guy trying with very little luck to create a sustainable distributor out of his extremely niche import brands (yes, even more niche than He'brew). I picked up another small guy down in Monterey and one in Sacramento, and I just kept on pushing the goods every day.

Southern brought a couple pallets to L.A., and I went down to see some old acquaintances across southern California. Changing over my SKU and UPC codes from 22s to sixes took some time and effort, but nothing like the initial, relentless push of the first few years.

With three or four dollars per case of my five-dollar profit going straight to truckers, I barely made enough to justify spending time and money on California sales. I figured that with my jigsaw-puzzle wholesale map, I was just trying to keep my business moving forward, so that as sales grew I could once again arrange for production on the west coast. I haven't yet brought on a west coast brewer, but it was still the right strategy.

By then I had about eighteen wholesalers across the country. With no experience at being spread so thin, I needed to figure out how I would manage and maintain them all.

With the rumblings of an idea, I looked at a map. Since I had first road-tripped with Maggie, a family friend from Palo Alto, to New Orleans many years before, I always wanted to see more and more of the U.S. I thought, What if I jump in the car and put together some kind of cross-country sales and marketing tour?

Maybe I could get sponsored by companies that would help cover the cost of the "tour" -- cell phone carriers, hotels, Starbucks, Apple... I had what I thought was a compelling, legitimate opportunity, but I needed an angle.

How often do you see small business owners on billboards or TV ads? I could pimp out my beer for a few grand and some free lattes and Wi-Fi.

The number of wholesalers I had – eighteen -- happened to coincide with the sign of life in Jewish mystical numerology (see also: number of chapters in *Craft Beer Bar Mitzvah*). And *Chai* (as in *L'Chaim* -- to life! -- and the giant gold chai adorning those noble hairy Jewish chests) -- the numerical value of those letters add up to the number eighteen.

The high holidays and the Jewish New Year were coming up. Shortly into the new year, Sukkot, also called the Festival of the Tents, commemorates the wandering of the Jews in the desert on their way out of Egypt to the Promised Land. Revelers gather for festive meals in a *sukkah*, a temporary hut, often set up in the backyard (suburbs) or rooftop (Williamsburg). In a kosher sukkah, palm fronds loosely covering the roof allow a glimpse of the stars. I realized my '93 Pathfinder had a little moonroof that should do the trick.

I figured I'd take my two-ton sukkah on the road, leaving at Sukkot. I thought I could make the trip in five or six weeks, which meant I'd be in New York by Thanksgiving.

That year, the time span between Sukkot and Thanksgiving was almost exactly forty days. Once in a while, the stars align. I thought the ultimate marketing shtick had just been handed to me. I called it "40 Days and 40 Nights: The Wandering He'brew Beer Tour of America."

I sent emails to the business development people at companies like Wells Fargo, Apple, and Starbucks, but got absolutely nowhere. Instead of landing any sponsorships, I ended up calling every person I could think of at stops across the country, asking for a couch to crash on while I pursued this personal and professional odyssey.

I contacted stores, bars, Jewish groups, and personal friends who might be able to help organize events to promote my cause. I let my wholesalers know I'd be coming to as many sales meetings and ride-withs as they could offer in a day or two per city. I loaded up a new press release with as much shtick as I could fit on two pages, and Matt generously donated Web time to create the template for a rudimentary blog to chronicle the trail.

Much like my first months in New York, with no strategic plan beyond selling the three thousand cases necessary to cover my credit card bill, I had no grand scheme for the 40 Days expedition. I knew I needed to spread the He'brew gospel every step of the way, attempting to inspire people along the route to join the roadshow by buying a case or two.

As it turned out, I was embarking on what would become a four-and-a-half-year tour of America and a life on the road.

✡   ✡   ✡

DEAR DIARY: OUTTAKES FROM THE ORIGINAL 40 DAYS AND 40 NIGHTS JOURNAL. A LITTLE LOOSE RE-WRITE OF THE ORIGINAL, BUT YOU'LL GET THE IDEA:

Genesis 12:1: LECH LECHA -- Leave your country, your people and your mother's household and go to the land I will show you... and I will bless you.

OPENING NIGHT: *Friday, October 11, 2003.* **SAN FRANCISCO, CALIFORNIA.**

In the beginning, there was a Happy Hour (well, several hours... into the wee hours). Chopped liver, potato latkes, Prison Whiskey, and the opening-night appearance of Genesis Ale and Messiah Bold in twelve-ounce bottles for the first time over the bar at San Francisco's Hotel Utah Saloon. And the Wandering He'brew Beer Tour is ON!

Big thanks to Joanna, Will, and the Utah posse, Laurence and Vic's 110-proof dynamic duets, and of course to all the local He'brew faithful who turned up to send me out of my garden of San Francisco Eden in true Shmaltz style. Fortunately, no one ended up like Noah, drunk and naked in his tent after the flood. So now I'm off for five more weeks of communal celebrations, endless retail sales presentations, and blissful taste-bud exaltations. Come out to join the tour, taste the Chosen Beers, buy an official limited-edition Wandering Beer Tour t-shirt, and enjoy the festivities with the Shmaltz tribe.

LOS ANGELES:

Rolling into Hollywood for a Three's Company-style flop off Sunset with Blyth and Tara, the hostesses with the mostesses, and the first of many not-quite-Zen-style sleeping spots on the floors and couches of generous friends across the country. No wall-to-wall carpets for Zen masters, and no Regal Beagle down the street for me. Just mile after mile of L.A. pavement, freeway, corner liquor stores, and lots of delicious Jewish delis.

SAN DIEGO:

Some warm San Diego hospitality once again from Melanie Rubin at the JCC, and the rest of the staff and local art collectors who sampled He'brew. Over to City Deli for a casual beer tasting, a World Series game and delicious cheese blintzes, with the smooth, dark malt of Messiah Bold. What a match. Oren Patashnik came by and may get the award for Most B'nai Mitzvot featuring the Chosen Beers. He writes, "Our three He'brew celebrations were for two bar mitzvahs -- Josh, October 1997; Jeremy, December 2002 -- and a bat mitzvah -- Ariel, August 2000." Too bad Shmaltz didn't start until 1996. Could've had a Patashnik bris as well!

PHOENIX, MESA, and TUCSON:

Anyone who says the Wild West of Arizona has been paved over and co-opted by strip malls and fast-food joints hasn't had a run-in with a certain Arizona badass: the low-hanging awning at Bruce and Dee's Little Guy Distributing compound in Mesa. I wish I could say that my sliced eyebrow came from a payback brawl with the drunken, lederhosen Weinstephan reps from Munich ("This one's for the Beer Hall Putsch!"), who were celebrating Oktoberfest at Papago Brewing the night of my arrival.

DENVER:

Hey Denver Mayor (and Wynkoop Brewery owner) John Hickenlooper: The main complaint from everyone in town, and now from me, too, is that you promised to lower the meter fees downtown from twenty-five cents for ten minutes. Just another broken promise from a politician?! Shouldn't we expect more from our elected Beer Officials?

Two thousand miles traveled already, and now off to Vail for a day of sales with the pros at High Point Brewing. The Chosen Beer in Vail? Where's my full-length sable fur when I need it?

MILWAUKEE:

If you're going to do one thing as a Wandering Jew beer salesman in Milwaukee, it's gotta be kickin' it in a bowling alley. Shlemiel, shlemazzel. Though the carpets leading to the basement may overwhelm the novice with the unmistakable waft of soiled diapers, one of the best dive bars of the "40 Day and 40 Nights Tour" was undeniably Landmark Lanes.

Most honorable mention goes to a certain ex-swimming champion, Matt Polacheck's dad, for bear-hugging me (I am still 6'1") in front of a room full of JCC locals with jaws dropped, ready to flee the madman before he turned on them. A parting thanks to Brad from New World Wines, who mail-ordered a case of the very earliest version of He'brew to celebrate the birth of his twin girls six years ago. Guaranteed that he brought the first case of the Chosen Beer into Wisconsin. After crossing half the country to hear him retell the story, it left me proud and grateful. Buy He'brew at Brad's beautiful wine and boutique beer shop.

CLEVELAND/KENT:

As the debate rages over who has the best corned beef in Cleveland, the thrilling fact for me is that both Jack's and Corky and Lenny's are stocking both styles of He'brew. I leave the judging to the locals, and simply request that you all order the Chosen Beers to accompany your sacred and secular deli rituals.

Survived yet more semi-apocalyptic weather -- a freezing ice and windstorm that brought six-foot swells to Lake Erie, outside the Rock and Roll Hall of Fame. (Boy's entitled to an hour of vacation along the way. Tried to smuggle a He'brew in for a promo shot with Jimi, Jim, Janis, or Jerry. Damn tight security!)

PHILADELPHIA:

Only one thing to say about Pennsylvania on this segment: Road Kill. Attention Deer in rutting season: Stay away from long stretches of Pennsylvania highways. Save yourselves!

Oh, yeah, and the Italian Market in Philly is sweet. Visions of Rocky on his first morning, after the raw eggs, barely able to run up the library steps. Three weeks later, in the ring with Apollo. Classic. Moira, my queen of crucifix kitsch, provided warmth, comfort, and whiskey to the weary traveler at the neighborhood basement dive Twelve Steps Down. So good to join you in my first taste of Ommegang's Three Philosophers, courtesy of Tom at Monk's. I feel smarter.

Hitting the end of the far-from-homestretch. Thanksgiving, here I come.

The sophisticated strategic plan for the re-invigorated Shmaltz 2.0 for the end of 2003, into 2004: Extend the 40 Days tour indefinitely. Sell as much beer as possible. Spend as little money as possible. Solid.

Between couches and floors, thankfully, it would be well over a year before I would have to sleep the night in my car. At that point I feared that I didn't have the money to cover a Motel 6, so it was a constant scramble. With those first two batches of Genesis and Messiah, I was just about breaking even and starting to cover setup charges. Though merely "on the cusp" of profitability, at least I wasn't losing money. No apartment, no office, no landline -- not even voicemail anymore -- a free Yahoo email address. My entire overhead was a cell phone bill and some Internet charges for Wi-Fi along the way. No rent and no fixed address, other than a four-inch-square P.O. box in my old neighborhood in San Francisco, where they could forward me mail around the country every couple of weeks. Gas, car insurance, food, beer. One business card, one sell sheet, one promo postcard. The leanest Jewish contract-brewing company in the world.

Early in the new year, I returned to Brooklyn, grabbed my car from Matt (who'd been car-sitting), and I drove south to see my wholesaler in Florida. I arranged meetings and some work days with my distributors along the way, in D.C., Virginia, North Carolina, and potential new business in Georgia.

For years I'd been trying to decide: was He'brew a community project? An arts organization? Yeah, it was a beer company, but I thought I could also do all these creative projects for my peoples. But the business was never successful until I put my head down and decided I was really a salesperson.

The marketing kept happening, but it became much less of a priority. The best marketing, I realized, came from having the beer on the shelf -- not in my car, or in a distributor's warehouse, or at a synagogue fundraiser or the brewery.

After a few ride-withs and catching up with some distributors (DOPS in Maryland/D.C. and Hop and Wine in Northern Virginia), I headed south, with a brief stop in a frozen Richmond to see the Edgar Allan Poe Museum. Poe seems to be claimed as native son by several east coast cities, many of them great craft beer stops. Coincidence? I did not manage to "quaff this kind nepenthe" (an elixir that chases away sorrow, from Poe's "The Raven," which was itself taken from Homer's *Odyssey*). But I toasted his honor and kept on moving.

A few specific events stand out along the early 2004 wandering as teachable moments. After rolling through the head office and hooking up with a couple of reps from Tryon in North Carolina, I headed over to Chapel Hill for what turned out to be an absurd double-header promo. I set up a tasting beginning at eight at a great little neighborhood joint with a decent selection of better beers, and it went well. I mixed with the locals and a few Jewish community folks, who pledged to spread the good word.

At eleven, seven or eight guys from Sparks, the energy drink-malt liquor combo, rolled in for *their* promo. They were beefy, macho guys, and they began egging on the customers to party down, all the way, with them. They rolled up in their bright orange-wrapped van, put up banners everywhere, plastered the place. Bought rounds, dropped tons of free samples, and took over. I respectfully took a quick sip of a sample and got the hell out of there.

That week I also had the single worst-attended promo ever in Shmaltz Brewing history, at the University of Georgia in Athens. The event was organized by the on-campus Jewish student organization. Cute, smart young Jewish woman invites you to a renowned music and party town. Hell, yeah, I'm on my way.

I walked in at Happy Hour and stayed for a couple hours. Literally not one person, other than the coordinator and me, showed up. Again: zero people.

Not every stop was so dismal. A dedicated and scrappy new craft beer wholesaler in Florida called Microman had brought my beers to the state, along with Mendocino's brands, when I'd first introduced the six-packs. Founded and managed by two buddies with a double passion for good beer and brutally long hours, my first few days with them were pure craft-beer-dude hang-out sessions. I talked smack, tossed off endless punchlines, and even made a few sales with the two reps that covered Orlando, Tampa, and the surrounding hundreds of miles between -- Mike Fouch, former bar owner, onetime president of the Tampa homebrew club, and current member of renowned bluegrass performers Hot Carl and the Shrimpers, and Johnny V, another fervent lay student of theology (much like Angelo of S.K.I.), though with a wild streak of banjo and entrepreneurship.[12]

On that first time down, Mike and I tried to pitch the Holy Land Experience, a "living Biblical museum," built to replicate the Jerusalem of 2000 years past, including the Dead Sea Scrolls, a model of the Temple on Mt. Moriah, and the Church of the Holy Sepulchre. All this just a few miles from Orlando city limits. Perfect fit, we felt, for Genesis and Messiah. But the pimply adolescent, no doubt a true believer, wearing his safety vest and directing traffic at the entrance, shattered our dreams, albeit apologetically:

---

12 Attn: Reader. Please hit the Independent in St Pete and now also in Tampa, spectacular beer spots created with his fantastic wife, Veronica, also of rural Florida bluegrass banjo fame, and tell them I said Yo! Quick aside for pure product placement right here for JB from Mr. Dunderbak's and Steve at New World who've welcomed me year after year with food, treats, and open taps. Nothing but pure fun and homebrew club style love in that posse, and they've paid for it ever since by hosting me for years on my annual treks south.

"Wow, that sounds terrific, fellas. But we don't sell any beer inside."

Steve and Ina, family friends from my bar mitzvah congregation, generously donated a stint at their condo in another heartland of the Jewish diaspora: Boca. I walk into the clubhouse to grab the key, and a small pack of *bubbes* and *zeydes* straight out of central casting have congregated before heading to early-bird seating. As I approach (and I am not making this up), one of the mensches, with rising timbre and disbelief, shouts, "If they're not gonna have lox at the memorial, *then what are they gonna have??*"

Finally, I did a presentation for a Jewish community fundraiser for Livnot (my Israel program folks) at a country club in West Palm Beach. After a couple weeks of cranking out work with my new wholesaler in Florida, I'd given myself a couple days off and moseyed down to Key West, where I stayed on Marathon Key, at the brick bunker apartment of my friend Heather's younger brother, Val. Driving back north, I stopped at a cute roadside café and grabbed a quick tuna sandwich.

Midway through the drive, I realized that I was not feeling so good. I started to feel bloated and a little moist, a bit gassy in several body cavities.

When I pulled up to the country club, the place was gorgeous, meticulously groomed, with marble and mahogany everywhere. It was straight out of *Caddyshack*: "Hey, Wang, it's a parking lot! And don't tell 'em you're Jewish."

My stomach was feeling terrible. I met the woman who organized the fundraiser, and she pulled me aside and said, "There's something I need to tell you. This club started after they built a huge Jewish golf club across the way, because the original club wouldn't let Jews in. You need to be a little *sensitive*."

Yeah, sensitive. I'm on it. I wandered off in a queasy daze, struggling to keep down a Sprite. When my time came, I gave my spiel. I talked about why Livnot was so important to me, how profound the experience was on my Jewish consciousness. I survived, barely.

When everyone was finally walking out, I sprinted in the other direction, through this gorgeous marble entryway into these midtown-Manhattan-style bathrooms with heavy floor-to-ceiling doors. I slammed the stall door and retched up my guts. Damn tuna sandwich. In a rare pay-for-stay travel night, I spent the next twenty-four hours in a Motel 6, purging my disease.

From spring into summer 2004, my wandering continued in earnest. I took ride-withs and sales meetings and threw promotional events wherever possible. As I never fail to tell my staff today, the initial sales pitch is so important, but if there's no follow-up, you haven't done your job all the way. Without follow-up, the chance of staying on the shelf is geometrically reduced. Then it's that much harder to get *back* on the shelf the next time.

Even with my best-laid plans, I just recently heard the complaint from an account we have in Coney Island: "Why should I bother with you guys? I gave you a shot, and I never heard back. All romance and no follow-through." The owner was absolutely right, and I made sure he heard from us every week for the rest of the summer. The initial pitch needs to be powerful, succinct, and compelling, but in some ways the follow-up is much more important.

As with many industries, we call it "filling the pipeline." There are empty shelves out there somewhere when you're the new flavor of the week. You can generally guarantee that, as long as your product doesn't suck (and even if it does suck, if you have enough incentive dollars), a lot of buyers will take a shot on that first case.

They've seen a slew of brands come and go. They may not trust that we're going to be in business forever. Plenty of entrepreneurs do the song and dance, and then they never hear from them again. In the first generation of the craft-brewing community, a lot of people were great brewers, but many couldn't, or didn't, focus that much on sales and follow-up.

The companies that spent money on sales reps -- putting a body and a voice in front of sales managers, retailers, chain buyers, bar owners, and customers -- thrived. Insert cliché here: boots on the ground, feet on the street, pressing the flesh. The clichés are annoying but the idea is the truth: *emmis!*

Once the distribution network exists, if they're given the correct attention, that doesn't go away. Those buyers remember it -- that Lenny Bruce joke you told, or how you talked about the woman's group of homebrewers in college. There's always some little nugget. My goal was to try to revisit people in the more distant markets every six to nine months.

Another cliché, also undoubtedly true: Nobody sells your product like you do. But I also think there are a lot of different ways you can sell your own product, beginning with the base-level humanity of a person sharing something they made, and talking about why they think it's special.

CRAFT BEER *Bar Mitzvah*

When I look back at my 2004 calendar, the traveling was non-stop. (The same would be true for 2005-06-07.) I went from Boston to Rhode Island, New Jersey, New York, Ohio, Missouri, Indianapolis, Detroit, Chicago, to Milwaukee, back to New York and San Francisco. In Kentucky, I had the chance to get into a handful of the biggest stores in the state, giant party stores, that somehow stock almost everything but also manage to *sell* almost everything. They had thousands of products stacked everywhere. Though He'brew was one tiny widget inside a huge operation, that was the place to be, and the buyers and staff there knew good beer and hand-sold it every day.

On one of my passes through Kentucky, I traded myself some comp time to stop into the Woodford Distillery. I had never been to a distillery, and I didn't really know much about the process. One more thing I'd need to research: Thank you, sir, may I have another?

Embarrassing to admit, but I guess I never thought about it enough to realize whiskey was made essentially from beer (except that beer brewed for distilling generally has no hop additions). The base grains -- usually corn, barley, rye, sometimes wheat -- are ground into what's called grist and then soaked in hot water to create the wort, much the same as with beer. Yeast is added to begin fermentation and this malt soup, also called the wash, will go into the complex of copper pots and tubes of the still, where it's boiled to perfection to achieve ideal alcohol transformation. Poured into charred oak barrels to age, for flavor and coloring from the wood, the liquor will emerge from two to four to many years later, after the beer caterpillar has morphed into its liquor butterfly.

By law, Kentucky bourbon must use at least fifty-one percent corn. Woodford Reserve used seventy-one percent corn, thirteen percent barley, and sixteen percent rye. The increased percentage of rye gave the bourbon its robust and assertive spice. It's a little bit harsh at first, a little rugged, but it smooths out nicely as your palette gets accustomed.

As a nice Jewish beer guy, I loved the fact that the original whiskey cooked up by the founding fathers was made from rye. Back in San Francisco, Anchor created a couple of delicious spirits using rye malts, including a fire-hot version of what was an 18th century whiskey recipe from revolutionary times. That trip to Kentucky inspired my thoughts for the recipe for our future double IPA (Bittersweet Lenny's R.I.P.A.), which builds an aggressive hop profile around the intrinsic character of rye.

Also that summer, I made a seemingly harmless stop in Missouri for a couple of ride-withs with Missouri Beverage. When I'd first come through on the 40 Days and 40 Nights tour the year before, the beer manager, Bill, had personally brought me around town to his best accounts. He showed me a new sell sheet that had He'brew on the cover -- "Shmaltz Brewing, Welcome to Missouri." The entire first page of the sales book used our tagline: "Christ, that's good beer!" Though these were somewhat understated Midwestern guys, their pronounced sense of humor permeated the entire operation.

After hitting key accounts in town, I took an afternoon off to see a good friend from the beer world before heading to Indianapolis the next day. My buddy suggested a couple beers at the taproom, aptly named the St. Louis Brewery, at local heroes Schlafly Brewing. We enjoyed a couple pints of their offerings around two in the afternoon. Then we proceeded to go on an eighteen-hour tear.

Early in our bender, we popped into the oldest standing bar closest to the original Budweiser brewery to hoist a round for history. After heading around to the corner lot and getting way too high, we jumped on a Happy Hour brewery tour. At one point, we were standing in an alleyway looking up at the pipes running from the brewhouse to the cellar. These pipes were maybe a foot in diameter. This wasn't even one of Bud's bigger breweries, and we joked that just the amount of beer in that pipe running across the path was probably more beer than He'brew made in an entire batch.

We were headed to the racetrack for the infamous one-dollar beer night (that beer unfortunately being the recently introduced light beer for connoisseurs, Michelob Ultra). What better way to enjoy race night, naturally, than to buy some crack cocaine in the ghetto of East St. Louis?

At the time I figured, what the hell -- I'm a guest, and I'm on a road show. Rock and roll, baby.

Through the tiniest of slits in a lowered driver's window, we scored said specialty items from a wild-eyed, strung-out Rastafarian. We got so high, we figured it'd be a good plan to buy some powder cocaine *to come down*.

This next dealer's name was Cool Breeze. Waiting for him, we were parked in an abandoned parking lot, a former supermarket, apparently, in a totally blown-out part of town. Cool Breeze was taking longer than we expected -- a lot longer. In between jabbering and solving the problems of the universe, I wondered if we were about to get car-jacked or taken hostage. Finally, Cool Breeze's brother shows up in a brand-new, sparkling metallic green Caddy, casually waves us over, and hooks us up.

At the track, we're flying. For absolutely no justifiable reason, we keep alternating between the dollar beers and the dollar hot dogs. Since my last college fraternity party, this was definitely the most Budweiser product I'd ever consumed at one sitting. (Well, sitting and standing, pissing like a furiously dehydrating racehorse.) There are, I dunno, hundreds, maybe thousands of people there, bands rocking, grandstands bumping, but we're in a crystal fog of our own little private party. All of a sudden I spot a guy I think I know.

Perhaps it's a mirage, but I think I sold that guy beer at a deli in town. As we walk by, he says, "Hey, man, what's going on?"

Where do I start? We sit down and drink with him and his buddy's friends for a while, yammering like Heckle and Jeckle.

After the track, someone in the crew has a local favorite in need of his monthly attention, so he drags us all to the Hustler Club. Still rolling, my friend suggests we go even deeper.

East St. Louis is evidently notorious for having some of the dirtiest fun you can have. Though I usually attempt to carry myself as a sensitive, progressive member of society, the nether regions of East St. Louis were undoubtedly a one-of-a-kind den of hedonism and iniquity. (And cheap. Recall that I was still "on the cusp" of breaking even.) A few more outposts on the tour with late night turning to mid-morning, drug-addled conversations with strangers turned best friends at a dance club called Pop's, and we finally stumble into my buddy's house long after sunrise, at 9:45 in the morning. I'm supposed to be on a ride-with in Indianapolis at 11 a.m.

I certainly won't be driving anytime soon. I call my man in Indiana and apologize profusely for having to cancel on him (without disclosing the less professional details). Then I crawl into the guest room and pass out.

I snuck in just enough sleep to slink out of bed mid-afternoon and drag my ass to Indianapolis. The next day I set up at a festival run by a bunch of folks from the Indianapolis Craft Brewers Guild, a true class act. At one point in the fest I realized that a couple of cute ladies kept coming back to my taps. For the first time in my whole history of owning a beer company, I was suddenly struck with the fairly certain notion that a woman was about to pick me up at a beer festival. And she seemed smart, fun, and sexy. I could not have been more surprised, or happier.

After the event, we went to a blues concert in a nearby city park. Then she said the magic words: "Why don't you crash at my place?"

She had a huge, three-bedroom tract home, startlingly under-furnished, on the outskirts of town. It all seemed far too good to be true -- I was more than a little uneasy, waiting for her boyfriend, or maybe her pimp, to pull up while we were butt-naked in the hot tub.

Eventually she explained that she was just breaking up from a relationship, and it seemed I'd been in exactly the right place at exactly the right time. Despite the paltry furnishings, she had an incredible stereo system piped through the entire house, and all night she cranked a local modern-rock station. Weirdly, every fourth song or so was clearly some kind of loosely-masked Christian rock. "Soaring now... I feel the power... you light up the sky... and I know you're there," etc. She had a cross hanging from the rear-view mirror of her cream Murano, and another cross hanging between her spectacular breasts.

Dear Penthouse: I never thought it would happen to me, but...

CHAPTER 14

Miraculous Jewbelation
This Chanukah, Candles Won't Be The Only Thing Getting Lit

If the big beer companies would just stick to sports, tits and ass, and talking cartoon animals to market their brands, I wouldn't be so offended. I am happy to laugh at good shtick, whatever the source. However, when the slogans move toward declaring Quality and Taste as a differentiating factor between any of them, I plead for America to call "Bullshit."

As corporate narcissism goes, misleading beer ads are not as nefarious as, say, weapons-of-mass-destruction-style lies, or as disingenuous as oil-companies-as-environmental-champions. Still, we should all be weary of, if not outraged by false claims, starting with the product packaging itself. Approved for generations by the federal government and ritually memorized by willing minions of underage boys building "beeramids," the can reads, *"This is the famous Budweiser beer. We know of no other brand produced by any other brewer which costs so much to brew and age. Our exclusive Beechwood aging produces a taste, a smoothness, and drinkability you will find in no other beer at any price."*

Since one of every two beers sold in the U.S. is a Bud product, perhaps by "costs so much" they mean the total dollars spent to produce that sheer mass of yellow, fizzy liquid. But by any reasonable measure, the cost per barrel or case to brew their beers clearly falls far below the cost of any authentic

210

craft beer. Of course they know that. A recent ad for the new Bud Light Golden Wheat ("HUGE FLAVOR… Light Beer") asserts that retailers can expect the "combined advantages of light beer volume and craft beer margins" (*Beverage World*, July 2010).

We should find it equally aggravating (especially, I assume, to St. Louis residents, so reliant on the jobs and corporate-donor largesse of the King) when A-B runs a multi-multi-multi-million dollar campaign, literally everywhere we look, declaring Bud the "The Great American Lager" (as if there's only one) -- a campaign that started just months before the family dynasty cashed out to the world's largest beer conglomerate, based in Belgium.

Perhaps it is our own fault as consumers, so well-trained by big advertising budgets for so many brands, to slurp up products we know are being sold to us purely as style over substance. Known in England as the "wife beater" beer because of its well-documented connection to binge drinking, aggressive behavior, and particularly cheap retail pricing, Stella Artois (owned by InBev, now also the masters of Anheuser Busch) spends massive advertising and promotional dollars to ensure the exact opposite status in the U.S. They demand that bar servers call their custom logo'd glass a "chalice." Ubiquitous billboards, bus-stop posters, and full-page print ads declare *"Perfection has its price."* An impressive marketing coup.

I recently heard a rep for one of my Coors/Miller distributors mention that Blue Moon has done incredibly well "for a craft beer, especially given that they don't even advertise." By any accepted industry definition, Blue Moon is not a "craft beer." The brands are simply a line extension of Coors Brewing (now even bigger as the merged MillerCoors) -- and they do, in fact, advertise. Compared to the truly minimal advertising budgets of any real craft beer company, other than Sam Adams (and maybe New Belgium and Sierra Nevada, but only recently), with millions of dollars worth of Blue Moon ads appearing in nearly every metropolitan culture newspaper and every national beer publication, as well as on radio, bus stops, taxi tops, and sports stadiums, it's telling that the rep can only have been surprised that Blue Moon wasn't advertised *on TV.* One extremely successful chain of beer bars recently shared data that listed Blue Moon as the top selling "craft beer" they carried, far above anything from Sam Adams or Sierra Nevada, the number one and two top micros in the country.

Blue Moon's tagline is "Artfully Crafted." The imagery of the TV ad (yep) featured on their website shows only the hand of a fine art painter creating a portrait of a beer masterpiece from malts, hops, and a final addition of an orange wedge. The stated mission of Blue Moon Brewing Company at Sand Lot Brewery in Denver aims to create "uniquely-flavored handcrafted beer." And, "more than a decade later," they claim, "word has started getting out." Though everyone but the owners seem to be fine with the knowledge that Blue Moon is a wholly-owned product line from the Denver giants, why would Coors Brewing be embarrassed to acknowledge that they are simply trying to make better beer?

Our biggest fear as small brewers is that the biggest guys will one day realize they could do both -- make truly high caliber beer *and* advertise the hell out of it -- and act on it. Perhaps we're lucky that giant companies rarely can, or will, innovate based on quality, and not simply marketing. For decades, their budgets have focused on churning out mass-marketed ads much more than increasing the complexity of ingredients. The other side of the marketing house at Coors (actually, their ad agency, Foote, Cone & Belding) perhaps says it all: "Coors Light -- The coldest tasting beer in the world."

While spending enormous sums on lifestyle marketing surrounding their glowing green bottle, for Heineken to boast "It's all about the beer" stands in direct contradiction to the fact that green bottles (as opposed to brown) are specifically bad for protecting the flavor and shelf life of beer.

Why can't they just stick with claims that are, if not scientific, at least self-aware, like the retro ads for Colt 45: "Works every time." Thumbs up to the new Billy Dee designs that loosely reference the Obama HOPE posters now marketing the malt liquor (owned by PBR) to white hipsters across the country. A truly ballsy attempt to create artificial authenticity, but at least it is, in fact, a very cheap way to binge.

The nationally broadcast advertising campaign for Pawtucket Patriot Beer -- on *Family Guy* -- remains my favorite: "If you drink it, hot women will have sex in your backyard."

In our tiny corner of the beer marketing world, I'm undoubtedly drawn to mocking the lies of the big guys who have all the resources to either make better beer or simply be honest about what they decide to produce.

I'm consistently thrilled to hype Shmaltz Brewing as the World's Smallest or Largest, Most Award-Winning or Fastest-Growing, Jewish, and now Freakshow-Themed, Craft Beer in America. The tagline for our Jewbelation Bar Mitzvah beer bragged its storied history, but of course was also undeniably true: "The Most Extreme Chanukah Beer Ever Created."

The beers that were exciting to me were always the ones that were the most ambitious, aggressive, and unique. For several years they've been lovingly (or sometimes dismissively) referred to as "Extreme Beer." Beer like Dogfish Head's World Wide Stout, Allagash Curieux, Lost Abbey's Angel's Share, Firestone Walker's anniversary offerings, Avery Maharaja -- beer that is ten to twenty bucks for a twelve-ounce bottle, or even more for 22s and 750s. And still a steal, compared to similarly complex and exceptional wines.

When I first started, one from way back was Eye of the Hawk from Mendocino Brewing. I poured He'brew at a rather boring music festival in Marin County, headlined by two leftover members from the Jefferson Starship, where I just kept sipping Eye of the Hawk in sixteen-ounce keg cups. It was a hot, sunny day. Rich, malty, hoppy, and eight percent alcohol. Sneaky stuff, encouraging a nice early-evening siesta in the cargo van before heading back over the Golden Gate.

On a trip to Ann Arbor for Tracy's sister's graduation, I came across Bell's Cherry Stout and Expedition Stout, both $16.99 a six-pack in 1997. (I'm nothing but jealous, even now). Taste buds blown away, in all the right ways. Anchor Old Foghorn and Sierra Bigfoot, so close to home, but like nothing I'd ever imagined before. Then there was Old Rasputin from North Coast, my first experience with an early and iconic "extreme" beer, before they were concerned with the definition. Stoned on the floor of a Mendocino County getaway with those explosive-yet-beckoning flavors knocking you back, then summoning you for more... It'd been a long journey from drinking three-dollar, thirty-two-ounce Abita Turbodogs in the French Quarter, or shift drinks of Black Forest at the Crescent City Brewhouse.

After the doldrums of the late '90s, by 2003 a resurgence of craft beer was definitely rolling. Stone and Dogfish Head led the way, with regional rock stars like Three Floyds, Great Divide, Avery, Lagunitas, and Victory cranking out amazing offerings. Over the previous years, many of the less ambitious, less innovative east coast regional breweries had disappeared. The survivors were making interesting beers that could now stand up to the products of the pioneering west coast brewers, and some were even better, setting new standards and creating wild new styles.

And through my many travels in the Midwest, I watched the craft beer scene there expand from successful "old timers," true innovators such as Bells, Great Lakes, New Glarus, to a whole new wave of diverse brewing swagger from companies such as Founders, Surly, New Holland, Two Brothers, Dark Horse, Arcadia, and Jolly Pumpkin.

In some ways, the boutique side of the craft beer industry has recently leapfrogged the middle-of-the-road beer drinker to target the passionate connoisseur. Even the larger regional micros such as Harpoon, Boulevard, Goose Island, or New Belgium, as they've become more and more widely distributed, have introduced their own high-end beers. Especially with a regional focus, many have seen tremendous growth, catering to the vast majority of more mainstream beer drinkers. But to get some attention and to capture the imagination and passion of those we lovingly call "beer geeks," you need to have some beautiful specialty beers. You gotta brew with some *chutzpah*.

By 2003, the concept of Extreme Beer had gained national notice:

Extreme Beer

by: Alström Bros. on Wednesday - October 08, 2003 - 13:47 UTC
First published in: Boston's *Weekly Dig*

Often style defying - from beers with alcohol contents that rival spirits, beers aged in bourbon barrels, beers made with enough hops to rip your tongue from your mouth, beers from yore and beers employing exotic ingredients that make one ponder - there's a bold new concept of brewing in America, and it's called Extreme Beer.

Extreme literally means that which exceeds the ordinary, usual or expected. And as such is a great way to describe these types of brews when approaching them from a mainstream point of view, where most beers that aren't fizzy, yellow and bland are indeed extreme to mainstream palates. And despite the media's recent usage of the term as a buzzword to solely describe high alcohol beers, many brewers and consumers have embraced Extreme Beer as something that pushes the boundaries of brewing and the palates of beer lovers.

We see it as the continuing evolution of the US beer industry and perhaps the second shot heard round the world for the American craft beer revolution. It's not just a pissing contest to see who can make the world's strongest beer; it's a movement - a movement to showcase the craft and how complex and versatile beer can actually be.

These aren't fancy imports from faraway lands, but rather handcrafted examples of beer being brewed right here in the US. They are highly artisan and diverse, obtainable in many markets, and they tweak the minds and palates of not only beer drinkers, but appreciators of wine and spirits - a positive crossover conversion for the beer industry.

And no, this is not a new beer trend. The concept of Extreme Beer, although new to many, has actually been around for quite a few years. Although it's been documented that Jim Koch of the Boston Beer Co. first used the term to describe the release of Sam Adams Triple Bock in 1994 (then the strongest beer at 17.5% ABV), home- and pro-brewers have been testing the limits of their craft since the '70s. We can only assume that adventurous brewers have been doing the same since the discovery of brewing beer.

Respect beer.

For me, this was where the excitement could be found – and, coincidentally, where the profit margins existed. I watched with increasing interest as the prices on twelve and 22 ounce bottles rose to heights no one thought possible just a few years before. Yes, extreme beers take more time, materials, ingenuity, and artistry to conceive, not to mention pull off. But the most adventurous and capable brewers were also growing more deservingly rewarded. Could we possibly do something like that?

The truth is, the only way Shmaltz Brewing became viable was by embracing the concept of extreme beer, and pushing what I think has been our unique angle on the movement. More ambitious recipes, more ingredients, often higher alcohol content (though even lower alcohol beers can be truly creative and "extreme" in their own right). We try to use more intense, or at least unexpected, flavors, more complicated brewing techniques. Multiple yeast strains, barrels from different sources around the country -- whatever the brewery was willing to indulge me in my newfound experimenting phase.

It all started with Miraculous Jewbelation, for He'brew's eighth anniversary. To celebrate the miracle of Chanukah (and the personal miracle of still having a beer company after eight craaazy, long, grueling, years), the idea gave a nod to Stone's Vertical Epic, which had its initial tasting on 02/02/02, continuing to 03/03/03 and beyond.

I love numerology, which has long been a vibrant element of Jewish culture and tradition. I pitched the idea to Paul, the brewer at Olde Saratoga, and he sort of laughed: "Are you serious?"

We brewed a beer with eight malts and eight hops at eight percent alcohol: eight thousand pounds of grain with eight hop additions of eight pounds each, every eight minutes, for a sixty-four minute boil. Each year since, we've added one more malt, one more hop, and one more percentage point on the alcohol ticker. Jewbelation[13] has become our winter seasonal-slash-anniversary beer, available after the Jewish holidays in the fall through Chanukah and into early spring.

Starting with year one of Jewbelation, Leah -- my most trusted long-term (and finally of legal drinking age) intern -- has served as my numerology research guru. With the number eight, an overflow of incredible shtick lit up the Internet. As always, I loved mixing Jewish history, text, and thought with pop culture, intellectual history, and rock music trivia. Traveling through late summer, I'd sit at truck stops or some grubby motor hotel to work on bullet-point one-liners, trying to tie them all together for a coherent and evocative story to cram onto the beer label.

I remember crashing at a no-tell motel outside Des Moines, the walls cheaply decorated with faux-finish six-shooters and other cowboy motifs, thinking about the symbolism of Chanukah. In the U.S., Chanukah is more or less thought of as Christmas for the Jews. You get a few presents, maybe sing "Dreidel, Dreidel," eat a latke, and request Adam Sandler's "Chanukah

---

13 At the time I came up with the name, I honestly don't remember having seen or heard of Avery Brewing's winter seasonal, Old Jubilation. I just thought Jew B. Elation would provide appropriately shmaltz-y fodder. Sincere apologies to Mr. Avery. As a side note to the footnote, at the launch party for Jewbelation 9 at Falling Rock for GABF, they only had one sixtel of He'brew Jewbelation, so every time I kept trying to order a pitcher of it to share with friends and beer peeps, I kept getting rounds of Avery Jubilation. Do eight pitchers of the wrong beer cover the offense?

Song" on the local FM morning show.

As a story of rebellion and honor, Chanukah commemorates the victory of the dedicated, far-outmanned and outgunned family of Maccabees leading a revolt against a Syrian empire determined to crush Jewish power and practice in the second century BCE. This band of religious warriors took back the Holy Temple in Jerusalem, but only after the retreating army ransacked the holy shrine. The Maccabees found remaining only one small flask of sacred oil to keep the eternal flame alive, enough for only one night. They lit the oil, and it burned, amazingly, for eight nights.

The typical reading suggests it must have been a miracle that God gave them enough light to last eight days. But while in Israel, I'd heard a different interpretation, one that I found much more compelling. The real courage in the Chanukah oil story falls to the individuals themselves. When they found that last vial of oil, instead of turning it into a fetish piece or a totem, they chose to use it. To light it. To risk the uncertain, and to start real life over again. They got everything they could out of whatever they had.

Purely as a literary inspiration, I think a lot of small business owners could identify with the attempt to squeeze everything possible out of the limited resources at hand, in order to pursue one's visions and obsessions.

With Leah's expert findings and few rounds of my own effort, we managed to mash up references from Chanukah, Passover, and Sukkot with the flood of Noah, something from Maimonides (one of the deepest Jewish thinkers), and bits about circumcision and King Solomon. Oh, and Winona Ryder.

From the label of Miraculous Jewbelation, 2004:

8 is a miraculous number in Jewish life. Chanukah, Passover, and Sukkot span 8 days. 8 humans survived the deluge on Noah's ark. Maimonides delineated 8 levels of *tzedakah* (charity). A *bris* (circumcision) comes on day 8. King Solomon completed the First Temple in the 8th month of the 8th year... *Seinfeld* ran 8 years. Dylan has 8 Grammys; Babs, 8 Golden Globes. Einstein couldn't write until age 8. Freud, the eldest of 8 children, took 8 years to complete his medical degree. Mel Brooks stole a cap gun from Woolworth's at age 8, and *The Producers* won 8 Outer Critic Circle Awards. Winona Ryder had 8 prescription medications in her purse when arrested for shoplifting.

2004 brings a most personal miracle: The 8th anniversary of HE'BREW – The Chosen Beer! *Miraculous Jewbelation* celebrates all the dedicated souls with the *chutzpah* to rise up and to risk lighting those final precious drops of sacred oil. To the courageous and the curious, the clowns and the creators. To all the Tribe of Shmaltz... To Life! *L'Chaim!*

Writing the shtick for all the anniversary Jewbelations since (nine through thirteen) has been profoundly satisfying for me. But whereas number eight really flowed, number nine proved to be a subtle scavenger hunt.

For weeks, I struggled with what I was trying to say. The sophomore slump was a constant fear. The number nine in Jewish tradition is a lot less unified than the number eight. Still, with Leah's digital archeology and Google's evolving algorithms, we found plenty to work with -- from nine blasts of the shofar to the ninth candle at Chanukah, nine planets, nine justices on the Supreme Court. I worked in references from Adam Sandler and Danielle Steele to Chaim Witz, better known as Gene Simmons, and Rodney Dangerfield, who'd died the year before. From Rodney, we jumped to our father Abraham circumcising himself at age ninety-nine, then pulled it all together with George Burns, my step-grandfather's doppelganger. Burns once famously quipped, "Sex is one of the nine reasons for reincarnation. The other eight are unimportant."

Doing the new packaging became so much fun every year, a break from the grind. Beginning with our eighth anniversary, Matt has designed all the labels. I considered having my onetime San Francisco designer, Nick, do it. He'd been so generous to me and crucial to Shmaltz. But I really felt like I had something growing with Matt.

For starters, he had redone my whole website for free and managed the updates throughout the year, gratis. He'd fixed my point-of-sale materials, sell sheets, shelf-talkers and new business cards. Only for a very generous and creative soul would it sound like a "reward" to get to do a beer label -- *for free* -- but Matt jumped right in. With his wife, Laura, also a designer, we sketched out a rough idea on a napkin at their apartment in Brooklyn, and he got to work.

I've worked with a lot of designers over the years (including my ex-wife), and there are always potential pitfalls. It's not easy trying to calibrate your own aesthetic with another person's, but over the course of several projects, Matt and I became an intuitive battery. I'd make a suggestion, and he'd do it in a way that was not what I was thinking, but so much better than anything I could've imagined. Today we have a level of communication I've never had with another creative person. We can be critical and supportive, totally honest and flexible with each other. That process has been exhilarating. Biased for sure, but I truly think he's creating some of the best designs in the beer world (and beyond): twenty-three labels (and now a book) and counting.

Back at the brewing ranch, Miraculous Jewbelation would demand a lot more malt than the average beer being brewed at Olde Saratoga. We planned to use eight thousand pounds and I remember being up on the brew rack, watching the counter showing how many pounds are going into the mash tun -- six thousand, seven thousand, seventy-five hundred. And then... it started slowing way down. The water was almost at the top of the stainless lip, and the grain was jammed coming in from the roof silo. We had to grab a broom handle and literally shove the rest of the grain into the brew kettle by hand.

My interest and pursuit of these more aggressive beers brought a new working relationship with Paul the head brewer, who is my guardian angel, my master artisan. Jewbelation is not a stout, or a porter. It's just a giant, ambiguous brown ale. I didn't want the flavors to force people to think, "Oh, I know what this is." I wanted to leave room for interpretation.

From the beginning, we put the brew recipes on our web site. It was antithetical to what I'd learned from the guys at Anderson Valley and Rogue, who thought it was completely unacceptable to put your recipes, or even much more than the basic ingredients, out in the world. Anderson Valley wouldn't even tell me how they made *my* beer.

But I'd been to a lot of Grateful Dead shows, and I saw all those people bootlegging recordings of the concerts. They seemed to be spreading the word -- expanding, not limiting, access. There's a particular benefit to having homebrewers who can see what you're doing: some will try to recreate it.

In Indianapolis, I talked to two women brewers about our rye double IPA. They said, "We absolutely adore this beer." They couldn't believe the recipe was on our site. They said they'd tried to make it at home. I asked how it came out.

"It was miserable. It was a brutal beer to try to homebrew. But it was totally fun." I, of course, encouraged them to keep trying and drinking the original, for research.

Today, good commercial craft brewers can more or less brew whatever they want, including knockoffs, and even clones. But they could brew the exact same recipe at Stone, Dogfish Head, Allagash, Russian River, and F.X. Matt, and it's going to taste a little different, if not very different, in each case.

I've never feared that somebody is going to steal our beer. Doesn't matter. Even if they do make a nut brown ale, it's not going to have a dancing rabbi on the label, or quote the Torah. The mother carton will not likely say "Do Not Store Fresh Beer in Saddlebags of White Donkey."

Because of the higher alcohol level, the first batch of Miraculous Jewbelation ended up being eleven hundred cases. Normally we'd get fourteen to fifteen hundred from a batch. It took me about three or four phone calls per wholesaler to get an order for a half-pallet or a pallet each, which I was able to sell for two to two-and-a-half times the margin of our regular six-packs. It took about two weeks to get everyone on board. At the time, it was the easiest, fastest-selling, most in-demand product we had in the lineup, for sure.

It's a simple lesson, and a life-changing one for Shmaltz Brewing. If you do something special and keep it a bit limited, you can charge a little more for it. If you do something incredibly special and even more limited, you can charge even more for it. That was the real beginning of my digging deeper into the shtick of He'brew and Shmaltz.

From there, I just wanted to get more and more outrageous, but all within the personality and framework of the brand we'd created. And that's where the success came from. It didn't come from watering down our names or our message, or making a blander product to reach a broader audience. Exactly the opposite: The more complex the beer and the more intense the shtick, the better the company did.

In 2004, He'brew served as the official beer sponsor of the New York Jewish Music and Heritage Festival, held at the South Street Seaport. That year they booked Matisyahu, the Jewish reggae star, shortly before he became a worldwide sensation. I'm looking over at a beer vendor, this big African-

American bartender. He turns around when Matisyahu gets up there and says, "This is incredible. Where's the Rasta? I just see some skinny Jewish dude up there."

I have a few great shots from that event including a very senior gent in a driving cap ordering a Messiah, and a very bronzed, flamboyant, shirtless New Yorker, all greased up in tiny running shorts, drinking a Genesis and dancing on roller skates to the New Orleans Klezmer All Stars.

It was a good time to be expansive. I had a friend from college whose buddy in L.A. sent me TV ads he'd done for the brand, unsolicited. A director who wanted more ads for his reel, without even talking to me he pulled together an entire cast of actors and filmed a hilarious spot for He'brew, which has been on our site ever since. "Oh, so you're a *doctor?* Zak, can you take a look at my lump?"

Late that summer, a fellow entrepreneur and Jewish bar owner whom I'd met the winter before on the beach in Miami (for a beer fest, not frisbee) offered to be the first to launch He'brew draft in New York at all three of his neighborhood beer-and-wine-bar jewels in Manhattan. Craig has since become a much-loved friend and colleague and a long-time supporter of our beers. We had a blast, marching with a handful of friends (and even Marty, then the S.K.I. rep, now manager) through the West Village, Soho, and Tribeca alternating Genesis and Messiah pints.

For Chanukah, I kept the trickle of draft flowing for my anniversary party, the first one I'd staged in New York. I'd met the producer of a group of delicious, slightly dirty gals called Nice Jewish Girls Gone Bad. Susannah "The Goddess" Perlman (who has since become a steady friend of mine and the He'brew family) emceed the night, juggling continuous costume changes and shephardessing the show from Catskills riffs to Jewish camp songs. The party climaxed with a half-naked accordion player leading a room full of Chanukah revelers hollering "Hava Nagila," and indulging in Miraculous Jewbelation.

✡   ✸   ✡   ✸   ✡

Parties, good. Staffing, bad. The first new He'brew guy I tried to hire in nearly five years turned out to be a failure. But I did get a new swear word out of the deal. Should I have been wary? I met this guy's dad in a bagel shop around the corner from my sublet off First Avenue. "You need some help?" he said. "I got a kid." So I gave him my business card.

This nice Jewish boy from the neighborhood seemed to have the perfect experience: sales and marketing for a specialty bakery in Manhattan. But I should have known the first time I asked him to get on the phone and call some accounts.

I asked, How do you say your last name?

"Well, my dad says Finkel-*stine*. I say *–steen*. Or *–stine*. Whatever."

This kid doesn't know how to pronounce his own last name. On the phone, he opens with, "Hi, this is so-and-so Finkel-*stine*. I'm calling from Shmaltz Brewing." He waddles through the pitch, then says, "OK, thanks. I'm so-and-so Finkel-*steen*."

I kept hoping it would work out, when he clearly had neither the skill nor the ability to pull off even the limited tasks I needed. In what would prove to be his last week, I somehow stupidly deposited his paycheck before he suddenly simply disappeared, taking with him my only logo'd fleece jacket I'd loaned him to wear at a demo. From then on, my friends and I started shouting "Finkelstein!" whenever we wanted to say "I can't believe that just happened" or "I got screwed" or "Fuck me!"

Apart from the many things I did poorly, including staffing, accounting, contract negotiations, and maintaining a meaningful long-term personal relationship, one thing I did well was PR. Alan Kaufman's early advice about pitching the media still rang true for me. With effort and hustle and a compelling story to tell, you get a ton of "free" advertising.

Of course, it's not really free. It takes hours and hours of time, focus, and follow-up. It takes writing and pitching, emails, calls, networking, scrambling. It's an investment, and it works best when plotted out as a long-term commitment. Just like so many other things in the sales and marketing world.

Living on the road, I continued to cobble together press releases whenever I could come up with a good angle, spreading them around as best I could. Compared to the faxing and mailing that had been the necessary time and expense of my PR efforts just a few years before, my laptop and the coffee-shop Wi-Fi, or even a stolen signal from a password-free Netgear or Linksys router in a nearby office or apartment, allowed me to run nearly paperless campaigns everywhere I traveled.

At the end of 2004, I roped in two great PR hits in a row. I got a couple of leads from a good friend I'd reconnected with in California. She was finishing journalism school at Berkeley, and she passed along contacts at National Public Radio in Washington D.C. and at *Time Out New York*.

Back on the east coast, I called the front desk at the magazine. I brought in a bottle of Jewbelation 8 to the office and had a killer conversation with this guy, their beer writer, who ended up featuring the product in a holiday review. By stroke of luck, he also freelanced for *Playboy*, and he gave the beer another spectacular hit on their website. Five stars, baby! I was amazed at how many people evidently really do read *Playboy* for its content. I got more responses from guys in the beer business out of that one little feature than so much of the more in-depth things I'd ever done.

But the real fun began when I planted a seed with a couple of calls to the NPR office in D.C. Traveling south on 95, I got through to a producer and said, I'm driving down to an event off 14th Street. Can I bring you some beer?

The producer called back and said, "OK, come on in. Scott is going to record a bit with you."

Scott is Scott Simon, a beloved media character on NPR's "Weekend Edition." Based on the staff response, he was definitely not used to drinking much beer on the radio. I got him cracking jokes and popping caps.

The piece ran during the holidays, and it was by far the biggest media hit I'd had up to that point. Close friends, old friends, mothers of friends, and, most importantly, strangers and potential customers called and emailed for weeks. Who knew how many beer drinkers were up at 7:45 a.m. on a Saturday morning.

That kind of energy and enthusiasm often leads directly to opportunities for more. When you can put something like NPR in your portfolio of media hits, other organizations start thinking you're a legitimate story. The wire services tend to pick up on it. And so many smaller outlets just run portions of your press release verbatim.

Because who doesn't love the story of a small business, a sole proprietor, trying to make it happen? And free booze!

CHAPTER 15

Pomegranates And C*cksuckers

A t the beginning of the new year I came back to San Francisco for a couple of months. It would be the longest stretch I'd had at home in several years. Mom's den again, and out to sublets in San Francisco, again.

Around this time I made a very important move for the business in California, consolidating my distribution from six or seven indies to one statewide distributor. That had an immediate impact. Whereas I used to make twenty to thirty phone calls to get seven distributors to do a price promotion or a push for a holiday, now I could have one point of contact spanning the entire state for certain key accounts.

Sometimes you sacrifice depth for breadth. Much like my national distribution model, my new wholesaler, Wine Warehouse, did not penetrate much beyond specialty shops and high-end chains, but they high-spotted at the key accounts that would do the vast majority of my business. For a company my size, this was a very effective strategy.

For the first time in years, I tried to focus on getting bars and cafes in the Bay Area to pick up the beers. It turned out to be a long, arduous task that never really took off. I had a target list of about a hundred accounts, and I got a few here and there to carry the goods. But it was eye-opening how painful it was to try to get into places that already had their setup. Micros had been a major slice of the beer pie in northern California for twenty years, and people were pretty happy with what they had -- Anchor Steam, Sierra Nevada, North Coast, Speakeasy, Lagunitas, Anderson Valley. Trying to break into that world proved to be a real challenge.

So I bailed. More than a few advisors have said, with conviction, "Play to your strengths." I went back to the original premise, which was to focus on grocery stores and on customers who are going to bring the beer home. In most of the beer world, suppliers concentrate on bars, sampling the beer, getting it and keeping it on draft. I tried to focus where I thought the model made the most sense for He'brew, instead of beating the business into someone else's mold.

To this day, we look for the niches. We now sell a respectable amount of draft around the country, with many permanent lines in various territories, though the largest number are in New York City, mostly with the Coney Island Lagers. In general, we try to make sure we're simply in the rotation in the beer bars that sell the best-quality craft beers in each market around the country.

On-premise sales demand time, attention, nurturing, and constant upkeep. It's a long sell cycle to get in, finding just the right moment when a tap line opens up, or the bar manager gets pissed at another wholesaler who dropped the ball or bailed on a promise. The spoils generally fall to those who are in that account regularly, and who invest in that relationship on a consistent basis.

Getting in is time-consuming enough, but then the real work starts. Staff trainings, bar promos, happy hour rounds for regulars. Dropping by with coasters or bottle openers, aprons, t-shirts, neon signs.

Of course, the bigger beer world set the standards, with sales reps who can afford to be in an account several days a week to check on Bud or Coors Light kegs or Heineken or Corona bottles. So many of the bars that specifically want to focus on craft beer, however, realize that small brewers, and often their distributors, can't give them the level of attention and service that the big guys can. But being craft beer people, they are generally very understanding, and appreciate the difference. They know they want to offer their customers

DECEMBER 12-18 Week 51 2005

NOVEMBER 2005	DECEMBER 2005	JANUARY 2006	FEBRUARY 2006
S M T W T F S	S M T W T F S	S M T W T F S	S M T W T F S
1 2 3 4 5	1 2 3	1 2 3 4 5 6 7	1 2 3 4
6 7 8 9 10 11 12	4 5 6 7 8 9 10	8 9 10 11 12 13 14	5 6 7 8 9 10 11
13 14 15 16 17 18 19	11 12 13 14 15 16 17	15 16 17 18 19 20 21	12 13 14 15 16 17 18
20 21 22 23 24 25 26	18 19 20 21 22 23 24	22 23 24 25 26 27 28	19 20 21 22 23 24 25
27 28 29 30	25 26 27 28 29 30 31	29 30 31	26 27 28

12 Monday

8:00

9:00

10:00

11:00

12:00

13 Tuesday

8:00

9:00

10:00

11:00

12:00

14 Wednesday

8:00

9:00

10:00

11:00

12:00

ExpressTrack

email all list (merch, 5 Star, Seattle, ·) (Bravo, parties, newsite)
50 tea/sleeve
2500 perbox
8k each
Rich new trips
Ryan Flying Dog
MN Beer to Mark
email coaster addresses
WI/FL/Chi/OH NY/CA
Brewery/Mon
WW CA Post Off

CA 59 kegs
13
2 Room
2 Tornado
2 Pac Coast
2 21st Am
Amnesia
Cards
Raleighs/Barclays/Ben's Nick's
Jupiter
Bistro Vic
HOTEL Utah

#Beer for Investors Chabad
Russ Tao Ephraim Ju Jon

Bruce's Bittersweet CT RIPA
Lenny
349/016

Cutting Room (Rob Sk.
Tornado 5-gal?
1:00

Mccommon handles
2:00

10:00 DAM Connie Ho
882 Emerson St StB
Channing
Steak roll + Reader
The Room Jacobee
3:00

prep NY email
DC email
T F email
4:00

Billy Cohen Purim Mar 13
Coaster addresses
Shirts to Tina
Stickers/posters
Yahoo 5:00

16 Friday Brian /Peter kegs
Ski older Baa 13
8:00 email SF party
Dops Valducis
9:00 five Rooms
Tom Bar B
10:00 McommonHandles
350/015
shirts for Matt Kinkos
shirts embroidery
SWS
1:00
2:00
Susie Bev Mo
3:00

11:00 11am SC ALAMO
Russ Beer
12:00 TAD? Rick 650-802-1689
San Rafael
2/4pm potter trips
4:00
5:00

17 Saturday 351/014
Mi Aidas Party
Call Susie Montalvo SF 3 Salons
call Susie

18 Sunday 352/013
5pm Concert Mtg
Amnesia
Hotel Utah

100% Recycled Products/Soy Inks
30% Post-Consumer Fiber

DEC

DAMN, DID I FORGET TO DO THAT...?

something out of the ordinary, based more on quality, curiosity, and flavor than on promo girls in tank tops giving away blinking plastic junk. Traveling so much, I rarely had the time to invest in building stronger relationships in any one spot.[14]

As a man who loves a good neighborhood hangout, I completely understand and respect the owner who wants to see his or her vendors and suppliers on a consistent basis. Bar people, after all, generally *like people*. They've purposefully created a clubhouse. They like to talk shit and swap tales. I often have more in common with bar buyers than grocery store buyers, who frequently have structured lives, families, regularly scheduled responsibilities. I'm a night owl, and though my internal alarm jolts me awake in the morning, I'm happy not to have to be too chipper till well after bagel time.

It wouldn't be until 2006-'07-'08 that a sea change would roll through so many parts of the country, encouraging a whole new round of small-business risk-takers and craft beer lovers to open their dream bars. The pantheon of originators, from the Toronado on Haight Street to Bleecker Street's Blind Tiger, set the standard for specialty beer destinations. (Apologies to all the brilliant beer bars, many of them very good friends and dedicated Shmaltz supporters, but there are far too many to rattle off here so please indulge the geographic bookends.) Often far ahead of the times, these iconic destinations (OK, OK! Brickskeller, Sunset, Horse Brass, Stuffed Sandwich, Roman's, Falling Rock, Monk's, Hop Leaf...) carved out an educated niche for themselves in their respective cities, and few dared compete.

But as I moved around the country, I started to see some truly impressive spots popping up in nearly every city and town I went through, with incredible selections of beers from the U.S. and international boutique breweries. These days, almost all my wholesalers have recently-opened beer bars that have skyrocketed to the top of their account lists, immediately becoming one of their top grossing accounts in the territory -- from small college towns to such well-established craft cities like Seattle and Portland, southern cities in states that popped the cap on alcohol percentage restrictions to previously slim better-

---

14 There were certainly exceptions around the country of many friends that I met along the way who brought Genesis or Messiah in on tap or bottles, who generally loved the quality of the beer -- the quality of the shtick enough to cover my butt and do my job for me, hand-selling to their own customers and again giving me support that might otherwise not be completely justified.

beer pickin's in southern California. There has been explosive growth even in top-tier beer cities like San Diego, Chicago, Philadelphia, Boston, Milwaukee, and New York. For the last couple of years, basically every work trip I've gone on -- Missouri to Madison to Missoula, St. Petersburg to Saratoga Springs to home in San Francisco -- I have been lucky enough to visit several new beer bars with standout beer selections, always with something I've never tasted, or even seen before. What a treat.

I'd been scheming about how to make my tenth year in business, 2006, a blowout. My wallet, my calendar, and my bedside table all held scraps of airplane napkins, torn corners of newspaper, and yellow stickies full of scribbled ideas.

My original thought was that each year of Jewbelation had gone so well -- why not do ten times more than that? We could put out ten different beers over the course of the year. The Jewish mystic tradition of Kabbalah holds that the Ten Sephirot form the basis of the universe. Why not ten beers?

I had no problem coming up with the shtick for ten different beers. I cooked up more than enough names, styles, and vision for the products in my head. But thinking through label design, packaging, production, recipe development, the contract-brew schedule, and of course my wholesalers' and retailers' interest in giving my little Shmaltz baby an entire extra shelf -- all of that was doubtful. Even in my true believer's head it soon became obvious that this idea was unattainable. Sometimes biting off more than you can chew can be exciting, but choking on it isn't so delicious.

I eventually whittled it down to two ideas for new beers, plus we would have the new Jewbelation. Going old shul, back to the roots, we put out a tenth anniversary edition of our flagship beer, Genesis Ale. Similar to how we'd taken the Messiah Bold recipe and cranked it up for the first Jewbelation, we would use the Genesis recipe as the starting point for something much bolder.

If you ever want to get sick of doing something, make just one thing, and talk about it, over and over. I'd been repeating the same pitch -- "It's a light brown ale, in between a pale ale and an amber. It has a nice, malty sweetness with good hop balance" – for the better part of a decade. I imagine Gary Coleman must have dreaded the moment he knew was coming when he MC'd the KSJO Shoreline Beer fest, when he eventually had to offer up the catch-phrase that was his signature, and his albatross -- "What'chu Talkin'bout, Shoreline Amphitheater!"

I poked around in the Torah, and the literary heavens simply opened up, revealing the obvious path: The anniversary beer would be called Genesis 10:10. Genesis chapter 10 lists the generations of Noah's children who got fruitful and multiplied, recreating civilization after the catastrophe of the Flood. *(Genesis 10:32: These are the clans of Noah's sons, according to their lines of descent, within their nations. From these the nations spread out over the earth after the flood.)*

For Shmaltz, Genesis 10:10 would be a new beginning, a reference to and a culmination of the company's progress. It felt like a self-initiation into much more aggressive, ambitious brewing goals.

For Genesis 10:10, Paul brewed the strongest beer we'd made to that point, sailing in at ten percent alcohol. For the first time since that first batch ten years earlier, we used pomegranate juice again, which made the beer beautiful, elegant, and unique. I called it a Pomegranate Strong Ale.

Paul and I worked on the flavor profile, and I sourced some wonderful pomegranate juice. We thought it would come in big metal drums. Unfortunately, it came in one-gallon glass bottles. Whereas the brewers thought it was funny, and not too annoying, to add nine pounds of hops every nine minutes to the ninth year Jewbelation, opening four hundred fifty glass bottles of pomegranate juice the morning before brewing was not their idea of an amusement. I couldn't blame them. They suffered for me, and they generously agreed not to revolt when I asked for a second batch as the first was selling out.

With memories of cutting the crowns of eight crates of pomegranates and squeezing them by hand, I ballparked some quick math. It turned out we'd use the juice of at least ten thousand pomegranates for each hundred-barrel batch. At least I didn't ask them to squeeze them all by hand.

Meanwhile, Jewbelation 10 was a total blast to work on. The bombastic nature of the number ten worked perfectly in cooking up the shtick. Ten thousand pounds of grain simply wouldn't fit in the kettle, but we used ten malts and ten hops and got it up to ten percent alcohol.

Each year of Jewbelation seemed to be leapfrogging the last. We went from a big, delicious brown ale for Jewbelation 8 to a much more nuanced, deeper flavor that emerged for number 9. Number 10 took it even further. It had a gorgeous, complex malt profile, with layers of intricate flavors. The mouth-feel had a lusciousness in the center, just enough coffee roast and dark chocolate, with a big, mouth-watering, caramel and milk chocolate sweetness. And the hops helped create parallel levels of flavors submerged gracefully into the beer. We were creating a multilayered narrative for the experience. It was unlike anything we'd done before.

Designing the beer label for what I coined Monumental Jewbelation was probably the most fun Matt and I had on the Jewbelations. Marking the decade anniversary, the beer demanded the ostentatious, the grandiose, the epic. For the movie *The Ten Commandments*, Cecil B. Demille had pulled an elaborate publicity stunt: he asked a conservative judge from the Midwest to help him put up memorials to the Ten Commandments all over the country. They got community groups to help, and soon there were hundreds of monuments engraved with the Ten Commandments installed in town squares nationwide. Many survived, and one even inspired the legal battle about public monuments with religious overtones. All this to hype ticket sales.

Leah, the rock of my numerology shtick, cranked out another installation. The label referenced the ten plagues in Passover. Every Jewish kid remembers dipping his or her pinky in grape juice and yelling, "Flies! Locusts! The killing of the first born!" There were ten generations from Adam to Noah, and ten from Noah to Abraham. The Kabbalah reveals ten core elements of the deepest mystical traditions of creation. I also found room for my favorite not-so-guilty pleasure, the band Rush, and I included Jack Black and Ali G, Mae West and Sandy Koufax.

From the label of Monumental Jewbelation, 2006:

In Jewish tradition, the number 10 demands Monumental gestures. As a publicity stunt for his 1956 film, Cecil B. DeMille got a Midwestern Judge to help erect hundreds of granite monuments of the Ten Commandments nationwide. 10 Plagues finally let Moses' people go. Deut. 26:12 obligates Jews to give 1/10th of their earnings to charity. 10 generations span Adam to Noah and Noah to Abraham. 10 Sefirot in Kabbalah symbolize the core elements of Creation. Father of the Bomb, Robert Oppenheimer was blacklisted in 1953 for 10 years for his family's alleged un-American activities. 10% of Nobel Peace Prize winners are Jewish. On Rush's 10th album, *Grace Under Pressure* (#10 on Billboard), Geddy Lee sings of his parents surviving the Holocaust. After Sammy Davis Jr.'s 1990 death, the lights on the Vegas strip went dark for 10 minutes - the first time since JFK's assassination. A minyan of 10 is necessary for communal prayer. Jack Black's parents joined a polyamorous group before divorcing when he was 10. In his *Belief* episode, Ali G confessed losing his virginity at 10 to an Italian supermodel. Mae West got 10 days in jail for obscenity for her 1927 play "*Sex*". She served eight, with two off for good behavior. 10 High Holy Days of repentance begin on Rosh Hashanah. 10 years after his Major League debut, Sandy Koufax, refused to pitch Game 1 of the 1965 World Series on Yom Kippur. To mark 10 years of Shmaltz Brewing, behold *Monumental Jewbelation*, HE'BREW's epic celebration of the most memorable moments in life. *L'Chaim!*

But the crowning glory of the year was the creation of the beer that would become our longest-touring rock star, Bittersweet Lenny's R.I.P.A. I'd noticed a couple of years earlier that the fortieth anniversary of Lenny Bruce's death was coming in 2006. He'd been alive for forty years and dead for forty years. I had an idea that I could pay tribute to one of modern America's most significant Jewish firebrands with our first-ever tribute beer.

For a long time I'd felt a strange affinity for Lenny Bruce, like a famous distant cousin I never knew. Certainly not for his tragic heroin addiction and shattered relationships, but absolutely for his audacity, satiric outrage, and love of language. And also because of a couple simple family anecdotes.

When I was about twenty-three, I was reading Lenny's book *How to Talk Dirty and Influence People*. I happened to be carrying it with me on a visit to see my grandmother, who wasn't getting around very well at the time. I always had a special relationship with my grandmother. She loved to tell stories about hurtling down the avenues of the Upper West Side as a kid on her in-line roller skates ("We only needed two wheels!") and going dancing with my grandfather in San Francisco as newlyweds. I loved picking her brain about different eras in L.A., New York, and northern California. Funny enough, as a very modern woman and an assimilated Jew, she was my family memory of the immigrants who landed in the U.S. and spread from New York City to the midwest and the west coast. Growing up down the street from her, her house was my special sleep over getaway, with movies in my own little fort in the den and, always, M&Ms on the dominoes table. As a teacher in high school and community college, she'd written a number of technical grammar books and classroom teaching manuals. I still have copies of them and love looking at her name on the spines.

So on this visit, I stroll in with my long hair and what I thought was my alternative sensibility. She sees the book and says, "Oh, you're reading Lenny?"

Uh, yeah. You've heard of Lenny Bruce?

"Oh, yes. Your grandfather and I used to go see him all the time at the clubs in North Beach."

In my head, I'm recalling that "the clubs" he was playing were slightly spiffed-up strip clubs -- the "burlesque" houses of the '40s and '50s. Here I am thinking I'm pretty cool for reading Lenny Bruce, this underground icon, and my elderly Granny shows me how much cooler she was, far ahead of my time. Humbling, but funny.

Years later, my mother told me that when she was a young girl in L.A., my grandmother used to take her across town to go to a certain shoemaker, whose shop was rather inconvenient and out of the way. One day she said, "Do you know who that man is? That's Mr. Schneider -- Lenny Bruce's father."

I had plenty of reason to offer tribute to the late comedian. Like Genesis 10:10 and Jewbelation 10, Paul brewed our R.I.P.A. at ten percent alcohol. For inspiration, I was looking at beers brewed with rye. Seemed only appropriate that a nice Jewish beer company should finally be brewing with the sacred grain of our deli birthright. I loved Bear Republic's Hop Rod Rye, and Founders in the Midwest had some strong rye-recipe beers that were different from the intense double IPAs made by Dogfish Head, Stone, and Russian River.

After my trip to the distillery in Kentucky, where I saw how much rye was used in bourbon, I basically pulled my English-major version of describing what I wanted to Paul (much as I'd done with Simon in the beginning, when I'd said I wanted to experience the beer like "the best reuben sandwich"). I said, Make it as big and raunchy as you can, slightly obnoxious, but at the same time penetrating and profound.

And Paul looked at me and said, "Soooo... hoppy? Malty?"

Like Lenny Bruce himself, I wanted the beer to have an element of explosion and punch. Lenny Bruce was said by some to be a bit of an asshole, and he was clearly self-destructive. However, many have commented on a definite sweetness, a tenderness, a pronounced romantic streak about him personally. His sense of love and sincerity, I think, clearly came through in his yearning for a world without hypocrisy and hollow sentiment. As a performer, he had a great balance of strength and aggression, and also a palpable sense of idealism and hope. He loved to play with words, to claw at the American landscape, with the deepest sense of his own humanity and self-exploration. Was it unreasonable to aim to bring those elements together in the brewing?

Up to that point we had not made an IPA, though the style had become the fastest-growing style in American craft beer. Again, there were some existing rye IPAs, but I wanted to make a beer that would be uniquely He'brew. What Stone, Dogfish Head, Russian River, Lagunitas, and Bell's had done so beautifully was to build these giant, aggressive IPAs around hops. They tended to be a little lighter in color and body, even though the flavors were rich and intense. They focused on the bitterness and the hop flavor, and the floral and citrus pop, forward and unmistakable.

I loved drinking those beers, but I thought, Shmaltz is not going to compete with these guys. Why would I even want to? Let's do something different.

I talked with Paul about building this double IPA around the rye malt -- multiple rye malts -- and what I believe in brewing the technical term is a "shitload" of hops. I asked Paul to forge the hop profile to accentuate, complement, and contrast with the earthy, spicy nature of the rye malts. It ended up almost copper in color, just like a nice, swarthy Jewish beer should be.

When Paul designed this beer, he'd never used that much rye malt before. We knew that Bear Republic used fifteen to seventeen percent rye malt, so I said, Let's make it twenty!

When we put the rye malt into the mash the first time, it slurped up the water, forming an unwelcome, sticky paste, as any homebrewer will know. Of course, our double IPA would be dry-hopped (dumping in even more hops at the very end of the boil, as the wort cools) for a final blast of aroma and a touch of flavor. When the rye malt is absorbing more and more liquid, it leads to pretty big losses, and dry-hopping makes it even worse.

The losses were frightening. In the beginning, it was fifty to fifty-five percent yield -- forty-five percent loss. For the single batches, which generally kicked out about 1400 cases of original Genesis Ale, we'd end up packaging a little over seven hundred cases.

Gradually it got a little better. The brewers were great with experimenting. Dropping a healthy lining of rice hulls in the mash eased the process (though an early batch managed to freeze the rake of the lauter tun, and Chris, the lead brewer, had to crawl into the vat and grain out by hand something like eight hundred pounds of hot, wet, spent grains. Not fun). Longer and longer aging in the conditioning tanks, so the yeast would fall out more effectively, also helped ease the losses during filtration. But since I didn't own the brewery, there was only so much time I could ask to monopolize the tanks.

With a few tricks and a bit of nature, eventually they just had big losses, as opposed to catastrophic numbers. During the "hop crisis" of 2008-'09, when prices would go through the roof and we were caught with our pants firmly around our ankles, just the cost of the hops used for R.I.P.A. came to five dollars per case of packaged beer, more than even the packaging, or all the other ingredients combined.

With appropriate shock and awe, and what I thought was also truth in advertising, I wrote that our R.I.P.A. was brewed with "an obscene amount of malts and hops," far beyond "community standards" of taste and flavor. Being a rye double IPA -- an R.I.P.A. -- it connected beautifully as a memorial beer. The beer itself is bittersweet, as was Lenny's sense of satire and squandered optimism. Here's a guy who left an incredible comic legacy. Without him, there's no George Carlin or Richard Pryor, Eddie Murphy, Chris Rock, Dave Chappelle. He was literally a martyr for his cause. And of all the places he was arrested, the first time was in San Francisco, where he was charged with obscenity -- long after midnight, at an adult club, for saying *cocksucker*. "So I see there's a lot of cocksuckers here tonight. You know I wouldn't marry anyone who wasn't a cocksucker!"

All these places I hold as dynamic urban areas, cities I'm proud to be associated with -- San Francisco, New York, L.A., Chicago: in each city, the cops would threaten to revoke the alcohol licenses of club owners who dared to book him. That's how they silenced him -- booze laws. By putting a new beer into the world, I felt we were doing our tiny part to add to the meaning of Lenny Bruce's life and work. I have no idea how many people pick up on the whole shtick, but people have certainly loved the beer, which has become a staple of our lineup.

I sort of stumbled into one of my biggest launch events when I took part in another Jewish Music and Heritage Festival, this time at the 92nd Street Y. The festival producer Michael Dorf had started his avant-garde nightclub, the Knitting Factory, in the '80s at the age of twenty-three with his bar mitzvah savings. When I first realized we were going to put out a Lenny Bruce tribute, I had an idea much like the "40 Days" tour. I wanted to call it "Dirty Jews: A 40-Year Tribute to Lenny Bruce." In my mind, we'd get the coolest, most aggressive satiric comedians in the country. We'd do a Lenny Bruce circuit with people like David Cross and Sarah Silverman. I actually pitched this idea to the comedy team at Bill Graham Presents, who book some of the biggest comedy tours in the country. But in the end, much the same as my overtures toward Apple, Starbucks, and American Express, nothing came of it.

The year before at the Jewish Heritage Festival, I'd mentioned to Michael that 2006 would be the fortieth anniversary of Lenny Bruce's death, and that I was thinking about doing a tribute of some sort. Maybe we could tie in some comedy the next year?

Being the quintessential idea guy, I think he channeled my idea, and honestly forgot I'd said anything about it. When I talked to him in '06, he'd already put together the beginning stages of his own Lenny Bruce tribute event. He was even using the same picture of Lenny that Matt and I were using on our neck label -- the infamous mug shot from Miami, when Bruce was arrested for impersonating a priest. Perfect!

Michael is a marketing guru, and he has to be one of the most connected guys I've ever met. He pulled together a lineup of talent so far beyond anything I could ever manage that I quickly jumped aboard as the beer sponsor. He generously allowed us to make the night our national launch party.

The night would be the first big event of so many more that my new publicist Jesse would help to make so wildly successful. I had been introduced to him through an ex-girlfriend who mentioned he was planning to leave his PR job at a boutique record label in San Francisco to pick up free lance clients and to craft a small business for himself. After doing all my own PR, it was the perfect time for me to bring him on. As I'd mentioned earlier, committing to a long term PR strategy can be an very effective way to get the word out about niche brands and a small company, especially instead of advertising. I'd flirted with the idea of using publicists in the past but the usual routine of sending out an unimaginative one-sheet to the PR wire services had failed for me before. I needed someone with more personality and commitment. As an artist, himself -- a talented musician -- as well as an extremely nice guy, he brought the perfect balance of fun, creativity and determination to our media push. The Shmaltz Brewing shtick lent itself particularly well to Jesse's talents: cranking down phone and email lists and pitching new product releases and unusual promo events. He was and still is a PR machine.

I signed up as one of Jesse's first clients on retainer, and we built a media plan for our tenth anniversary rollout. He hounded journalists with just the right sense of urgency and brought in an impressive response to our R.I.P.A launch.

The emcee was Lewis Black, and the event featured comedians Todd Barry and Jeff Garlin, Judy Gold and Eugene Mirman. Jonathan Ames told one of the dirtiest, most hilarious stories I'd ever heard. And somehow, at the last minute, Michael managed to get Sarah Silverman as the headliner.

In 2006, I had a major hard-on for Sarah Silverman. I thought, If there's one woman I'm prepared to worship, she's the one.

After the show -- both Matt and I busted out suits for the occasion -- I'm in the V.I.P. reception area, and suddenly there she is, walking straight toward me.

Holy shit! Sarah Silverman! Genius, gorgeous, hilarious, Jewish!

She had on a face of stage makeup, and she was a little shorter than I imagined. Stumble, lunge -- I jump in front of her and blurt out, Thanks so much for doing this. I'm the beer sponsor. We make the Lenny Bruce beer.

Pause.

Here comes the magic moment. She'll look into my soul (or maybe my beer label) and see that my shtick is perfect for her, and that we're perfect for each other. She'll dump altar-boy Jimmy Kimmel, and we'll soar off to our own Promised Land.

She looks up, a bit glassy-eyed. Of course, I can't imagine how many people must accost her like this pretty much every day. And she says, "Oh, um, OK... Yeah." And she was gone.

Our sponsorship notwithstanding, using Lenny's image proved to be a bit of a tricky process. I knew his wife and his mother had long since passed away, and that he had one daughter who might be alive, but I could not track down any information about her, or who might control the estate.

I called Fantasy, the company that put out his recordings. No leads. I called HBO, which had produced a recent documentary. Nothing. At one point it seemed as though the estate of Frank Zappa was somehow involved – he and the Mothers opened the last concert Lenny Bruce ever performed at the Fillmore in San Francisco in 1965. Since I was unable to get in touch with anyone, I planned to donate some of the proceeds from the event, and later from beer sales, to free speech and civil rights organizations, including the Center for Constitutional Rights and the ACLU, which had originally been interested in my idea for the "Dirty Jews" tour.

After two years, I finally got an email from a lawyer in L.A. who said he was working with Lenny's daughter, Kitty. They were trying to get in touch with anyone who was using Lenny's images. We went through a quick, productive discussion about donating a portion of the proceeds to projects in L.A., and then I never heard back from him.

Before the Lenny Bruce idea, I generally shied away from specific celebrity overlap with the company. I want people to drink the beer on its own merits. People are always asking, "Have you sent the beer to Seinfeld? Mel Brooks? The Beastie Boys?" When I first started He'brew, it seemed like everywhere

I went someone claimed to know Mike D from the Beastie Boys, and could *"hook me up, bro."* Nothing ever came of any of it.

I sent a bottle through a connection to Steven Spielberg. Got a note back from a PR assistant that said, "Steven thanks you for the beer. L'Shana Tova." Surprisingly sweet, and I appreciated that they even bothered to send a note -- but not exactly a bankable endorsement. (See Appendix.) I knew none of these people needed me, and none of them needed free beer. It was also insightful to hear how many comedians and entertainers over the age of thirty had management who said that their client didn't drink alcohol, or was in "a program." Based on the comedians who came though the club I worked at in New Orleans, at some point every one of them seemed to be enjoying the hell out of their vices.

Around this time I got a one-paragraph taste of my own semi-exalted position in the Jewish community when I was asked to write a blurb for the highly anticipated launch of *Judaism for Dummies.* I read the advance copy they sent, and it was surprisingly good, with interpretations of holidays or Torah stories that remained open-minded and engaging, and a few clever bits about Jewish food and pop culture. When it came out, the inside cover featured blurbs from then still-Democratic Senator Joe Lieberman, three nationally known rabbis who were writers, a professor and the head of a foundation, and me. Evidently, a few beer labels and shtick-y press releases qualified me to comment on five thousand years of tradition. Happy to be invited to the party.

One of my best friends, Jim, had a magnificent wedding in Woodside, at his family's house, where we'd spent so many hours of our youth lounging by the pool, throwing the frisbee, playing quarters, and returning for late night cool-downs after Dead shows. That same weekend, my college class of 1991 gathered for our fifteenth-year reunion. Even then almost all my closest friends had at least one, if not two or three, kids.

At the reunion there were kids in Baby Bjorns, kids in red wagons, kids in little Stanford shirts. I couldn't help but think about my own arrested development. Taking a little look at my peers suggested that it might be an appropriate time to consider accelerating the transition from my vagabond life on the road. I didn't even own a plant I had to worry about, and I wasn't doing such a great job of taking care of myself.

When Matt and I went to the Great American Beer Festival that fall, we absolutely damaged ourselves. It was a rookie move. For a ten-year veteran, I should've known better. Wednesday night, thanks to my beer broker Sean, who made arrangements with Chris, the owner of Falling Rock, we had our ritual pre-GABF party to launch our new beers and hype of the progress of the company. That year we were promoting Genesis 10:10, R.I.P.A., and Jewbelation 10, all ten-percent beers. I was wrecked before the official festival even started.

At the convention center on Thursday, I snuck into the closed-off downstairs, found a darkened coffee stand and curled up in one of their booths. I napped for forty-five minutes before the evening session started. At our table at the fest, a generous soul came by, took one look at Matt, and gave him an Emergen-C.

For the first several years of the business, constantly overwhelmed and stressed about the new venture and also in a committed relationship, I really didn't drink that much. For the four and a half years on the road in the second era of Shmaltz Brewing, I was trying to figure out the balance between working all day and night and weekends surrounded by beer, and remaining effective and productive working sixty to eight to often many more hours per week. Like so many entrepreneurs, my life was my work. The fact that I didn't have a home for that whole period perhaps added to the exertion.

On ride-withs, the accounts love to taste the goods while you're standing there -- especially when you're the owner of the company -- and they love to bust out something special to try, to say thanks for coming in. Trying to sell and sip all day, and then promote at events or Happy Hours with wholesale reps; wanting to taste all those interesting beers that you can't get outside the region; even just seeing good friends around the country -- it's exciting to catch up with everyone, and they all want to show you a good time in their home town, and to bring you to the good beer spots. Many have day jobs, so it's a great excuse for them to kick out the jams for a night or two.

That was pretty much every night for me... for years. I would reward myself with a juicy vacation, usually for a couple of weeks in the spring, and then get back on the road to try to keep it all cranking. Whether it was the demands of the beer job or my particular disposition, indulging too much became routine.

I'd been operating for years on a river of energy. Sometimes I'd be running on autopilot (even with new beers, the pitches can get a bit repetitive), but often I just felt completely fired-up. Learning to drink for a living is like working out a muscle: you get better at it.

I'm not saying it's a lofty, long-term strategy for business or life. I'm just saying that Frank Sinatra said it, and he was the Chairman: "I feel sorry for people that don't drink. When they wake up in the morning, that's the best they're gonna feel all day."

CHAPTER 16

Step Right Up!
Welcome To The Freak Show

"Your body is not a temple, it is an amusement park."
-- Anthony Bourdain, *Kitchen Confidential*

"I guess if circus sideshow freaks are more mainstream than Jews, Shmaltz is going mainstream."
-- My response to a question from a Brooklyn journalist in 2007

In the fall of 2006, a lawyer in New York, a nice Jewish boy from Manhattan, approached me about a client he represented. A licensing specialist who'd been at our Lenny Bruce tribute event at the 92nd Street Y, Dave said he'd been impressed by the product and by what we pulled off. He said he was charged with the task of obtaining licensees for a non-profit arts organization called Coney Island U.S.A.

Now celebrating its thirtieth anniversary, Coney Island U.S.A. stands as a landmark and a cherished institution. The maestro, Dick Zigun, who started the non-profit, serves as *de facto* mayor of Coney Island, strolling the neighborhood to see friends and hoods alike, quoted in every article that comes out about the death, the rebirth, and the eternal controversies of Coney.

Coney Island somehow seems to be in a constant, inconclusive period of profound transition. Every year has been either the end of an era or the dawn of a new age, or both. From the long-lost days of Elephant hotels, giant public baths, and enormous amusement parks serving millions of New Yorkers escaping the heat, Coney Island has long been known as "America's Playground." Through divisive attempts at large-scale urban planning mixed with an obvious air of decay and neglect, the neighborhood remains packed with families and tourists -- literally millions of visitors still assuming Coney Island is their kinda town.

Years before they became our new collaborators in the Craft Lager project, CIUSA began hosting a giant arts event called the Mermaid Parade. Tens if not hundreds of thousands of revelers flock to the farthest edges of Brooklyn to star in a sweaty, anarchic pageant of tattooed, roller-skating, hula-hooping, half-naked mermaids, pirates, and sea goblins, with board-member judges expecting to be bribed with treats and trinkets and a New York pop-cult celebrity king and queen reigning over the festivities. It's a spectacle.

But CIUSA's main attraction involves running the last remaining circus sideshow in a fixed location in America -- what's known in traditional lore as the Freak Show. Renowned staff performers include Heather Holliday, the world's most petite yet provocative sword swallower; Insectavora, a face-tattooed, whip-cracking, nationally recognized fire-eating artist; and Serpentina, the house snake-dancer with her partner, a seventy-five-pound, twelve-foot albino python.

Coney Island had seen it all -- beds of nails, an electric chair stunt, contortionists, and a new array of genetic oddities each summer. Natural-born freaks such as the Wolfman, Black Scorpion, and Seal Boy, Mat Fraser, with his dashing British charm, drumming talent, performance art sensibility, and Thalidomide-induced flipper arms. Nic Sin, the three-foot, 6.66-inch rock-star midget and straightjacket escape artist, would soon join us to brew the inaugural batches at Coney Island Brewing Company, the World's Smallest Brewery.

The superstar emcee, Donny Vomit, showcases a signature piece known as the Human Blockhead, originally credited to Melvin Burkhardt, a famed (and Jewish) carny from the '50s and '60s. Story goes that Robert Ripley coined the phrase, remarking, "Wow, Melvin, you sure are a blockhead." Eight performances a day during the summer months, Donny opens by hammering a sixty-penny nail into his skull, "All for the demented pleasure of you fine folks sitting here today." Taking it up a notch, Mr. Vomit then jams a running power drill into his face: "Hey, look at me, I'm *at work!*"

Dave, the licensing lawyer, approached me and said, "What you did with the Lenny Bruce beer was fantastic. Would you consider doing a tribute beer for Coney Island?" I'd never thought about anything like that before. When people asked, "The beers are really great. Have you ever considered a more generic brand?" I'd reply that I hadn't started this just to be Jeremy's Beer Company. I started it to make He'brew.

We were completely slammed at that point, consistently up eighty to one hundred percent every year. I had hired Angela as my full-time assistant, Jesse was on retainer for some part-time PR help, and Matt, still at his full-time job, served only occasionally as my on-call art director for specific projects. The concept of taking on an entire new brand seemed pretty absurd.

Joining me to hit a holiday beer night, Matt and I drove down to D.C. On the trip, we started kicking the Coney Island idea around. I told him the first time I'd been to Coney Island was probably in 2003, when I went to the Mermaid Parade. It was a rainy day, and I took the Q train with Peter to check out the scene. The rain limited the crowd, though it never dampened the enthusiasm for the pageantry.

Afterward, we went to a bar called Ruby's on the boardwalk. The place was full of dudes who looked like they'd been working out in jail. I kept thinking of that part in *Dazed and Confused*, when the guy named Clint says, "I came here to do two things -- kick some ass and drink some beer." Luckily, Ruby's never runs out of beer.

I'd never really dreamed of running off to join the circus, and I didn't have some lurid fetish for clowns. It wasn't like my grandmother grew up in Brighton Beach. My father, though a prankster in his own way, would probably have been more a mark than a carny. My good friends the Mullin brothers were both born with six fingers and/or six toes, as was their sister, though all had them removed, and they rarely seemed to regret losing that potential career path. Generally speaking, the closest things to sideshows I'd participated in were the parking lot scenes at Grateful Dead shows. That freak show had quite a different vibe, with hacky-sack circles, miracle tickets, and veggie burritos -- not foot-long Polish sausages, funnel cake, and potential gang fights.

What we did have, however, was a sensibility about artistry and uniqueness, mixed with sincerity... and shmaltz. As Matt and I talked about the idea of starting another brand, we sensed the rivulets, the tributaries of potential. My first thought was, What if we did a whole line of Coney Island freak beers?

We were selling six-packs of our originals, Genesis and Messiah, but by then we also had three other beers we felt ranked up there with some of the best craft beers in the country in terms of creativity, recipe, design, and execution. I figured, what if we used this as an opportunity to go totally bonkers?

I thought about contacting some of our favorite craft brewers, like the guys at Allagash, Elysian, Ithaca, and Terrapin, and asking them to do a beer they probably wouldn't make for themselves -- something that was too weird or experimental, something that didn't fit their portfolio. I thought the idea would highlight just how far contract-brewing could go. I liked the concept: A craft-beer freak show.

To this day, I get excited about it. People in the business are doing some bold collaborations now, and in 2007 we would have been right in the forefront. But I knew it would have been harder than it needed to be, with multiple packaging lines, labels pallets, bottle styles, case configurations, shipping, and potential distribution conflicts.

I don't remember how it started, but we were beginning to think of Coney Island as something potentially a little more... "mainstream." The Cyclone, the Wonder Wheel, Houdini, the Marx Brothers -- there'd been a literal parade of star power through the place's well-documented history. In its heyday, Coney was where the escalator was invented for moving masses, through parks lit up way ahead of Times Square. And of course there was America's annual freedom binge, Nathan's Hot Dog Eating Contest, held in the birthplace of the world-famous invention.

There are over eight million people in greater New York, a bit more than the population of the entire Bay Area, which boasts nearly fifty breweries. New York City has four. Brooklyn Brewery has been leading the cause for over twenty years, dominating local craft beer in the city. Chelsea Brewing, on the west side of Manhattan, has purposefully stayed pretty small and doesn't distribute much packaged beer.

The only other brewpub to not only survive but thrive in New York is Heartland Brewing, then with four locations (now seven) in the tourist-heavy commercial areas. They began brewing the beers in the restaurants as traditional brewpubs, but several years before, they opened a production plant in Brooklyn to feed all the locations from a central facility. The relative newcomers at Six Point Craft Ales were making big waves in the New York craft beer scene, a welcomed, and much-enjoyed, draft option at the local bars we frequented.

With only four breweries in the whole city, we started thinking: What if we didn't go so far out, but made a beer that might appeal to a lot of different people, instead of our usual hyper-niche target? From somewhere in the cosmic soup, the word "lager" made an appearance in our conversation for the first time.

As much progress as we've made in craft brewing in the last thirty years, ninety-five percent of the beers consumed in this country are still mass-marketed lagers. More than anything, craft beer is seen as an alternative to those styles. Generally speaking, great craft breweries make wonderful ales[15].

I can, of course, recognize that most of the country, still in the early stages of American beer evolution, asks for a light lager, the closest thing to Budweiser they can get[16]. But that doesn't mean I necessarily want to give it to them. There are plenty of examples of very flavorful lagers -- bocks, schwartz beers, dopplebocks, eisbocks, rauchbiers. Some breweries had already started making imperial pilsners and extreme Octoberfests -- bigger, stronger, hoppier. We thought, what if we did a whole line of lagers? We could leave He'brew to be pretty much all ales. If we did some interesting, unusual lagers, we'd have an obvious point of differentiation. The progression could parallel what Anchor

---

15 Though much to our excitement, many of the best regional craft breweries are now starting to introduce ambitious, innovative lagers. There seems to be an interest in truly demolishing the myth that American lagers need to be watered down, adjunct-ridden, and forgettable. Night of the Lagers with Beer Advocate and Manitou Craft Lager Festival -- keep it rolling. Let's make Bud's claim as "The Great American Lager," as irrelevant as it is insincere.
16 True story from bartending at Crescent City Brewhouse in New Orleans, circa 1992. This happened almost daily. Guy walks up to the bar: "Hey man, gimme a Bud Light." Sorry, sir, we make all our own beers here. "Oh. man, no problem. Gimme a Coors Light, then." No I mean we actually brew all the beers right here on the premises. Can I pour you a pilsner? "I'm really sorry. Just give me a Miller Lite instead."

Steam and Sam Adams had done the generation before: taken recipes for European lager styles, and upped the ante. We thought, why don't we take it one step further, bringing American craft ale sensibility to traditional lager brewing?

It was clear we had a real opportunity, something that fed off the notoriety of Coney Island. Unlike He'brew, the Chosen Beer, the brand "Coney Island" already existed in people's minds across the country and around the world. Coney Island unquestionably suggested an image of something fun, perhaps historical -- a little wild, an escape. A chance to "come out and *playy-ayyy*." Matt, Paul, and I decided to focus on creating a line of craft-brewed lagers with ambitious recipes. They'd be craft-brewed lagers for connoisseurs. I took to calling our flagship Coney Island Lager a "pitcher beer for beer geeks."

The idea was not necessarily to get the Bud drinkers to drink our beer. The microbrew industry has this notion of "gateway" beers, which help ease the transition from mass market to craft brewing. I always kind of disliked that idea. Why make something medium for the sake of being medium?

On the other hand, if you drink a double IPA or an imperial stout (or a barrel-aged, multiple-yeast-strain, funked-up wild-fermentation lacto-bretto one-of-a kind-o), sometimes it's nice to have a few more beers, whether they be a bit lower in alcohol or just a bit more subdued in flavor, in between.[17]

As Matt and I were thinking this through, we had a couple of meetings with the folks who ran the Sideshow. They wanted to leave the beer styles up to us, as long as we included the shtick and the energy of the Sideshow in the marketing. For us, that's a no-brainer. That's what we get off on.

They thought we'd design the beer labels from their existing Sideshow banners. They had an extremely talented house artist on their board, Marie

---

17 A quick, vehement written comeback for all those critics/writers/beer pundits lately decrying "extreme" beer and calling for a return to "session" beers as proof of true craftsmanship -- and because they get too loaded and can't drive home. 1. To those of us who simply like robust and flavorful beers better, most session beers are *boring*; 2. There are already a ton of session beers out there, many brutally bland, though some flavorful, nuanced, and delightful. Why add more?; 3. Session beers will not make anyone other than pub owners any money. Few consumers care enough about a well-balanced, subtle English mild or quaffable bitter to pay a craft-beer premium for it. If one operates a pub (or a brewery that was paid off before the 20th century), then sessions can certainly be useful -- go for it. If you have a packaging operation, you already know that the shelves do not need another middle-of-the-road six-pack that your distributor doesn't want to carry, that you'll need to sell for $10.99 anyway if you want to have health insurance and a car allowance for your sales reps. This, by the way, is coming from a guy whose fastest growing product is a 5.5% amber lager.

Roberts, who'd painted an ongoing series of brightly-colored carnival banners. They'd licensed the art to a company for bike messenger bags, coasters, and t-shirts, but none of those projects got very far off the ground. Remembering what a headache it was to transfer Tracy's real-world artwork to the original labels, I pushed Matt to seek our own artist, who could work directly in the digital medium.

Matt's wife, Laura, had a friend who worked with her at a teenybopper fashion catalog company, a guy who recently had been named one of the top ten tattoo artists in New York. We asked him to start with the unofficial logo of Coney Island, the original logo for the famed Steeplechase Park from the 1880s, known as the "Tillie" face.

The Tillie face was by then in the public domain: The hair parlor, the dry cleaner, the sausage vendors, and pretty much everyone in and around the area of the amusement park were using it. What we didn't want to do was just recreate it. We asked Dave, the artist, to take that logo and create an edgy, modern version -- something proprietary and truly unique. He abstracted a kid's face with a huge smile and a pointy haircut, with piercings and face tattoos loosely referencing snake patterns, Donny's handlebar mustache, Angelica's vertical streak, and a Riddler-style question mark spiral.

In early spring of 2007, I came back from Morocco on a two-day stopover in New York before returning to San Francisco. I thought I'd use the time to button up some of the details for Coney Island, so I went to talk to my wholesalers, S.K.I. We were thinking about putting out the first Sideshow lager for the summer, but we hadn't decided yet whether we'd do it in six-packs, 22 ounce bottles, or draft only. I think S.K.I. saw it as an opportunity to have what would become one of a small handful of genuine New York brands in the market.

Ralph saw the vision. Actually, the moment we showed an early draft of the logo and mentioned the brand name to Ralph and a few colleagues -- Paul, the off-premise manager, and Claude, the on-premise manager -- I knew we were on to something. Their eyes lit up. Ralph suggested, "It would be so great if you could get the beer brewed in Brooklyn or New York City somewhere. That would be the perfect hook."

The problem was, there were only four functioning breweries locally.

Brooklyn Brewery didn't have enough capacity to brew even its own beers. As mentioned earlier, Brooklyn brews a little of its own beer, some of the draft and more of the very special releases and 750s, in New York City, while the majority comes from F.X. Matt upstate. Chelsea was out: they were too small, and I didn't really want to deal with brewing on the side of town farthest from Coney Island. It also wasn't the right fit for the Coney Island shtick. And Six Point was booming, and already could not keep up with demand.

So Ralph says, "What about that guy at Greenpoint? He might have capacity." Of all the local breweries, I really knew next to nothing about Greenpoint Beer Works. They made the Heartland beers for the chain of centrally located brewpubs. Those restaurants seemed incredibly successful, in some of the most popular spots in New York.

Though neither of us had any idea, Greenpoint's production facility turned out to be five blocks from Matt's house in Prospect Heights. They were producing about five thousand barrels just for the restaurants, which is an amazing success, especially given New York's otherwise unsuccessful brewpub past. By contrast, my production for the entire country, for thirty wholesalers and a couple thousand retailers and bars, only surpassed five thousand barrels in 2008. At the time, it was even less.

When we went to meet with the brewery manager at Greenpoint, it was hard for me to project how much beer we were going to need. I had never done anything intended for a wider audience, especially a lager. Would we need twenty kegs a month, or two hundred? It was a draft-only brewery, so we planned to do kegs in Brooklyn and, later, bottles up in Saratoga. They were typically scrappy, small-production brewery guys. I really liked the whole crew. Greenpoint had a thirty-barrel system with a few 30-bbl. fermenters, a couple of sixties and, later, one ninety. By contrast, Saratoga started at one hundreds and had a 300-bbl. bad boy. Given the smaller batches, Greenpoint could easily crank up, or scale back, on, production, as demand set our needs.

Kelly at GPBW had brewed in the Pacific Northwest, and he'd been in the business longer than I had. He was a west coast beer kind of guy, about my age. We nailed down the basics within forty-eight hours. Matt and I couldn't believe how quickly it came together.

The association with a local brewery gave us instant credibility in the neighborhood. We could walk in anywhere in Brooklyn and explain that we were sharing profits with a beloved local arts organization, with a staff, designers, and brewers who all lived and worked right here in Brooklyn. That really got us off the ground, and it was one hundred percent Ralph's idea. I hadn't even known about or considered Greenpoint.

Eventually both the business relationship and the brewing would turn sour, but in the beginning things were great. For all the pain and suffering He'brew had gone through over the years, this seemed like it might actually be a relatively smooth project. A first!

The plan was to make a robust amber lager, light enough to have "drinkability," but also complex enough that real craft drinkers would find it interesting. The recipe ended up being a bit of a blend between a darker amber Munich lager Paul had designed for Olde Saratoga (a Great American Beer Festival award-winner) and a hoppier, lighter-colored lager Kelly had been making, which had more of an aggressive pale ale hop profile, but was brewed with a Czech Pilsner yeast. We bulked up the malt profile a bit, bumped up the hop recipe, and dry-hopped with Cascade, the mother of all American craft hops. It turned out to hit just the right balance, as I wrote for the label: "a mashup of European brewing tradition and strongly characteristic of American craft." A damn tasty and very balanced beer. I was excited.

In the beginning, everyone played nice. Kelly and Paul were having easy conversations. Things were done on time, and the Sideshow was supportive and helpful. Everyone was very positive and optimistic.

At first we were draft-only. Then we decided to add 22 ounce bottles as well up in Saratoga. The logo was so kick-ass, we just had to get it on a bottle. In Brooklyn, we were making thirty-barrel batches, sixty kegs at a time. It took off right from the beginning, and Kelly threw in the second and third batches right away. We were selling maybe a hundred kegs a month that first summer.

Creating the branding, the naming, and the marketing for Coney surprisingly felt a lot like He'brew, but with a completely different sense of history and context. On the original Coney Island Lager label, I barked: "Step Right Up and Witness the Delectable Alchemy! Discover the Thrill of Old-World Brewing Conjoined with Beguiling New-World Flavor!" It was a combination of old and new, funky and bizarre, yet open and approachable. A freak-show version of family-friendly. We couldn't have done it if we hadn't already gone through all this with He'brew. Remember the three pillars of Shmaltz? Really, the same three applied to Coney Island -- quality, community, shtick.

He'brew will always be a niche product. That's what I like about it. As I've said, I'd rather be the big (or only) fish in a small pond.

It's interesting that outside of New York, in most places, He'brew still leads Coney Island in sales. Within New York, however, Coney Island was clearly going to take off in a big way for our portfolio. It quickly grew to be significantly bigger than He'brew for us in New York, which was bittersweet for me, for sure. I couldn't believe I'd spent eleven years of my life creating equally high-quality products and promoting the hell out of them. And then this clown-faced beer waltzes in poised to outsell my dancing-rabbi babies, in just a matter of months, by a margin of ten to one in certain neighborhoods. Don't get me wrong -- I'm thankful it's working. But part of me was like, Come on! Where have you sales people and buyers and customers been the last ten years?

For whatever reason, my juju never fails to hit its share of speed bumps. One of the first days we launched the original Coney beer was for the Mermaid Parade, in June 2007. It was a glorious, sunshine-y summer day. I didn't know the Sideshow very well yet. They were operating their concessions out of a tiny space called the Freak Bar, with maybe three bar stools and a pass-though window. I had no idea what to expect.

With at least a hundred thousand people in Coney Island for the parade, this was by far the most high-profile thing we'd ever done. We had to fight our way to the bar just to check it out.

When we get there, the Sideshow bar staff is totally overwhelmed, completely unprepared. And the beer is warm. There's no ice, and no beer in the fridges as backup.

I lost my shit. The problem was, I didn't know who I was supposed to be mad at -- myself for not seeing this coming? The Sideshow, for the same? Standing in front of Matt, I just needed a moment to scream. Then I pushed

251

my way down the sidewalk to the bodega on the block, asking if they had ice.

They did, so I ran back to the Sideshow and grabbed an intern, a long-haired rocker kid with a nose ring. I gave him a hundred dollars to run out to get all the ice I'd secured from the bodega. He came back and filled buckets to try to chill the beer. And then they ran out of cups.

I'm thinking, You've got to be kidding me. Finally, they simply ran out of beer.

I've done my best to convince myself over the years that the little injustices don't really matter. I want to be a perfectionist, as do Matt and most of the people I try to work with. But it doesn't mean the world needs you to be, or somehow rewards you for all your anxious attention.

In the Sideshow's defense, this was a scrappy, non-profit arts organization that was essentially running a snack counter. They were winging it, and nobody was prepared. All in all, it was a terrible success. They sold a lot of beer, and we got a ton of new customers in exactly the right setting for our new brand, as well as lot of media coverage, including Russian TV and a Japanese newspaper article. In the end, the Mermaid Parade kicked off our launch summer with a bang.[18]

From the very beginning, Coney Island was sort of liberating for me. I used to tell the sales reps, you can hurt my feelings with the things you say about He'brew, but you can't hurt my feelings with the things you say about Coney Island. He'brew is my soul and my passion. Coney is our jam. It's *supposed* to be a party.

One of my favorite accounts was Manitoba's, in the East Village. Handsome Dick Manitoba was one of the true icons of the New York punk rock scene, with his notorious Jewish Afro. His band, the Dictators, were essentially a punk-rock bar mitzvah band. The bar had six draft lines, and when we first walked in, the guy running it was wearing a Coney Island belt buckle. Turned out to be a Coney Island fanatic. Kevin added our beer in place of Yuengling, "America's Oldest Brewery." He even went online and sourced a

---

18 Perfect timing for Shmaltz: CIUSA had recently received help from the city of New York to purchase their building, which allowed them to take over the Army Recruiting Center in the front corner on Surf Avenue. They have since expanded the Freak Bar into the previous Coney military outpost and have become our number one account during the summer months, flying through bombers of all our styles. Draft has started to make a more consistent appearance, and we've found the perfect home for our craft lager lineup.

killer backlit Coney Lager sign (paid for it himself!), and the place has carried Coney Island ever since. We regularly do events with them, sponsoring punk-rock DJ nights and the Gotham Girls roller derby team's after-parties.

Those were the kind of guys we were appealing to with Coney Island, at East Village places like Doc Holliday's, the Riviera, and Marshall Stack. As the local beer-drinking scene in New York grew more sophisticated in its tastes, as new accounts were opening every month, and with restaurants finally coming around to better beer, we were perfectly primed to participate.

By early '07, I'd completed (survived) the ten-year anniversary of Shmaltz Brewing Company. We'd put out Jewbelation 8, 9, and 10, as well as Genesis 10:10 and Bittersweet Lenny's R.I.P.A. After all those years of making the distributor and retailer rounds, I'd lashed together what proved to be a rather solid distribution network.

After several years of working with these same wholesalers, the few that had dropped off because of slow payments, weak sales, or buyouts left me with a reliable group to whom I could feed these new products. The beer company that had started in Jewish delis and at bar mitzvahs was becoming more about creating ambitious, high-end craft beers than simply confining itself to gatherings of members of the tribe.

Even as the brand seemed to expand its reach to the better beer enthusiasts around the country, I am so pleased that I never had to compromise my vision for He'brew as a truly *Jewish* brand. In fact, digging deeper into the traditions and adding even wilder layers of shtick only seemed to complement our efforts to make even more ambitious beer recipes, flavors, and labels.

You don't have to be Jewish to love He'brew (this slogan stolen straight from Levy's Rye), but if you're interested in or willing to engage in the reasons the shtick informs the beer, and vice versa, there's a narrative to the interplay between the malts and the punchlines that I hope inspires a deeper investigation. Very few (if any) "Jewish" products on the shelves at the grocery store have tickled these same ribs.

As the shtick got more intense, so too did the booze. In 2006, three of our beers were ten-percent alcohol, and they would continue to rise, depending on the occasion. Among other things, that did a fair amount of damage to my body. My taste buds were constantly titillated, and our sense of our success was more apparent than ever, but my body wasn't in the best of shape.

I'd been asked to speak at the Extreme Beer Festival, sponsored by the guys at *Beer Advocate* in Boston. Begun by the Alström brothers, Jason and Todd, *Beer Advocate* started around the same time as I did. Methodically building their reputation over the years, they now preside over an empire of craft-beer junkies from around the country and the world. They do reviews, tastings, and events to foster this community. Smartly, they do a little bit in every part of the country, helping their devoted following find each other, from beer cellars to neighborhood bars and well-loved specialty festivals. *BA* (now a website and a nationally distributed magazine) stands as both cause and effect of what many of us have experienced as a sea change in our boutique beer world. They've created a sustaining buzz in the industry, and some occasional healthy controversy. Their success (along with Rate Beer, another hugely influential, social-networking beer-enthusiast site) has reflected, as well as driven, the broader success of craft beer in the U.S.

My talk for Extreme Beer Fest that day was "How It Took Ten Years of Radical Jewish Brewing to Create a National Success." (Hey, it worked that day. Why not keep it rolling?) For me, the invitation to speak crystallized so many elements of my business that had changed so much in such a short time. I was thrilled. I was being asked to speak as the warmup act for arguably the biggest celebrity in the craft beer world, Sam Calagione from Dogfish Head Brewing. He'd started a couple of years before I did. I read his book, *Brewing Up a Business* -- we're the same age, we graduated the same year, we studied mostly the same things. He got into brewing as a hobby, which grew into a passion. He distributed his own beer in the beginning. He somehow did everything I had done -- starting a brand and putting out a few beers at first -- but then he did everything that I'd done *while also* starting a brewery, personally brewing much of the beer, changing legislation in Delaware, starting a restaurant, and even making all his own tap handles. All while I'd ... contract-brewed... and stressed all the way out, just from that.

To this day, I have a bit of a complex about some of the top craft guys -- Sam, Vinnie, Adam (yeah, yeah, don't *tell* him), Rob at Allagash. So many of us are around the same age. Greg and his partner Steve started Stone Brewing the same year I began Shmaltz. The two Floyd Brothers and their dad Floyd opened in 1996. Same with Jim and Jason Ebel at Two Brothers. The Norgroves at Bear Republic started the same year as I did, and run a multi-million-dollar pub and beloved national craft brand. A lot of people around my age were a lot more financially successful, and had created a lot more buzz. They were often the minds, if not also the hands, behind the actual brewing. I knew that they were they were the pioneers, building the excitement and the demand, for the larger craft beer movement and what Shmaltz has been able to participate in over the last few years.

The audience at Extreme Beer Fest was a hardcore group, many of whom likely knew a lot more about beer than I even did. They're the guys at the epicenter of the scene – beer geeks, *BA*ers and Rate Beer fanatics, homebrewers, and avid enthusiasts. Meanwhile, I represented the two dirty words in craft -- contract brewer.

I made sure to create some rapport from the get-go, so we could have some fun. I wasn't about to make any claims, telling these people what they should think about my products. If I'm at a tasting in a store, I'll gladly tell people what they're tasting and why they should respect and buy our beers. But this was a different situation.

Starting with my self-deprecating dirty-word intro, I told some tales from the road and some punchlines. I said, It's important to realize I am advocating for this family of small businesses called craft beer everywhere I go, in every pitch to every grocery store buyer, every bar owner, at every community event. With enough shtick, enough sincerity, and enough flowing pitchers of ten percent R.I.P.A. and Jewbelation, the crowd seemed to appreciate that we were serious about making outstanding beers.

Then it was Sam's turn -- the main event. One of the Dogfish managers, a big tall guy, helped Sam wade through a throng of well-wishers. It looked like the heavyweight champ making his way to the ring, like the parting of the Red Sea. Matt and I looked at each other. A beer guy on one side of the room, referencing one of Dogfish's best known IPAs yelled out sports-stadium-style, "NINE-ty MIN-ute!" Clap, clap, clap clap clap. Someone on the other side shouted out, "ON-ne TWEN-ty!" Clap, clap, clap clap clap. Back and forth, rising to a fever pitch. People were going nuts.

Though the craft beer community is typically a very friendly, supportive community, I sometimes get a bit of flak. Someone will ask, "If you're not a brewer, where do the recipes come from?" Or, "Don't you want to make your own beer?" And those are legitimate questions. My honest answer is that I love to taste the flavors, but I didn't want to be the brewer. I absolutely love to eat, but I really don't have any interest in cooking. I didn't know how to design a website, either, so I hired someone to do it. (Actually, first Christopher and then Matt did it for free, for a long time.) I hired a trademark lawyer (eventually), and an accountant (finally -- twelve years in). Label printer, publicist, t-shirt maker... I describe what I want, and if I do it right, eventually we end up with something much better than I could ever have done myself, or even imagined.

I'd come a long way from the early days of my turkey reuben analogy. Working with Paul on new beers, I got to the point where I could clarify directions to the balance of flavors, the overall malt profiles, alcohol content, and the specific hop varieties. I'll say, I'd like to stay away from black patent malts and focus more on caramels. Let's add some oatmeal or wheat, pilsner malt, pale rye or crystal rye. And so on. Paul and I sampled a lot of different beers together, and he's been able to calibrate his recipes to my tastebud preferences -- much the same way Matt has been able to fulfill, and far surpass, my vision for the aesthetics of our brands.

It's really just an evolving version of exactly what I've been doing since I started. In 2008, Jay Brooks wrote an article for an issue of *Beer Advocate* that profiled six "Bad-Ass Beer Advocates." He wrote, "Shmaltz is arguably making some of the best contract-brewed beer in America." There are caveats in that sentence, but there are a lot of companies that contract brew part, if not all, of their beers, including Sam Adams, Brooklyn, Harpoon, Blue Point, Southampton, 21st Amendment, Six Point, Pretty Things... And I drink them all. Great company to keep.

Matt came down with me to Washington D.C. for the Strong Beer Festival at the Brickskeller, a big supporter of ours over the years. I did my song and dance for another family of beer fanatics at the Brick's annual gathering. Super-mensch Dave Alexander generously hosted us, as always, offering what will likely be called the Michael Jackson suite for eternity (the iconic beer writer, not the pop king). He also mentioned that the room had recently served as the Tomme Arthur suite (of Lost Abbey and Port Brewing).

Anyone familiar should fight off the mental image of Michael Jackson, Tomme Arthur, and me snuggling in one of those Brickskeller faux-brass twin beds. I certainly did.

Why a dozen high-alcohol samples of the region's finest extreme beers wasn't enough to satisfy our evening's pleasure, I cannot say. But when our waitress, Kristin, bought us double shots of Jack Daniels and suggested a group move to the freak-show-themed bar Palace of Wonders for Coney Islands and more whiskey, we bounced through the rabbit hole and headed for the existential hangover certainly awaiting on the other side.

Also that month, Big Daddy Dave Keene's infamous Barleywine Festival at San Francisco's Toronado offered seventy or more ways to leave your lover and punish your liver. I did both. Or rather, I punished my liver and my girlfriend prepared to leave me. A whirlwind romance had started with a slightly buzzed cell-phone conversation outside Falling Rock at GABF in the fall with a soon to be not-completely-blind date. She would receive the first "I love you" I'd said to anyone since my divorce. She also challenged me to think about money, family, and a future beyond the road that would continue to elude me and compromise our relationship.

I was inspired, however, to throw all the modest profits from two years of Shmaltz into a IRA for myself and begin a commitment to a life of more Priceline hotels and fewer foldouts couches. Progress?

Perhaps you can see where this is heading: south. I went on from San Francisco to L.A., to Craig and Jsun's warm hospitality and cold He'brew at the new The Other Room on Abbot Kinney in Venice for a Jewish community event that we'd been planning a long time. The crowd was too busy with each other to care about my shpiel, so I ended up yelling over the din a quick history of the company. Then I let them go strap on the Jewish beer goggles.

We partied the night away, and when I woke up, my body rejected me. After weeks of beer festivals and tenth anniversary goblets, I don't believe I had one molecule of hydration in me. Gingerly traveling north, somewhere outside San Luis Obispo, I managed not to throw up on the poor college girl serving me soup and dry toast, and I drove on to Monterey to see my cousin.

Stumbling to his door, I said, I think I need to go lie down. Now.

For a much-needed break from the self-inflicted damage, that spring I celebrated Passover in Morocco, a several-thousand-year-old Arab empire where alcohol is generally illegal, and what beer that does exist is rather undesirable. Family friends invited me to visit one of the few remaining Jewish families in Meknes, where we commemorated, with only four small cups of libation, the liberation of the Hebrews.

CHAPTER 17

They Came, They Tried To Kill Us, We Survived, Let's Drink: Crisis, Resolution, Crisis, And The Ultimate Excel Spreadsheet

While I was specifically not rocking the casbah in Morocco, Matt was finishing the label for Origin, hand-drawing the art and emailing me drafts to review over mint tea and tagines. We planned to launch early that summer. We were evolving the idea of Genesis 10:10, our limited-edition anniversary beer, dropping the alcohol content to eight percent, having decided to produce a more "sessionable" imperial pomegranate amber ale. It would be the first new permanent addition to the lineup since Messiah Bold.

We had already started work on a new beer that I coined Rejewvenator. The entire idea hadn't yet crystallized in my head, but I knew Rejewvenator would tie directly into the sacred species listed in Deuteronomy, by incorporating a different sacred fruit into the brewing each year. As I walked though foothills and valleys, towns and villages throughout Morocco, these same sacred fruits grew in abundance everywhere I went. Hiking through outposts of forgotten sand and stone fortresses, or on treks through the lush oases beyond the gorges and into mountain valleys high above the desert, every day revealed stunning vistas and even more beautiful groves, overflowing with all the sacred species -- pomegranates, figs, dates, olives, grapes -- everywhere I turned. Tiny tributaries pulled off the river coming out of the mountains, feeding small farmers' plots and sustaining the strings of tiny villages that stretched far into the landscape. I assumed this was what Eden must have looked like.

For Shmaltz Brewing, Origin thematically represented a new beginning. Genesis was our flagship, our first creation. Genesis, Chapter 10, charts the descendants of Noah's sons. We tend to think of ourselves as descendants of Adam and Eve, but in reality -- or the reality of mythology -- all people are more directly descended from Noah and the presumably hearty (and biblically unnamed) Mrs. Noah. When the dove brings the olive branch, revealing the dry ground after the receding of the flood waters, Noah first offers up a little charbroiled sacrifice, but then, immediately after receiving a renewed covenant from the divine, he plants a vine, the first act marking the renewal of life[19].

After ten years of He'brew, we were moving into a new phase for the business, hopefully from a more established and experienced place. Origin would be our first permanent new product. (At the time, we didn't realize that Bittersweet Lenny's would become a year-round offering. But you just kept ordering it, so we just kept brewing it.) Today, with its balance of a big, rich malt profile, plenty of hop presence, and just a hint of unique tart and sweet from the pomegranates, Origin continues to be a real favorite of people at beer festivals and trade shows. The beer recently won People's Choice Award at the wildly attended Atlantic City Beer Festival.

With Coney Island Lager coming for summer, we were preparing to go into the draft business in a much bigger way for the first time in the company's history. At exactly that moment, we ran into a major crisis.

I'd had been working with Microstar, the only keg-leasing company in the business, for nearly a decade. I got an email from the C.E.O. saying they were canceling my contract.

I'd started taking a few kegs a month when I was with Anderson Valley, and I probably averaged ten or fifteen kegs a month over the seven years I'd been under contract, with an occasional bump from a round of seasonals. When they threatened to cancel, I had nothing but excuses: I was so bad at bookkeeping -- living on the road, having mail forwarded, and writing checks

---

19 Of course, he then unfortunately proceeds to get tanked, before his sons find him naked on the floor of his tent. In a rage, or because of predestination or tribal narrative, he blesses two, curses one (Ham, the source of the Canaanites – hmmm, that ain't kosher), and still manages to live another 350 years, dying at age 950.

from diner counters and friends' coffee tables -- that I was constantly behind on my payments.

Ken at Anderson Valley often thundered about the keg problem. I can hear every brewer thinking about how to track rogue kegs, how to pull empties out of basements or backyards, to load onto trucks to bring back to the brewery. Especially for a small producer with wide distribution, Microstar is simply the only option. If they don't lease kegs, breweries have to buy their own. When they ship them around the country, they inevitably start losing them fairly quickly. They're an asset that starts hemorrhaging.

New kegs cost about seventy or eighty dollars until 2003 or so, when the prices started going up. Even used kegs jumped from forty to fifty, mirroring the increase for new ones. In perfect shit-storm fashion, the minute Microstar started rumbling about my contract, the price of new kegs began to skyrocket. Part of the problem was that the scrap-metal value of a keg had gone up to thirty dollars, and bars and retail customers still only paid the ten-dollar deposit that was industry standard across the country. People were simply taking them to scrap yards to cash in. As a result, kegs were disappearing all over the country, every month.

At the same time, one of the major keg-manufacturing facilities closed down completely. Suddenly, buying a new keg rose from eighty dollars to a hundred twenty to one-eighty in a flash. Used keg prices followed suit. That meant if you were even selling a couple hundred kegs a month, you might need well over a hundred thousand dollars' worth of kegs to maintain that float, many of which were likely going to be lost, stolen, or scrapped.

I, of course, freaked out. Then I got on the phone, and I managed to beg and plead and scrape together just enough kegs to prepare for Greenpoint's first run. I bought old kegs in any condition from defunct breweries that were still sitting at some of my wholesalers around the country, and I paid the cost of shipping them to Brooklyn. (Any remaining inventory would all be gone shortly, when all the small brewers hit the same hysterical call buttons.)

At the height of the mayhem, in a dumb-luck moment of timing, Kelly and I happened to be online the same day, and we found out that a couple of German breweries had consolidated and were selling off old kegs. Rick at Schaefer, another in a long line of superheroes to save my butt at exactly the right moment, said, "We'll sell you as many as you want, for X dollars a keg." (Not that it was some profound trade secret, but I promised I wouldn't mention it. Suffice to say it was way below new keg pricing, and significantly below any load of used kegs we could find.) We bought two container loads from them, which meant, for my portion, I had to come up with about a hundred grand -- in thirty days.

Without owning a brewery, I certainly didn't want to own my own kegs. We agreed that Kelly would start buying them back from me as we needed them for contract brewing, hopefully putting several hundred into rotation right away and growing from there.

At that point, Matt stepped up in a huge way and saved me. Several months before, after a beer fest and a few late-night samplers, I'd called him and blurted something I'd been thinking for some time: I think you should quit your job (of ten years, full benefits) and work with me full-time (way more than full-time, and no benefits). I'm not sure what the hell might happen, or when we'll get health insurance (October, 2010), but come on, man! Let's blow this thing up! Let's make history!

Though Matt had been my creative partner for some time, crafting much of the visual character of the brands, he now threw himself all-in, becoming the other Shmaltz guy and my New York and east coast general. He also took out fifty thousand dollars from his and his incredibly indulgent wife's home equity line, and he handed me a check for half the keg cost. I called every credit card balance-transfer option sitting in my P.O. box, fudged some income numbers to bump up my credit lines, and got the rest from zero percent offers that would last a year or so.

Without a brewery, or even an office, or a landline, Shmaltz Brewing owned fourteen hundred kegs, with nowhere to put them. So we stacked them to the rafters at the brewery at Greenpoint, and Ralph agreed to store them in a giant locked yard at S.K.I. We even stacked them in a parked big rig in Saratoga. At eight kegs to a four-foot-square pallet, fourteen hundred kegs made... a lot of stacks.

The keg issue was a big deal, even beyond my little universe. It was reported in the major media across the country. To its credit, the beer industry, led by the big beer companies and the big beer wholesalers, recognized the problem and moved on it quickly. Deposits were tripled, to thirty dollars per keg. Laws were passed making it illegal to sell kegs to scrap yards. Impressively, everyone pulled together, and the problem was soon overcome. Three years later I still own over a thousand kegs, though I will be selling them all shortly. Any takers?

Until that point, we were moving five or so kegs a month in New York City, and about twenty around the country. I knew draft was about to pick up for us, so I begged, pleaded and, most importantly, agreed to pay Microstar C.O.D. To their credit, and through the steady helmswomanship of Lauri, the C.E.O., they gave me another shot. We've grown our draft business substantially since, year after year, up from those twenty a month to well over four hundred per month with Microstar and another four hundred or so per month of my own kegs in New York.

Back in San Francisco at the end of that winter, the I.R.S. came knocking with my first official tax audit. For our first meeting, I was once again crashing at my mom's for a few weeks. By our second, I'd found a sublet back in San Francisco, on the corner of 17th and Mission, just down from the rent-by-the-hour flophouses and two hundred feet from the donut shop that doubled as the local crack-addict and heroin-junkie encampment. Thanks to two musicians touring Europe and the magic of Craigslist, I actually had a great little apartment, just a few blocks from some of my favorite bars and restaurants in the city. But the auditor was, understandably, more than a little skeeved by the neighborhood. I told him not to leave anything in view inside his car, and to bring a lot of quarters for parking meters if he planned to stay awhile.

For 2005, I'd gotten my sales up to about $350,000, up from maybe a hundred and thirty grand at the height of my 22 ounce business days. All I had to show at year's end, however, was $12,000 left over as profit -- my "salary." Michel, the I.R.S. investigator, who reminded me a little of Inspector Clouseau, came to my mother's house for our initial meeting. He explained that I had a small business that was growing a lot, and there were certain things that set off investigations -- the dreaded "red flags." "You've gotten big enough for us to be curious," he said. True, the business had grown, but I was still spending any gross profits, traveling constantly, and just scraping by.

Michel said, "Please let me take a look at the receipts, so I can start building a file." I said, Here's my tax return. Well, did I have my backup paperwork? No sir, that's it. No bank statements, no credit card receipts. No invoices, no purchase orders, no proofs of payment. For the last couple of years I'd joked with Matt every time a receipt made an appearance. What's the point? I figured, It's just more stuff to shlep around. And break even is break even. I told the auditor, Seriously, I don't have a single receipt. He was astounded.

"Er, this is somewhat of a unique situation for me," he said. Most of the time, he joked, people were so angry with the auditors, they open the door to a dank basement stuffed with boxes containing years of receipts, none of them marked, and say, "Go ahead."

Over the course of several meetings, we slogged through. I had the brewery run a report for the invoices I paid. I asked my vendors to send statements for the year, and I got my bank statements from Wells Fargo. I said, You can see how much went in and out of my business bank account. My personal bank account was equally unimpressive -- a few grand here and there, matching up with the business profits.

Your Earnings Record

Years You Worked	Your Taxed Social Security Earnings	Your Taxed Medicare Earnings
1984	$ 1,040	$ 1,040
1985	550	550
1986	1,894	1,894
1987	1,061	1,061
1988	1,501	1,501
1989	1,635	2,241
1990	0	0
1991	3,417	3,417
1992	8,682	8,682
1993	23,842	23,842
1994	14,021	14,021
1995	12,443	12,443
1996	38,108	38,108
1997	6,943	6,943
1998	5,987	5,987
1999	442	442
2000	0	0
2001	12,821	12,821
2002	14,120	14,120
2003	5,940	5,940
2004	0	0
2005	12,374	12,374
2006	41,675	41,675
2007	57,825	57,825
2008	46,798	46,798
2009	Not yet recorded	

QUITE A RUN FROM '97 - '05.
NOT TO MENTION THE REST.

It went back and forth like that for several months, a bit of a war of attrition, for some time before Michel and I finally came to a settlement. In the end it came down to about eight thousand dollars I couldn't "prove" I'd spent. Michel got promoted and, having reported back about my mother's guest room, the crack-corner sublet, and a reasonable effort to reconstruct an entire year of my life, they closed the file and moved on. The end result: $1252 in income tax for the I.R.S. locked and loaded, for weeks, if not months, of this guy's attention.

Happily, I survived my first audit with my sense of humor intact. And the episode did inspire me to start thinking about changing my bookkeeping practices.

I've begrudgingly learned to take better care of my paperwork. I tell all my vendors that I run a "paperless" company. Most are happy to use email, though somehow I still manage to get piles of unnecessary envelopes forwarded to me whenever I'm on the road for work.

Similarly, for ten years I received my depletion reports -- wholesalers' statements of the amount of our product they're selling -- and promptly threw them away. Again, neither trained nor predisposed as a sales manager, I figured I'm on the phone with these guys or selling beer in their cars with them fairly regularly, and I know if there's a problem. Let's just go sell as much as we can, and we'll worry about the numbers one day, when I'm not just scrambling for survival.

After a basic template that Angela and I created to start tracking this "stuff," and after probably two hundred phone calls just to get all the depletions sent monthly (you know who you are, you naughty non-reporting distributors), we evolved to the next step with the help of intern-turned-post-biz-school whiz Kevin Friedman. My old "vice president" helped his cousin Leah and me create a monster Excel file to track our wholesalers' monthly, quarterly, and annual sales.

That spring, on Mother's Day, I had a business meeting with a potential employee at a well-worn, well-loved, bike-messenger, dope-smoking, Mission beer garden called Zeitgeist (their motto: "Warm Beer, Cold Women"). Zak would end up becoming my west coast regional sales manager. The year before, he'd hired me for an event at U.C. Davis through Hillel, the on-campus Jewish student organization. After ordering pints of Racer 5, we had a great discussion about Jewish entrepreneurship. Later, we ran into each other at a beer festival in San Francisco, and Zak was putting out the feelers with tech companies. Within a few months I had hired him to work for me part-time, which quickly became full-time.

It was wonderful to have somebody so young, enthusiastic, and capable, someone who was also interviewing at Google and Yahoo, who somewhat astonishingly considering Shmaltz Brewing as a "legitimate" career direction.

Compared to the days when Rob had the same thoughts, slowly but surely, Shmaltz was crawling toward becoming an actual company. We were starting to have enough products, revenue, and mojo in place. I still, however, had my entire marketing plan on a Post-it note in my wallet, where it had already been squirreled away for years.[20]

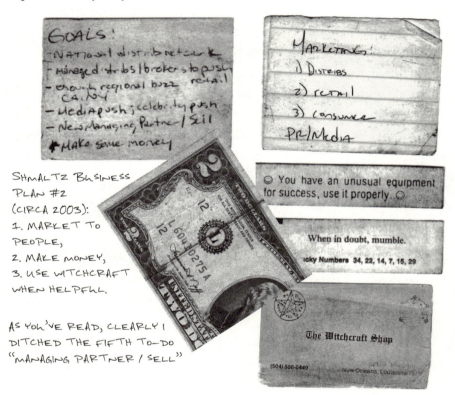

With fifty thousand dollars of his home equity at risk, Matt officially came on full-time as my art guru and east coast sales manager, better known as "the other Shmaltz guy." He'd been working at a small Midtown design firm churning out trade show booths, UPC code changes on packaging for sample boxes, and anything that needed to be communicated by various members

---

20 Also squirreled away for well over a decade, and through several wallet transfers: a business card blessed with a witch's spell from a long-defunct witchcraft shop in New Orleans, circa 1993; a two-dollar bill offered as a good luck charm from a close temp-job friend; and a fortune cookie from Chinatown tour days reading, "When in doubt, mumble." (20a)

(20a) Holy shit, I'm putting a footnote to a footnote (sweet): Not to confuse the fortune cookie advice with Lagunitas's long-standing mantra: Beer speaks, people mumble. Great shtick.

of extremely-corporate America. I said, It sounds like you could use a bit of creative inspiration -- every day.

Typical of Shmaltz: The things that have been most successful for me have started casually and personally. Very rarely is there a well-thought-out, pre-planned business decision. I don't necessarily advise this for everyone, but it's worked for me.

Matt and I had been introduced by our mutual friend, Peter. They grew up together in Milwaukee and continued to watch every Packers game together at the Kettle of Fish in the West Village. One spring break, visiting Peter at college, Matt received a rush offer at a frat house at Stanford -- though he was still a senior in high school. He was just visiting the campus, had not even applied to Stanford, and had no intention of going to school there. Repeated beer bongs filled with goldfish floaters and slash marks on faux-samurai headbands marked his "progress." Making friends and drinking beer -- early talents.

After redoing my website, Matt designed the first Jewbelation label for my eighth anniversary in 2004. By 2007, he had created more beer labels, business cards, sell sheets, posters, and postcards for the company than any other designer, and it continues to this day -- twenty-three beer labels and counting. He has created the entire visual landscape of Shmaltz Brewing, and made it spectacular.

Matt had a friend in New York he'd grown up with who was an investment banker. We met this friend at the Kettle of Fish so I could ask him one question: How do I finance this business?

Sales were growing, and I simply needed more money to cover it all. I'd passed the "cusp" of breaking even every year for the past couple, and every month the bills for the contract-brewed cases increased as our sales continued to increase. Good problems to have, for sure, and certainly better than the alternative scenarios of my first seven years in business. However, with the keg purchase tying up so much of my working cash, I needed to find a solution to buy more beer -- more inventory -- so I could keep it rolling to my wholesalers and the market.

As I'd explored previously but couldn't quite clarify in my head until those few pints with Matt's buddy, my options were few. 1) I could gather my life savings -- of which there were none; 2) I could raise equity by trying to sell a portion of the company, once again asking friends and family, or look for angel investors like I'd done in 1999 (though the memories of that first round were still painful, and I was far from clearing those assumed obligations); or 3), I could take on more debt.

In order to get a bank loan, a small business owner needs to personally guarantee that the lender can liquidate your life and all your assets, if necessary, to cover the nut. I had nothing to offer a bank other than a couple years of slightly profitable and aggressive growth. No house or brewing equipment, or anything else more tangible than my best intentions. So the only solution I could see was to crank up my credit cards once again.

There's no question that if our country hadn't been so ridiculously overzealous about feeding the economic bubble before the current recession, I never would have made this whole enterprise work. It's the only way I survived. When I'd call about another credit card offer that came in the mail, they'd say, "Mr. Cowan, could you please tell me your annual income?"

And I'd say, Oh, sure. $286,000. "OK, great. Here's a $37,000 credit limit." Then I'd turn around and spend it all -- on beer.

My old investor Russ – the same Russ whom I bailed on for breakfast in the year of the bender -- once said something that sticks with me to this day: "To make any business work, you need to be prepared to do the everyday work, every day. So much of this kind of stuff is just doing the blocking and tackling."

Blocking and tackling -- that sounded to me like the worst possible part of the job. Reminds me of my head in the scrum in college, with a broken pinkie and a bloody schnozz.

By this time, I was routinely fighting the fact that the job demanded so much blocking and tackling. My friend Jon, who owns a wine company, has become a wonderful advisor over the years, and he's heard me complain about it. To this day, he'll call and ask for the "Blocking and Tackling Department" of Shmaltz Brewing, just to piss me off.

It's simple stuff: checking in with customers, and reminding the market over and over about yourself and your products. Checking the costs of your ingredients, and packaging and negotiating better deals. Watching trucking costs. Keeping your receipts. Being consistent in your plans and demands from wholesalers and reps. Paying bills and, most importantly, getting paid on time -- and then turning around to buy more beer and more packaging. And keeping a steady pace, without letting too much fall through the cracks.

In short, for a restless entrepreneur, brutal. But *so important*. Consistency and reliability -- they're no secret to so many success stories. I suppose the words are on those glossy corporate posters at Office Max for a reason.

Blocking and tackling doesn't mean, however, that you've got to stand still. After many years of having one and then just two beers, that's what made the more recent growth of the company so exciting. Yes, things were stressful, and we were constantly behind. Yes, the new products were likely creating distractions and spreading everyone way too thin. But the industry loves what's new, and we loved whipping out what we considered fresh art projects in the form of beer.

Right from the beginning, we had a great response from the community for Coney Island. I had been selling maybe five or ten kegs of He'brew a month in New York City. In the first month with Coney Island, S.K.I. sold probably eighty kegs. The next month it was a hundred and ten, and the next one-twenty-five. Same distribution, same quality of product, just a different name and different shtick.

It did change our ability to reach a lot more people. The reputation and experience of He'brew made people respect and appreciate, and become aware of, Coney Island rather quickly. Conversely, the familiarity of the Coney Island name got us into a ton of bars, and we were able to bring He'brew into many of them. It was a good symbiotic relationship.

That summer, despite the unearned largesse, my buddy Craig's close friend Cathleen rented me her Brooklyn apartment way below fair market cost. Her generosity landed me my best sublet ever: air conditioning, multiple bedrooms, elliptical machine -- a huge advance in Shmaltz sublet history.

In this spirit of expansion, and with a guest bedroom to offer, I asked my friend Eva, who happened to be coming from Minneapolis to visit family in

New York, to help me plan the entire future of Shmaltz Brewing... for free. A good friend from our New Orleans post-collegiate youth, Eva had worked for several consulting firms, and by this time she was running her own one-woman show, charging large sums of well-earned dollars. Again, angels share much more than I can repay.

She created a master spreadsheet for the company that connected the costs of all the products to sales dollars from each brand, and then she outlined the potential expenses necessary to achieve three scenarios. We plotted conservative to moderate to aggressive sales increases to get a sense of the money landscape that could roll out before Shmaltz Brewing. With many of the products in place or in the final planning stages, and with enough sales history to loosely ballpark what might happen if things went poorly, well, or gloriously, I saw a reasonably understandable bottom line emerge for the first time in over a decade. That blessed spreadsheet quickly became my Shmaltz Torah.

Armed with a little bit of knowledge, a lot more credit card debt, and very large sales growth, in the fall of 2007 I hired one more salesperson to cover the south and, I hoped, an even wider territory. Just when I was realizing the new hire wasn't working out, one of the brewers from Olde Saratoga called me and told me he was moving to Atlanta. So Darren just kind of happened. Sometimes things work out perfectly -- you get the feeling the universe is smiling down on you.

While brewing at Olde Saratoga, Darren had run the production for our first-ever barrel aging of Bittersweet Lenny's. He'd grown up in Florida before landing in Atlanta, where he worked for a financial company. He was a homebrewer who wanted to go into the beer business, so he gave up his career-path job in the financial world to wash kegs at Sweetwater Brewing in Atlanta, where he started apprenticing. At Saratoga, he became a production brewer, and in addition to all his other full time responsibilities there, he single-handedly managed this great little barrel-aging project for me, pulling R.I.P.A. into Rittenhouse 100 rye whiskey barrels and babying that beer through to its glorious conclusion. That successful experiment grew into our current barrel-aging program kicking out R.I.P.A. on RYE, Vertical Jewbelation, Barrel Aged Blockhead, and 2011's Genesis 15:15. Darren continues to be our special brewing project coordinator, and a key source of production knowledge to the company and to me personally.

While, on the one hand, the heavens seemed to be opening up for me on so many fronts, the other hand was preparing to spank my ass with a lot less love. In October I went to the brewery and had a meeting with Bob, the G.M., and Paul, the head brewer. That was the first time anyone mentioned the words "hop problem" to me.

As a contract brewer, I'd never taken the time to learn how hops were bought and sold. I knew that the intricate buds grew on vines, and I knew we used a huge array of them in our beers. I'd touched and smelled them whenever I was bouncing around the brewery "helping" brew up a batch of beer (read: staying out of the way). In the whole time I'd been in business, I'd never been involved in a single hop purchase, and I had no idea who the companies involved were. I had certainly never heard the two words that would haunt, in horrific fashion, myself and so many other small brewers: Hop Contract. Horrific, because we didn't have one.

By November, people in the business were calling it a "hop crisis."

Evidently, the year's hop harvests in the U.S. and around the world had been exceptionally poor. To make matters worse, there had been a huge fire at a key hop supplier's warehouse. On top of that, the craft industry had created a marked increase in demand for hops. Just about every small-to-regional-size microbrewery was making stronger single and double IPAs -- Stone, Dogfish Head and so many others, creating the innovative products that new craft followers craved. Sierra Nevada, Sam Adams, even Red Hook and Goose Island had cranked up their hoppier offerings, slurping up pounds at a scale much beyond our modest annual needs. Suddenly, we had a big problem on our hands. And there was panic.

Conspiracy theories were rampant. For years, hops had been priced between two and four dollars a pound. Almost overnight they went up to ten, then sixteen, then twenty-three dollars. At the height of the situation, the only way I could get *any* Cascade hops (used in nearly all our recipes) was to touch my toes and evacuate thirty-six bucks per pound from my credit card -- and that was for committing to pretty decent volumes of over a thousand pounds.

For a while, no matter how little quantity we wanted, it was impossible to get a full order. The brewery told me they weren't even sure what they could get for their own beer, and they had no contract in place for mine. Like so many new waves of extreme (or just more flavorful) brews, most of our new beers used a lot of hops. The guys at the brewery said, "We don't want to scare you, but you need to be terrified."

Chanukah came early in 2007 – or, as my people like to say, Christmas came late on the Hebrew calendar that year. I'd been working with my PR guy, Jesse, for about a year at that point. Almost like a one-year anniversary present, we received an inquiry from the nationally broadcast program *The Big Idea with Donny Deutsch* on CNBC.

Though I'd never seen it, everyone I talked to seemed to know all about it and thought it was clever and fun. The week before Chanukah I shot the producer a follow-up email: What are you doing for the holiday? I think she lived in hyper-producer mode. I'd get three words from a Blackberry.

"Working on it."

"You available?"

"Hold tight."

"Dec. 11?"

It turned out the day she wanted me was the day of our eleventh anniversary party at the Toronado. I told them I had to get back in time for the party and they said, "No problem. We'll fly you out on the red-eye and back that day. We shoot at three p.m. Wear something respectable. No logos."

Before I went, I had to figure out what the show was. Evidently Donny Deutsch's father had owned an ad agency that Donny took over. A hotshot kid, he blew it up and made it a widely recognized success. He cashed out of the business and started the show, which featured small business stories from around the country.

One of the guests who was going to be on the same episode with me reigned as the Mattress King of infomercials. A very hospitable guy in person, his business was grossing $800 million every year, selling mattresses, one at a time, on TV. The show also featured more modest entrepreneurs, like the couple from the Midwest who made sand candles in their garage.

THE CAME, THEY TRIED TO KILL US, WE SURVIVED.

Though I was excited to do the show, it proved to be a profoundly disturbing experience. By coincidence, I bumped into a guy at the airport bar who said, "Hey, aren't you going to be on *Donny Deutsch*?" He was scheduled for the same show -- he owned a guitar-pick company in the Central Valley. Talking to him relaxed me a bit; I found myself uncharacteristically nervous.

The car service picked me up from the corporate hotel where we were being put up during the day and brought me to the studio that afternoon. I was thrown into the makeup room with a couple of hotties, who tried to make me look acceptable for TV. It was the end of the Jewish holiday season. I'm sure I looked pretty damn tired. They coated my entire face with heavy brown foundation, then started recreating it from scratch, with a spray gun and wands of colors and creams.

So it was myself, the guitar-pick guy, and the mattress king. I was going to be on a segment called "Is This the Big Idea?" In it, the featured guests and Donny would discuss the idea of my business, and whether or not they felt it was a Million Dollar Idea. Very quickly (even for television), they go over some basic information about the business -- gross sales, the business model, some information about the product, a little bit of past PR. They critique it, and then they give their "informed" judgment.

Meanwhile, the actual businessperson gets about nine words by way of introduction. The whole segment lasts maybe three minutes. I'm used to spouting off with the shotgun approach, usually with print writers, or even radio. You banter a bit, and eventually the right stuff will come out. I'd watched the last two guests, who got time for two quick sentences to define their life's work.

Still, before we cut the segment, I thought it sounded like an amazing opportunity. Donny had just been in a very public pissing match with Ann Coulter, who was notorious for her "slash and burn" punditry. She'd been quoted as saying something to the effect that it would be a better world if everyone were Christian and Republican. When she went on his show, Donny called her on it. She'd said essentially that evangelical Christianity taught that Christians were "perfected" Jews, and she suggested that Donny give up Judaism and come to church with her. He was furious, and vehemently stood up to her.

Three weeks later, the whole episode was still coming up daily on media segments and blogs. I thought, well, perfect Chanukah present for us to chat about on national TV.

But I got to the set, and it was clear from the start that we were all just preprocessed fodder for the show. I could have been a guy selling garbage cans in New Jersey. There was nothing authentic about the moment or the content. It just filled the time.

I walked in, and the host didn't even look up. I didn't need a big hug and a "Hey, thanks for coming across the country on such short notice, in the middle of your busiest sales push of the year." But some vaguely human gesture would have been appreciated.

I mumbled something about hoping to say happy Chanukah to my mom, and he said, "Yeah, fine."

We ran through the segment, and it was eleven years of my life condensed into about eight seconds of me, and then these two guys and Donny. To his credit, the owner of the guitar-pick company did a great job of plugging for me, mentioning the high quality of the beers and pointing out how many awards we'd won. But they all agreed that He'brew would never be a million-dollar idea. They said, "You can't make a product for such a niche market. You've got to expand your focus. If you want to make this beer, make it for everyone."

Ironically, by the end of 2007 we would sell $875,000 of He'brew for the year. So the "million-dollar idea" we were apparently never going to hit on was already pretty fucking within reach.

My friends who were watching said they could see me steaming. I did force my way into a couple of exchanges. I argued, Well, you don't need to be Irish to drink Guinness, and I slapped Donny on the back and made a wisecrack about him being my bar mitzvah boy. In the end, I was at least given a moment to wish my mom a happy Chanukah.

PR-wise, it was such an eye-opener. Jesse and I are constantly talking about trying to get on wider-audience TV shows such as this one. I specifically remember sitting up in bed with Tracy when we first started, thinking He'brew could surely get featured on Letterman. Leno, Oprah, *The Daily Show* -- what better product are they going to bring out for Chanukah, or Rosh Hashanah, or Purim?

But it's astounding how many people saw me on *Donny Deutsch*. For a while the episode ran in repeats, so my ignominy was saved for posterity.

That week, I saw another episode with a similar segment, a woman whose business had done about a million bucks in 2006. She came on gushing about how much she loved the show and how, inspired by Donny's advice and enthusiasm, she was going to do a million and a half in '07. That's fifty percent growth -- pretty huge.

And Donny said, "Well, that's great. But you gotta think BIG! Why not shoot for two million, five million, ten million!"

This poor lady was busting her ass to grow her company – her *million-dollar company*. Apparently it wasn't enough to think, Wow, this woman is really succeeding. Did her expenses go up too? Net profits? Vacation time? Benefits for staff or investments for the future? Evidently, you just need to sell more and more. The *why?* is never addressed on the show. Are you going to work harder just to accomplish the same thing?

The year after I was on the show, we grew eighty percent. I made a little more and spent a lot more, building a foundation for the next phase of growth.

This guy was so blind to people's real lives. In my opinion, it's not about making a million dollars if it doesn't make your life better, more dynamic, more interesting, if it doesn't bring something better into your world. Let's be honest: very often, work kinda sucks. Work is not the payback -- it's the pay. Donny Deutsch should have been celebrating this woman's hard-won success. Instead, he was ranting about an abstract number.

Art should be for art's sake, but money needs to be for something different. Something specific. Something meaningful. Something morally sound. Something worth earning.

I flew back to San Francisco that night, missed the party, but arrived for a couple of beers with Zak at midnight. Despite the vote of no confidence from Donny Deutsch, I believed we were onto something special. A few remaining friends and the Toronado beer posse were a better jury anyway.

Before soaking in my self-satisfied bowl of cherries, though, I pulled one last bonehead move for the holidays. Prior to hiring Darren, I'd hired a beer industry friend as my sales rep in the south who had clearly not worked out. I'd been struggling with the frustration through the last three months of the year. By the end of December, I was just burned out on the situation.

I worked myself into a frenzy, convincing myself that I needed to fire her immediately. Instead of taking a deep breath and waiting until the holidays were over, one night I wrote an email about how disturbed and upset I was. I told her I had to fire her. I hit "send" and walked to the shower. The momentary hot-water relief was shattered by a realization: It was Christmas Eve. She was half-Jewish, and I knew she celebrated Christmas with her significant other, her friends and family, even some work acquaintances.

I was overcome with a sickening sense of self-loathing. I wanted to crawl into the Internet and somehow get that email back.

Luckily, she managed to find a new job quickly, and we've remained friends from afar. I know we wish each other the best. But that doesn't excuse my utter lack of judgment and my behavior. One more suggestion to do as I say, not as I did.

When the New Year began, all I could see was the black cloud of the hop crisis growing larger and darker. Paul, the head brewer, and I were on the phone pretty much all the time, emailing, calling, begging, and pleading with anyone who could find us some hops. Yet again, I had to inflate my credit card debt to stay afloat. I also hit up my *mishpocha*: Peter loaned me twenty-five grand, my mom cobbled together ten thousand, another friend offered fifteen more.

Paul was an absolute lifesaver. He worked overtime to help me keep in constant contact with the hop suppliers, desperately searching for anything that might become available. Through his contacts we eventually found half the hops we needed to keep brewing.

We were paying between five and ten times the cost, and we had to buy it all up front, something that was totally unheard of previously. Cascade, the mother of all Pacific Northwest hops, went from three to four dollars a pound to twenty, to thirty-six. All the other varieties we used across the brewing board went to eighteen, then twenty-four and up.

THE CAME. THEY TRIED TO KILL US. WE SURVIVED.

I got some very kind responses from several brewers I'd become friendly with over the years, including Brian at Dogfish Head, Matt from Magic Hat, and Jeff, the "Chief" at Ithaca. My buddy Brian, who was managing brewing for Spanish Peaks, did me a huge favor in the form of nearly five hundred pounds of Crystal. Still, what we got was nowhere near the many thousands of pounds I'd need.

After months of nail-biting and wrangling, Paul finally secured what became known as the "supplemental hop" purchase: sixty-five thousand dollars worth of hops that nine months before would have cost about nine grand -- a few boxes of this, a few boxes of that, a load of insanely priced Cascade, and some other crucial varieties. I remember so clearly a very tense call with the brewery C.E.O., who gave me the final dollar amount while suggesting I should simply not go through with it -- not introduce new products and stay smaller, for now.

But I really had no option. If we didn't make this beer, we wouldn't hit my projections. I'd already hired Darren, whose wife was pregnant with his boy Kane. Matt's wife had just given birth to their first baby, Lillia, and at the moment he was the family breadwinner. Zak, Angela, and Jesse had all put their trust and labor toward the company, and toward me. I remember so clearly being on that call, outside a bar in Athens, Georgia, during a lunch stop on a ride-with the first time I visited Darren to get him started with Shmaltz. There was no choice. It simply had to happen.

So many voices pay so much lip service to the "market" in this country. We believe it will take care of everything. The saddest part about the whole disaster was that, in hindsight, it doesn't look as though it needed to happen at all. There were clearly just enough hops to go around for a year or so. The following year there were even more, and now this year there are plenty for everyone -- and hop prices have dropped fifty to seventy-five percent, with futures back down to prices from before the crisis occurred.

Of the fifteen hundred small breweries in the U.S., there were very few, if any, reports of people going out of business because of this enormous calamity. The people who could least afford the massive hit -- the small guys who had not negotiated long-term contracts -- had to severely limit the hops they used, change the recipes of some of their most important brands, and swallow the crazy price increases. People lost a huge amount of money.

With the panic, the uncertainty, and the lack of meaningful information from anyone who really should have known the situation, I desperately bought anything I could get my hands on, regardless of price. Perhaps I should have rolled even more risky dice and waited it out. Unlike one hop supplier who looks to have taken maximum advantage of the situation, thankfully, my primary vendor, who fought to get me enough to survive without gouging the little guys, literally saved my business. I've since signed a long-term contract, securing a big chunk of our future needs at much more reasonable prices.

All said, however, in those two years of price insanity I lost almost $200,000. And that was just my little forty-five-hundred-barrel operation at the time, which grew to six thousand barrels by the time the crisis was on its back slope. *Two hundred grand* -- and you've seen my Social Security statement. Many others must have lost much more.

The financial rules of the beer world have been set by much bigger companies than ours -- much bigger, in fact, than even the biggest craft brewers. If a craft brewer is buying anything, from bottle caps to glass, paying for trucking, brewing equipment, or raw ingredients, the logic is set on a much bigger scale. Though not an M.B.A., I do understand the concept of economies of scale.

But for an industry as vibrant and multi-dimensional as the over-fifteen-hundred small brewers in the country selling an estimated $3.5 billion of product, it's shocking to realize how few options -- how few suppliers -- really control the vast majority of materials needed to run this industry. Trying to scale that supply chain down to craft beer on the artisan side, the numbers barely make any sense.

Admittedly, I made a ton of bad decisions along the way. But even without a brewery and other overhead common to the industry, it took me nearly ten years to start making any profit -- and what profit there is has been rather modest. From conversations with many fellow brewers -- many of your and my favorite brands -- this is not uncommon. That is one hell of a lot of risk and investment and labor with which to pursue one's passions in a for-profit venture.

Still in the throes of survival mode, while reeling from the monster expense of the hop crisis, we amazingly managed to keep production rolling and barrel through to hit my "aggressive" sales targets from Eva's master Excel file. Coming to the company with varying professional experience but a similar disposition for obsessive commitment, both Zak and Darren grew into their roles and responsibilities as regional sales managers in very different ways -- but both to hard-earned stellar success. Their distributors were up big numbers, many well over one hundred percent. After my poor record of retaining past co-workers, I was relieved, then thrilled, that these guys threw themselves into the job with such vigor and focus. I have repeatedly told them I want them both to be so much better at the job than I ever was -- and they seem to be working their asses off to make my demands come true.

The Coney success in New York City helped our overall growth significantly, and we somehow managed to pull through the shit-storm building stronger relationships, more excitement about our products, and a core team of over achieving staff. This seemingly basic idea -- that if we simply had the ingredients to make more beer and the zealous staff that could push the hell out of it -- was actually happening. By 2008, we were doing a little over $1.5 million in sales -- still small, but up ten times what it had been just five year before. In 2009 we'd hit just shy of $2 million, and 2010 is looking like a similar trajectory. In my mind, at least, I can hear Donny Deutsch hollering, *"I don't care what the sales are. It's still not a million dollar idea!"*

✡   ✶   ✡   ✶   ✡

It was finally time to roll out our first summer seasonal from He'brew: Rejewvenator. Originally, I'd planned to release it for Rosh Hashanah, the Jewish New Year. (As the *Los Angeles Times* had riffed so many years before about He'brew, "This beer could give new meaning to the term 'High Holidays.'") But instead of creating an entire new release in such a short time period before our fall-release Jewbelation, I realized we could flip seasons between two beers by releasing Rejewvenator in spring and running it through the autumn High Holidays instead.

The seal for the deal came in the form a letter from a lawyer representing, of all people, Sierra Nevada Brewing Company, many months before our

Rejewvenator was even planned to launch. With very uncharacteristic planning, Matt and I had already just about finished the label the year before. We'd printed an advance description with a tiny, mocked-up product shot, along with the rest of our lineup, on our small promo postcards, which we handed out at beer fests and other events. This was the only place the information appeared. I'd told Matt we needed a small secondary descriptor for Rejewvenator, a tidbit to clarify the seasonal as an alternative to Jewbelation, which we called our Anniversary Ale. I threw out the line "Annual Celebration Ale," and he slapped it down.

Yes, *of course* I knew about Celebration Ale from Sierra Nevada. It had always been one of my favorite special releases, another "extreme" beer far ahead of its time. But the word celebration seems to be ubiquitous when it comes to beer-related fun. There's Celebrator beer from Ayinger and *Celebrator Beer News* and... Honestly, it just never occurred to me.

The law firm representing Sierra clearly did not agree. "Dear Mr. Cowan: It has come to our attention... ipso facto... whereas aforementioned to the extent that... blah, blah, blah... Cease and Desist Now."

I was shocked. Sierra Nevada? Couldn't they have just sent an email? A quick note from the brewery -- "Hey, wondering about this postcard we saw. How about we trade you a name change for a case of Celebration for Chanukah?" I would have been happy to oblige.

Instead, I got this series of aggressive and intimidating legalese missives, on expensive swanky law-firm linen paper, no less.

Late one night, I banged out an extraordinarily sarcastic response I thought I would send Sierra management and the beer media. But then, in an unusual show of restraint, I realized I'd better just shut up and change the name. Harvest to Harvest Ale, it is. No one's trademarking that, gents.

Perhaps I should be grateful that the lawyer saved my shtick. Suddenly it all came together. From the label -- "Jewish tradition celebrates two New Years: The first calendar month in Spring historically comes after the barley harvest. The High Holidays in Fall mark the creation of the world. Harvest to harvest -- the perfect bookends for deliciousness!"

The mirroring of the new years, this doubling effect of the seasons, stirred my question to Paul: Could we use two yeast strains, a lager and an ale?

THE CAME, THEY TRIED TO KILL US, WE SURVIVED.

From the label of Rejewvenator Year of the Fig, 2008:

"The winter of bondage has passed, the deluge of suffering is gone, the Fig tree has formed its first fruits, declaring all ready for libation."
– Song of Solomon

Jewish tradition celebrates 2 New Years: The 1st calendar month in Spring historically came after the barley harvest. The High Holidays in Fall mark the creation of the world. Harvest to harvest - the perfect bookends for deliciousness! Arise noble Rejewvenator, infused for '08 with the sacred succulent Fig. O the history, O the shtick: Gen 3:7: "And their eyes were opened, and they knew that they were naked; they sewed fig leaves together and made themselves aprons." Time to get cooking! "Professed Wrestlers and Champions were in times past fed with figs." -Pliny, Roman naturalist. Romulus, mythic founder of Rome, and his twin Remus were nursed by a wild she-wolf under a fig tree. In 1857, Queen Victoria commissioned an 18 inch plaster fig leaf to adorn her cast of Michelangelo's *David*. "The statue that advertises its modesty with a fig leaf brings its modesty under suspicion." -Mark Twain. Buddha gained enlightenment meditating beneath a fig tree. Zechariah/Micah: "Nations shall beat their swords into plowshares...all will sit with his neighbor under his fig tree, with no one to be afraid." Fear not Shmaltzers - Grab your Newtons, rub your happy belly, strap on your fig leaf and your championship belt, and prepare to blow your *shofar*...tis a new HE'BREW Beer season to rejoice. *L'Chaim!*

I've always been a fan of malty, dark beers, with the thematically appropriate names doppelbock (often called "liquid bread," a rich lager to help the German monks get through Lent) and Belgian dubbel (or double, a classic monastic strong brown ale). Why not pinch from acclaimed, sacred European brewing tradition to create some new Jewish brewing history, and an only-in-America craft beer?

The "-ator" ending for all beers in the style comes from the original doppelbock, Salvator, or savior, with its obvious religious connotations. We already had the He'brew Messiah, so it would be the Rejewvenator to begin the new year after Passover in the spring -- liberated from bondage and ready to indulge in *chametz* (leavened or fermented grain, i.e., beer), which is forbidden till after the holiday.

The totem animal of the doppelbock style is a goat, usually with large horns reminiscent of (and genetically related) to the ram, which appears in Jewish text as the substitute for Isaac in Abraham's near-sacrifice of his only son. The story of the binding of Isaac is read every year for Rosh Hashanah, when the ram's horn, or *shofar*, blasts its annual spiritual wake-up call to the congregation. The *shofar* also looks a little like a small beer bong.

In keeping with the sacred species theme, Angela had sourced an exquisite fig concentrate, pressed straight from luscious mission figs near Indio, CA. I'd had the salesman's contact information scribbled in a margin of an email buried in a folder. I sent him an note and didn't hear back. I sent him another -- no answer.

Suddenly we were only six weeks away from brewing the beer. I called the supplier and he said, "Sorry. I changed my email address." One other thing: he could no longer get the concentrate.

We all started making desperate phone calls, and I soon reached a very cordial older gentleman grower, a broker in upstate New York. He informed me there apparently had been a "fig crisis" the year before, and there would be no fig juice until next harvest in the fall. I respectfully replied, Sir, the word "crisis" is currently reserved for hops. You'll need to find a suitable substitution, such as catastrophe or apocalypse.

Miraculously (I don't know how he does it), Paul called a company in California's Central Valley and managed to procure the exact fig concentrate that we'd previously sourced. They'd already told us they were completely sold out, but Paul charmed them into selling us two fifty-five-gallon drums. Bob sent a truck, and they arrived three days before we were scheduled to brew.

The Rejewvenator series is now one of my favorite beer projects that we make. In 2008, it was the year of the fig. The following year was the year of the date, which was recently awarded a gold medal at the World Beer Championships. For 2010 it's the *bubbe* of all sacred Jewish fruits, the Concord grape.

That leaves one sacred species we haven't used yet -- olives. Oily, and not even vaguely a flavor to pair with any beer we've thought of lately, olives will be a serious brewing challenge for everyone involved in the next round of Rejewvenator, slated for 2012. The fruit of the branch brought to Noah by that innocent dove, who never imagined how complicated she would make the lives of a handful of brewers trying to create a unique beer recipe with a product that is seemingly unusable in the brewing process: This is what it sounds like, when the brewers for contract-brewers cry...

CHAPTER 18

The Promised Land-ish

The 40 Days and 40 Nights beer tour, starting in fall 2003, had stretched across four and a half years of my life. Shmaltz Brewing had sold more He'brew beer than I'd ever thought possible. We'd introduced a second brand, Coney Island, that I'd never foreseen. I'd risked more credit destruction than any lender should've deemed reasonable.

I may have damaged my body a bit, but the distribution and marketing foundation built over those years would make viable all the new products, the new PR plans, and the aggressive revenue growth that followed. The intuitive business plan, incubated on a couple of stickies and hatched on one Excel spreadsheet, was working.

I decided it would be a good time to go home. At least for a few months.

With a few more real-life classes of business math under my belt, I took a look at the rents in San Francisco, which had more than doubled since I'd started my enterprise. I realized I'd be better off scraping together everything I could to buy the smallest apartment I could stomach to house myself and the global headquarters of Shmaltz Brewing. Sneaking in during the final death throes of "stated income" mortgages, in the spring of 2008 I put ten percent down on a 420-square-foot studio in one of the city's eternally "transitional" neighborhoods, South of Market. "Transitional" in San Francisco means equal parts crackheads, junkies, and the associated social services of rehab centers, homeless shelters, and low income housing, all sitting directly next to the well-intentioned gentrifiers with cool shoes and a taste for a better latte. Specifically in SOMA, the economic step far above (but not far away from) the indigent included the longstanding leather-daddy bars, high-end scooter showrooms, and a cluster of dance spots hosting Asian club kids and Burning Man theme campers. Fortunately, a gourmet grocery store with a prepared foods section and an overstuffed salad bar sat at the end of my block. Even more importantly, my studio came with a deeded parking spot.

What my friends called my live-work cube did not come with any closets (the modernist/minimalist architect who designed the building was serious when he advised, "Just get rid of everything"). They'd generously installed a dishwasher, which I immediately sold on Craigslist, figuring the chances of me needing to do more than one or two dishes at a time were pretty close to zero. I put an all-in-one washer-dryer in its place -- one of the best executive decisions I've made. Parallel to my brewing plans, my eating regimen remained almost exclusively contract-eating. My "cooking" at home entailed preparing an occasional bowl of cereal or a bagel toasted under the broiler.

I've eaten out nearly every meal for close to fifteen years. In 2010, having relocated my apartment and home office to the heart of the Mission, I challenged myself to eat two to three meals a day out, never at the same place, for sixty days. Success -- I made it to seventy-five before returning to my first duplicate, appeasing a friend in dire desire of the chicken liver appetizer at Serpentine on Third Street. Over one hundred fifty different spots, mostly in the neighborhood, and I never came close to running out of eateries to explore.

In 2008, at age 38, I bought my first couch and my first new bed, as well as two plates and two sets of silverware and six beer glasses to serve the maximum number of friends I calculated could fit in the forty or so square feet of my "living room." Coincidentally, my mom would soon be retiring to Montana, meaning the long-running storage facilities of Shmaltz Brewing would be closed forever when she sold her garage, along with the rest of her condo, in Palo Alto.

Leah secured us the smallest, cheapest rent-by-the-month storage locker we could find beneath the off-ramp of the 101, and we loaded in the boxes of old -- I mean "vintage" if you see them pop up on eBay -- Shmaltz materials, from promo posters to limited-edition baby shirts to early hand-painted tap handles.

Global headquarters consisted of a four-foot stainless steel desk, one three-drawer filing cabinet, and of course a collection of yellow stickies to track company priorities. An upgraded Macbook, a USB wireless card, and an unlimited-use cell phone meant no need for a landline or a cable connection. I'd make it three months in my new slice of the American dream before heading to New York for the summer and subletting my own apartment to someone else for the first time in my life.

I'd heard the cliché many times in the context of business-speak: "Plowing the profits back into the company." Even after well over a decade of ostensibly being a "businessman," I don't think I could have defined exactly what it meant on paper, or in practice. Likely not a coincidence, since I had so little experience with profits. I aced that real-life class in 2008.

Following the plan from Eva's prophetic spreadsheet to my profit-and-loss statement, now generated quarterly by the recent addition of a freelance bookkeeper, Shmaltz Brewing started making money. And as fast as it started rolling in I started spending it -- on the business.

I'd done three to four ride-withs each day and several evening and weekend events nearly every week for almost five years. Managing twenty-five or so monthly distributor orders, event planning, marketing materials, press release edits, and media interviews, all the accounting, the ongoing landslide of customer emails, donation requests, compliments and constructive criticisms, and making time for the new products we were cranking out -- all while on the road. I was cooked.

Whether coincidence or confluence, the company started generating the profits that allowed me to hire talented and committed people to push the Shmaltz vision beyond anything my one-man show could handle.

Still purposefully without an org chart, I had gathered a posse of co-workers. Leah inherited the virtual office mantle from Angela to handle admin and the zillion projects that the company (or I) would cook up repeatedly; Matt split time on art and sales in and around New York; Darren in Atlanta covered the South, and Zak in San Francisco juggled the West. Everyone cranking throttle. On monthly retainer for Shmaltz, perched above Mission Street at the modest headquarters of his own entrepreneurial outpost, Jesse spun out press releases and media blasts, lighting up the phones and cajoling journalists, from the biggest nationals to the neighborhood Jewish newsletters. In my head, (and I suppose outside my head as well) Shmaltz Brewing suddenly became a real company.

Yet with the new employees, I was becoming what I always feared: a manager. For so many years, customers, distributors, and buyers simply referred to me in the singular as "the He'brew Guy." Having had so much practice without staff, I continued to think of myself less as the Boss than as simply a creator, or perhaps the Producer.

Even after three years, the role of manager still feels new to me, and sometimes awkward. I wanted to create a company more like a family than an organization. I'm realizing as I write this that I'm unconsciously mimicking my primary role model: not a business leader, but a Jewish mother. With high expectations for those around me and high hopes for their own personal development, my response to shortcomings and missed opportunities commonly sounds something like, "I'm not angry, I'm just disappointed."[21]

Whenever I meet people and mention that I run the company, the response is usually the same: "Wow, this is your *job?* That must be the best job ever!"

I often say that I don't want to taint the glamorous image of the freewheeling small-beer business owner with gritty details of real struggles (other than the three hundred or so pages here), so I encourage the fantasy and suggest they *buy our beer* to touch the magic.

However, there are certain moments that even I can appreciate: *Wow, is this really my job?*

Tasting a box full of our favorite beers from around the country and around the world as part of serious R&D for designing new beers is just such a moment.

From the first round with Simon at a table outside Brewmakers to the dozen times I've been responsible for "research" with Paul, the process has

---

21 When mentioning this to Matt, he remarked, "Yeah, that's about right. Though since most families are rather dysfunctional anyway, that's probably why companies try to run like a real business. You know, with rules and stuff."

been the same: instructive and scrumptious.

For Albino Python, I grabbed a sample of everything I could find stocked at Bierkraft in Brooklyn that seemed within the realm of white or wheat beers. We tasted probably eighteen different micros and imports, searching for the elements in each that reflected our aspirations for our own creation.

Much like any "proper" beer tasting, we go through the elements of a formal beer judging, starting with clean glasses and a quiet moment of anticipation.

From here I'll borrow from the non-profit Beer Judge Certification Program (BJCP) official guidelines. Hit their website for tons of great info at bjcp.org.

Appearance: Simple enough: Look at the beer. But is it simple? Color, clarity, lacing of the foamy head. Some beers are designed to be crystal clear, others to be light but cloudy, with dense stouts to completely block out the light. Does the beer achieve its intention?

Aroma: A distinct size advantage for some members of my tribe -- bury your nose in the smell of it all. For purposely hoppy beers, the floral and citrus notes of a strong IPA, especially when dry-hopped, bring first enjoyment even from afar. Moving closer, explore the malts – bready, biscuit, sweet or spicy grains. The smell of a neighborhood bakery, or the brew pub down the street.

Flavor: Finally -- drink it! Sweet or bitter up front. Chocolate or grapefruit, raisins or cornmeal -- the flavors, especially over the last several years, have expanded exponentially. Let the liquid explore your mouth and seek out the nooks and crannies of the subtle -- or extreme -- spectrum of tastes to enjoy.

Mouthfeel: Light on the pallet or thick, viscous, and chewy. Does the carbonation help or hurt experiencing the flavors? Smooth textures or rough edges -- important for both the intention of the brewer as well as the enjoyment of the drinker.

Overall Impression: Did you like it?! Did it accomplish what the label/ brewer stated as the goal? Do you want to keep sipping, quaffing, gulping?

Work, work, work!

For Albino Python, we whittled it down to Hitachino white, Allagash white, and Hoegaarden as points of reference. I love tasting beers right next to each other that I might otherwise think seem pretty similar. Sip to sip, the variations come through so clearly, revealing a world of difference even within comparable styles. The intensity of the wheat profile, various spices, the mouthfeel and carbonation, and the overall flavor directions of the three offered perfect points of departure for my discussion with Paul. And they tasted so good.

As with nearly all our beers, we decided to go for a hybrid version of several styles. Every year this decision proves painfully problematic at Great American Beer Festival, since none of our beers are brewed to classic "style guidelines." Comments every year come back something like, "Great overall beer, but not close enough to style for medal consideration." The awards we've won, which have been enough to justify bragging, usually come from wider categories such as "Best in Show" or alternative catch-all groupings such as "Alternative Lager" or "Experimental Belgian." Not a huge concern -- we usually just brew to impress our friends, beer cohorts, and, most importantly, ourselves.

Paul designed the Python flavors to come through as a bastardized Belgian *wit* with a touch of German *hefe*, though with a heavy dose of American craft taste and attitude. The grain bill included specialty two-row barley, about forty percent wheat malt, acidulated malt, pilsner malt, and oatmeal. Hops included warrior to bitter, and saaz and summit for flavor and aroma.

Paul suggested we include spices from well-known beer styles but not in any traditional combination: ginger, sweet orange peel, and crushed fennel seed. I said, Hell yeah, go for originality. Even at six percent alcohol, Python could be considered an "extreme" beer because of the unusual ingredients and brewing process.

All the beers I'd brought and could find were brewed with top fermenting Ale yeast. However, this mashup of styles and ingredients would be brewed with lager yeast. As far as we knew, Albino Python would be the only White Lager... *in the world!* (Not positive, but happy to hype it as such until proven wrong. Please send samples for confirmation to address at front of book.)

The day we poured the first cold Pythons at S.K.I., the Italian salesmen loved the spices and were ready to bring it home to drink with pizza and family recipes. Because of its multi-layered flavors, we continue to use the beer at nearly every beer dinner we do, pairing with dishes like sushi-grade smoked salmon and wasabi crème fraiche and house-made, chorizo-stuffed calamari with squid ink risotto. At Brouwer's for Seattle Beer Week in 2010, they even prepared an actual python as a special dish for the night. Scary, but tasty.

Since Heather, the Coney Island sword swallower, tended toward sweeter tonics, I warned her ahead of time that our tribute to her might be a little rough on her palette. But her performances offered the perfect foil for an aggressive hoppy lager: sharp, strong and steely but also delicate, poised, well-composed. Paul designed a seven-percent robust IPA recipe for Sword Swallower, with barley, rye, wheat and pale Vienna malts for the lightest colored (yet still complex) beer we offered. The hops drew from European sources but served up a huge helping of Pacific Northwest flavor and aroma hops, dry-hopping with IPA favorites, crystal, cascade and amarillo. We weren't sure how the lager yeast would affect the overall beer, but the characteristic clean finish and slightly softer texture have made Sword probably my favorite "session-ish" (for seven percent) beer in our portfolio. And we love working with Heather whenever possible, even if she prefers a Mermaid Pilsner or a vodka and pineapple juice.

And the maestro of the whole beer carnival: Mr. Donny Vomit, the MC of the Sideshow with his signature act the Human Blockhead. When the shtick can so beautifully inspire the beer, Shmaltz Brewing shines.

Powerful, intense, raucous, a standout. And -- as with the Sword -- alarming, precise, and graceful. Commanding.

I looked to the strong European lagers for inspiration, buying a box of boozy options from our pals at City Beer in San Francisco. Zak and I sampled the medley, and I narrowed down my scheme to something in the neighborhood of the fabled and noble high gravity legends, Eku 28 and Samiclaus Helles.

Kelly and I had banged out a loose idea for a recipe the year before, and he threw together a test batch one-off at Greenpoint that had turned out well and sold through at several bars in New York City. Over the phone, Paul and I worked to refine the flavors, preparing for the national launch as our lead Coney seasonal. We went though our five steps of "pro" beer tasting simultaneously, over the phone.

We knew we could not afford the many months of brewing and aging of the coveted originals, but the grain bill aimed to coax a luscious adaptation of what we knew we could create: our own bad-ass American version of a strong European lager. Munich and Vienna malts, pale and crystal rye, wheat and flaked oats gave the Blockhead a huge, complex malt foundation. Warrior, horizon, tettnang, palisade, crystal and hallertauer displayed a cornucopia of both continental and clearly U.S. craft hop flavors. Donny (and many others) loved the beer. I knew Paul had nailed it.

The summer of 2008 marked my sixth annual pilgrimage to New York for the summer selling season. To launch our Coney Island Craft Lagers, we organized a bash at the Gate on Fifth Avenue in Park Slope, one of our favorite bars in Brooklyn. We brought in the sideshow acts, Donny (Human Blockhead), Heather (Sword Swallower), and Stephanie (Albino Python) to perform in the standing-room-only inside bar.

The crowd was pretty well boozed up, and I jumped on the bench seats and started yelling MC-style, hollering about the great craft beer scene in Brooklyn, barking about the evolution of Shmaltz. I introduced the maestro Mr. Donny Vomit, who jumped on the bar and jammed a power drill into his nose. The place went nuts.

Coney looked to be a bit of a different beast than He'brew.

Matt and I glanced at each other across the rocking bar and mouthed "H-O-L-Y S-H-I-T."

In addition to putting the performers in front of every room we could manage, it also seemed like a good plan to start protecting our Shmaltz assets and my evolving enterprise.

My friend Jon had been pounding me year after year to get my trademarks in place. I made one brief attempt to handle it myself a few years earlier, and then I accidentally let the trademark for He'brew slip. I didn't realize renewal is mandatory every five years. After all the headache of going through the buyout in 1999, I essentially owned nothing: no recorded copyrights, no registered trademarks, no intellectual property. I had common law rights from simply using the marks, which carried some legitimate weight, but in the scheme of rock-solid protection of goods, I had zilch.

Jon gave me the name of his trademark lawyer in New York, saying, "For this kinda stuff, I want a pit bull of a Jewish lawyer with a Manhattan address." Fitting the spirit of Jon's colorful commentary towards foes of her clients though absolutely lovely in person, Barbara has become one of my most gracious and truly invaluable vendors.

Perhaps it's lucky I started investing in a lawyer as the recession slammed New York City: She has been very understanding of my own financial limitations, and she and her firm have been incredibly flexible in working within my budget. Even so, they've been completely professional and thorough in protecting my brands.

I knew it was going to be tricky for Coney Island -- in general, geographic names cannot be easily trademarked. Several years back I'd had the idea to make a light beer and call it Israelite: "Tastes great, more fulfilling... You shall be a Light unto the Nations (Isaiah 42:6)." Perfect shtick for the lineup, but the U.S. P.T.O. sent back the trademark application, rejected based on the geographic reference. Since I wouldn't have likely wanted to drink much of the beer, they saved me the effort.

Still, Brooklyn Brewery seemed to have gotten their trademark, as had Sam Adams for Boston Lager. Then I saw an article about somebody who was marketing, of all things, a Coney Island perfume. Ah, the invigorating scent of the sea... and sweaty amusement park operators, knife fights, sausages...

I told Barbara about it and she said, "Actually, that was my client." In a city swarming with lawyers, Jewish or otherwise, this was unbelievable -- kismet, my legal *beshert*.

At the time of this telling, we've trademarked just about everything we make -- all the brand names and company marks, "Coney Island" for beer and brewing services[22], even soda pop (coming soon). We registered

---

22 No longer intent-to-use since we've opened Coney Island Brewing Company, the World's Smallest Brewery. Inaugural batches brewed by Nik Sin the 3 foot 6.66 inch tall self identified rock star midget of the freakshow. One gallon at a time, since 2010.

"Freaktoberfest" and "Geektoberfest" for both the beers themselves that we produce and the festivals we've promoted in Brooklyn and around the country. The entourage of He'brew Beers have finally all been filed into the P.T.O. hall of trademark justice. After negotiation with a Mexican tequila company and an evangelical Christian spring water bottler, one final loose end should get tied up momentarily to finally register our flagship brand, Genesis Ale, nearly fourteen years in.

For all the right reasons, Barbara has me right where she wants me. Now we have to protect all these trademarks. Over the past year we've had multiple incidents demanding legal attention for our marks. Coincidence? She's like the trademark drug dealer: she gave me the first few for free, and I just keep coming back for more. Intellectual property junkie -- *hit me.*

My first run-in with trademark complications came very early in the business, right when I started, from a guy who ran a snack company called Meshuganuts. Much like I had, he started the venture at home, in his garage in San Francisco. A couple months after I started He'brew, I'd asked his advice about the business, and he had been really helpful (though he warned me he'd seen very few examples of Jewish products the community supported over the long haul). He gave me leads and contacts, and overall was a great resource. And I loved the name -- seriously, Meshuganuts?! Wish I'd thought of it... and felt like selling nuts all day long.

Maybe four weeks later, I got a letter from either him or his lawyer, I can't remember which: "Dear Mr. Cowan: Please cease and desist your entire project. Using Jewish humor, illustrations, and puns in branding is owned by Meshuganuts." He was making pecan shortbread cookies. We should have been co-marketing at the grocery store, not waging a war of words. He sold his company a couple of years later to a national confectionary giant, likely relieved of his burden.

I got another absurd cease-and-desist over the graphics for Origin. Matt hand-drew an abstracted pomegranate tree, for the background and Poma Liqueur sent another three-pager on heavy linen cream paper stock, filled with bluster and accusation, demanding we remove the image. They charged that we'd stolen their logo.

1. Matt personally drew ours, and we'd not even looked at the Poma bottle

or their marketing other than in passing as one of a hundred bottles on most back bars. 2. Come on, guys -- dancing rabbis blowing a *shofar* and floating in a kiddie pool of pomegranates... I just don't think anyone will be *confused*.

When it comes to trademark disputes, you will inevitably find yourself on both sides. In the spring of 2009, I was contacted by a guy who was leaving his head brewer's job at a larger regional brewery to start his own packaging microbrewery in upstate New York.

The town name, Canandaigua, is an Iroquois word meaning "chosen spot." He told me he wanted to call the brewery Chosen Spot Brewing and wanted to confirm with me that I wouldn't have a problem with the name. I said I appreciated him getting in touch, and that, yes, I owned the federal trademark for the phrase "Chosen Beer." I'd used the phrase on every bottle and every marketing piece for the brand and my company for thirteen years. I see it as a fundamental element to our identity. (I didn't explain the nightmare of retaining the phrase through the early ATF label approval insanity.) I pointed out that there is not one other beer of the tens of thousands of beer names from over 1500 breweries in this country that uses the word "chosen" in the brand. In closing, I really needed to discourage him from using it.

He said, "I've got to tell you, my lawyer says it's going to be fine." I was pissed.

Over several months I repeatedly urged him to reconsider and even offered to find a compromise. Maybe he could just use it as a descriptive line attached to the brand specifically in town, since that was where people would recognize the slogan.

Simply the *potential* for customer confusion is the test for trademark infringement, and I couldn't imagine that if we had big banners reading "The Chosen Beer" next to "Chosen Spot Brewing" in the New York section at Great American Beer Festival, no one would come up and say, "Hey, are you guys connected?"

Barbara looked it up, and she saw that he hadn't trademarked the name yet. We figured it was going to cost me between $25,000 and $50,000 to sue him after he opened. So I decided to take another tack and put out a beer of our own called Chosen Spot.

At the tail end of my summer sublet in Brooklyn, in the shower one morning, I came up with the shtick for a fake brand. The next week, Matt and I designed the label in five hours.

We had a batch of Coney Island Mermaid Pilsner coming up, so Bob at the brewery pushed through label approval. We shipped a pallet to our local wholesaler and we had cases of Chosen Spot Pilsner in the guy's hometown within forty days. It was definitely ruthless and sneaky, but better, I thought, than us spending $100,000 arguing in court.

I never heard back from him. I did what I thought was necessary -- what I thought was the cheapest and most efficient solution to protect myself and the company. I also felt conflicted about it the whole time. After years in the business, clearly this guy was finally pursuing his own craft beer dream, and before it even opens he's got this giant mess.

"WELL, I MEAN, WHO CHOSE IT?"

Months later I read an article that said he was spending close to a million dollars to open his brewery. It turned out he was going to change the name anyway. With plenty of experience and resources behind him, I'm sure he'll do well.

Interestingly, for a while both Chosen Spot and Mermaid Pilsner were reviewed on Rate Beer and Beer Advocate with rather varied ratings, given the fact that they were the same beer. I still love the real t-shirts we got printed out for the fake rollout.

Right from the introduction of our new white lager from Coney Island, Albino Python got up and started running… before it crawled. I'd asked Paul to design a robust, unfiltered, unpasteurized wheat beer brewed with cold fermenting lager yeast. The brewery had produced many different white beers over the years for themselves and their contracts such as Southampton. But all the ales had been processed with top fermenting ale yeast. We thought it should work as planned; however, since there weren't any other white lagers we'd found, we had nothing to go by.

The first batch tasted so lovely. As I mentioned, the day we poured samples for the S.K.I. reps, the Italian guys tasted basil and chided us for not bringing *quattro stagione* pizza or primavera to pair with it. The whole crew loved the aroma and the complexity of the herbal spices and floral hops.

They went out and just *sold* the beer. We shot straight to twenty-five, then fifty kegs for the month, growing every day. Only a year earlier, we'd been selling maybe ten to fifteen kegs per month of our entire portfolio. Having a hot seller jump straight to number two in sales for us was a great sign. And I simply loved to drink that beer.

About six weeks after the launch, The Python suddenly curled up and refused to move -- literally. Whether it was the lager yeast dropping to the bottom of the keg and clogging the flow of beer through the stem, or whether the lager yeast still active enough at the cold temperature was going through secondary fermentation in the keg -- likely both -- it simply wouldn't pour. Chunks of clotted yeast or endless foam would spew out of every keg online in the city. Within two weeks sales plummeted.

Even after over a decade in the beer business, I did not know enough technical details to respond quickly or effectively. We stumbled through apologies and begged for patience as we flipped the kegs upside down to move the yeast away from the stem. We asked the bars to gently roll the kegs to try to get the yeast back into suspension so it would pour correctly. You can imagine the response of the average New York bar owner when asked to manually massage a keg several times a day inside his already jam-packed cold box. The t-shirts on Bleecker sell here for a reason: *Fuck you, you fucking fuck.*

The kegs turned out to be an ominous sign. Clearly enough yeast remained active to over-pressurize even the bottles. The first report came from one of our most important accounts in the Midwest, Binny's in Chicago. Two bottles displayed in the cold box exploded with enough force to shatter the entire cooler door.

They pulled all the bottles off all the shelves of the chain, and we scrambled to figure out what the hell was going on and how the hell we might fix it. Rather remarkably, I'd never experienced a brewing problem before -- never a spoiled batch and never a packaging concern.

I called my business liability insurance company, who'd specifically targeted small brewers by marketing through the Brewers Association. They told me recalls were not covered by my insurance. I was shocked. Isn't this exactly why we have coverage for worst-case scenarios?

They said I was covered for any damages that might occur if someone got injured after the fact -- lost an eye or cut open a hand -- but the decision, and the cost of trying to prevent that catastrophe, fell completely on me.

Over my years of bartending, I'd had plenty of bottles blow up from much bigger companies such Bud and Heineken. We all knew it was a part of the business. But this was *my* baby. Trying to explain the situation to concerned buyers and wholesalers felt almost as painful as imagining what I stood to lose if the situation got much worse.

In this case, being so small turned out to help my cause. Since we hadn't packaged all that many cases and the beer had been a big hit from the start, not much remained from the early batches on shelves or at wholesalers.

I stopped shipping and destroyed what was left of the batches at the brewery, and we took back problem cases from wholesalers and retailers. Particularly perplexing, it seemed not all bottles were experiencing the problem, so we'd never know where the next report would come from.

As of fall 2010, we filter and pasteurize the beer, just to be safe. I know some craft beer brethren are shaking their heads in disappointment at the "killing" of our beloved "live" beer. But I've tasted both versions, and I still absolutely adore the current flavor. And I especially love that we won't harm anyone, or our own future, in the process.

The ad campaign for our new addition to the Coney family of beers should have read: *"Don't order yet, Friends. Once you've enjoyed the explosive taste of Coney Island Albino Python, you also get, thrown in at no extra charge -- a frivolous lawsuit! Cheers!"*

Just as I was coming up for air on the recall, a completely unexpected kick to the nuts: The snake-dance performer depicted on the label filed a lawsuit against me for $250,000. She had emailed me that winter that she thought she wasn't making enough money from the product. Was I just another person who was going to screw the Sideshow, like so many had in the past?

My agreement was with the Sideshow itself, the arts organization that employed the performers. The organization was supposed to work out separate agreements with the performers; Shmaltz wasn't supposed to be involved in those negotiations. (However, as everyone involved regularly quips, "It is a freak show, after all.")

I forwarded her email to the Sideshow management with a note to please respond and take care of her concerns. Six months after the email, I got a letter at my P.O. box in San Francisco from her lawyer. They were suing me personally (not the company, and not the Sideshow) for a quarter-million dollars. I remember I called him from my cell phone as I left my studio apartment on Howard Street in my '97 Pathfinder. I got straight through to him -- strange for a lawyer with a midtown Manhattan address not to have a secretary. The moment I mentioned who I was and why I was calling he launched into a tirade, screaming, "LISTEN, MR. BIG SHOT! YOU BETTER COME OUTTA YOUR FANCY OFFICES AND THAT EXPENSIVE CAR AND TELL YOUR INSURANCE AGENT THAT YOU'VE BEEN SCREWING A TALENTED ARTIST. NOW YOU'RE GONNA PAY!"

I replied with rare calm, given the situation, "Sir, your letter is the first I have even heard of the lawsuit. You need to stop screaming at me." Loved the "fancy offices" bit.

I've definitely been responsible for plenty of negativity in the world, and I'm culpable for many failings. This, one hundred percent, was not one of them. I'd been approached by a non-profit arts organization for a licensing project that would generate needed funds. I'd done my part. Now one person they employed was blaming me, and holding the organization unaccountable for a perceived injustice. She was suing me for far more than the total sales of the entire product line.

But the goddess of conflict resolution was smiling on Shmaltz that summer. Maggie, who was friendly with the Sideshow, miraculously saved the entire situation from utter calamity. A Manhattan corporate lawyer for years, she decided to change her career and help non-profits and small businesses whenever possible. She patiently responded to the lawyer's absurd bluster, gave the Sideshow time to regroup, and urged the people involved to settle the dispute among themselves. I can't thank her enough.

I was terrified that the other performers were thinking the same way and that the whole project would unravel. I was so relieved to find out they were not in any way feeling taken advantage of, and we've continued to work together whenever possible in New York City and around the country.

Surviving the madness offered the chance to make my working relationship with the Sideshow much healthier. We've been able to achieve a more productive level of communication, and, as I mentioned, they are our number one account in the country. When the world gives you exploding lawsuits of lemons, make lem-... no, wait -- just make more beer.

Our tiny company was growing exponentially. At the end of 2008, Jesse could legitimately send out a press release announcing that Shmaltz Brewing sales had grown ten times what they'd been just five years before. Shmaltz had a staff around the country, distribution in nearly thirty states, and a growing appreciation of our diverse lineup. The company had come a long way from the two 5.5% ales I'd sold on a solo mission crisscrossing the U.S. We'd been able to participate with the best craft beers in the country at special events, from Extreme Beer Festival to GABF to high-end beer dinners and boutique beer pairings.

S.K.I. had a strapping young street rep with great intentions and a mouthful of urban dictionary-isms. He handled the East Village and the Lower East Side, crucial territories for our brands. Tired of selling so many brands and chasing down so many bad checks, Sean told Matt and me that he was planning to leave S.K.I., and he wondered whether we could make some room for him on our supplier side. He loved the idea of working with a smaller portfolio, and ours was the one he was most excited about. He was a non-Jewish guy who just really loved great beer.

I'd spent so long thinking of the company as my personal project that the idea of someone not already connected to me approaching us for a job still seemed astonishing. Sure, I'd get the occasional blanket email looking for a position in the "organization," or in the "warehouse" or the "marketing department." Hated to burst their bubbles. Why would someone venture their career and their paycheck on the dancing rabbi and the Sideshow freaks?

I asked Ralph's permission to talk to Sean about a job with us. The last thing I wanted to do was risk my relationship with one of our most important customers. Ralph was very cool about it and knew Sean was ready to leave, so I hired Sean part-time and sent him outside of S.K.I.'s territory.

I'd gotten used to asking new employees to pay their dues in a part-time role. My strategy was to force them to force me to hire them. And every one of them did it. Sean was no exception.

After a few months working on our surrounding markets, he came back to focus on S.K.I.'s territory. He knew their system -- the schedule, the ordering, the reps and the manager's expectations. He would prove extremely valuable helping us grow to make S.K.I. our biggest distributor, particularly with the expansion of the Coney brands through specialty beer bars and, most important, neighborhood hangouts. He would stay passionate about the beers and committed to the company throughout our growth. However, unfortunately, as Ralph later remarked, sometimes a company's needs outgrow the individuals that got it there. This would be the case with Sean, who needed to move on over the past summer.

In the fall of 2008, Leah took over from Angela as my official administrative go-to. Leah had interned for me for years, many of those while still underage, while she was going to Emory University. She'd done all the research for the numbers eight, nine, ten for Jewbelation, and for pomegranates, figs, and dates for Rejewvenator. Her cousin Kevin had been my first-ever intern. I knew I could rely on her. The family tree was growing stronger and stronger.

None of us are exactly sure whether Jesse thought he was hitting on Melissa at *Beer Advocate*'s American Craft Beer fest in Boston. But after a final buzzed chat (this was the month before he met Robyn, the love of his life), Melissa got in touch about entering the sisterhood of the Shmaltz Internship.

We put her to task immediately, and her talents and sensibility became an obvious fit for our small but growing tribe. She would take on full-time responsibility for Massachusetts before moving down to New York to help with S.K.I. and juggling Indiana, Michigan, western Pennsylvania, a bit of Ohio, and even some of Nebraska. She's also become our Twitter queen on the East Coast.

From the day I wrote my first business plan, my mom has always encouraged me that one day I'd have enough help that I'd be able to focus on the stuff I'm good at (and want to do). If I didn't have a new product, a big event, or some other distraction-slash-evolution-slash-challenge, I'm not sure how I would have stayed alive through the grind. It's the whole reason I did this in the first place: *Wouldn't it be cool if …*

Perfect example: Freaktoberfest. Our buddies Pat from the Gate (now the Smuttynose sales manager) and Ben, the grand poobah of my (and many small breweries') long time top account, Bierkraft, had been kicking around the idea of a Park Slope beer festival.

With years of experience and beer connections and an impossible-to-miss ZZ Top beard, Pat served as the dirty rock 'n' roll Santa Claus of the Brooklyn craft beer scene. And Ben, one of the most enthusiastic and sophisticated beer-and-cheese geeks I've ever met, brought the grassroots network of customers, potential volunteers, and technical skills needed to pull it together.

Matt and I pitched them on doing a fest with us. We didn't mean to take over the branding of the event, but the guys were totally into it.

To fill out the team, we recruited Erica, who managed a burlesque bar in Prospect Heights, the too-short-lived Barrette, and DJ Mikey Palms, co-owner of Southpaw and Public Assembly, our Jewish homeboy and hookup to the local underground music scene.

On one of many brainstorm-filled drives we took together, on our way back from D.C. earlier that summer, Matt and I had thought of an idea for a beer festival specifically focused on the Coney Island beers that would bring all our very favorite brewers from around the region and across the country to Brooklyn for a craft beer rager.

Though I loved the name, *Shocktoberfest* wouldn't reflect the quality of the great beers we wanted to present. *Shocktoberfest* sounded way too Clear Channel rock jock.

Freaktoberfest fit the bill perfectly. We could pimp our seasonal Halloween release as well as brand a killer party.

Since we didn't own a brewery, Matt and I figured if we had our own beer festival, it would give us an excuse to bring people to us to present the beers in the way we wanted to showcase them. We wanted to remind our fellow beer geeks that beer is still supposed to be *fun*. Step inside and experience great craft beer, with go-go dancers and brass bands and rockin' DJs.

At the same time, we wanted to expose ambitious micros to people who might not otherwise be all that interested -- people who might be drinking PBR or Red Stripe, or whatever's on special -- but who would love the rocking party. People who already respect indie music and indie movies and like local restaurants and alternative culture -- those people should be drinking indie beer as well.

Once you expose those people to the complex, wild, and exciting flavors of the most creative beers coming from independent small breweries -- whether a barrel-aged American brown sour brewed with exotic spices and multiple yeast strains that might take six months to two years to produce, or an American take on a European low gravity fruit beer, or a mead/malt blend unlike anything they'd tasted before -- they usually realize, "Damn, this is amazing stuff!"

We figured the perfect place to kick off what we'd hoped would grow into an annual gathering (coming up on our third annual as I write) would be at the Sideshow at Coney Island U.S.A.

Once we got the posse in place, we had about a month to pull it together. Even with so little time to plan, the night came together beautifully. We had a blast.

Mikey nailed down the music acts and the bands set up in front of the historic old bank building on West 12th Street across from the Sideshow. Erica booked the best burlesque and go-go dancers she knew. Ben pulled together a crew of volunteers and worked with Pat and me to nail down the brewery lineup. Matt jammed out the graphics and designed the website with online ticket sales. Jesse pounded down his phone lists and invited the media.

The breweries who came brought only their specialty beers. Downstairs, we asked for styles more on the sessionable side, four to seven percent alcohol, but no flagships of widely distributed brands. The V.I.P. room upstairs featured only rare and obscure beers from our favorite breweries, with special burlesque performances just for the private room. We had one unbelievable beer after another -- Lost Abbey, the new Dogfish Head, Southampton, Hair of the Dog, Allagash, Firestone Walker.

I was blown away. I'd been hitting festivals for thirteen years, and I'd never seen the stunning selection we were able to pull together. Great beer, roller derby women, dancing girls, rocker chicks, and the men who love them all. Spectacular.

While we were pulling in the Brooklyn beer freaks and beer geeks, we also got an invitation from a local staffer, who loved our beers, to join the Brooklyn Chamber of Commerce.

I figured it seemed like an appropriately grown-up business decision to make, so we joined as a networking opportunity, hoping to connect with some retail accounts in the borough. Though my disposition is generally not pro-business of the kind that seems to dominate many Chambers of Commerce, everyone in Brooklyn was surprisingly nice, helpful, and supportive.

Just a few months later, we ended up winning the Distinguished Business award for community-based small businesses and organizations. The honorees at the annual gala were the president of Pratt Institute, a hip new downtown hotel, and Shmaltz Brewing.

I'd seen Marty Markowitz, the president of the Borough of Brooklyn, on TV for so many years, typically holding a Junior's cheesecake in one hand and a Brooklyn Lager in the other. It was a treat to be introduced by this flamboyant Jewish icon at the ceremony at the Brooklyn Museum.

After all my tongue-in-cheek braggadocio spewed out over the years of Shmaltz Brewing, the freeway signs along the BQE (Brooklyn-Queens Expressway) took on a slightly different feeling:

"Believe the hype!" (westbound, at Kosciuszko Bridge)[23]

We had our first company-wide meeting during San Francisco Beer Week that winter. Leah and I planned all-day staff meetings, and then the crew

---

23 Other delights: "Oy Vey!" Williamsburg Bridge, westbound, at entrance; "Fuggedaboudit!" Gowanus Expressway, westbound, approaching the Verrazano Narrows.

went to events that Zak had pulled together every night. Beer dinners, happy hours, pub crawls -- a jam packed calendar to highlight so many things we'd accomplished as a company. We barely survived. By the last afternoon of Toronado's famed Barleywine Festival, we were all ready for a vacation.

Still, in some specific ways, we got more accomplished in one week than I had in years. I printed out profit-and-loss statements for us all to review and sales reports by distributor, by territory. Line by line, we went over what the company spent, what it made, and where we spent it and made it. Everything was open for discussion, and everyone could see the bottom line.

My friend Jim donated his loft for our off-site. When we first sat down, I looked up, and everyone was looking at me. I'd made such a scramble to get all the data together, I realized I hadn't given one second of thought to what I should say as a manager, or what I should do as a leader.

So I opened my mouth, as I tend to do, and started yapping. I tried to speak from the truth of the moment. I told them how bizarre and exciting, and how meaningful, it was for me to have this group of people bring their talents, their time, and their energy to a project I felt like I'd been doing alone for so long.

The week was a huge success and a turning point for me. I saw the staff throwing themselves into their jobs, and began to see that I could delegate and truly rely on them to follow through with a similar care and commitment that I'd demanded of myself.

Unfortunately, one area I couldn't toss off my plate were the huge credit card debts that I relied on to keep us afloat. Given that I'd seriously exaggerated my income in the first place, perhaps I should not have been so self-righteous in my fury when the recession started my credit lines receding. However, I'd made payments every month and paid the necessary interest and balances and kept in great standing -- with a credit rating much higher than my Stanford-qualifying SAT scores.

With literally five working days' notice, the credit card that I used to pay for company expenses just closed. I had been using the one card for several years to pay for everything from hops to travel to FedEx to pint glasses, point-of-sale materials and so much more. Not a bankruptcy or buy-out, they sent a one-page letter in the mail that simply stated the lender would no longer extend credit and my account would be terminated. Thirty-five thousand dollars of cushion ripped out from under me.

After receiving TARP funds from the taxpayers to allow for their own survival, Chase unilaterally changed the terms of a balance transfer offer I'd accepted and had been paying down every month for eighteen months. The minimum monthly payment went up one hundred and fifty percent, and the payout changed from five years to two years. The balance was still sixty thousand dollars when the accelerated payments began, which meant just the increase added up to nearly my mortgage.

It didn't need to happen overnight, but I knew I should start planning to cover my butt as our sales continued to grow and my financial resources continued to dry up.

Throughout the first two years of the recession, with front-page lip service paid by government and bright new billboard ads by banks targeting small business as the "engine of growth" and "driver of new jobs," yadda yadda, I figured it must be a good time to approach banks to help finance what now had been five years of profitability and growth for Shmaltz.

For all the economic hardship of 2009 and into 2010, all the suffering and unemployment, the foreclosures, the widespread problems in the country, craft beer continues to grow. One nagging problem continues to be that small businesses haven't been able to come up with the resources to support their growth or to get out from under the debt they've created.

It hasn't been a lack of demand. In 2009, overall U.S. beer sales were down two percent and import sales were down nearly ten percent. In contrast, craft beer dollar-sales grew ten percent in 2008 and 2009 and look to be on the same pattern for 2010. Shmaltz's numbers have auspiciously stayed well above that pace.

When we were named one of the "Top 20 Fastest Growing Companies" in the Bay Area by the *San Francisco Business Times*, I received multiple inquiries from local lenders claiming just such small-business loan expertise. One well-wisher quickly dropped out when they realized we didn't own a brewery, real estate, or equipment.

I went to the local bank that I've used since my first month in San Francisco, when I opened a little personal savings account in 1995. Originally on the upper floors of the Bank of America building downtown with an breathtaking panorama of San Francisco, they'd been so inviting: "Why don't you bring your friends up for the view?"

Fifteen years later, with my business looking to break two million in sales, I was greeted by a silver-haired, sixty-something gentleman in a three-piece pinstripe blue banker suit. Sitting at a conference table, he opened by saying, "I have to tell you how impressed we are. After thirteen years of business, you've really paid your dues. And I can tell from talking to you, and looking at your business, the company is clearly on a roll. My local BevMo has eight of your beers at eye level, in stock at all times. I've looked at your profit-and-loss statement, and I've been reading about you in the local media."

Frustratingly, for the last three months of the previous year, this same banker would not even return my phone calls. I finally had to threaten that if he didn't call me back by "this afternoon," I'd be pulling the rest of my paltry savings account out of this bank and never coming back. This meeting came a month into our renewed negotiation.

I think he was sincere in saying some of the nicest things anybody's said to me in a professional setting that I can remember. But in the end they ran me through a relentless series of fiery hoops, until a botched accounts payable audit on their end undid the whole deal. After four months of hours and hours of answering questions, providing documentation, running and re-running reports -- all wasted effort.

The same thing happened in New York with a lender who, according to their small-business loan specialist, was a "very enthusiastic and extremely well-funded, working people's bank." After many more painfully detailed demands, they pulled a flawed real estate appraisal off the Internet, which skewed all our numbers and undermined the agreement, dashing nearly five months of work.

But the worst insult probably came from the bank I'd been doing business with for the entire history of my company, Wells Fargo.

In a year in which I would deposit over two million dollars and carry a healthy daily balance at all times, Wells Fargo would not even extend a ten-thousand dollar business credit card to me -- at *any* interest rate -- to buy the shirts and merchandise we wanted to stock at the storefront brewery for summer in Coney Island.

My much bigger concern -- the hundred and fifty thousand dollars I needed to support our inventory growth -- for them was out of the question. One of their reasons for turning me down: too many requests for credit increases on my credit report. Most of the requests, however, had come *from them.*

Finally, a smaller San Francisco-based bank that focuses on green tech companies and some New Age beverage products threw me an eight-percent-interest bone for a hundred thousand dollar unsecured line of credit. I had to close out some credit cards, so my total available debt may have even gone down from the deal.

Thankfully, this past year has been by far the most prosperous period in the history of the company. We sell more beer in one month now than I sold in my first year and a half in business. At the end of 2009, still plowing the profits back into the company, I found myself with $125,000 in checks to deposit the last week of December.

I remember seeing the total on the bottom of the deposit slip. I thought, There's the possibility that everything is going to be manna from heaven from here on out. Or the chance that it'll all come crashing down, as I'd feared for so long.

The most likely scenario, however, remained: "blocking and tackling."

The next day I turned around and paid my final invoice of the year: $97,000 for beer inventory.

I tried to pay it online, as I had so many times before, but the dollar amount was too big to process through Bill Pay. I had to write the check by hand. Spelling out the numbers (n-i-n-e-t-y s-e-v-e-n t-h-o-u-s-a-n-d) and holding up the check in my hand, I mouthed the letters to myself (for one last time in this book): H-o-l-y s-h-i-t.

For the first time in over thirteen years, Shmaltz Brewing broke even in the first six months of 2010. With profits growing and debts shrinking, this summer I printed the healthiest balance sheet I'd ever seen with our business name at the top. Sink or swim? Swim!

For Jewish New Year, which fell during New York Craft Beer Week in the fall of 2009, my mother came to visit. Alan, the owner of the Blind Tiger, hosted her and my lawyer Barbara at the bar, for the featured barrel-aged pomegranate experimental strong ale, which had gone from a nearly unpourable disaster to one of my favorite beers we've ever accidentally made. Josh, our on-call guru for all the barrel aging, cask conditioning, and blending that goes on after-hours at the brewery, had pulled off another minor miracle.

Post-apples-and-honey, my mom and I went to an alternative synagogue with an occasionally cross-dressing comic rabbi for Rosh Hashanah at City Winery in Tribeca. A sweet beginning to the new year.

I had heard my *shofar* wake up call and prepared for our Jewbelation Bar Mitzvah anniversary marathon, stretching from the Great American Beer Festival in Denver later that month to San Francisco Beer Week in spring. I was confident that our thirteen-percent-alcohol monster brown ale would rise to the self-generated holiday challenge: "Chanukah versus Christmas: The Battle Royale of Beers."

For the Great American Beer Festival, the biggest craft beer gathering in the country, Leah sourced commemorative yarmulkes with the Shmaltz logo on gorgeous silk of various colors. Underneath our "best anniversary" wishes, just to be clear, we screen-printed: "This Is Not a Frisbee."

Joe Carroll, owner of Spuyten Duyvil and the sister BBQ joint across the street, Fette Sau (named top barbecue in New York City), FedEx'd several pounds of meat out to GABF to join me in a presentation in the food-and-beer-pairing pavilion. Jewbelation-glazed brisket, pulled barbecue chicken with pomegranate seeds, caraway-crusted beef tongue, and Kobe beef hot dogs partnered with Jewbelation 13, Origin, R.I.P.A, and Albino Python. Zak cooked up the soundtrack, only slightly reminiscent of Hot Borscht at my bar mitzvah. We got the crowd to yell Lenny Bruce-isms and toast the World's Largest Beer "L'Chaim."

The national promo crawl ran straight into the second annual Freaktoberfest the next week in New York. Our V.I.P. tasting paired rare and obscure craft beer euphoria with a jazz group jamming heavy metal covers and Blue Note solos. The party downstairs raged. The Stumblebum Brass Band marched from North Sixth Street in Williamsburg into the middle of Public Assembly, with a standing-room-only crowd. One of the go-go dancers said, "What should we do?" and Erica hollered, "Just jump up on the pedestals and shake whatcha got." The whole place was *jamming*. Our favorite breweries from all over the country and such special beers from around the world, with our friends in the band, Workout, rocking a Flying V in hot pink spandex and headbands. A thrilling sophomore effort.

The Freaktoberfest season rolled straight in Chicago. For several months, I'd been hearing from a gravel-voiced and endlessly energized guy at what he said was a "haunted bar" just west of downtown. His messages, which began "Hey, it's Ronnie from Cigars and Stripes," inevitably included some wild description of sideshow acts, fetish performers, and more and more great beer.

He'd scored an actual sideshow tent from Ringling Brothers, circa 1940. This gregarious ex-wrestling promoter said that every year he attached the tent to the backside of his bar and booked whatever crazy acts he could come up with. Big hits of the night's twisted lineup included the Human Pincushion and a guy who invited hot girls to come onstage and kick him in the nuts. Matt and Anthony, from my wholesaler Glunz, pulled together just about every craft beer in their book to sample for the festival goers. Even the pouring rain couldn't drown the carnival enthusiasm.

Mostly for fun, but with just enough business scheduled to justify the write-off, I dropped into New Orleans for Halloween. My date had a full-body rubber jumpsuit and a taste for Cochon. One of the biggest distributors in town had a new craft beer manager who was eager to close a deal. At Great American Beer Festival he'd said, "Yes, we're Coors, Miller, Abita, Sam Adams, Brooklyn, Harpoon, and Stone, but we want to bring the Shmaltz to NOLA."

It'd been about twenty years since I'd lived in New Orleans, chugging 32-ounce Turbodogs and sweating out cheap domestic drafts by funking out at Tipitina's and the Maple Leaf. More so in the last few years than the twenty previous, New Orleans has a growing high-end beer scene at places such as Avenue Pub, Stein's Deli, Barley Oak, and Martin's, even at music venues such as Howlin' Wolf, and most shockingly, on Bourbon Street[24]. It was a great excuse to catch up with some old friends and make a few new ones.

---

24 What the hell, after everything we've been through in all these pages, why not one last footnote to marvel at the great beer scene at the Delachaise, Cure, Lüke, Butcher, Acquistapace's. We've both come a long way in our beer lives -- looking forward to more.

I've been promising my co-workers we'll have company meetings there at some point, and I'm sure they'll hold me to it.

I feel only slightly guilty saying that my favorite part of the most recent San Francisco Beer Week this year was that I did almost nothing besides showing up. I made some suggestions to Zak, Leah, and Jesse, and they pulled together some of the best parties this company has thrown, by far. At the same venues we've been doing business with for years, the parties were a smash. Standing room only, and we sold out of beer at every event.

And the craziest part for me was that I looked around, and out of the whole crowd I recognized only a handful of my closest friends. I knew hardly anybody. Packed with happy beer partiers and flowing pints and bottles of our goodies passed repeatedly over the bar -- to strangers.

Who were all these people? I hadn't emailed them, and I hadn't stood in a beer aisle and hand-sold our beer to them. Were they Jewish or carnies or beer freaks -- or just there for the show? Yes, to all the options.

In spring, Mayor Bloomberg announced that a highly regarded vendor had signed a ten-year lease at Coney Island to open multiple new amusement parks over the coming years. And the mayor of New York City, one of the richest, most powerful individuals in the entire world -- Jewish or otherwise -- held up *our beer* at the Coney Island press conference. He said that the city and the new park operator would spend tens of millions to upgrade and renovate America's Playground.

I had just received final trademark confirmation on "Coney Island" for beer, brewing services, and soda. During the summer we opened Coney Island Brewing Company -- the World's Smallest, non-commercial, non-production brewery, with a rotating lineup of nano-brewers, starting with Nic Sin, rock star, impersonator, and midget. Is Shmaltz going "mainstream"?

2010 marks a lineup of He'brew beers far beyond anything I could have described even just a few years ago. It's inconceivable that I could have imagined any of it with Simon in those early "turkey reuben" days. R.I.P.A. on RYE, our first packaged barrel-aged offering this spring, followed by Rejewvenator's Year of the Grape for summer, onto the fall to the Vertical Jewbelation project for winter, and our anniversary.

I thought it would be fun(!) to re-brew (yes, re-contract-brew) each of the recipes for Jewbelation 8 through 13. Plus brew a new recipe for J14. And then take a portion of each batch and barrel-age them in our second use Sazerac barrels from the R.I.P.A. on RYE project to release as Vertical Jewbelation. Another in a lineup of *"wouldn't it be cool if…"* projects.

The Vertical Jewbelation gift pack will have one twelve-ounce bottle of each recipe, Chanukah candles, and instructions on how to make your own beer menorah. Delicious beer, delicious shtick. Buy it, drink 'em, celebrate. Like the miraculous sacred oil of the Maccabees, it's meant to be used!

And there are plenty of projects that continue to tickle my entrepreneurial bone, including a brew pub in San Francisco, a west coast home for the Shmaltz offerings after all these years of wholesale wandering -- rotating matzoh ball soup specials, Kobe beef bagel dogs, corned beef knishes, the best damn free-range organic funnel cake west of Coney Island…

And possibly the same in Brooklyn. We're always on the lookout for the right fit. I still need a spot to commission the black velvet homage to Lenny Bruce, and the same could work for Donny and Heather from the Sideshow as well.

All to be continued. I'm excited to read what the next chapters have in store for myself, my family of co-workers and our craft beer *mishpocha*.

Earlier this year, trying to get back to the plan to take a break from Shmaltzville and see a bit more of the world, I spent a couple weeks out of the country. On my last stopover, at the airport bookstore, I spotted Howard Zinn's *A People's History of the United States*. Reading the work inspired waves of questions in my head about what the significance of my labor might be. What does it all mean?

As Greil Marcus writes in *Lipstick Traces*, "Real mysteries cannot be solved, but they can be turned into better mysteries." My deepest intuition, drawn from Jewish tradition and other explorations, leads me to a related thought: Interpretation is the only absolute truth.

I've tried to understand the sources that I have come across, and I've chosen to produce offerings that I hope both reflect and add to our evolving narrative -- through craft beer.

In his analysis, Zinn points out the importance of the transition this country made from the Declaration of Independence to the Constitution. The Revolutionary document entitles us to "life, liberty, and the pursuit of happiness." In the Constitution, the Founding Fathers rewrote the phrase as "life, liberty, and property." Was it prophetic, this change from the pursuit of happiness to the protection of property?

I look at the time and effort that has gone into creating this book, and even more so, into creating this company. As I'm finishing these last few lines, I think it finally feels good to consider this project a real business. Though there was never any guarantee that in the thirteenth year, we'd have grown into a mostly-legitimate, mostly-thriving enterprise, this has indeed proven to be our bar mitzvah year. Well past the cusp of some things, still on the cusp of others.

For the moment, I'll grab myself a Mazel Tov cocktail and hoist one with you in a toast to the tribe. To life… *L'Chaim!*

APPENDIX

CRAFT BEER *Bar Mitzvah*

TABLE OF CONTENTS
WITH BEER PAIRINGS

CHAPTER 1...... Genesis, Act 1: Beers In The Garden

Theme appropriate but not encouraged: Coors Light, Bartles & Jaymes wine coolers
First beer of the night: HE'BREW Origin Pomegranate Ale

CHAPTER 2...... The Old Country

Theme appropriate, also not particularly encouraged: Maccabee, or only slightly
better, Goldstar
Sentimental favorite now long sold out, but nectar: Rejewvenator, Year of the Fig
in honor of my grandmother who loved figs... and grammar

CHAPTER 3...... Let There Be Rock, Blood, And Revelation

Theme appropriate and historically relevant: Abita Turbodog in a 32-ounce go-cup
Fertile Crescent City evolution: R.I.P.A. on RYE, our Bittersweet Lenny's R.I.P.A. aged in
Sazerac 6-Year rye whisky barrels

CHAPTER 4...... Underwater Kabbalah And A Mission Burrito Of Love

Theme appropriate at a Mission St. taqueria: Negra Modelo though I'd probably just go
strawberry or melon agua fresca
Welcome home to Bay Area Hop School: Anchor Liberty, Speakeasy Big Daddy, Magnolia
Proving Ground, 21st Amendment Brew Free or Die, Russian River Pliny the Either,
Moylan's Hopsickle

CHAPTER 5...... Genesis, Act 2: West Of Eden aka Exile Never Tasted So Good

Hear O' Israel, The Beer is One: Genesis Ale

CHAPTER 6...... Conan The Distributor

Self-distributed delights: Stone Sublimely Self-Righteous, Captain Lawrence Extra Gold

APPENDIX

CHAPTER 7...... Business School 001: Catholic School Girl Meets The Candyman

Theme appropriate but not encouraged: Red Bull

Encouraged but should I be offended?: Lost Abbey Judgment Day.

Back in time at the Crow Bar in North Beach or wherever you find yourself:
the Sammy Davis Jr. (Black and Tan with Guinness and Genesis. Even better, sub
North Coast Old #38 on Nitro)

CHAPTER 8...... Business School 002: Success For Dummies

*Theme appropriate, scientifically impossible without a time machine, likely to taste very bland,
but Jewish :* Gablinger's (Rheingold Light. Thanks Dr. Joe!)

From my first year with wholesalers: Lagunitas Brown Shugga, originally released in 1997

CHAPTER 9...... Finally, Business School 101, Hold The Viagra

Theme appropriate, not encouraged, and thankfully not in existence: Evan's He-brew or
He-brew Is-real Good Beer

As a shout-out to Forties at Homeboy Liquors: Dogfish Golden Shower/Era

As a shout-out to inspirational Stouts: Bell's Expedition, North Coast Old Rasputin

CHAPTER 10.... Snatching Defeat From The Jaws Of Victory

Theme appropriate and almost my career, twice: Mendocino Red Tail Ale (I'd probably go
with Eye of the Hawk or Talon Barleywine)

As a huge Thank you to Brooklyn Brewery for bringing He'brew to NYC: Local Number 2

Mazel tov to all those who submitted Beers Brewed for Weddings: Belgian Frambozen
from Dennis at CB&Potts (CO), hopped up wheat from Jon at Power House Brewing
(OH), Wedding Belle Ale brewed by the bride and maid of honor with Brewdude Dixon
now at Dunedin (FL), Wedding Alt (and every year for 11 anniversaries and counting)
from Tom at Brewers Alley (MD), Scott's Offering for Joe and Leah at Shorts (MI), Gift
for Sophia from Kelly at Kelso/Greenpoint (NY), Luciernaga (The Firefly, originally
O'Schneider Wedding Ale) from Ron at Jolly Pumpkin (MI), and Nectar of the Hops
for David from Redstone (CO) who points out that mead, not beer, stands as the original
inspiration for the "honeymoon."

Only one beer brewed for a divorce (I guess one would be enough): Burned and Bitter,
smoked IPA from George at Water Street (WI)

APPENDIX

CHAPTER 11.... I Don't Have The Cash For The Guns And Ammo, But I Do Have $50,000 Of Credit For The Beer

Theme appropriate but do they serve beer in prison? Bagel Beer
Perfect beer for vacation in Hanoi: Bia Hoi (fresh, local draft delivered daily)
Beer to say I was very upset but then I got paid and recently you've been very nice to send me birthday cards the last few years, and I liked meeting your son who's now the boss: Rogue Imperial Pilsner or Hazelnut Brown

CHAPTER 12.... Genesis, Act 3, And The Messiah I'd Been Waiting For

Truly the beer I was waiting for and still love: Messiah Bold
For Darren my co-worker and Brent at Red Light Red Light: Barrel Aged Messiah in first-use fresh Rittenhouse 100 rye whisky barrels

CHAPTER 13.... 40 Days And 40 Nights… And 40 Days And 40 Nights And… Repeat.

Theme appropriate, but not encouraged: Michelob Ultra and Crack
Favorite beer to debut the week before my tour stop in Philly at Monk's, November 2003: Ommegang Three Philosophers

CHAPTER 14.... Miraculous Jewbelation (This Chanukah, Candles Won't Be The Only Thing Getting Lit)

Umm hmm well, lemme see, wait, I know: Miraculous Jewbelation. Ok well any Jewbelation since each successive year can claim to be The Most Extreme Chanukah Beer ever created.

CHAPTER 15.... Pomegranates And C*cksuckers

Bittersweet Lenny's R.I.P.A.: Though this beer failed as my ticket to making Sarah Silverman fall in love with me, it remains the totem beer for Shmaltz Brewing and possibly my life. Drink responsibly and please avoid arrest for verbal obscenity.

APPENDIX

CHAPTER 16.... Step Right Up! Welcome To The Freak Show

A Four-In-One Beer Spectacle:

- ★ Start the dance with an Albino Python (one that doesn't blow up or sue you, see Ch. 18)
- ★ throw down a Sword Swallower (our hoppy yet silky smooth tribute to the World's Hottest and Nicest Sword Superstar),
- ★ arise and take possession of a blood red Freaktoberfest (ideally at our Freaktoberfest festival), and
- ★ nail it home with a Human Blockhead (luscious and dangerous, just like the MC himself).
- ★ Somehow find yourself waking up in the Michael Jackson suite at the Brickskeller in D.C., happy, and without any (more) face tattoos.

CHAPTER 17.... They Came, They Tried To Kill Us, We Survived, Let's Drink: Crisis, Resolution, Crisis, And The Ultimate Excel Spreadsheet

Beer we need to support: anything from a small brewer who got royally screwed by the Hop Crisis of 2007-2009 (and ongoing) but survived to brew again
A couple favorites: Ithaca Flower Power, Terrapin Hopsecutioner, Bear Republic Hop Rod Rye

CHAPTER 18.... The Promised Land-ish

Thematically appropriate and strongly encouraged: Better and better craft beer.
As Mike from Founders put it in his *Beer Advocate* column, it's not "extreme" beer, it's simply evolution and progress.
Last Call: Shmaltz Liquor: Jewbelation, R.I.P.A. or Blockhead whiskeys, micro distilled with the help of St. George's Spirits, coming soon; oh, and with a goblet back of Vertical Jewbelation, a barrel aged blend of all 7 Jewbelation recipes.

Enjoy the manna, *L'Chaim!*

APPENDIX

For Immediate Release (Go Tell Your Mother, Please)
Contact: Jeremy Cowan
Headquarters: 415-550-8424
Hotline: 415-3-HEBREW

PLEASE HYPE   PLEASE HYPE   PLEASE HYPE   PLEASE HYPE

In The Beginning, There Was An Idea...
HE'BREW—THE CHOSEN BEER

February, 1997, San Francisco, CA -- After 3000 years of civilization, a microbrew to complement the Jewish American experience hit Bay Area shelves, just in time for Hanukkah. By the end of the eight day holiday, nearly all the first batch of He'Brew—The Chosen Beer miraculously leapt off the shelves into the enthusiastic hands of local residents.

Why is this beer different from all other beers? Genesis Ale is the first creation of Shmaltz Brewing Company, a local labor of laughs and love begat by Bay Area native, 27 year-old, Jeremy Cowan. He'Brew is a celebration beer meant to accompany the rites and rituals of life, both sacred and secular. A hint of pomegranate in Genesis Ale evokes a subtle, sweet taste of the Land of Milk and Honey (with a crisp, smooth finish): a smidgen of Middle East, a dash of American West. Then we tasted it, and it was very good......

The Chosen Beer proved to be a tasty holiday tidbit for the media as well as for consumers. The *Jewish Bulletin of Northern California* featured He'Brew in its Hanukkah guide. A mention in the *San Francisco Chronicle* was picked up by the *New York Times* wire: calls and emails poured in from Ft. Lauderdale to Nashville, St. Louis to Denver, Manhattan, Reno, and Modesto. The nation was thirsting for holiday shtick, and He'Brew provided a shmaltzy punchline.

In addition to creating high-quality, hand-crafted products, Shmaltz Brewing is committed to active community involvement. In accordance with Jewish tradition, ten percent of all profits will go to *tzadakah*--charity (we are eagerly anticipating the first dollar of profit, expected some time around Purim!!). Shmaltz has already donated The Chosen Beer to events for the

"ON THE CUSP" OF
PROFITS RIGHT FROM
THE BEGINNING

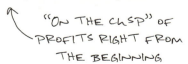

316

APPENDIX

Jewish Museum San Francisco, the Traveling Jewish Theater, and Challapalooza, a festival for *Davka*, a locally-published Jewish literary magazine. In March, pints of He'Brew will flow freely at a fund-raiser to support Women's American ORT, a global, not-for-profit educational organization.

Genesis Ale is just the beginning. During 1997, Shmaltz Brewing plans to be fruitful and multiply our offerings to several beers and microbrewed soda as well. He'Brew is currently available at select markets and Judaica shops throughout the Bay Area, from Santa Cruz to San Francisco and Marin to Berkeley. The Chosen Beer is ideal for weddings, parties, bar mitzvahs (ID required), or anywhere people are kibitzing or cavorting.

New batches of Genesis Ale are bubbling to life and emerge from their stainless garden monthly. For more information about He'Brew—The Chosen Beer or Shmaltz Brewing Company (or to order a t-shirt or to reserve beer for Purim) please contact:

Jeremy Cowan
Shmaltz Brewing Company
3435 Cesar Chavez, Suite 227
San Francisco, CA 94110
Headquarters: 415-550-8424
Hotline: 415-3-HEBREW
cowberg@sfo.com
www.shmaltz.com

DON'T PASS OUT....PASS OVER

APPENDIX

TWO PILLARS OF THE JEWISH COMMUNITY

DEC-24-1996 09:37   ANTI DEFAMATION LEAGUE   1 303 8301554   P.01/02

Anti-Defamation League®   **ADL** Anti-Defamation League®

1120 Lincoln Street, Suite 1301 • Denver, Colorado 80203-2136 • (303) 830-7177 / FAX 830-1554

December 23, 1996

Jeremy Cowan (or is it Tracy Ginsberg?)
He'brew
San Francisco, CA

Dear Jeremy:

Attached is the article from the Denver Post which prompted my contacting you.
You can add it to your growing collection. I agree that your idea is both creative and
pro-Jewish. No surprise that every Jew in America doesn't have a good sense of
humor - and a strong enough sense of self esteem to handle this one.

My best to you in your enterprise. If you get to Denver give us a call.

Sincerely,

Saul F. Rosenthal
Regional Director

SFR/ds

cc: Barbara Bergen, ADL
       San Francisco

DREAMWORKS
SKG

October 13, 1997

Jeremy Cowan
Shmaltz Brewing Company
3435 Cesar Chavez Street, Suite 227
San Francisco, CA 94110

Dear Jeremy,

Although other commitments keep Mr. Spielberg from being able to write
personally, please know how much your wonderful beer, ushering in the New
Year, was appreciated.

On Steven's behalf, we thank you so very much for thinking of him and giving
him a laugh with the "Chosen Beer!"

L'Shana Tova!

Kris Kelley
Director of Public Relations

KK/tr

APPENDIX

EMAILS FROM THE TRIBE

From: ▓▓▓▓▓▓▓▓▓▓▓
Date: Tue, 1 Jan 2002 21:03:29 EST
Subject: a note of thanks
To: hebrew@shmaltz.com

Just wanted to let you know how much I enjoyed your Messiah Stout. I got it at Safeway in Aptos, Ca. to go with some cracked crab. There are hardly any dark beers on the shelf anywhere any longer. I only buy dark beer just like I only buy dark roasted coffee. For this reason alone I was thankful.
First your label caught caught my eye. What chutzpa calling your HeBrew the choosen brew.
Then, Messiah stout. OY !
Your label...so irreverent. Don't get me started.
The photo/artwork, so utterly defiant. I love the joy of nudity and the naked truth of your convictions and the symbolism of the map telling us about who you are and what you stand for.
The read on the back...SUPURB. I only feel sorry for you for not being able to get the web address schmaltz.com
I just want to acknowledge your brilliance.
You have captured the archityple spirt of what it means to be completely and unabashedly Jewish in America. I applaud you in a standing ovation.
Shalom and carry on with every success a victory and every victory a defeat of those who say you can't be yourself.

You should really read this one because it shows much-loved enthusiasm. The "cool things" part after the recycling can is precious. ↙

Date: Mon, 3 May 2004 16:33:52 -0400
Thread-Topic: Love your beer
Thread-Index: AcQxTfKvtBcshCgvSESMlietJz+8Cw==
From: "Wasserman, Michael" ▓▓▓▓▓▓▓▓▓▓▓
To: <tastychutzpah@hebrewbeer.com>

Dear Beer Jews,
      I recently came across your beer in the liquor store while buying beer for the bar in my house at school in Providence, RI. I was delighted to find a beer that understands my heritage and the struggle we go through every day to find new humorous ways to express our Judaism. Of course right away I hear my grandmother's voice in my head, "Of course this beer you should try! How nice it will go with the well-balanced diet I know you're keeping at school as you continue to work towards being a doctor." And while the med school and the well-balanced diet may not ring so true, of course I took my grandmother's voice-in-my-head's advice and I bought some to bring back so all my housemates could try it. Because so many of us are Jewish, as it so happens, we were all thoroughly amused by the humor, but the bond of brotherhood that lies beneath all of that. It was almost as if the beer sweat that dripped off the bottles as we took them out of the refrigerator represented the tears our ancestors shed in egypt, and the bitter tasting beer, the bitterness of those years of bondage.
      In any event, to make a long story short, the beer we love. And so, I figured I would let you guys know that. And then it occured to me that maybe you had some cool stuff you could send me to decorate our bar with. It's a really great room. There is pine paneling all around and we have a bar counter and a dartboard and a trash can, and recycling, and other cool things. But what we don't have is any awesome He'brew paraphernalia. I know some companies send out free stuff for people to put up in their bars as advertising and stuff, and I think it would be great if we had a big He'brew sign, or some He'brew pint glasses or something. So, if you do that kind of thing, then I have my address at the bottom, and I know everyone in the house would think that was great.
      Even if you can't do that, just responding to this e-mail with a nice hello to all of the people at my house that I can read to them would be very pleasant indeed. So, thanks for taking the time to read this e-mail. I hope it finds you well and in good health. And in the words of Rabbi Ben Eliezer, "Stay Jewish, yo."

Date: Thu, 29 Apr 2004 09:54:29 -0700 (PDT)
From: mike lupton ▓▓▓▓▓▓▓▓▓▓▓
Subject: i love this
To: tastychutzpah@hebrewbeer.com

messiah bold is one of the greatest beers known to man. thank god that someone, somewhere was blessed enough to create such a fine drink. i may not be a jew (or a christian for that matter), but i think that by drinking messiah bold i am going to be good with god.
thanks for the great beer, come to orlando on your next wandering jew tour,
mike lupton
beer fan

APPENDIX

The following are the 613 commandments and their source in scripture, as enumerated by Maimonides:

To know there is a God Ex. 20:2
Not to even think that there are other gods besides Him Ex. 20:3
To know that He is One Deut. 6:4
To love Him Deut. 6:5
To fear Him Deut. 10:20
To sanctify His Name Lev. 22:32
Not to profane His Name Lev. 22:32
Not to destroy objects associated with His Name Deut. 12:4
To listen to the prophet speaking in His Name Deut. 18:15
Not to test the prophet unduly Deut. 6:16
To emulate His ways Deut. 28:9
To cleave to those who know Him Deut. 10:20
To love other Jews Lev. 19:18
To love converts Deut. 10:19
Not to hate fellow Jews Lev. 19:17
To reprove a sinner Lev. 19:17
Not to embarrass others Lev. 19:17
Not to oppress the weak Ex. 22:21
Not to speak derogatorily of others Lev. 19:16
Not to take revenge Lev. 19:18
Not to bear a grudge Lev. 19:18
To learn Torah Deut. 6:7
To honor those who teach and know Torah Lev. 19:32
Not to inquire into idolatry Lev. 19:4
Not to follow the whims of your heart or what your eyes see Num. 15:39
Not to blaspheme Ex. 22:27
Not to worship idols in the manner they are worshiped Ex. 20:6
Not to worship idols in the four ways we worship God Ex. 20:6
Not to make an idol for yourself Ex. 20:5
Not to make an idol for others Lev. 19:4
Not to make human forms even for decorative purposes Ex. 20:21
Not to turn a city to idolatry Deut. 13:14
To burn a city that has turned to idol worship Deut. 13:17
Not to rebuild it as a city Deut. 13:17
Not to derive benefit from it Deut. 13:18
Not to missionize an individual to idol worship Deut. 13:12
Not to love the idolater Deut. 13:9
Not to cease hating the idolater Deut. 13:9
Not to save the idolater Deut. 13:9
Not to say anything in the idolater's defense Deut. 13:9
Not to refrain from incriminating the idolater Deut. 13:9
Not to prophesize in the name of idolatry Deut. 13:14
Not to listen to a false prophet Deut. 13:4
Not to prophesize falsely in the name of God Deut. 18:20
Not to be afraid of killing the false prophet Deut. 18:22
Not to swear in the name of an idol Ex. 23:13
Not to perform ov (medium) Lev. 19:31
Not to perform yidoni ("magical seer") Lev. 19:31
Not to pass your children through the fire to Molech Lev. 18:21
Not to erect a pillar in a public place of worship Deut. 16:22
Not to bow down before a smooth stone Lev. 26:1
Not to plant a tree in the Temple courtyard Deut. 16:21
To destroy idols and their accessories Deut. 12:2
Not to derive benefit from idols and their accessories Deut. 7:26
Not to derive benefit from ornaments of idols Deut. 7:25
Not to make a covenant with idolaters Deut. 7:2
Not to show favor to them Deut. 7:2
Not to let them dwell in the Land of Israel Ex. 23:33
Not to imitate them in customs and clothing Lev. 20:23
Not to be superstitious Lev. 19:26
Not to go into a trance to foresee events, etc. Deut. 18:10
Not to engage in astrology Lev. 19:26
Not to mutter incantations Deut. 18:11
Not to attempt to contact the dead Deut. 18:11
Not to consult the ov Deut. 18:11
Not to consult the yidoni Deut. 18:11
Not to perform acts of magic Deut. 18:10

Men must not shave the hair off the sides of their head Lev. 19:27
Men must not shave their beards with a razor Lev. 19:27
Men must not wear women's clothing Deut. 22:5
Women must not wear men's clothing Deut. 22:5
Not to tattoo the skin Lev. 19:28
Not to tear the skin in mourning Deut. 14:1
Not to make a bald spot in mourning Deut. 14:1
To repent and confess wrongdoings Num. 5:7
To say the Shema twice daily Deut. 6:7
To serve the Almighty with prayer Ex. 23:25
The Kohanim must bless the Jewish nation daily Num. 6:23
To wear tefillin (phylacteries) on the head Deut. 6:8
To bind tefillin on the arm Deut. 6:8
To put a mezuzah on each door post Deut. 6:9
Each male must write a Torah scroll Deut. 31:19
The king must have a separate Sefer Torah for himself Deut. 17:18
To have tzitzit on four-cornered garments Num. 15:38
To bless the Almighty after eating Deut. 8:10
To circumcise all males on the eighth day after their birth Lev. 12:3
To rest on the seventh day Ex. 23:12
Not to do prohibited labor on the seventh day Ex. 20:11
The court must not inflict punishment on Shabbat Ex. 35:3
Not to walk outside the city boundary on Shabbat Ex. 16:29
To sanctify the day with Kiddush and Havdalah Ex. 20:9
To rest from prohibited labor on Yom Kippur Lev. 23:32
Not to do prohibited labor on Yom Kippur Lev. 23:32
To afflict yourself on Yom Kippur Lev. 16:29
Not to eat or drink on Yom Kippur Lev. 23:29
To rest on the first day of Passover Lev. 23:7
Not to do prohibited labor on the first day of Passover Lev. 23:8
To rest on the seventh day of Passover Lev. 23:8
Not to do prohibited labor on the seventh day of Passover Lev. 23:8
To rest on Shavuot Lev. 23:21
Not to do prohibited labor on Shavuot Lev. 23:21
To rest on Rosh Hashanah Lev. 23:24
Not to do prohibited labor on Rosh Hashanah Lev. 23:25
To rest on Sukkot Lev. 23:35
Not to do prohibited labor on Sukkot Lev. 23:35
To rest on Shemini Atzeret Lev. 23:36
Not to do prohibited labor on Shemini Atzeret Lev. 23:36
Not to eat chametz on the afternoon of the 14th day of Nissan Deut. 16:3
To destroy all chametz on 14th day of Nissan Ex. 12:15
Not to eat chametz all seven days of Passover Ex. 13:3
Not to eat mixtures containing chametz all seven days of Passover Ex. 12:20
Not to see chametz in your domain seven days Ex. 13:7
Not to find chametz in your domain seven days Ex. 12:19
To eat matzah on the first night of Passover Ex. 12:18
To relate the Exodus from Egypt on that night Ex. 13:8
To hear the Shofar on the first day of Tishrei (Rosh Hashanah) Num. 9:1
To dwell in a Sukkah for the seven days of Sukkot Lev. 23:42
To take up a Lulav and Etrog all seven days Lev. 23:40
Each man must give a half shekel annually Ex. 30:13
Courts must calculate to determine when a new month begins Ex. 12:2
To afflict oneself and cry out before God in times of calamity Num. 10:9
To marry a wife by means of ketubah and kiddushin Deut. 22:13
Not to have sexual relations with women not thus married Deut. 23:18
Not to withhold food, clothing, and sexual relations from your wife Ex. 21:10
To have children with one's wife Gen. 1:28
To issue a divorce by means of a Get document Deut. 24:1
A man must not remarry his ex-wife after she has married someone else Deut. 24:4
To perform yibbum (marry the widow of one's childless brother) Deut. 25:5
To perform halizah (free the widow of one's childless brother from yibbum) Deut. 25:9
The widow must not remarry until the ties with her brother-in-law are removed (by halizah) Deut. 25:5
The court must fine one who sexually seduces a maiden Ex. 22:15-16
The rapist must marry the maiden Deut. 22:29

613 MITZVOT

He is never allowed to divorce her Deut. 22:29
The slanderer must remain married to his wife Deut. 22:19
He must not divorce her Deut. 22:19
To fulfill the laws of the Sotah Num. 5:30
Not to put oil on her meal offering (as usual) Num. 5:15
Not to put frankincense on her meal offering (as usual) Num. 5:15
Not to have sexual relations with your mother Lev. 18:7
Not to have sexual relations with your father's wife Lev. 18:8
Not to have sexual relations with your sister Lev. 18:9
Not to have sexual relations with your father's wife's daughter Lev. 18:11
Not to have sexual relations with your son's daughter Lev. 18:10
Not to have sexual relations with your daughter Lev. 18:10
Not to have sexual relations with your daughter's daughter Lev. 18:10
Not to have sexual relations with a woman and her daughter Lev. 18:17
Not to have sexual relations with a woman and her son's daughter Lev. 18:17
Not to have sexual relations with a woman and her daughter's daughter Lev. 18:17
Not to have sexual relations with your father's sister Lev. 18:12
Not to have sexual relations with your mother's sister Lev. 18:13
Not to have sexual relations with your father's brother's wife Lev. 18:14
Not to have sexual relations with your son's wife Lev. 18:15
Not to have sexual relations with your brother's wife Lev. 18:16
Not to have sexual relations with your wife's sister Lev. 18:18
A man must not have sexual relations with an animal Lev. 18:23
A woman must not have sexual relations with an animal Lev. 18:23
For men not to use sex to gain 'ownership' over other menLev. 18:22
Not to have sexual relations with your father Lev. 18:7
Not to have sexual relations with your father's brother Lev. 18:14
Not to have sexual relations with someone else's wife Lev. 18:20
Not to have sexual relations with a menstrually impure woman Lev. 18:19
Not to marry non-Jews Deut. 7:3
Not to let Moabite and Ammonite males marry into the Jewish people Deut. 23:4
Not to prevent a third-generation Egyptian convert from marrying into the Jewish people Deut. 23:8-9
Not to refrain from marrying a third generation Edomite convert Deut. 23:8-9
Not to let a mamzer (a child born due to an illegal relationship) marry into the Jewish people Deut. 23:3
Not to let a eunuch marry into the Jewish people Deut. 23:2
Not to offer to God any castrated male animals Lev. 22:24
The High Priest must not marry a widow Lev. 21:14
The High Priest must not have sexual relations with a widow even outside of marriage Lev. 21:15
The High Priest must marry a virgin maiden Lev. 21:13
A Kohen (priest) must not marry a divorcee Lev. 21:7
A Kohen must not marry a zonah (a woman who has had a forbidden sexual relationship) Lev. 21:7
A Kohen must not marry a chalalah ("a desecrated person") (party to or product of 169-172) Lev. 21:7
Not to make pleasurable (sexual) contact with any forbidden woman Lev. 18:6
To examine the signs of animals to distinguish between kosher and non-kosher Lev. 11:2
To examine the signs of fowl to distinguish between kosher and non-kosher Deut. 14:11
To examine the signs of fish to distinguish between kosher and non-kosher Lev. 11:9
To examine the signs of locusts to distinguish between kosher and non-kosher Lev. 11:21
Not to eat non-kosher animals Lev. 11:4
Not to eat non-kosher fowl Lev. 11:13
Not to eat non-kosher fish Lev. 11:11
Not to eat non-kosher flying insects Deut. 14:19
Not to eat non-kosher creatures that crawl on land Lev. 11:41
Not to eat non-kosher maggots Lev. 11:44
Not to eat worms found in fruit on the ground Lev. 11:42
Not to eat creatures that live in water other than (kosher) fish Lev. 11:43
Not to eat the meat of an animal that died without ritual slaughter Deut. 14:21
Not to benefit from an ox condemned to be stoned Ex. 21:28
Not to eat meat of an animal that was mortally wounded Ex. 22:30
Not to eat a limb torn off a living creature Deut. 12:23
Not to eat blood Lev. 3:17
Not to eat certain fats of clean animals Lev. 3:17
Not to eat the sinew of the thigh Gen. 32:33

Not to eat mixtures of milk and meat cooked together Ex. 23:19
Not to cook meat and milk together Ex. 34:26
Not to eat bread from new grain before the Omer Lev. 23:14
Not to eat parched grains from new grain before the Omer Lev. 23:14
Not to eat ripened grains from new grain before the Omer Lev. 23:14
Not to eat fruit of a tree during its first three years Lev. 19:23
Not to eat diverse seeds planted in a vineyard Deut. 22:9
Not to eat untithed fruits Lev. 22:15
Not to drink wine poured in service to idols Deut. 32:38
To ritually slaughter an animal before eating it Deut. 12:21
Not to slaughter an animal and its offspring on the same day Lev. 22:28
To cover the blood (of a slaughtered beast or fowl) with earth Lev. 17:13
To send away the mother bird before taking its children Deut. 22:6
To release the mother bird if she was taken from the nest Deut. 22:7
Not to swear falsely in God's Name Lev. 19:12
Not to take God's Name in vain Ex. 20:7
Not to deny possession of something entrusted to you Lev. 19:11
Not to swear in denial of a monetary claim Lev. 19:11
To swear in God's Name to confirm the truth when deemed necessary by court Deut. 10:20
To fulfill what was uttered and to do what was avowed Deut. 23:24
Not to break oaths or vows Num. 30:3
For oaths and vows annulled, there are the laws of annulling vows explicit in the Torah Num. 30:3
The Nazir must let his hair grow Num. 6:5
He must not cut his hair Num. 6:5
He must not drink wine, wine mixtures, or wine vinegar Num. 6:3
He must not eat fresh grapes Num. 6:3
He must not eat raisins Num. 6:3
He must not eat grape seeds Num. 6:4
He must not eat grape skins Num. 6:4
He must not be under the same roof as a corpse Num. 6:6
He must not come into contact with the dead Num. 6:7
He must shave his head after bringing sacrifices upon completion of his Nazirite period Num. 6:9
To estimate the value of people as determined by the Torah Lev. 27:2
To estimate the value of consecrated animals Lev. 27:12-13
To estimate the value of consecrated houses Lev. 27:14
To estimate the value of consecrated fields Lev. 27:16
Carry out the laws of interdicting possessions (cherem) Lev. 27:28
Not to sell the cherem Lev. 27:28
Not to redeem the cherem Lev. 27:28
Not to plant diverse seeds together Lev. 19:19
Not to plant grains or greens in a vineyard Deut. 22:9
Not to crossbreed animals Lev. 19:19
Not to work different animals together Deut. 22:10
Not to wear shaatnez, a cloth woven of wool and linen Deut. 22:11
To leave a corner of the field uncut for the poor Lev. 19:10
Not to reap that corner Lev. 19:9
To leave gleanings Lev. 19:9
Not to gather the gleanings Lev. 19:9
To leave the gleanings of a vineyard Lev. 19:10
Not to gather the gleanings of a vineyard Lev. 19:10
To leave the unformed clusters of grapes Lev. 19:10
Not to pick the unformed clusters of grapes Lev. 19:10
To leave the forgotten sheaves in the field Deut. 24:19
Not to retrieve them Deut. 24:19
To separate the "tithe for the poor" Deut. 14:28
To give charity Deut. 15:8
Not to withhold charity from the poor Deut. 15:7
To set aside Terumah Gedolah (gift for the Kohen) Deut. 18:4
The Levite must set aside a tenth of his tithe Num. 18:26
Not to preface one tithe to the next, but separate them in their proper order Ex. 22:28
A non-Kohen must not eat Terumah[clarification needed] Lev. 22:10
A hired worker or a Jewish bondsman of a Kohen must not eat Terumah Lev. 22:10
An uncircumcised Kohen must not eat Terumah Ex. 12:48
An impure Kohen must not eat Terumah Lev. 22:4
A chalalah (party to #s 169-172 above) must not eat Terumah Lev. 22:12
To set aside Ma'aser (tithe) each planting year and give it to a Levite Num. 18:24

APPENDIX

613 MITZVOT

To set aside the second tithe (Ma'aser Sheni) Deut. 14:22
Not to spend its redemption money on anything but food, drink, or ointment Deut. 26:14
Not to eat Ma'aser Sheni while impure Deut. 26:14
A mourner on the first day after death must not eat Ma'aser Sheni Deut. 26:14
Not to eat Ma'aser Sheni grains outside Jerusalem Deut. 12:17
Not to eat Ma'aser Sheni wine products outside Jerusalem Deut. 12:17
Not to eat Ma'aser Sheni oil outside Jerusalem Deut. 12:17
The fourth year crops must be totally for holy purposes like Ma'aser Sheni Lev. 19:24
To read the confession of tithes every fourth and seventh year Deut. 26:13
To set aside the first fruits and bring them to the Temple Ex. 23:19
The Kohanim must not eat the first fruits outside Jerusalem Deut. 12:17
To read the Torah portion pertaining to their presentation Deut. 26:5
To set aside a portion of dough for a Kohen Num. 15:20
To give the foreleg, two cheeks, and abomasum of slaughtered animals to a Kohen Deut. 18:3
To give the first shearing of sheep to a Kohen Deut. 18:4
To redeem firstborn sons and give the money to a Kohen Num. 18:15
To redeem the firstborn donkey by giving a lamb to a Kohen Ex. 13:13
To break the neck of the donkey if the owner does not intend to redeem it Ex. 13:13
To rest the land during the seventh year by not doing any work which enhances growth Ex. 34:21
Not to work the land during the seventh year Lev. 25:4
Not to work with trees to produce fruit during that year Lev. 25:4
Not to reap crops that grow wild that year in the normal manner Lev. 25:5
Not to gather grapes which grow wild that year in the normal way Lev. 25:5
To leave free all produce which grew in that year Ex. 23:11
To release all loans during the seventh year Deut. 15:2
Not to pressure or claim from the borrower Deut. 15:2
Not to refrain from lending immediately before the release of the loans for fear of monetary loss Deut. 15:9
The Sanhedrin must count seven groups of seven years Lev. 25:8
The Sanhedrin must sanctify the fiftieth year Lev. 25:10
To blow the Shofar on the tenth of Tishrei to free the slaves Lev. 25:9
Not to work the soil during the fiftieth year (Jubilee)Lev. 25:11
Not to reap in the normal manner that which grows wild in the fiftieth year Lev. 25:11
Not to pick grapes which grew wild in the normal manner in the fiftieth year Lev. 25:11
Carry out the laws of sold family properties Lev. 25:24
Not to sell the land in Israel indefinitely Lev. 25:23
Carry out the laws of houses in walled cities Lev. 25:29
The Tribe of Levi must not be given a portion of the land in Israel, rather they are given cities to dwell in Deut. 18:1
The Levites must not take a share in the spoils of war Deut. 18:1
To give the Levites cities to inhabit and their surrounding fields Num. 35:2
Not to sell the fields but they shall remain the Levites' before and after the Jubilee year Lev. 25:34
To build a Temple Ex. 25:8
Not to build the altar with stones hewn by metal Standard->Ex. 20:24 TLT Yemenite->Ex. 20:23
Not to climb steps to the altar Ex. 20:27
To show reverence to the Temple Lev. 19:30
To guard the Temple area Num. 18:2
Not to leave the Temple unguarded Num. 18:5
To prepare the anointing oil Ex. 30:31
Not to reproduce the anointing oil Ex. 30:32
Not to anoint with anointing oil Ex. 30:32
Not to reproduce the incense formula Ex. 30:37
Not to burn anything on the Golden Altar besides incense Ex. 30:9
The Levites must transport the ark on their shoulders Num. 7:9
Not to remove the staves from the ark Ex. 25:15
The Levites must work in the Temple Num. 18:23
No Levite must do another's work of either a Kohen or a Levite Num. 18:3
To dedicate the Kohen for service Lev. 21:8
The work of the Kohanim's shifts must be equal during holidays Deut. 18:6-8
The Kohanim must wear their priestly garments during service Ex. 28:2
Not to tear the priestly garments Ex. 28:32
The Kohen Gadol 's breastplate must not be loosened from the Efod Ex. 28:28
A Kohen must not enter the Temple intoxicated Lev. 10:9
A Kohen must not enter the Temple with his head uncovered Lev. 10:6

A Kohen must not enter the Temple with torn clothes Lev. 10:6
A Kohen must not enter the Temple indiscriminately Lev. 16:2
A Kohen must not leave the Temple during service Lev. 10:7
To send the impure from the Temple Num. 5:2
Impure people must not enter the Temple Num. 5:3
Impure people must not enter the Temple Mount area Deut. 23:11
Impure Kohanim must not do service in the temple Lev. 22:2
An impure Kohen, following immersion, must wait until after sundown before returning to service Lev. 22:7
A Kohen must wash his hands and feet before service Ex. 30:19
A Kohen with a physical blemish must not enter the sanctuary or approach the altar Lev. 21:23
A Kohen with a physical blemish must not serve Lev. 21:17
A Kohen with a temporary blemish must not serve Lev. 21:17
One who is not a Kohen must not serve Num. 18:4
To offer only unblemished animals Lev. 22:21
Not to dedicate a blemished animal for the altar Lev. 22:20
Not to slaughter it Lev. 22:22
Not to sprinkle its blood Lev. 22:24
Not to burn its fat Lev. 22:22
Not to offer a temporarily blemished animal Deut. 17:1
Not to sacrifice blemished animals even if offered by non-Jews Lev. 22:25
Not to inflict wounds upon dedicated animals Lev. 22:21
To redeem dedicated animals which have become disqualified Deut. 12:15
To offer only animals which are at least eight days old Lev. 22:27
Not to offer animals bought with the wages of a harlot or the animal exchanged for a dog Deut. 23:19
Not to burn honey or yeast on the altar Lev. 2:11
To salt all sacrifices Lev. 2:13
Not to omit the salt from sacrifices Lev. 2:13
Carry out the procedure of the burnt offering as prescribed in the Torah Lev. 1:3
Not to eat its meat Deut. 12:17
Carry out the procedure of the sin offering Lev. 6:18
Not to eat the meat of the inner sin offering Lev. 6:23
Not to decapitate a fowl brought as a sin offering Lev. 5:8
Carry out the procedure of the guilt offering Lev. 7:1
The Kohanim must eat the sacrificial meat in the Temple Ex. 29:33
The Kohanim must not eat the meat outside the Temple courtyard Deut. 12:17
A non-Kohen must not eat sacrificial meat Ex. 29:33
To follow the procedure of the peace offering Lev. 7:11
Not to eat the meat of minor sacrifices before sprinkling the blood Deut. 12:17
To bring meal offerings as prescribed in the Torah Lev. 2:1
Not to put oil on the meal offerings of wrongdoers Lev. 5:11
Not to put frankincense on the meal offerings of wrongdoers Lev. 3:11
Not to eat the meal offering of the High Priest Lev. 6:16
Not to bake a meal offering as leavened bread Lev. 6:10
The Kohanim must eat the remains of the meal offerings Lev. 6:9
To bring all avowed and freewill offerings to the Temple on the first subsequent festival Deut. 12:5-6
Not to withhold payment incurred by any vow Deut. 23:22
To offer all sacrifices in the Temple Deut. 12:11
To bring all sacrifices from outside Israel to the Temple Deut. 12:26
Not to slaughter sacrifices outside the courtyard Lev. 17:4
Not to offer any sacrifices outside the courtyard Deut. 12:13
To offer two lambs every day Num. 28:3
To light a fire on the altar every day Lev. 6:6
Not to extinguish this fire Lev. 6:6
To remove the ashes from the altar every day Lev. 6:3
To burn incense every day Ex. 30:7
To light the Menorah every day Ex. 27:21
The Kohen Gadol ("High Priest") must bring a meal offering every day Lev. 6:13
To bring two additional lambs as burnt offerings on Shabbat Num. 28:9
To make the show bread Ex. 25:30
To bring additional offerings on Rosh Chodesh (" The New Month") Num. 28:11
To bring additional offerings on Passover Num. 28:19
To offer the wave offering from the meal of the new wheat Lev. 23:10
Each man must count the Omer - seven weeks from the day the new wheat offering was brought Lev. 23:15

APPENDIX

613 MITZVOT

To bring additional offerings on Shavuot Num. 28:26
To bring two leaves to accompany the above sacrifice Lev. 23:17
To bring additional offerings on Rosh Hashana Num. 29:2
To bring additional offerings on Yom Kippur Num. 29:8
To bring additional offerings on Sukkot Num. 29:13
To bring additional offerings on Shmini Atzeret Num. 29:35
Not to eat sacrifices which have become unfit or blemished Deut. 14:3
Not to eat from sacrifices offered with improper intentions Lev. 7:18
Not to leave sacrifices past the time allowed for eating them Lev. 22:30
Not to eat from that which was left over Lev. 19:8
Not to eat from sacrifices which became impure Lev. 7:19
An impure person must not eat from sacrifices Lev. 7:20
To burn the leftover sacrifices Lev. 7:17
To burn all impure sacrifices Lev. 7:19
To follow the procedure of Yom Kippur in the sequence prescribed in Parshah Acharei Mot ("After the death of Aaron's sons...") Lev. 16:3
One who profaned property must repay what he profaned plus a fifth and bring a sacrifice Lev. 5:16
Not to work consecrated animals Deut. 15:19
Not to shear the fleece of consecrated animals Deut. 15:19
To slaughter the paschal sacrifice at the specified time Ex. 12:6
Not to slaughter it while in possession of leaven Ex. 23:18
Not to leave the fat overnight Ex. 23:18
To slaughter the second Paschal Lamb Num. 9:11
To eat the Paschal Lamb with matzah and Marror on the night of the fourteenth of Nissan Ex. 12:8
To eat the second Paschal Lamb on the night of the 15th of Iyar Num. 9:11
Not to eat the paschal meat raw or boiled Ex. 12:9
Not to take the paschal meat from the confines of the group Ex. 12:46
An apostate must not eat from it Ex. 12:43
A permanent or temporary hired worker must not eat from it Ex. 12:45
An uncircumcised male must not eat from it Ex. 12:48
Not to break any bones from the paschal offering Ex. 12:46
Not to break any bones from the second paschal offering Num. 9:12
Not to leave any meat from the paschal offering over until morning Ex. 12:10
Not to leave the second paschal meat over until morning Num. 9:12
Not to leave the meat of the holiday offering of the 14th until the 16th Deut. 16:4
To be seen at the Temple on Passover, Shavuot, and Sukkot Deut. 16:16
To celebrate on these three Festivals (bring a peace offering) Ex. 23:14
To rejoice on these three Festivals (bring a peace offering) Deut. 16:14
Not to appear at the Temple without offerings Deut. 16:16
Not to refrain from rejoicing with, and giving gifts to, the Levites Deut. 12:19
To assemble all the people on the Sukkot following the seventh year Deut. 31:12
To set aside the firstborn animals Ex. 13:12
The Kohanim must not eat unblemished firstborn animals outside Jerusalem Deut. 12:17
Not to redeem the firstborn Num. 18:17
Separate the tithe from animals Lev. 27:32
Not to redeem the tithe Lev. 27:33
Every person must bring a sin offering (in the temple) for his transgression Lev. 4:27
Bring an asham talui (temple offering) when uncertain of guilt Lev. 5:17-18
Bring an asham vadai (temple offering) with guilt is ascertained Lev. 5:25
Bring an oleh v'yored (temple offering) offering (if the person is wealthy, an animal; if poor, a bird or meal offering) Lev. 5:7-11
The Sanhedrin must bring an offering (in the Temple) when it rules in error Lev. 4:13
A woman who had a running (vaginal) issue must bring an offering (in the Temple) after she goes to the Mikveh Lev. 15:28-29
A woman who gave birth must bring an offering (in the Temple) after she goes to the Mikveh Lev. 12:6
A man who had a running (unnatural urinary) issue must bring an offering (in the Temple) after he goes to the Mikveh Lev. 15:13-14
A metzora must bring an offering (in the Temple) after going to the Mikveh Lev. 14:10
Not to substitute another beast for one set apart for sacrifice Lev. 27:10
The new animal, in addition to the substituted one, retains consecration Lev. 27:10
Not to change consecrated animals from one type of offering to another Lev. 27:26
Carry out the laws of impurity of the dead Num. 19:14
Carry out the procedure of the Red Heifer (Para Aduma) Num. 19:2

Carry out the laws of the sprinkling water Num. 19:21
Rule the laws of human tzara'at as prescribed in the Torah Lev. 13:12
The metzora must not remove his signs of impurity Deut. 24:8
The metzora must not shave signs of impurity in his hair Lev. 13:33
The metzora must publicize his condition by tearing his garments, allowing his hair to grow and covering his lips Lev. 13:45
Carry out the prescribed rules for purifying the metzora Lev. 14:2
The metzora must shave off all his hair prior to purification Lev. 14:9
Carry out the laws of tzara'at of clothing Lev. 13:47
Carry out the laws of tzara'at of houses Lev. 13:34
Observe the laws of menstrual impurity Lev. 15:19
Observe the laws of impurity caused by childbirth Lev. 12:2
Observe the laws of impurity caused by a woman's running issue Lev. 15:25
Observe the laws of impurity caused by a man's running issue (irregular ejaculation of infected semen) Lev. 15:3
Observe the laws of impurity caused by a dead beast Lev. 11:39
Observe the laws of impurity caused by the eight shratzim (insects) Lev. 11:29
Observe the laws of impurity of a seminal emission (regular ejaculation, with normal semen) Lev. 15:16
Observe the laws of impurity concerning liquid and solid foods Lev. 11:34
Every impure person must immerse himself in a Mikvah to become pure Lev. 15:16
The court must judge the damages incurred by a goring ox Ex. 21:28
The court must judge the damages incurred by an animal eating Ex. 22:4
The court must judge the damages incurred by a pit Ex. 21:33
The court must judge the damages incurred by fire Ex. 22:5
Not to steal money stealthily Lev. 19:11
The court must implement punitive measures against the thief Ex. 21:37
Each individual must ensure that his scales and weights are accurate Lev. 19:36
Not to commit injustice with scales and weights Lev. 19:35
Not to possess inaccurate scales and weights even if they are not for use Deut. 25:13
Not to move a boundary marker to steal someone's property Deut. 19:14
Not to kidnap Standard->Ex. 20:14 TLT Yemenite->Ex. 20:13
Not to rob openly Lev. 19:13
Not to withhold wages or fail to repay a debt Lev. 19:13
Not to covet and scheme to acquire another's possession Standard->Ex. 20:15 TLT Yemenite->Ex. 20:14
Not to desire another's possession Standard->Deut. 5:19 Yemenite->Deut. 5:18
Return the robbed object or its value Lev. 5:23
Not to ignore a lost object Deut. 22:3
Return the lost object Deut. 22:1
The court must implement laws against the one who assaults another or damages another's property Ex. 21:18
Not to murder Standard->Ex. 20:13 TLT Yemenite->Ex. 20:12
Not to accept monetary restitution to atone for the murderer Num. 35:31
The court must send the accidental murderer to a city of refuge Num. 35:25
Not to accept monetary restitution instead of being sent to a city of refuge Num. 35:32
Not to kill the murderer before he stands trial Num. 35:12
Save someone being pursued even by taking the life of the pursuer Deut. 25:12
Not to pity the pursuer Num. 35:12
Not to stand idly by if someone's life is in danger Lev. 19:16
Designate cities of refuge and prepare routes of access Deut. 19:3
Break the neck of a calf by the river valley following an unsolved murder Deut. 21:4
Not to work nor plant that river valley Deut. 21:4
Not to allow pitfalls and obstacles to remain on your property Deut. 22:8
Make a guard rail around flat roofs Deut. 22:8

APPENDIX

613 MITZVOT

Not to put a stumbling block before a blind man (nor give harmful advice) Lev. 19:14

Help another remove the load from a beast which can no longer carry it Ex. 23:5

Help others load their beast Deut. 22:4

Not to leave others distraught with their burdens (but to help either load or unload) Deut. 22:4

Conduct sales according to Torah law Lev. 25:14

Not to overcharge or underpay for an article Lev. 25:14

Not to insult or harm anybody with words Lev. 25:17

Not to cheat a convert monetarily Ex. 22:20

Not to insult or harm a convert with words Ex. 22:20

Purchase a Hebrew slave in accordance with the prescribed laws Ex. 21:2

Not to sell him as a slave is sold Lev. 25:42

Not to work him oppressively Lev. 25:43

Not to allow a non-Jew to work him oppressively Lev. 25:53

Not to have him do menial slave labor Lev. 25:39

Give him gifts when he goes free Deut. 15:14

Not to send him away empty-handed Deut. 15:13

Redeem Jewish maidservants Ex. 21:8

Betroth the Jewish maidservant Ex. 21:8

The master must not sell his maidservant Ex. 21:8

Canaanite slaves must work forever unless injured in one of their limbs Lev. 25:46

Not to extradite a slave who fled to (Biblical) Israel Deut. 23:16

Not to wrong a slave who has come to Israel for refuge Deut. 23:16

The courts must carry out the laws of a hired worker and hired guard Ex. 22:9

Pay wages on the day they were earned Deut. 24:15

Not to delay payment of wages past the agreed time Lev. 19:13

The hired worker may eat from the unharvested crops where he works Deut. 23:25

The worker must not eat while on hired time Deut. 23:26

The worker must not take more than he can eat Deut. 23:25

Not to muzzle an ox while plowing Deut. 25:4

The courts must carry out the laws of a borrower Ex. 22:13

The courts must carry out the laws of an unpaid guard Ex. 22:6

Lend to the poor and destitute Ex. 22:24

Not to press them for payment if you know they don't have it Ex. 22:24

Press the idolater for payment Deut. 15:3

The creditor must not forcibly take collateral Deut. 24:10

Return the collateral to the debtor when needed Deut. 24:13

Not to delay its return when needed Deut. 24:12

Not to demand collateral from a widow Deut. 24:17

Not to demand as collateral utensils needed for preparing food Deut. 24:6

Not to lend with interest Lev. 25:37

Not to borrow with interest Deut. 23:20

Not to intermediate in an interest loan, guarantee, witness, or write the promissory note Ex. 22:24

Lend to and borrow from idolaters with interest Deut. 23:21

The courts must carry out the laws of the plaintiff, admitter, or denier Ex. 22:8

Carry out the laws of the order of inheritance Num. 27:8

Appoint judges Deut. 16:18

Not to appoint judges who are not familiar with judicial procedure Deut. 1:17

Decide by majority in case of disagreement Ex. 23:2

The court must not execute through a majority of one; at least a majority of two is required Ex. 23:2

A judge who presented an acquittal plea must not present an argument for conviction in capital cases Deut. 23:2

The courts must carry out the death penalty of stoning Deut. 22:24

The courts must carry out the death penalty of burning Lev. 20:14

The courts must carry out the death penalty of the sword Ex. 21:20

The courts must carry out the death penalty of strangulation Lev. 20:10

The courts must hang those stoned for blasphemy or idolatry Deut. 21:22

Bury the executed on the day they are killed Deut. 21:23

Not to delay burial overnight Deut. 21:23

The court must not let the sorcerer live Ex. 22:17

The court must give lashes to the wrongdoer Deut. 25:2

The court must not exceed the prescribed number of lashes Deut. 25:3

The court must not kill anybody on circumstantial evidence Ex. 23:7

The court must not punish anybody who was forced to do a crime Deut. 22:26

A judge must not pity the murderer or assaulter at the trial Deut. 19:13

A judge must not have mercy on the poor man at the trial Lev. 19:15

A judge must not respect the great man at the trial Lev. 19:15

A judge must not decide unjustly the case of the habitual transgressor Ex. 23:6

A judge must not pervert justice Lev. 19:15

A judge must not pervert a case involving a convert or orphan Deut. 24:17

Judge righteously Lev. 19:15

The judge must not fear a violent man in judgment Deut. 1:17

Judges must not accept bribes Ex. 23:8

Judges must not accept testimony unless both parties are present Ex. 23:1

Not to curse judges Ex. 22:27

Not to curse the head of state or leader of the Sanhedrin Ex. 22:27

Not to curse any upstanding Jew Lev. 19:14

Anybody who knows evidence must testify in court Lev. 5:1

Carefully interrogate the witness Deut. 13:15

A witness must not serve as a judge in capital crimes Deut. 19:17

Not to accept testimony from a lone witness Deut. 19:15

Transgressors must not testify Ex. 23:1

Relatives of the litigants must not testify Deut. 24:16

Not to testify falsely Standard->Ex. 20:14 TLT Yemenite->Ex. 20:13

Punish the false witnesses as they tried to punish the defendant Deut. 19:19

Act according to the ruling of the Sanhedrin Deut. 17:11

Not to deviate from the word of the Sanhedrin Deut. 17:11

Not to add to the Torah commandments or their oral explanations Deut. 13:1

Not to diminish from the Torah any commandments, in whole or in part Deut. 13:1

Not to curse your father and mother Ex. 21:17

Not to strike your father and mother Ex. 21:15

Respect your father or mother Standard->Ex. 20:13 TLT Yemenite->Ex. 20:12

Fear your father or mother Lev. 19:3

Not to be a rebellious son Deut. 21:18

Mourn for relatives Lev. 10:19

The High Priest must not defile himself for any relative Lev. 21:11

The High Priest must not enter under the same roof as a corpse Lev. 21:11

A Kohen must not defile himself (by going to funerals or cemeteries) for anyone except relatives Lev. 21:1

Appoint a king from Israel Deut. 17:15

Not to appoint a foreigner Deut. 17:15

The king must not have too many wives Deut. 17:17

The king must not have too many horses Deut. 17:16

The king must not have too much silver and gold Deut. 17:17

Destroy the seven Canaanite nations Deut. 20:17

Not to let any of them remain alive Deut. 20:16

Wipe out the descendants of Amalek Deut. 25:19

Remember what Amalek did to the Jewish people Deut. 25:17

Not to forget Amalek's atrocities and ambush on our journey from Egypt in the desert Deut. 25:19

Not to dwell permanently in Egypt Deut. 17:16

Offer peace terms to the inhabitants of a city while holding siege, and treat them according to the Torah if they accept the terms Deut. 20:10

Not to offer peace to Ammon and Moab while besieging them Deut. 23:7

Not to destroy fruit trees even during the siege Deut. 20:19

Prepare latrines outside the camps Deut. 23:13

Prepare a shovel for each soldier to dig with Deut. 23:14

Appoint a priest to speak with the soldiers during the war Deut. 20:2

He who has taken a wife, built a new home, or planted a vineyard is given a year to rejoice with his possessions Deut. 24:5

Not to demand from the above any involvement, communal or military Deut. 24:5

Not to panic and retreat during battle Deut. 20:3

Keep the laws of the captive woman Deut. 21:11

Not to sell her into slavery Deut. 21:14

Not to retain her for servitude after having sexual relations with her Deut. 21:14

MORE EMAILS FROM THE TRIBE

Subject: funny story...
Date: Thu, 26 Aug 2004 03:20:00 -0400

im hanging out at my apartment and someone leaves one of your genesis ales behind...i dont know who brought it, but I will find out early tommorrow...
my friend and i, who are on mushrooms, will now laugh at your bottle until we sleep....thank you, jew it up, my friends, gary

Date: Thu, 11 May 2006
Subject: Hebrew Mugshots

Dear Hebrew Beer,
The members of the 353rd German Infantry Division thought you might like to see what our WWII Reenacting group drinks after a hard day on the battlefield. Nothing but the best! *HE'BREW BEER!* **Our beer of choice, or the "Chosen Beer". No disrespect intended. Yes, some of us are of Jewish decent. We thought you might like a "little different" type of picture as opposed to the usual Drunk Dudes and Tattood Chicks for your Mug Shots section.** *"L'Chaim!"*
Sincerely, *Wilhelm Larsen*

Hi Jeremy!
I have been watching He'Brew beer grow over the past few years and I think it is great. However, there is one thing you are lacking, and that is a spokesmodel. Every beer needs a spokesmodel and I am the perfect girl to do it! When I meet guys, and they find out I am Jewish, I usually get a response of, "You don't look Jewish!" or "Jewish girls don't look like this!" and even "Jewish girls are usually ugly!" It makes me SO angry! So here is a chance to make a good showing for all the Jewish girls out there. If you are interested, please feel free to contact me.

HI Sharli--
I couldn't agree with you more and so glad to hear from such an enthusiastic supporter. Well, what do you have in mind? Happy 2005-

Date: Thu, 06 Jan 2005 23:23:00 -0500
From: sharli ▓▓▓▓▓▓▓▓▓
Subject: RE: suggestion
To: 'Jeremy Cowan at HE'BREW Beer' <jeremy@hebrewbeer.com>
Thanks for getting back to me Jeremy! I have a lot of ideas. Most of them are about print advertising. I don't know what your ultimate goal for the company is, but teaser campaigns sure work wonders! Even just plastering a picture of something everywhere makes people want it. Perhaps you have something in mind. I haven't really seen any ad campaigns from you guys, just your website. I also visualize a print ad, it is part of a girl (me) from her chest to her nose. Her cleavage is peaking out of a low cut sweater and there is a medium sized diamond Jewish star handing around her neck. She is holding an ice cold Genesis Ale up to her glossy red lips and the condensation from the bottle is starting to drip. And the tag line says something like "Being Jewish has never looked so cool" or something like that. Hey, I I'm not an ad exec Anyway, Please let me know your thoughts.

APPENDIX

HANGOVER RATINGS

EMAILED APRIL 11, 2006 FROM R. TODD MANAHAN, MARIETTA, GA

ONE STAR HANGOVER *

No pain. No real feeling of illness. You're able to function relatively well. However, you are still parched. You can drink 5 sodas and still feel this way. For some reason, your are craving a Philly sub and steak fries.

TWO STAR HANGOVER **

No pain, but something is definitely amiss. You may look okay but you have the mental capacity of a staple gun. The coffee you are chugging is only increasing your rumbling gut, which is still tossing around the fruity pancake from the 3:00 AM Waffle House excursion. There is some definite havoc being wreaked upon your bowels.

THREE STAR HANGOVER ***

Slight headache. Stomach feels crappy. You are definitely not productive. Anytime a girl walks by you gag because her perfume reminds you of the flavored schnapps shots your alcoholic friends dared you to drink. Life would be better right now if you are home in your bed watching Lucy reruns. You've had 4 cups of coffee, a gallon of water, 3 iced teas and a diet Coke -- yet you haven't peed once.

FOUR STAR HANGOVER ****

Life sucks. Your head is throbbing. You can't speak too quickly or else you might puke. Your boss has already lambasted you for being late and has given you a lecture for reeking of booze. You wore nice clothes, but that can't hide the fact that you only shaved one side of your face. For the ladies, it looks like you put your make-up on while riding the bumper cars. Your eyes look like one big red vein and even your hair hurts. Your sphincter is in perpetual spasm, and the first of about five shits you take during the day makes the eyes water of everyone who enters the bathroom.

FIVE STAR HANGOVER *****

You have a second heartbeat in your head, which is actually annoying the employee who sits in the next cube. Vodka vapor is seeping out of every pore and making you dizzy. You still have toothpaste crust in the corners of your mouth from brushing your teeth in an attempt to get the remnants of the poop fairy out. Your body has lost the ability to generate saliva so your tongue is suffocating you. You don't have the foggiest idea who the hell the stranger was passed out in your bed this morning. Any attempt to defecate results in a fire hose like discharge of alcohol-scented fluid with a rare 'floater' thrown in. The sole purpose of this 'floater' seems to be to splash the toilet water all over your ass. Death sounds pretty good about right now.

APPENDIX

EARLY COUCH SURFING: 1996-2002

Cousin Hildy and Alan, cousin Melinda, Rebecca
and Dustin, Greg (friend of a friend from college
shortly after he edited Skang Mag), Louise Caplan,
Henry, Andy, The Mullins, Samantha, Gabe, Peter
of course

2003-2009-ISH - SUBLETS:
- Williamsburg-Itamar, several times
- 1st apartment in Chinatown, Israeli musician
  connection, coincidence
- Ina and Steve's Boca condo: twice
- John and Yanghee in SF
- Nicole's studio in Cole Valley (during her trip
  to India)
- All Peter's apartments
- 5th and President in Park Slope w/ Amber/
  Darren and the cats and dancers
- Tina's apartment- Fall '04 (Spring 2005)
- John's studio in Cole Valley
- Woman's house in Skokie, Chicago for 2 weeks;
  off Craigslist
- Will and Sady in Park Slope
- Debbie and Grant's – Williamsburg- summer '06
  Yonis and anything goes
- Pearl's apartment: 19th and 1st
- Kathleen's on Carleton-Summer/Fall '07
- Dovid and Erica's on Potrero
- Jim's loft on Shipley
- Seattle Week in basement of nice Dutch hippie
  and girlfriend
- Cathleen in Brooklyn
- Chris and Tim's Ft. Greene
- Albano and Ellen, Prospect Heights

COUCHES, FLOORS, AND GUEST ROOMS:
- Mike and Popy Fouch, house, and Winnebago,
  Tampa
- Johnny V and Veronica, St. Pete
- Moira, Philly
- Steph, Portland
- Julie Rice, Detroit
- Blyth in LA and Minneapolis

- Alan Shapiro, repeatedly, Seattle
- Bruce, Little Guy Dist., Mesa, AZ -
  In Winnebago - stitches not incl.
- Craig, the Room, LA
- Chris, Indianapolis wine buyer and Dead
  bootleg for the road
- Beer Ninja, Indy, Lay-Z-Boy
- Vail sales rep Jeff – killer cook and
  amazing wine
- Aaron, Dayton, OH-with dog
- Dana Sade, DC
- Robin and Don, DC and Palo Alto
- Paige and Mark, DC
- floor of Jeff's house in DC
- Jeff and the co-op, Boston
- Jen in Chicago
- Rebecca in Tucson
- Robin's cousins in Cleveland
- Eva in Minneapolis
- Vanessa and Shanta in Madison
- Jamie in Colorado
- Wendy in Colorado
- Bill from Little Guy in Mesa, AZ
- Jack in Louisville
- Val, Heather's brother in Marathon
- My Pathfinder in Miami in parking lot,
  after The Room, 1st visit
- Nikki's parents in Lancaster
- Trevor's house in St. Augustine
- Heather's mom's house in Miami
- Hank's house in Atlanta: Midtown car
  break-in, one hour
  ↳ Bag of He'brew shirts and favorite
    sandals only things stolen
  ↳ Decided not to do "Israelite" that night
- Floor of some Hillel girl's apt @ Duke
- Les Lupo's house near Baltimore
- Couch of sales kid for Cavalier IN
- Christina's in Indianapolis
- Mike Shnarsky's sweet guest suite
  Milwaukee

INDEX

PLEASE GO TO:
CRAFTBEERBARMITZVAH.COM
TO DOWNLOAD YOUR VERY OWN COPY
OF THE INDEX

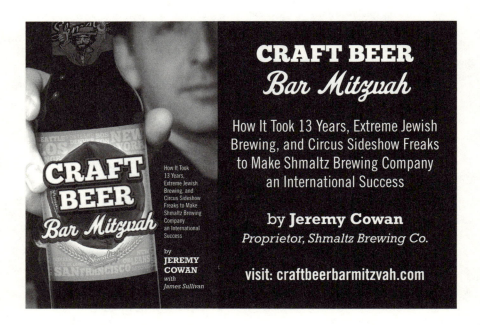

BEER!

Tasting Notes:
Insert comments about suggested beer pairings... or whatever fine, authentic craft beer you find yourself enjoying.

Taste like a pro:

1) Look

2) Smell

3) Drink

4) Reflect

5) Repeat

SHTICK!

Suggested Beer Names for Future Shmaltz Brewing Projects
(Throw in your own punchlines and send us an email:
info@shmaltzbrewing.com)

 HE'BREW BEER

 CONEY ISLAND CRAFT LAGERS

DEAR DIARY:

Make a wish for your ultimate Mikveh prayer... substitute hot tub if necessary:

Lyrics or stolen quotes from inspirational sources most relevant to your seventh grade drama, wedding vows, or other rites and rituals both sacred and profane:

Worst Hangover memory:

Best Hangover memory:

WORK!

Scribble a Business Plan for your own venture... be it a Jewish Celebration Freak Show Beer Company, a different inside-joke-turned-life's-work obsession, or even a legitimate entrepreneurial enterprise. As Rabbi Hillel said two thousand years ago, *If not now, when?!*

ABOUT THE AUTHORS

Jeremy Cowan is the founder and owner of Shmaltz Brewing Company. For more information about the author, please refer to the previous 332 pages of *Craft Beer Bar Mitzvah*.

James Sullivan is the author of three books, including *Seven Dirty Words: The Life and Crimes of George Carlin* and *The Hardest Working Man: How James Brown Saved the Soul of America*. He is a regular contributor to the *Boston Globe* and a former staff writer for the *San Francisco Chronicle*.